MOOSE PASTURES AND MERGERS:
THE ONTARIO SECURITIES COMMISSION
AND THE REGULATION OF SHARE MARKETS
IN CANADA, 1940–1980

CHRISTOPHER ARMSTRONG

Moose Pastures and Mergers:

The Ontario Securities Commission
and the Regulation of Share Markets
in Canada, 1940–1980

UNIVERSITY OF TORONTO PRESS
Toronto Buffalo London

© University of Toronto Press Incorporated 2001
Toronto Buffalo London

Printed in Canada

ISBN 0-8020-3510-8

Printed on acid-free paper

National Library of Canada Cataloguing in Publication Data

Armstrong, Christopher, 1942–
  Moose pastures and mergers : the Ontario Securities Commission
  and the regulation of share markets in Canada, 1940–1980

  Includes bibliographical references and index.
  ISBN 0-8020-3510-8

  1. Ontario Securities Commission – History.   2. Securities – Ontario –
  History.   I. Title.

  KEO407.5.A92 2001   346.713′092′09045   C00-933142-5
  KF1439.A92 2001

University of Toronto Press acknowledges the financial assistance to its
publishing program of the Canada Council for the Arts and the Ontario Arts
Council.

This book has been published with the help of a grant from the Humanities
and Social Sciences Federation of Canada, using funds provided by the
Social Sciences and Humanities Research Council of Canada.

University of Toronto Press acknowledges the financial support for its
publishing activities of the Government of Canada through the Book
Publishing Industry Development Program (BPIDP).

For Valerie

Contents

Illustrations to follow page 198

Acknowledgments

Many people and institutions have assisted me. The staff of the Ontario Securities Commission has always acceded cheerfully to my requests, but this book is in no sense an official history, the views presented being mine alone. Archivists at the Archives of Ontario and the National Archives of Canada have supplied many boxes of records from their collections. Both the Montreal and Toronto Stock Exchanges have allowed me to examine records that were still retained at the exchanges and given me space in which to work. Among private individuals, Donald McNeill, the former executive secretary of the Broker Dealers Association of Ontario, kindly presented me with the minute books of that organization to make use of as I saw fit. William Wismer read drafts of several chapters and lent me interesting photographs. The Social Sciences and Humanities Research Council of Canada gave me a grant which enabled me to travel across the country to consult archival materials, and the Faculty of Arts at York University provided aid towards publication.

The final manuscript has been much improved over earlier drafts thanks to a number of people. The reports of two anonymous readers for the Aid to Scholarly Publications Programme of the Humanities and Social Sciences Federation of Canada provided valuable critiques, and a grant in aid of publication is gratefully acknowledged. My old friends and colleagues Ramsay Cook and H.V. Nelles both read the first version and tactfully suggested that it was so long that readers were unlikely to have the time or energy to make their way all through it. Gerald Hallowell of the University of Toronto Press said the same thing. As a result, a considerable amount of detail was chopped out, to the ultimate benefit of author and (I hope) reader. Elizabeth Hulse did her usual keen-eyed job of copy-editing. If errors and omissions remain, they are my fault.

The book is dedicated to my wife, Valerie, for all the support she has given me.

MOOSE PASTURES AND MERGERS:
THE ONTARIO SECURITIES COMMISSION
AND THE REGULATION OF SHARE MARKETS
IN CANADA, 1940–1980

Introduction

Regulation is protean. Normally aimed at the protection of the public against fraud or exploitation, it can also be deployed to preserve desirable privileges for suppliers of commodities or services. This book focuses upon the regulation of share markets in Canada by the Ontario Securities Commission (OSC) during the period following the Second World War, when it emerged as the most important tribunal in the country. The study thus forms a companion volume to *Blue Skies and Boiler Rooms: Buying and Selling Securities in Canada, 1870–1940* (1997), which examined the period from the emergence of organized stock exchanges in Victorian Canada through the crash of 1929 and the depression that followed. The focus here is upon the changes in the world of finance confronted by the OSC and the methods that the regulators adopted in dealing with them.

Over the forty-year period covered here the problems preoccupying the regulators naturally shifted. Part I of this study shows that until the mid-1960s the major objective was to protect share buyers against fraud resulting from false and misleading claims and the manipulation of prices by brokers and promoters. These practices were particularly prevalent in the case of speculative ventures exploring for minerals, whose backers frequently predicted that finds of great value underlay the rocky, fir-clad hills and boggy lowlands of the Precambrian Shield, lands fit in the main only as 'moose pastures.' Yet in controlling such promotions, the regulators were constrained to some extent, since they, like many other people, subscribed to certain widely accepted myths about the nature of the mining world in Canada. Folklore had it that the most significant discoveries had been made by independent prospectors, and that raising money by selling penny stocks to fund exploration through public companies offered the ordinary investor an opportunity to get in on the ground floor, with the chance of huge gains. Buying such shares was undeniably a gamble, but one that many people were prepared to take in the hope of making a killing while at the same time patriotically promoting the development of Canadian resources. Such beliefs helped to pave the way for the Windfall Mines affair in 1964, which culminated in a great scandal that laid the groundwork for some important changes in securities legislation.

By the mid-1960s, moreover, other important developments in the business world were also occurring which are analysed in part II of this book. A growing number of corporate mergers focused attention upon the treatment received by small shareholders from corporate management and from other insiders. Demands arose that all investors should be treated as fairly and equitably as possible by restricting the use made of confidential information and by requiring public companies to make greater disclosure about their internal operations. During the 1970s attention turned to the structure of the brokerage and investment business itself. Were small investors well served by a fixed scale of commissions on share trades? Should foreign firms be permitted to enter this sector of the Canadian economy, or ought it to be protected as the preserve of domestic operators?

Throughout this period the declared objective of the securities regulators was 'investor protection.' But how was this to be achieved? An increasing emphasis came to be put upon the principle of 'disclosure,' whether through requirements that prospectuses be issued by public companies selling securities or through the insistence that corporate insiders must reveal their secrets. The fundamental objective of this form of regulation, in the words of the leading historian of federal securities regulation in the United States, was the 'remediation of information asymmetries,' so that all persons trading might do so upon an equal footing.[1] Or, to use the homelier language of the racetrack more familiar to the hopeful spirits in the brokerage offices along Bay Street in Toronto's financial district, to make sure that they all got a fair run for their money.

Regulation has, of course, been the subject of much study and analysis by scholars from a number of different disciplines: economics, political science, law, and information theory, as well as history.[2] A recent study of securities regulation by Mary Condon, entitled *Making Disclosure: Ideas and Interests in Ontario Securities Regulation* (1998), seeks to elucidate legal concepts and philosophy by a close study of formal documents such as statutes, regulatory rulings, and legal decisions, and the author summarizes the more recent literature on regulation in various disciplines. She points out that much of the analysis has been directed at understanding the goals of particular regulatory agencies and the degree to which these have been attained. Attention has also been devoted to explaining why regulatory agencies, once established, have behaved as they did. Both approaches therefore tend to focus upon the role of the various competing interests involved in the process. Condon contends that it is also important to examine ideas, particuarly the meanings attributed to terms like 'disclosure,' to see how and why they acquired a particular connotation. She suggests that an examination of the interplay between interests and ideas in specific circumstances is required to understand a given outcome.[3]

To the historian such a proposition seems unexceptionable. Ideas do not spring up full-blown: somebody has to think them, and those thinkers have their own particular interests. A notion such as the 'public interest' may thus have quite distinct meanings in different times and places. Sometimes, too, ideas are far from clear and may only be expressed in conduct, not in the abstract. Interests can also be messy, confused, and contradictory, sometimes resting upon firm ideological foundations, at other times upon crude rationalizations of self-interest. What this book attempts to do is to look more deeply into the historical record of that subtle interplay of ideas and interests,[4] in order to understand the regulatory context in which investors, brokers, company promoters, and politicians operated between 1940 and 1980.

Securities regulation was pushed towards centre stage by Canada's steadily increasing prosperity following the Second World War. During the depressed 1930s the gross national product (GNP), which had reached $6.1 billion in current dollars by 1929, dipped to only $3.5 billion by 1933 and recovered to just $5.6 billion in 1939 when war broke out.[5] The severe economic slump was reflected in the monthly index of Canadian share prices (1926=100), which fell from over 200 in 1929 to less than 50 by 1932, while the index for mining stocks dropped from a pre-crash high of 150 to about one-third of that value. When the war began, the share index was still hovering around 100,[6] and mobilization did not spark any rise. A new index covering the years 1940 to 1956 (1935–9 = 100) valued shares of industrials, utilities, and banks at just 77 and mines at 81 in 1940. As the Allies staggered from one military defeat to another until 1942, this index slipped to just 64 for industrials and 52 for mines. Only as military fortunes improved did a slow recovery commence, though it was not until 1945 that these indices reached pre-war levels. (See appendix, table A.1.)

The Canadian economy, however, grew rapidly during the Second World War, and the following three decades saw a period of almost uninterrupted expansion. By 1945 the country's GNP totalled $30 billion in constant (1971) dollars; it reached $40 billion by 1955, $70 billion by 1965, and $113 billion by 1975. Though the share-price index rose somewhat sluggishly during the late 1940s, it advanced rapidly thereafter. A new measure (1975=1000) shows a steady rise to 1970 before the index stabilized around the 1975 level. (See appendix, table A.2.) Thus during the period covered by this book, rising share prices helped to draw investors into securities markets as disposable income and personal savings increased markedly. Cautious investors, of course, could stick to well-established blue-chip companies that paid reliable dividends. Yet many people preferred to speculate in unproven 'junior' (non-dividend-paying) mining and oil shares, many of which were not listed on the stock exchanges but traded 'over the counter' through the offices of Toronto's numerous broker-dealers.[7] One attraction of such speculative securities was that they held out the promise of sizeable capital gains, which were not taxed in Canada before 1972.

The United States enjoyed equal prosperity in the post-war era. Not surprisingly, the problems facing securities regulators in Canada and the United States were often similar. Discussions about regulation in Canada normally proceed from the assumption that the rules in the United States were both stricter and more effectively enforced, but I should like to argue that such an assumption is not well warranted. Canadian regulators sometimes moved ahead of their American counterparts on certain issues, though at other times they lagged behind.

The demand for government regulation of the marketing and trading of securities arose in North America around the time of the First World War, after complaints began to be heard that smooth-talking salesmen were duping the unsophisticated into buying securites representing nothing more than 'building lots in the blue sky.' As a result, many American states and Canadian provinces enacted 'blue sky' laws that empowered their officials to vet the quality of new offerings in order to protect investors.[8] During the great boom of the 1920s most of Canada's provinces also enacted Security Frauds Prevention Acts requiring the registration of brokers and salesmen and specifying deceptive practices. In both countries the crash of 1929 was widely blamed upon stock-market operators, who engaged in practices such as 'wash trading' (where the same party was both buyer and seller) and 'bear raids' designed to drive down the price of particular stocks so that they could benefit from 'short selling' when shares were borrowed and sold in anticipation of a price fall, to be repurchased and returned later at a profit. As a result, there was an outcry for stricter regulation which gained force as share prices declined even further when the depression of the 1930s worsened.

In 1931 the government of Ontario responded by creating a specialized board to police securities dealings, an agency renamed the Ontario Securities Commission two years later. In 1934 George Drew, the first Ontario securities commissioner, propelled the merger of the Standard Stock and Mining Exchange, where many speculative issues had been traded in an atmosphere akin to a gambling den, with the more reputable Toronto Stock Exchange (TSE) in the hope of raising standards of conduct. Probably the most significant action taken by the OSC during the 1930s was a ban upon calling on private residences to sell securities which was aimed at outlawing both door-to-door marketing and telephone solicitation.[9]

When Franklin D. Roosevelt took over in Washington, his administration moved swiftly to pass the Securities Act of 1933, which required sellers to disclose all 'material facts' about any security being offered for sale in more than one state. The following year the Securities Exchange Act was passed to create a Securities and Exchange Commission (SEC) to oversee the activities of promoters and brokers. While relying principally upon disclosure to prevent fraud and deception, the commission also developed a range of administrative techniques reminiscent of the older blue-sky approach, in particular the use of 'deficiency letters' to deny registration to prospectuses deemed unsatisfactory. Still, despite complaints that the New York Stock Exchange (NYSE) continued to operate like a 'private club' with 'elements of a casino,' the SEC did little to intervene in its internal operations.[10]

Share prices in North America began to recover from their depressed levels when an Allied victory started to appear likely. Before long, promoters of speculative mining shares were once again hard at work in Canada, and the OSC did little to rein them in. The Ontario government decided to rewrite the Securities Act in 1945 by taking a leaf from the American book and requiring 'full, true and plain disclosure' of all material facts about a new issue of securities sold in a 'primary distribution' from a company's treasury. In an effort to improve standards, the OSC was also directed to review the registrations of all brokers and salesmen and to cancel the licences of anyone if the 'public interest' required it. Thus while adopting the American principle of full disclosure, Ontario also retained aspects of the blue-sky approach to protecting investors by excluding undesirables from the securities business.

Critics of granting sweeping powers to regulatory tribunals often argued that government intervention might disrupt the efficient functioning of markets and interfere with capital flows. Even bureaucrats admitted that there were certain activities, such as wash trading, which they were ill-equipped to police. The stock exchanges already possessed wide-ranging powers to compel their own members to comply with their rules, and the concept of self-regulation gained popularity. In 1947 the government of Ontario was persuaded that it should adopt the principle of self-regulation. The securities business was divided into three sections: members of the stock exchange, underwriters of blue-chip bonds and stocks, and the broker-dealers who handled over-the-counter issues. The TSE and the Ontario section of the Investment Dealers Association of Canada (IDA) were given statutory powers to discipline the first two groups, while the others were rounded up into a new Broker Dealers Association of Ontario (BDA). The OSC had overriding authority to deny registration to people guilty of dubious conduct, but this 'shotgun' proved too crude a weapon for many purposes.[11]

During the 1940s and 1950s American securities regulators complained persistently about the failure to control marketers of dubious shares based in Toronto. These 'stockateers' sold mining stocks by mail and by telephone all across the continent from 'boiler rooms' on Bay Street. Washington pressed for amendments to the Extradition Treaty between the two countries so that offenders might be brought to stand trial south of the border, but this remedy never proved effective. The OSC, meanwhile, complained that the Americans often failed to deliver conclusive proof of acts of fraud and deception to permit the imposition of discipline at home.

By the early 1950s the Ontario Securities Commission had been in existence for more than two decades. Regulatory historians have argued that such agencies often lose their sense of mission over time and even become subject to 'capture' by those whom they are supposed to control. Regulators, it is said, come to exhibit more concern for the stability of the regulated sector than for the protection of the public. Yet those who might seek to draw a sharp contrast between an activist SEC in Washington and a largely passive OSC in Toronto should note that the leading historian of the American agency identifies the Truman and Eisenhower years (1945–61) as its 'midlife crisis': 'During the Eisenhower administration, the Securities and Exchange Commision reached its nadir ... [I]ts enforcement and policy-making capacity were less effective than at any other period in its history.' The SEC failed in its efforts to end floor trading by members who operated on their own accounts on the NYSE and did nothing to interfere with the fixed scale of commissions charged for trades on the exchange, preferring to rely upon self-regulation.

Believing that the private sector was over-regulated, the Eisenhower administration sharply reduced the size of the SEC staff and de-emphasized enforcement activities, so that a mere seven convictions for misconduct were registered in 1955. The commission 'interpreted its statutory responsibilities narrowly, focussing primarily upon the noncontroversial tasks of administering a corporate disclosure system and preventing fraud.' In the early 1950s the United States was beset by a rapid increase in the number of boiler rooms, 'where typically twenty to thirty telephones would be manned by former carnival workers, pitchmen, confidence game operators or bookmakers, who would promote fraudulent or highly speculative securities to lists of unsophisticated investors.' But the SEC did not interfere much with the National Association of Securities Dealers in over-the-counter stocks, despite the fact that the organization proved casual about disciplining its members, who were often so lightly capitalized as to be proof against damage suits brought by aggrieved customers.[12]

The Ontario Securities Commission had its share of similar problems. Self-regulation proved to be no panacea. The board of governors of the Broker Dealers Association was often quite tolerant about misleading advertisements and high-pressure sales methods designed to dupe the unwary. The OSC was probably more dogged in pursuing fraud cases in the 1950s than its counterpart in Washington, but like the SEC, it remained faithful to the principle of self-regulation. The Toronto Stock Exchange was left to handle its own internal affairs except in a few cases where outrageous price fluctuations aroused a public outcry and the commission felt compelled to step in. Not until 1958 did the TSE take steps to tighten up its listing requirements, especially in the case of speculative mining companies. In 1961, under pressure from the government of Ontario the exchange finally appointed a full-time president from outside the ranks of its members to manage day-to-day affairs.

Problems with the stock exchanges persisted in the United States during the 1960s. First of all, there were serious scandals involving members of the American Stock Exchange (Amex).[13] During the 1950s Amex officials devoted much time to pursuing new listings, attracting a number of ventures whose soundness was suspect, including almost one hundred speculative oil and mining companies based in Canada. Nevertheless, 'Regulation of the American Stock Exchange by the SEC was largely passive,' and during the Eisenhower years the commission 'made no effective efforts to review or alter the exchange's governance, listing or floor-trading practices.' In 1961 an investigation revealed that the father-and-son team of Gerald A. and Gerald F. Re had been using its Amex membership during the previous five years to engage in insider trading, price manipulation, bribery of other brokers, and preparing false prospectuses. The Res were expelled, but an SEC staff study concluded that they were far from unique among Amex floor traders and 'specialists' (members supposed to ensure orderly trading in particular stocks), who were responsible for 'manifold and prolonged abuses.' Privately, one SEC official admitted that the commission 'should have realized something was seriously wrong considerably earlier than it did, probably in 1957 or early 1958, if not earlier.' The failure to act could be blamed upon misguided faith in self-regulation by Amex leaders.[14]

These scandals finally persuaded the SEC that there was a need for a thoroughgoing examination of the operations of the stock exchanges and the securities business in general. An internal study group was created whose *Special Study of Securities Markets*, submitted to Congress in 1963, proved to be the 'single most influential document published in the history of the SEC.'[15] Floor trading had always been defended as steadying markets and increasing liquidity, but the report concluded that own-account operators actually contributed to volatility by handling only active stocks on small fluctuations and ignoring lightly traded issues as unprofitable. The conclusion was blunt: 'Floor trading is a vestige of the "private club" character of the stock exchanges and should not be permitted to continue.'[16]

Serious problems were uncovered at the Toronto Stock Exchange at almost the same time. The furor surrounding the sudden rise and precipitous decline of the stock of Windfall Mines in the summer of 1964 led to the establishment of a royal commission. The investigation revealed the way in which promoters were marketing shares by manipulating prices through carefully-crafted rumours and leaks, how little attention was being paid to public orders by the floor traders, and the extent to which members were turning a blind eye to 'accommodation trades' designed to conceal the widespread sale of shares by brokers to their own customers without any disclosure. Echoing criticisms of the NYSE in the 1930s, the royal commission reported that many members treated the exchange like 'a private gaming club maintained for their own benefit.'[17]

Around the same time 'insider trading,' profiting from the use of information not available to the public, began to attract criticism. Though the 1934 Securities Exchange Act required traders to disclose all material facts about a security, this provision had never been applied to corporate insiders by the SEC. Only in 1961 did the commission hold in *Cady, Roberts and Company* that a broker-dealer must make disclosure to its customers. Not until 1965 was a major case launched against insiders who had profited from confidential corporate information. Ironically, *SEC v. Texas Gulf Sulphur Company* stemmed from the same huge mineral discovery in northern Ontario that had helped to spark the Windfall affair the previous year. The suit named not just company executives and directors but also 'tippees' who might have received advance news of the strike and sought to recover their gains.[18]

By the time the SEC laid charges, the government of Ontario was already contemplating an overhaul of its securities legislation. The wave of corporate mergers across North America in the early 1960s had sparked concerns that insiders were benefiting at the expense of ordinary shareholders. In 1963 the provincial government struck an advisory committee to consider the effects of such transactions; it recommended that any bid for more than 20 per cent of a company's shares should remain open for at least twenty-one days and that shareholders should be advised so as to permit them to make informed decisions on whether to tender their stock. A new Securities Act, passed in 1966, adopted these recommendations and required that senior corporate officers and large shareholders should be obliged to disclose their interests and any changes.

American law actually helped to encourage mergers. Not only could funds borrowed to finance takeovers be deducted for tax purposes, but aggressive conglomerators who acquired a wide range of businesses in diverse fields were permitted to use accounting techniques that made takeovers appear to generate additional earnings almost by magic, helping to fuel the 'go-go' share markets of the mid-1960s.[19] In 1968 the U.S. Congress did pass legislation requiring disclosure of any bid for more than 10 per cent of the shares of a company, a threshold lowered to 5 per cent in 1970. Yet the SEC refused to intervene in internal corporate governance by imposing stricter standards of accounting for acquisitions, and it also hesitated to require conglomerates to disclose more-detailed financial results for each operating subsidiary in order to permit investors to value their shares more accurately.

The Ontario Securities Commission had its own problems in regulating internal corporate affairs. Two major scandals in the financial services sector surfaced in the mid-1960s, when both Atlantic Acceptance and Prudential Finance defaulted, creating heavy losses for creditors and security holders. Investigations eventually revealed that the treasuries of both companies had been looted by dishonest senior executives. The OSC argued that there was little that it could do in cases of deliberate fraud, but angry investors remained unconvinced. In 1967 the commission began to prescribe the contents of corporate financial statements in more detail to protect investors.

A wave of corporate mergers in Canada beginning in the late 1960s raised renewed concerns because of the practice of financing such takeovers through 'private placements.' Sophisticated investors such as insurance companies were providing financing without a prospectus, despite the fact that such securities might subsequently be resold to the wider public. An OSC study concluded in 1969 that all companies issuing stock should be required to produce prospectuses that could be kept 'evergreen' by periodic updates to ensure continuous disclosure of material facts. Attempts to translate this proposal into legislation foundered, however, because of complaints from the financial community about the expense and complexity of preparing and updating the required information.

Still, as the number of corporate mergers in Canada continued to mount during the 1970s, the OSC persisted in trying to try to ensure that all investors received fair treatment. One particularly controversial issue was whether or not the owners of a 'control block' of shares in a company targeted for takeover should be able to sell out at a premium price not offered to other stockholders. Disgreement over this issue helped to block the revision of securities legislation.[20] Meanwhile, entrepreneurs attempting to engineer hostile takeovers sought to wrap up their deals before a target could recruit a 'white knight' to start a bidding war that might force up the price of the stock dramatically. Using the stock exchange to mount lightning strikes rather than following the formal bidding process became more and more appealing. The OSC did its best to see that investors had sufficient time and information to allow them to make informed decisions, but only in 1978 was the Ontario Securities Act finally revised in a way that was supposed to protect small shareholders in takeover battles.

Securities regulation served other purposes besides investor protection. Stock exchange members had always benefited from a fixed scale of commission charges on trades, which prevented any price competition for customers. When the SEC sought to reduce the domination of the New York Stock Exchange by its floor traders and specialists in 1938, it won the support of the retail brokerage houses with the promise that there would be no challenge to this system. For the next three decades this 'highly expensive compromise' endured.[21] But by the 1960s institutional traders such as mutual funds and insurers, which often executed large 'block trades' worth thousands of dollars, became increasingly restive about paying these commissions. Adding to the discontent was the NYSE's insistence on restricting membership to those whose 'principal business' was trading in securities and banning public companies from holding seats in order to prevent institutional traders from capturing the fees on their own dealings. As a result, block traders eventually began to seek alternatives to dealing with exchange members and over-the-counter brokers by establishing a 'third market.' In an effort to avoid losing business, NYSE members began to grant 'give-ups' to institutions, directing that part of their commissions be redirected to other exchange members as payment for sales campaigns and purported research services. Gradually, fixed commissions no longer came to apply to most institutional trades.

Price-fixing was also threatened by American anti-trust laws. The SEC was prepared to argue that the exchange rules should be exempt from anti-trust rules in order to permit effective self-regulation, but by 1968 the Department of Justice was threatening to prosecute. The NYSE defended its practices as essential to maintaining market liquidity and averting destructive competition, but it failed to make a convincing case for a commission scale linked to the value of a trade rather than to the number of shares involved. Moreover, analysis revealed that brokerage profits in the United States had risen sixfold during the bull markets of the 1960s. Economists argued that rate regulation was justified only in industries with large economies of scale relative to consumer demand, such as public utilities, and they predicted that lower commissions would likely increase trading volume, while competition promoted efficiency in the brokerage business. In an effort to deflect such criticism, the NYSE eventually felt compelled to grant volume discounts on all trades of more than one thousand shares and to outlaw give-ups, though it still refused to abolish the fixed commission scale.

Yet the issue would not go away. In 1971 the NYSE was pressured into authorizing negotiated commissions on all orders worth more than $500,000. The following year economist Paul Samuelson condemned the SEC's failure to promote competition as 'sad if not scandalous.'[22] Other critics pointed to rate-fixing as evidence that the commission had become a captive of those it regulated. The SEC concluded in 1973 that fixing a 'reasonable' rate of return on brokerage business was impossible, and in order to prevent action by Congress or the courts, it announced that fixed commissions would end on 1 May 1975. When 'Mayday' came, the predicted disaster failed to materialize: between 1975 and 1980 commissions paid by individual investors declined by 20 per cent and those paid by institutions by 60 per cent, yet volume increased steadily and third-market dealings shrank as brokerage profits rose handsomely.

Canada, of course, lacked the same strong anti-trust laws that helped propel the change south of the border.[23] The 1966 Securities Act made the OSC responsible for reviewing the by-laws of the stock exchange, apparently without anyone grasping that this would include approving commission rates. When the TSE proposed to raise charges the following year, the commission simply consented to the change. As inflation mounted during the early 1970s, brokers began discussing a further increase, but the debate in the United States guaranteed that any rise would be controversial. In 1973 the OSC ordered its first-ever hearings on commissions, and approval was eventually granted for an increase. Another round of hearings in 1976 produced a surprising result, however, as a majority of commission members agreed to a higher fixed scale but two commissioners registered strong dissent. Although fixed commissions survived in Canada throughout the 1970s, it was clear from the debates that those days were likely numbered.

Another issue that absorbed much of the time of regulators during the 1970s was the corporate structure of the securities business. Brokerage houses traditionally operated as sole proprietorships or partnerships since most stock exchanges forbade corporate memberships. With the passage of time, however, firms found their capital needs increasing as they began to undertake 'liability trading, – acting as principals rather than agents in block trades – as well as underwriting new issues and trading currencies. This problem was brought to a head in the United States by the 'back office' crisis after 1967, when many brokerages found themselves swamped with the paperwork involved in the transfers of share ownership. The number of 'fails' (trades that could not be completed) and 'short differences' (securities missing or stolen) mounted rapidly, and hasty shifts to computerized systems merely exacerbated the situation. When markets turned sour in 1969–70, the brokerage business suffered a severe shake-out as 160 members of the New York Stock Exchange went out of business, 80 disappeared through mergers, and there were another 80 liquidations or retirements. The inadequacies of self-regulation were highlighted by the failure of the NYSE to force its members to go out of business.

With the inadequate capitalization of brokerages underlined by the back-office crisis, the firm of Donaldson, Lufkin and Jenrette announced its intention to 'go public' in 1969 by selling shares to outside investors. The proposal, of course, collided with the NYSE's ban on corporate seat holding, but seeing that a challenge to the rule under the anti-trust laws was likely, the exchange decided to drop its prohibition in 1970. Within a few years about fifteen brokerages had become public companies.

The back-office crisis did not strike in Canada with the same ferocity, but nonetheless there were a number of mergers among brokerage houses, and a few firms began to consider going public. More alarming was the takeover of long-established Royal Securities Corporation by the American retail giant Merrill Lynch in 1969. Immediately the stock exchanges and the Investment Dealers Association formed a task force to consider the problem of ownership and capitalization in the Canadian investment business. The following year this committee recommended that foreigners should be excluded from controlling firms in this key sector, and at the same time it rejected the idea of dealers being allowed to go public. Eventually the Ontario government imposed a ban on industry outsiders (including non-Canadians) controlling more than a one-quarter interest in any securities firm. Yet the issue refused to go away; American brokerages continued to try to expand and inadequate capitalization remained a problem.

Mutual funds also created concerns for regulators on both sides of the border as their popularity with investors increased rapidly in the 1960s and 1970s. Though an SEC report in 1966 pointed out problems regarding management fees and raised concerns about conflicts of interest on the part of fund operators in choosing investments, historian Joel Seligman argues that this document 'must be accounted among the most poorly reasoned studies ever presented to the Commission, striking both for its failure to analyze central policy questions and for the extent to which the report's legislative conclusions were influenced by political expediency rather that the needs of investors or the theory of competition that elsewhere regulated the economy through the anti-trust laws.'[24] No action resulted. A study of mutual funds in Canada by a joint federal-provincial task force produced equally little result. In both countries the mutual-fund industry campaigned successfully against tighter regulatory control, the Canadian lobby group being particularly insistent that fund salespeople need not receive the same training or be subject to the same supervision as the sellers of other types of securities.

Neither the SEC nor the OSC devoted many resources to mastering theoretical issues. Seligman concludes, 'Throughout most of its post-World War II years, the [Securities and Exchange] Commission had interpreted its statutory responsibilities narrowly, focussing primarily upon the noncontroversial tasks of administering a corporate disclosure system and preventing fraud.'[25] Manuel Cohen, who joined the SEC staff in 1942 and became chair in 1964, preferred to evolve rules through case-by-case determination rather than the proclamation of sweeping new principles. The same applied to O.E. Lennox, who chaired the OSC for a remarkably long span between 1948 and 1962 and took a similarly cautious and conservative stance.

Revelations about scandal on the American Stock Exchange did bring about the *Special Study of Securities Markets* in 1963. Although this inquiry identified issues likely to cause future problems, such as the growth of institutional investing and fixed commissions, it stopped short of making recommendations for drastic changes in regulatory legislation. The SEC possessed no staff of economic analysts, nor did it believe that its role included making plans concerning the future structure of securities markets. The same was true of the OSC, which employed only a fraction of the numbers of its American counterpart. When the attorney general of Ontario created an advisory committee to study legislative revisions in 1963, he chose J.R. Kimber, who had succeeded Lennox as OSC chair, to head it up. The other members included civil servants and lawyers in private practice, and the result was a fairly conservative set of recommendations.

The regulators therefore operated empirically. The SEC was 'without an economic theory about the regulation of stock exchanges and mutual funds.'[26] Yet eventually a vigorous scholarly debate about the necessity and efficacy of regulating corporate conduct by requiring disclosure developed in the United States, following the appearance of an article by George Stigler in 1964. A number of other critiques of the underlying assumptions of U.S. securities law were soon published, arguing that 'a mandatory corporate disclosure system is unnecessary because corporate managers possess sufficient incentives to voluntarily disclose all or virtually all information material to investors.' Reviewing this literature, Joel Seligman concludes convincingly that criticisms of regulation based upon theories of efficient markets and other incentives to voluntary disclosure are 'unrealistic.' In particular he points out the failure to take sufficient account of the empirical evidence concerning securities fraud prior to 1929.[27] Economists and legal scholars in Canada did not participate extensively in such theoretical debates; like their counterparts in the United States, Canadian regulators simply proceeded on the assumption that extensive disclosure was essential to investor protection.

Despite its weaknesses, regulators in both countries demonstrated a continuing faith in the principle of self-regulation. Not only was this method of control seen as less invasive and disruptive than direct intervention, but it also fitted well with the desire of governments to control spending by curtailing the size of regulatory bureaucracies. Yet the SEC's William O. Douglas had pointed out in the 1930s that to be effective, regulators must possess ultimate authority and willingness to compel compliance in a pinch: 'Government would keep the shotgun, so to speak, behind the door, loaded, well-oiled, cleaned, ready for use but with the hope that it would never be used.'[28] Joel Seligman adjudges the back-office crisis of 1969–70 to be the clearest demonstration of the inadequacy of self-regulation. 'Far from being a panacea, SEC supervision of industry self-regulation has been effective in its major applications only when the Commission has been willing or able to threaten or actually use its regulatory authority to create incentives for industrial self-regulation.'[29]

The same judgment applies to the OSC's failure to force the Toronto Stock Exchange to end certain long-standing practices that operated principally for the benefit of members and insiders. The most glaring abuses arose from permitting speculative mining and oil companies to continue the primary distribution of their stock through the exchange at the same time as secondary trading in previously issued shares continued. Forbidden on exchanges in other countries, such marketing operations were a positive incentive to promoters and brokers to manipulate prices by wash trading, own-account dealing, and the release of false or misleading information, all aimed at drawing in unwary members of the public to purchase shares at inflated prices. Turning a blind eye to these abuses ultimately led to the major scandal over Windfall in 1964, which finally helped to bring about the reform of securities legislation and effectively ended the worst abuses on the floor of the exchange.

A generally protective attitude towards brokers and exchanges on the part of the regulators, evidenced by the unwillingness to force an early end to the commission price-fixing, was equally apparent in the response to new trading methods made possible by the development of electronic computers. Beginning in 1968, the National Association of Securities Dealers Automated Quotation (NASDAQ) system meant that 'At the touch of a few buttons, a broker or dealer could instantly see the competitive quotations of all market-makers in a given [over-the-counter] security.'[30] Many observers anticipated that stock exchanges would disappear altogether before long, but throughout the early 1970s the SEC allowed the New York Stock Exchange to obstruct the expansion of NASDAQ. Even after Congress granted the SEC power to modify the exchange's by-laws, the commission refused to act. In Canada stock exchange traders fought equally strongly against threats to replace their traditional methods of face-to-face dealings with electronic systems, and the Ontario Securities Commission declined to tackle the Toronto Stock Exchange over this issue.

Not surprisingly, the evolution of securities regulation by the SEC and the OSC since the Second World War displayed many similarities. The problems encountered by regulators in both countries were much alike and the solutions adopted often the same. The declared aim of regulation in both Canada and the United States was 'investor protection,' though the precise meaning of that concept changed over time. Investors, however, were sometimes reluctant to accept too much protection if they believed that such rules might deprive them of desirable opportunities to make profits. Particularly in Canada there was widespread acceptance of the notion that investing in penny mining stocks might net a huge pay-off. Even if the odds against success were very high, financing the exploration of the country's resources was worthwhile. Thus the amount of disclosure demanded for investor protection had to be balanced against the desire to get in on a hot stock on the ground floor and ride it up as far as it would go. How the regulators at the Ontario Securities Commission tried to balance the demands of investor protection against the desire for profit is the story that follows.

PART I

1

'The Canadian Problem'

Rupert Bain was one Canadian broker who prospered mightily, even during the dark days of the 1930s. Having founded H.R. Bain and Company in 1923 to deal in municipal and corporate bonds, he switched to gold stocks in the depths of the Depression. Between 1934 and 1936 Bain showed off his success with promotions like the Pickle Crow mine by building a $250,000 house on the northeastern outskirts of Toronto, the twenty-nine-room mansion with its ten-car garage and formally landscaped gardens adjoining a nine-hole golf course and a stable for his polo ponies and other bloodstock.[1]

Floyd Chalmers, editor of the country's leading business newspaper, the *Financial Post*, who had known Bain since their soldiering days during the First World War, observed that Bain and his salespeople were not above sharp practices. 'Most of his clients were small speculators on whom he unloaded, at a good markup, shares he optioned from the treasuries of developing mining companies. The operations were quite legal but the high-pressure tactics of his salesmen (particularly on the telephone) were deplorable. We exposed several of his operations and questioned if his salesmen had any right to be licensed at all.'[2]

In 1940 the Better Business Bureau received complaints that Bain was employing several salesmen who had previously fallen afoul of the authorities in the United States, but the Ontario Securities Commission reported that an investigation had not revealed any breaches of its regulations. Bain was eventually summoned before the Managing Committee of the Toronto Stock Exchange, and he promised to let go several of his more controversial employees. Since the OSC had already looked into his activities, the TSE board felt that it could hardly do much more to discipline him, as 'the exchange should not be asked to sit as a court of appeal over the commission.' Bain was also directed to sever his operations into two parts, Bain, Newling and Company to hold the seat on the TSE and H.R. Bain and Company to function as a brokerage for marketing unlisted stocks over the counter.[3]

During the Second World War the OSC received numerous complaints about Bain, and by 1946 it reported that its dossier was 'fairly formidable,' revealing patterns of conduct which 'speak for themselves.' His salespeople enthusiastically adopted the long-distance telephone for their high-pressure marketing, and complaints were registered against them from every province in Canada except Prince Edward Island. In particular, there were angry protests about the branch office in Buffalo, New York, set up to serve Bain's many customers in the United States, which indicated gross carelessness or fraud in its operations.[4]

Bain was not alone. After 1934, American law forbade the sale of issues not registered with the Securities and Exchange Commission in Washington, while separate state regulatory bodies required brokers to be licensed in order to operate, but most Canadian brokerages simply ignored these rules. In May 1940 the *New York Times* published a highly critical account of the Toronto boiler rooms running telephone sales campaigns. The *Times* claimed that at least thirty-nine stocks had been illegally offered for sale in the United States since 1938, and that twenty-five different Toronto brokers had been involved.[5]

In November 1940 *Time* magazine published an exposé about the activities of F.H. Marples and Company of Toronto. A salesman from Marples had telephoned a Chicago man and during a thirty-minute talk (costing $1 per minute) had touted shares in Payco Gold Mines, which he claimed were currently selling at 40 cents each but would soon to rise to $1. Unfortunately, the recipient of the call was W. McNeill Kennedy, regional administrator for the SEC in Illinois. The salesman falsely claimed that his firm was licensed by that agency, and U.S. officials quickly registered a formal complaint with the OSC.[6]

I

The Americans eventually dubbed this phenomenon 'the Canadian problem.' Why was it that Canada would not take action to prevent brokers from selling unregistered stocks in the United States? Why did regulatory agencies such as the Ontario Securities Commission connive in violations of American law by refusing to discipline boiler-room operators for marketing highly speculative mining shares? Why was Ontario ignoring complaints from other Canadian provinces as well as from south of the border?

The OSC seemed to show little interest in cracking down on the high-pressure marketing of speculative shares. Certain myths about Canadian mining held sway in the financial community. First was the belief that the discovery and development of major mineral deposits was usually the work of independent prospectors and promoters. Second was the claim that the sale of shares in public companies to finance mining exploration offered the investing public a chance to hit the jackpot when a major disovery was made. The fact that only a minuscule number of these mining speculations ever paid off and that many promoters simply exploited the gullibility of investors was ignored. Taken together with the assumption that resource development was a vital engine of economic growth in Canada, these notions created a powerful conservative bulwark against demands for reforms which might alter the status quo, even if the objective was to make mining finance more honest and transparent.

Among the believers in this myth were not only prospectors, promoters, and investors but also politicians, particularly in Ontario, where the growth of the mining industry during the early twentieth century had been so spectacular. Even the scandals that engulfed the stock market after the crash of 1929 had largely failed to bring about major reforms in the securities business. The Ontario Securities Commission was created in the early 1930s, and the Securities Act required the registration of brokers and dealers, but the very slowness of the recovery from the Depression provided arguments against tightening the regulations further.

For instance, the requirement that buyers of over-the-counter shares during a primary distribution of stock from a company's treasury by promoters or corporate insiders should receive a prospectus was watered down. In 1937 Ontario securities commissioner John Godfrey argued that 'very few, if any, of the customers were concerned so much with the detailed information relating to the company as they were with the possibility of making a profit on the stock from a market standpoint.' Buyers need only be advised where they might obtain a copy of the prospectus if they desired.[7] At that time the OSC did limit the amount of stock that could be granted to the vendors who sold mining claims to companies to 1 million shares (or one-third of the stock in a typical 3-million-share company). This vendor stock was to be placed in escrow and withheld from sale, to be released only at the rate of one share for every four treasury shares sold to the public in order to give the insiders an incentive to market the treasury stock if they wished to cash in by reselling their vendor shares. These escrow rules became a major grievance amongst mining men, and with the provincial economy remaining sluggish, the rules were relaxed in 1939 so that henceforth 100,000 vendor shares would be released from escrow immediately and the remainder on the basis of one share for every two treasury shares sold. Still, mining people complained that these regulations were interfering with development. Under pressure from the mining industry, Ontario's attorney general, Gordon Conant, who oversaw the Securities Commission, was persuaded to relax the escrow rules in the spring of 1940 to permit the release of vendor stock on the basis of one share for each one sold to the public.[8] Mining promoters thus continued to have access to large pools of low-cost stock in speculative companies, which they could market by mail and telephone at inflated prices using high-pressure methods.

Floyd Chalmers launched a campaign in the *Financial Post* demanding that the OSC mount a clean-up of Toronto's boiler rooms; he alleged that they were employing people who had fled from U.S. authorities.[9] In April 1940 Ontario premier Mitchell Hepburn invited Chalmers to a meeting with Attorney General Conant and Roy Whitehead of the OSC, and he demanded the names of securities salesmen who had been licensed in Ontario despite problems with the Americans. Lee T. Brooks, for instance, had been indicted in Michigan for violating securities laws and was now selling shares over the telephone for Rupert Bain. Were there others like Brooks, asked the premier? A list of eight names was produced. It included Denby Lloyd, who had several convictions for fraud, had served time in jail and skipped bail to reach Canada, and yet had been licensed by the OSC. Hepburn growled, 'He ought to be in jail. If I had my way I'd put him there.' Whitehead, however, insisted that most of these people had only been running tipsheets encouraging people to purchase speculative shares over which he had no jurisdiction. He had eventually required Lloyd to take out a brokerage licence, which at least gave him some hold over Lloyd's activities, and there had been no complaints about his operations in Toronto to date.

Despite Hepburn's rhetoric, Chalmers was not optimistic following the meeting. Attorney General Conant had contributed little, except to say he was concerned about the arbitrary authority of the OSC since there was no appeal to the courts from its decisions.That was typical of Conant, wrote Chalmers: 'He was a quiet, easy-going but very attractive lawyer ... who throughout his career avoided coming to grips with any unpleasant confrontation if he could avoid it. His only significant comment was on that question of appeal.'[10]

The *Financial Post* kept up its campaign for the next few weeks. Conant was reported as saying that the undesirables would be cleaned out. Already one man had been 'invited' to surrender his registration, another had done so voluntarily, and a third had had his licence revoked.[11] Yet *Time* magazine's embarrassing exposé about the case of F.H. Marples and Company in the autumn of 1940 showed that it was business as usual for the shadier types on Bay Street. Confronted by reporters, Marples had to admit that a telephone call had been made to an SEC administrator in Chicago, but he stoutly denied any impropriety. He insisted that under Ontario law any sale of shares would legally be consumated in Toronto, so that the quesion of offering stock not registered in the United States did not arise. Moreover, Marples asserted that Kennedy had written to his brokerage house within the past three months to request information on stocks and so was legally qualified to receive such calls. As to the salesman's claim that the shares would soon go as high as $1, Marples contended that while he tried to restrain his salesmen, he could not always contain their flights of optimistic fancy.

In this case, however, the evidence seemed so damning that the OSC could hardly refuse to act. Roy Whitehead tried to defend his actions, insisting that the commission did its utmost to cooperate with the Americans, and that most of the information they possessed actually emanated from Toronto. But he had to admit that the Marples firm had been the subject of previous complaints about high-pressure telephone selling in the United States, and the seriousness of the allegations compelled him to launch a hasty investigation, which led to the cancellation of Marples's brokerage licence within a fortnight.[12]

American officials, however, were convinced that the OSC had little intention of seriously tackling 'the Canadian problem.' If the provincial government could not be persuaded to act, perhaps Ottawa could be induced to deliver offenders against U.S. securities laws to stand trial in the United States. Unfortunately, the current Extradition Treaty between the two countries, dating from 1842, had no provisions to cover such crimes.[13] In January 1941 the chair of the SEC, Jerome

Frank, therefore wrote to Secretary of State Cordell Hull to propose that negotiations be opened to amend the treaty. [14]

The American minister in Ottawa commenced discussions with the External Affairs Department about an extradition agreement that would cover violations of the U.S. Securities Act of 1933 and the Securities Exchange Act of 1934. The Canadians responded by proposing that, rather than simply adding a convention covering these particular offences, a whole new Extradition Treaty be negotiated. The talks proceeded smoothly, and in the spring of 1942 an agreement was signed in Washington, ratified by the U.S. Senate within a month, and approved by the president ten days later. [15]

In Canada, however, the provisions covering securities offences aroused great controversy. Securities law differed markedly between the two countries. Criminal law was a state responsibility in the United States but a federal one in Canada, which had no equivalent to the U.S. laws passed in 1933–4 that required share sellers to disclose all material facts to prospective buyers and to register with the SEC if marketing of a stock was to take place in more than one state. Provincial and state laws concerning the registration of securities and their sellers bore a greater similarity to one another, but with forty-eight states and nine provinces involved, it was inevitable that there should be significant variations. Actions legal in some provinces of Canada were forbidden by certain American states.

Because of the general similarity of the Canadian and American legal systems, extraditable offences had always been confined to those acts illegal in both countries, the principle of 'dual criminality.' In order to meet Washington's wish to provide for extradition of all persons guilty of indictable offences under American securities laws (that is, those punishable by at least one year in jail), the drafters of the new treaty adopted an unorthodox approach. As the legal adviser to the External Affairs Department explained, 'Those engaged in the negotiation of the treaty were, therefore, reluctant to reject a proposal merely upon the ground that a type of conduct which was treated as a crime in the United States was not regarded as criminal in this country.' In order to provide 'complete coverage' of offences under American law (and any future Canadian legislation of a similar sort), article III of the 1942 treaty covered crimes 'against the laws for the prevention of fraud in the sale or purchase of securities,' but also all 'offences, if indictable, against the laws relating to (a) public securities markets ..., (b) registration or licensing of securities or persons doing business in securities.' [16]

When news of this wording penetrated the Canadian financial community in June 1942, it set alarm bells ringing. With dual criminality abandoned, 'technical' offences, such as failing to register a share issue in a particular state before marketing it there, might render a person liable to extradition even if such an act was not illegal in Canada. The board of the Toronto Stock Exchange hastened to retain Liberal back-bencher Arthur Slaght as counsel to raise the matter with the minister of justice, Louis St Laurent. Slaght pointed out that 'very substantial mining and security interests' were concerned that the treaty might prove a serious impediment to the raising of capital in the United States for Canadian ventures.[17]

By the autumn of 1942 a storm of protest had blown up aimed at blocking the ratification of the treaty; the presidents of the stock exchanges and the Investment Dealers Association were in full cry. There were objections in principle: acts legal in Canada might lead to the extradition of persons who had never set foot across the border, giving American law extraterritorial scope. Moreover, brokers in the United States might 'abuse the spirit' of the treaty by using it to monopolize the entire market for themselves. In addition, there were the practical consequences of compliance: the complexity and expense of registering securities and brokers in the United States might cut off the vital flow of foreign investment in a time of dire need.[18]

The government of Ontario was also enlisted in the fight against the new treaty. Provincial officials pointed out that attempting to make offenders against its Securities Act liable to extradition would achieve little, since such offences were not indictable. The OSC often received requests from the SEC to cancel the registration of Toronto brokers accused of operating across the border, but Roy Whitehead had adopted the policy of cancelling only when the transaction involved 'some element of fraud and not merely because the sale was made of an unregistered security.' Gordon Conant, now the premier, warned the federal justice minister that the province believed that Ottawa did not even have the constitutional authority to make such an agreement unilaterally since it invaded provincial jurisdiction. Moreover, the treaty would bind Canada to hand over those accused of 'using the mails to defraud,' which was not an offence under the Criminal Code.[19]

Having studied these protests, St Laurent admitted that SEC rules were 'very severe,' and that under the treaty the Americans might contend that a Canadian resident had committed an extraditable offence without ever leaving the country. He wrote, 'That does not seem to me to be in accord with the usual extradition practice, and I would like to guard against an interpretation of the treaty that could have that effect.' People who offended against the law in the United States and took refuge in Canada were one thing, 'but I do not think we should go farther than that.' The only exception might be those who set up a scheme to violate American law while operating in Canada, but honest, legitimate brokers need not fear falling afoul of U.S. regulations by mistake.[20]

The Ontario Securities Dealers Association, which had been formed in the spring of 1941 to represent brokers of over-the-counter stocks who were likely to be the focus of any enforcement campaign, put forward its own objections, noting that the completion of the Alaska Highway would open up a vast new area to be explored that would require American capital. T.A. Crerar, the federal minister of mines and resources (who was responsible for development in the Yukon and the Northwest Territories, being traversed by the highway), concurred that this issue had better be handled carefully. The Prospectors and Developers Association repeated similar warnings, and Toronto mining promoter Norman Vincent complained bitterly to Prime Minister Mackenzie King that he might be held to be a criminal in a state like Mississippi, where lynching was a not uncommon practice.[21]

The president of the Toronto Stock Exchange arranged to see the justice minister in January 1943 to set forth the concerns of his members, and the head of the Canadian Daily Newspaper Association conveyed fears that papers carrying advertisements for unregistered securities might face charges. Efforts were made to alert the finance minister to the possible adverse effects upon the flow of U.S. investments into Canada, a serious problem at a time when American dollars needed for the war effort were in short supply.[22]

All this high-powered lobbying had its effect upon a federal cabinet that had heretofore paid little attention to the new treaty. At the end of January 1943 Prime Minister King advised Parliament that the government had received representations from all across the country which must be studied before the new treaty could be ratified.[23] To the Americans, of course, it seemed that Canada had caught a belated case of cold feet about bringing well-deserved retribution down upon some crooks. Lester B. Pearson, the Canadian minister in Washington, reported that columnist Drew Pearson was ranting against the refusal to hand over a bunch of stock swindlers 'despite tons of Lend-Lease equipment now pouring into Canada.'[24] Brokers were particularly unhappy that the treaty might be applied retroactively. Having ratified the agreement, however, the Americans were unwilling to yield to demands for changes. Before long, Lester Pearson was reporting that Canada's failure to act was sparking further criticism in Washington.[25]

'The Canadian problem' continued. In the spring of 1943 H.R. Bain and Company was charged with illegally selling 250 shares of Gold Frontier Mines in Pennsylvania.[26] Officials in Ottawa did their best to justify the abandonment of the principle of dual criminality. To them it seemed 'virtually indefensible' to refuse to assist the American authorities in regulating the way that Canadians marketed shares in the United States. Any attempt to remove such offences from the Extradition Treaty would now be seen as an effort to maintain an unfair advantage for Canadian brokers. If American law continued to be flouted, capital markets might be closed off. Trying to alter the agreement to restore the principle of dual criminality would 'seriously emasculate' the treaty and would be rejected by the Americans. Nevertheless, the opposition was so strong that the government decided against trying to push the agreement through. The under-secretary of state for external affairs advised the prime minister, 'The conflict is an important one. Its implications do not appear to have been fully apprehended and certainly they were not resolved when the treaty was signed. In the circumstances, I am inclined to the opinion that we should try to get the treaty modified before submitting it to parliament.'[27]

In May 1943 a cabinet committee composed of Mines Minister Crerar, Finance Minister J.L. Ilsley, Justice Minister St Laurent, and Secretary of State Norman McLarty met with representatives of the stock exchanges, the Investment Dealers Association, and the Ontario Securities Dealers Association as well as the Prospectors and Developers Association, the Ontario Mining Association, and the Toronto Board of Trade. The federal ministers did not defend the agreement very forcefully. Pushing ahead with ratification of the treaty would clearly entail political costs.[28]

That truth became even clearer when the federal government convened a meeting of provincial securities regulators in Winnipeg a few days later. Every province except New Brunswick was represented. None of the provincial representatives felt at all happy about dropping the principle of dual criminality, and they called upon Ottawa to consult their attorneys general fully before proceeding any further.

Amongst themselves they agreed that the root of the problem was the OSC's failure to control its brokers, a proposition that not even the Ontario people seriously disputed.[29]

British Columbia's superintendent of brokers, E.K. DeBeck, came away from the meeting convinced that federal officials now recognized from this 'storm of protest' how seriously they had blundered. What was needed was a pretext for reopening negotiations, but it was going to be 'pretty awkward' to induce the United States to resume negotiations when the Senate and the president had already given their assent to the treaty. He predicted that External Affairs would not try to restore dual criminality but tag on some reservation in order to render the treaty provisions less far-reaching.[30] The reservation proposed by Canadian officials focused upon the intentions of the actors: people engaged in 'genuine business transactions' in compliance with local laws should not be liable to extradition despite conduct in 'incidental technical conflict' with the laws of the other country. Only persons who committed fraudulent acts or crossed the border to avoid punishment would be subject to extradition.[31]

The Americans were not impressed. The Canadian Legation reported, 'The representatives of the SEC seemed to be greatly disturbed by the provisions of the proposed reservation. They emphasized that the people they were after were not reputable dealers who may technically infringe US law; they are concerned only with crooks or occasionally with people who deliberately set out to flout on a large scale the registration provisions of the Securities Act.' Accepting the proposed changes would make it hard to extradite anyone.[32]

John Read, the legal adviser at External Affairs, concluded that any change of mind in Washington was unlikely. The SEC wanted to get its hands on the people who were swindling American investors, in particular, those who had fallen afoul of the SEC and retreated to Toronto to continue to peddle shares. These included American citizens who might employ as many as fifty telephone salesmen in their boiler rooms. 'They are determined to get these people and will, I think, apply the utmost pressure upon the government to force us to make them extraditable.'[33]

In August 1943 the State Department returned Canada's proposed reservation with some suggested changes. The deputy minister of finance, W.C. Clark, reported gloomily that the revised language would still make anyone who committed a fraud or wilfully violated any law subject to extradition.[34] Early in 1944 External Affairs concluded that there was little hope of progress, and the idea of solving 'the Canadian problem' through changes to the Extradition Treaty was dropped for the time being.[35]

II

In 1943 a provincial election in Ontario had brought the Conservative party to power. The new premier was George Drew, who had been Ontario's first securities commissioner back in 1931. As the likelihood of an Allied victory in the war increased, stock markets in Canada began to revive from a long slump. The new provincial attorney general, Leslie Blackwell, found himself under renewed pressure to crack down upon securities fraud. The *Financial Post* was particularly critical of the OSC's reliance upon restitution orders as a means of settling allegations of wrongdoing against brokers. While this might seem an efficient and equitable way of rectifying double-dealing, the paper pointed out that the OSC rarely imposed any further penalties on dishonest operators, leaving them free to prey on other unsuspecting customers. In January 1944 the paper detailed a number of such cases where brokers and their salesmen had avoided losing their licences by offering refunds to those who complained, while other victims got only partial repayment or nothing at all in some cases.[36]

Privately, Gordon Grant, the paper's mining editor, complained to the new attorney general about the way that Roy Whitehead of the OSC operated: 'Mr. Whitehead's practice of taking friends into his office for private settlements of undisclosed character would not seem to be a practice to be encouraged.' Telephone selling by boiler rooms must be at an all-time peak, said Grant, judging by the volume of complaints received by the *Post* and the Better Business Bureau. In the old days Whitehead had at least threatened to cancel registrations if there were serious complaints. Now 'he claims that long distance telephoning to other provinces will be stopped when drawn to his attention – but phone calls go on unchecked.' The American authorities remained eager to prosecute Canadian offenders, but Whitehead continued to waffle about whether or not he even possessed the legal authority to punish those calling across the border. Grant dismissed Whitehead as 'an apologist to those who use questionable practices' and demanded that he be replaced by someone with vision and courage.

The OSC seemed quite willing to allow various shady characters to continue in business. Brokers who had run afoul of the regulations were sometimes permitted to take over previously reputable firms without any name change to alert customers. Those who lost their registration might reappear, operating under new confidence-inspiring titles. If they could not secure a broker's licence, they sometimes restyled themselves as investment advisers, who did not require OSC registration. Grant also pointed out to Blackwell that these criticisms of the OSC were being widely echoed: he need only look at the reports of the conference of provincial securities regulators in Winnipeg in May 1943, where the blame for most of the activities creating friction with the United States and other provinces had been laid at the feet of Toronto brokers.[37]

Many abuses were rooted in the methods adopted since the mid-1930s to raise money for junior mining companies. A promoter or grubstaker might advance a small sum to a prospector. If the results were at all encouraging, a mining claim was filed and a 3-million-share public company incorporated, the property being paid for with one-third of the stock, 90 per cent of which was placed in escrow. Then the promoter would find a broker willing to acquire options to 'take down' the treasury stock. Blocks of 300,000 shares were commonly optioned for 5 cents apiece or less, with a 'step-up' for each subsequent 300,000-share block to 7.5 cents and 10 cents. As the stock was marketed to the public, the money received by the company treasury would supposedly be used to finance further exploration such as diamond drilling. If these results were promising, share prices would move upward, making it worthwhile for the promoters to exercise the successive options and raise more money. As this process proceeded, the insiders could apply to have their vendor stock freed from escrow on a one-for-one basis as shares were sold to the public. A successful company would end up with a producing mine, its shareholders a handsome profit.

In practice, however, option financing usually worked quite differently. First of all, rather than dealing at arm's length, the promoter and broker were often identical. Very low priced options (for as little as half a cent per share) were granted, and there were no effective restrictions on the prices demanded from buyers. The market price of an unlisted mining stock depended upon the general state of the economy and other securities markets, upon discoveries in the area of the claim, and upon news about the progress of exploration, such as drilling on the site, but promoters were skilled at spreading rumours to arouse interest in a particular stock. Wash trading (in which the same party was on both sides of the deal) could be used to push the price of a stock upward, yet when a member of the public tried to sell, there were often no buyers if the promoters refused to support the market.

Sometimes a broker or promoter arranged to purchase all the 900,000 escrowed shares for 5 cents each or less (at a maximum cost of $45,000) and to take down the three optioned blocks (at a maximum cost of $15,000, $22,500, and $30,000 respectively). The insiders then controlled a block of 1.8-million resaleable ('free') shares that had cost an average of 6.25 cents apiece. With the additional costs of grubstaking, exploration, and the incorporation of a public company, the total outlay might run to 7 cents a share, due over a period of a year or more as the options matured. Turned over to a boiler-room operator, these shares might be marketed starting at 10 cents initially, but as the price was pushed up by skilful manipulation, it might rise to 50 cents or more if all went well. The insiders would be left with handsome profits, plus enough shares to control a company's affairs in the improbable event that a valuable mineral discovery was actually made. Once the promoters and brokers failed to provide support to share prices, these typically dropped sharply, but the insiders were often able to make use of any money in the company treasury to launch other similar ventures.

An investigation by the *Financial Post* revealed that during 1943 at least eighty-eight deals to finance unlisted mining companies had involved the taking down of blocks of option stock for 5 cents or less. The public was rarely offered shares for under 10 cents, and towards the end of the year selling prices of 15 to 30 cents were common even when no work had been done on the properties. The Securities Act banned 'unconscionable and unreasonable' profits on promotions, but this prohibition applied only to stock in primary distribution being sold directly to the public from a company treasury. The OSC had shown no inclination to redefine the point at which a sale to the public actually took place to prevent insiders from reselling their shares at a large profit. The *Post* complained that the 'present complete lack of control prevents money going into the ground and has made Ontario a phony promoters' hangout.'[38]

British Columbia superintendent of brokers, E.K. DeBeck, was convinced that these methods were responsible for most of the problems facing the Ontario securities industry. 'The very principle of the option type of financing on a sliding scale of prices offers the strongest inducement or temptation to run a market on worthless or unproven stocks, particularly when the information upon which the increases are based is the result of diamond drilling only.' On the strength of little more than rumours, promoters were able to push up mining share prices to 'grotesque heights' and earn unconscionable profits while doing little or no exploration. Such stocks provided wares for the Toronto boiler rooms selling all across North America which had so angered the U.S. authorities, and in supporting the system, mining and brokerage men in Ontario seemed to 'have lost all sense of proportion.' DeBeck complained that the OSC was simply shutting its eyes to the 'exploitation of the public.'[39]

In October 1943 the Drew government created a provincial Royal Commission on Mining. Part of its mandate was to examine the financing of mineral exploration and development. The choice of broker Norman Urquhart, who had once headed that playground for speculators at the old Standard Stock and Mining Exchange,[40] as its chair, and the inclusion of a number of stalwarts from the mining comunity, like Toronto promoter R.J. Jowsey, who played an important role in the Prospectors and Developers Association, suggested that the commission was hardly likely to turn a very critical eye on abuses. The Conservatives were probably keener to defuse continuing criticism from mining brokers and promoters that the current regulations were seriously impeding the development of Ontario's mineral resources, since their minority government was likely to face the electorate again before long and was hoping to avert gains by other political parties in northern Ontario.[41]

The mining commission received over one hundred submissions. A brief from the Investment Dealers Association did point out that the debate over the changes to the Extradition Treaty had made it clear that 'the most pressing problem' was the boiler rooms preying upon American investors. If legitimate dealings were not to be interfered with, the authority of the OSC should be extended so that it could supervise registrants more carefully and refuse to approve dubious promotions.[42] However, when the commission began its public hearings in January 1944, it became clear that those who claimed that over-strict regulation of securities marketing was impeding mining development would receive a sympathetic reception. Urquhart opened the proceedings by asking whether door-to-door selling and unrestricted telephone marketing ought to be permitted. Should the escrow rules be relaxed? Not surprisingly, most witnesses answered with ringing affirmatives. The Ontario Mining Association recommended the out-and-out abolition of the OSC, a view echoed by the local branch of the Canadian Institute of Mining and Metallurgy, which claimed that the regulators had 'placed stupid, restraining and hurtful regulations in the path of the prospector until he is becoming disheartened.' Most people concurred with prospector Cyril T. Young that the present rules were 'rotten' and any change would be an improvement.[43]

Gordon Grant of the *Financial Post* recognized that the commission was likely to recommend a serious watering-down of the OSC's authority. He tried to warn Attorney General Blackwell privately, 'With the present boom in development mining stocks, lifting of securities regulation would be the signal for the greatest outbreak of organized fraud in the history of the country, it seems to me.' Why should Ontario choose this moment to drop the kind of regulation that currently existed in eight provinces and forty-three American states? If it did so, the angry Americans might even decide to cut off long-distance telephone connections, and in the circumstances, who could blame them? The Conservatives must be aware that 'Ontario needs effective securities control. Criticism of securities control comes from a very vocal but very *small* group within the industry whom I am sure do not control so many votes ... Undoubtedly securities control is an unwanted child left on your doorstep by a previous administration, but ... flowers will be in order if you can really clear this situation up and provide honest administration in this important department of government.'[44]

Within less than two months the mining commission delivered a preliminary report. Grant's worst fears were realized since its centrepiece was the abolition of the OSC's discretionary powers. In particular, it was proposed that the detested escrow provisions, which prevented insiders from unloading all their vendor shares upon the public without the corporate treasury receiving any benefit, should be abolished completely. The Ontario securities commissioner should be replaced by a much weaker part-time body composed of a mining expert, a lawyer, and a securities dealer, whose decisions could be appealed directly to the courts. Only a few bows were made in the direction of correcting abuses. Purchasers of shares in primary distribution ought to receive a prospectus and return a signed acknowledgment for a transaction to be finalized (though this would also make it much more difficult to prosecute salespeople for making false or misleading representations). The ban on selling in person or by telephone or telegraph at private residences in Ontario should be extended to all such calls emanating from the province to other jurisdictions because high-pressure marketing was harming sales of mining stocks.[45]

The over-the-counter brokers in the Ontario Securities Dealers Association expressed enthusiasm for the recommendations. Using prospectuses and disclosure rules to protect investors on the British model was much more satisfactory than American blue-sky laws, which only impeded development in a 'pioneer mining country like Ontario.' The OSDA argued that the current system of mine financing had evolved because banks and producing mines refused to assume the risks born by mining promoters. 'Of course, large corporations and men with money can develop properties. They do not need the public's money. It is only when they have made a success or a partial success that they ask the public to come in so that they can get their original investment back and still have a speculation. The ordinary small security issuer, however, must help the prospector by getting money from the public to develop his mining claims. We submit that he should not be so hamstrung at so many turns in the road.'[46]

Only a few people in the financial community expressed concern about dropping the escrow requirements on vendor shares, though one person observed, 'Some of us remember the days before the Ontario Securities Commission pooling arrangements when floods of vendor stock used to be sold at no benefit to company treasuries. It was not uncommon then for only 15% of proceeds of sale of shares to the public to reach a mining [company's] treasury.' Securities regulators in the other provinces were highly dismayed at the commission's proposals. Interviewed by the *Financial Post*, most of them declared (anonymously) that the time for a clean-up was long overdue and the main responsibility must fall upon Ontario, where the boiler rooms were located. Privately, Superintendent DeBeck of British Columbia complained that the preliminary report was quite unsound and simply reflected the fact that the mining and brokerage community in Ontario had 'lost all sense of proportion.' Federal officials were reported to be fearful that if the principles of the mining commission's report were accepted, regulation would become impossible. Moreover, the recommendations were bound to act as a red flag in Washington.[47]

Despite these criticisms the commission refused to bend. The nineteen-page final report, dated 6 September 1944, did not back down from the insistence that a complete overhaul of the regulatory apparatus was required: 'the Ontario Securities Commission has taken unto itself powers which this commission believes were never intended in respect to the regulation of mine financing. Intended as a fraud prevention measure it has developed, on the one hand, into a measure which tends to result in the strangulation of new mining development, and, on the other, into a measure which in some phases of its operation at least, would seem to do more to condone fraudulent practices than to discourage the same.' The OSC should be deprived of its discretion. 'From the evidence before this commission it is indicated that the greatest progress in the discovery and development of mineral resources in Ontario was made during a period in which there was no legislation requiring the escrowing of vendor shares.' The report also devoted an entire section to a vigorous denunciation of the proposed changes to the Canada-U.S. Extradition Treaty, which might permit charges to be laid for actions legal in Canada. If all the recommended changes were adopted, the commission concluded optimistically, the problems that had led the Americans to press for the new treaty would soon evaporate.[48]

The financing of junior mines was continuing apace. During the first half of 1944 the *Financial Post* reported that 114 option or underwriting agreements had been filed with the OSC, 69 of them calling for an initial block of stock at 5 cents a share, 1 at 2 cents, and 2 at 3 cents. The public did not appear to be deterred from buying these stocks, despite the fact that the spreads between option prices and public offering prices seemed even greater than previously. Brokers were listing prices for no less than 370 companies, with another 50 occasionally quoted, as well as the innumerable promotional issues for which there were no established markets. Each day the Toronto papers carried 'bid' and 'ask' prices for approximately one hundred unlisted mines and oils, chosen by a committee composed of representatives of nine leading over-the-counter brokers. The only way that the public could secure information about these companies was to visit the offices of the committee secretary at T.A. Richardson and Company. As a result, virtually all buyers of such shares remained completely dependent on what they were told by salespeople over the telephone.[49]

The *Financial Post* ran a cartoon showing a pen with black sheep being separated from white ones labelled 'March 31st: Ontario Security Salesmen's Licences Come up for Review and Renewal' and captioned 'Round-up Time Is a Good Opportunity for Some Sorting.' Roy Whitehead evidently concluded that the time had come to make the OSC's annual review of registrations in 1944 more than the usual formality. Eight licences were suspended, immigration officials in Ottawa were asked to investigate the background of securities salespeople applying to enter Canada from the United States, and three deportation orders were issued for failure to disclose a criminal record.[50]

Whitehead also decided that from 1 January 1944 all applicants for a sales licence would be required to have been resident in Canada for at least one year. When an American salesman appealed this ruling, Whitehead pointed out that during the past two years there had been a steadily increasing number of applications for registration by high-pressure salespeople, mainly from New York. The OSC had endeavoured to check up on the records of applicants by contacting the SEC, the police, and other informants, but requiring people to be resident in Ontario made it more difficult for them to conceal their backgrounds. However, the OSC's Board of Review[51] overturned the commission's decision on the grounds that the Securities Act did not provide explicitly for a residency requirement. Simply turning down an applicant without a hearing exceeded the discretionary power of a regulatory tribunal by preventing a person from stating a case. Evidently, cracking down on the denizens of Toronto's boiler rooms might be more difficult than anticipated.[52]

Meanwhile, the market for Canadian mining stocks continued to heat up. In the summer of 1944 the *Financial Post* reported that while there were some promising finds, such as the Giant Yellowknife gold mine in the Yukon, scores of new companies were being floated whose share certificates had little more value than 'wallpaper.' Prospectors were selling unpromising claims to promoters for between $3,000 and $5,000 without even bothering to take vendor stock. Buyers had so much money and were so eager to purchase shares costing brokers just a nickel for five or seven times that amount, the paper reported somewhat ruefully, that high-pressure selling methods were no longer required in many cases.[53]

At long last the Ontario government decided to undertake the reform of securities regulation. In June 1944 Roy Whitehead was transferred to the less controversial post of superintendent of insurance and replaced as chair of the OSC by its registrar (or senior administrator), W.A. Brant. As soon as the report of the Royal Commission on Mining was delivered in September, Attorney General Leslie Blackwell instructed Brant to begin drafting a new Securities Act. By the end of October, however, Brant was dead, leaving the commission with its two senior posts vacant; Blackwell took over as acting commissioner pending the appointment of a full-time replacement.[54]

At the end of the year the *Financial Post* commenced a whole series of articles on what it called 'stock racketeering.' Under this heading were lumped the misrepresentations made concerning speculative mining shares by promoters, brokers, and salespeople. Most common were outright falsehoods or gross exaggerations about the extent of development of a particular property. Common, too, were promises by salespeople that a particular stock would start to rise or soon be listed on the stock exchange. Buyers were told that reselling their shares would be easy, though the insiders commonly supported the market only for a short time during a price run-up before withdrawing, thus rendering the stock virtually unsaleable. Sometimes reluctant purchasers could be won over by sending them a false confirmation of a buy order. The final insult to investors might be the misappropriation of any funds remaining in the company treasury. The *Post* laid the blame for failure to stamp out these practices squarely upon the OSC.[55]

Leslie Blackwell was infuriated by this drumfire of criticisms. He insisted that he and his staff were only following the letter of the Securities Act. The attorney general grumbled that he had made the mistake of confiding in Gordon Grant, the *Post's* mining editor, about the problems facing the OSC, only to be repaid with an 'untrue' article stemming from 'unquestionable malice.'[56] Blackwell had in fact already ordered the commission to cease the practice of permitting brokers and salespeople to offer restitution to customers in order to escape punishment for wrongdoing. Yet he refused to be stampeded by a barrage of complaints. When R.L. Healy of the Wright-Hargreaves mine protested to Premier Drew that quick action was needed to clean up the securities business and flush out the shady Americans in Toronto's brokerages, the attorney general replied that the situation was not as serious as represented. He was not ready to start cancelling the registrations of brokers and dealers simply to satisfy the press.[57] ·

Blackwell had to admit that the time had come to bring in new legislation. By early 1945 a draft act had been prepared and shown to interested parties in the financial community, such as the Toronto Stock Exchange.[58] Yet he could not simply proceed at his own pace. At a federal-provincial conference on the uniformity of law the previous summer a number of attorneys general had expressed the view that uniform legislation was essential if securities fraud was to be stamped out, and Blackwell had therefore promised to consult the other provincial regulators before submitting a new bill to the Ontario legislature.[59] Not only the provinces but the federal government was concerned about securities regulation, since it too controlled valuable mining prospects, such as the recent uranium finds on Great Bear Lake and gold discoveries at Yellowknife. The Americans still remained deeply concerned about securities regulation in Canada, as an estimated $125 million in net investment had flowed north of the border during 1944 alone, much of it going into junior mining shares of doubtful value. So long as the revision of the Extradition Treaty hung fire, the United States could not force the handing over of offenders against its federal or state laws.[60]

Blackwell therefore announced a conference to be held in Toronto on 29 January 1945. The regulators met for two and one-half days. Not only federal officials attended, but also Ganson Purcell, chair of the SEC, and two of his senior officials, Edward H. Cashion and J.T. Callahan. Both British Columbia and Alberta sent their chief securities regulators, and officials came from New Brunswick and Quebec. Manitoba, Nova Scotia, and Saskatchewan were unrepresented, though the latter two had deputed British Columbia to speak on their behalf.[61] First to be heard from were Purcell and the SEC officials, who described the extent of the illegal marketing of Canadian stocks in the United States by Toronto brokers. In the course of this discussion, sharp criticism was levelled at the OSC by both the Americans and the officials from the other provinces. Then Blackwell and his staff explained their draft bill. Securities regulation had always rested upon the prohibition of various kinds of dishonest conduct and had granted the right to investigate where fraud was suspected. These powers were combined with registration of brokers and their salespeople, intended to ensure their good character and behaviour. Regulators were given relatively limited discretion over the kinds of securities offered for sale, though they could refuse to register an issue or demand that it be restructured. Following the recommendations of the mining commission and modelled upon the American Securities Act of 1933 and the Securities Exchange Act of 1934, Blackwell's new act adopted a different approach. Now promoters would be required to make 'full, true and plain' disclosure by a prospectus of all the material facts about a company to prospective purchasers of shares sold over the counter in primary distribution.[62] (For shares traded on the stock exchange, the TSE's listing requirements were assumed to be sufficient protection for buyers.) The OSC would not act as a judge about whether or not a company would succeed, but leave it to the investor to make an informed decision on whether to put up money. Failure to distribute a prospectus and secure an acknowledgment might allow the rescission of the transaction during a period of up to one year.

Yet the proposed legislation did not rely solely upon disclosure to protect investors. Brokers and salespeople must still be registered with the OSC, the courts having held in 1932 that the province could require such people to be 'honest and of good repute.' As a result, the commission would be granted wide discretion to refuse or cancel the registration of any person in the 'public interest.' In presenting the draft bill to the other regulators, Ontario promised a 'general purge' of undesirable types from the securities industry to put the boiler-room operators out of business.[63]

The response of the Canadians at the conference, however, was not enthusiastic. British Columbia's superintendent of brokers, E.K. DeBeck, took the lead in criticizing the proposed changes. G.M. Blackstock of Alberta backed him up strongly, while the Quebec officials privately endorsed these views but preferred to let the other provinces take the initiative. Central to the criticisms were doubts that disclosure would provide sufficient protection for investors. DeBeck thought that the experts who prepared prospectuses could easily lay them out so as to deceive the unwary about things like estimated ore reserves or markets for a product. Even if purchasers were willing or able to study these documents with care, they might fail to spot such pitfalls. It was pointed out that the Securities and Exchange Commission did not rely solely upon disclosure as a means of regulation: many applicants for registration were required by 'deficiency letters' to supply additional information, and stop orders or injunctions could be issued to halt the sale of any issue pending compliance. In addition, many American states had blue-sky laws that allowed them to regulate security sales directly.

DeBeck complained that curtailing the OSC's discretionary authority to refuse registration of an issue meant that, 'no matter how unreasonable or how loaded the setup of the company may be, it would be registered subject to full disclosure having been made in the prospectus.' The proposed legislation would do nothing to prevent mining promoters from optioning shares for 5 cents or less, which then could be marketed to the public for three or four times as much, even if no development work had been done on the property. DeBeck expressed the belief that every promoter in the country would flock to Toronto in search of higher profits. The peddling of worthless stocks across North America would give Canada a black eye and make it all the harder to raise money for resource development in future. The response of the Ontario officials was defensive; Blackwell closed the meeting with a promise that the proposed law would undergo further refinement.[64]

Yet few significant changes were made in the legislation. Tabling the bill in the assembly in February 1945, the attorney general harked back to the report of the Ontario Royal Commission on Mining, which had called for a relaxation of regulatory controls.[65] During the second-reading debate on the principles of his bill, Blackwell reiterated the long-standing criticism of blue-sky legislation that it required some bureaucrat to determine whether or not a joint-stock company was likely to succeed or not. No longer, he said, should approval to distribute securities to the public depend 'upon the state of some commissioner's liver at the time.' Officials were incapable of assessing the true worth of speculative mining shares, so the OSC would simply receive filings from promoters and ensure that full disclosure had been made to intending purchasers of any shares in primary distribution.[66]

In explaining the bill to the house clause by clause, Blackwell did admit that there were some elements within the financial community causing serious concern. Of 225 brokers registered with the OSC who dealt in over-the-counter stocks and were not members of either the Toronto Stock Exchange or the Investment Dealers Association, about 25 had 'some mark' against their records, and among the 1,327 salespeople they employed, 28 had likewise fallen afoul of the authorities. Around the start of the year the OSC had compiled a list of twenty-nine Toronto brokerages engaged in heavy telephone selling. For instance, during January one firm with six salespeople had made 500 calls within Ontario, 214 to other provinces, and 47 to the United States, while another with eight salespeople made 306 in Ontario, 24 outside it, and 244 across the border. Blackwell had to concede that the extent of such calling made it clear that the pitches were not directed only to current customers or to business numbers; calls must be being made to the private residences of strangers, a practice banned in Ontario since 1934. Moreover, since very few Canadian stocks were registered for sale in the United States, these calls must involve violations of American law.[67]

The attorney general argued that his aim was to ensure that members of the public 'do not play against a marked deck' when buying shares. The response of Opposition Leader E.B. Jolliffe was generally favourable, though he expressed doubts that investors would take the time to study and assimilate the facts disclosed in prospectuses. He contended that the OSC should retain wider administrative discretion since Ontario was 'quite likely to be overrun by a type of securities salespeople that you will never catch up with in any court.' Former Liberal premier Mitchell Hepburn was much less happy; he put forward the criticisms of organizations such as the Prospectors and Developers Association, which argued that the new act strayed too far from the principles recommended by the Royal Commission on Mining in 1944. Eventually Blackwell agreed that the Legal Bills Committee should hold hearings at which any interested parties could put forward proposals.[68]

Intense pressure was exerted upon Blackwell to modify the legislation. A leading securities lawyer claimed that share buyers would simply use the right to rescind transactions to try to cut their losses, because 'an investor who has lost money is ready to avail himself of any trick to get his money back.' The Prospectors and Developers Association attempted to demonstrate the immense practical problems created by the need to print and distribute prospectuses for popular new issues, which could only be marketed successfully if brokers struck while the iron was hot. Blackwell was also subjected to a powerful campaign to drop the ban on salespeople telephoning private residences. The Ontario Securities Dealers Association claimed that this prohibition was just a sop to the 'howling' from the SEC, which had already put a stop to all speculative mining finance in the United States and would now do so in Canada too. Why should Ontario impose a ban when no other province or state did so, especially since at least 50 per cent of the money invested in junior mines came from south of the border? Mining broker C.R. Blackburn went further, claiming that 98 per cent of the opportunities to raise money by selling unlisted mining stock would be ruined.[69]

Despite this lobbying, Blackwell stuck to his guns, and the bill emerged from the committee within a fortnight little changed. When he reported the legislation back to the full house, he pointed out that the only significant amendments involved the reduction of the period during which investors were permitted to nullify a purchase on account of failure to receive a prospectus from one year to sixty days. The attorney general insisted that critics of the requirements of disclosure by prospectus for stocks in primary distribution as being too arduous to comply with were really trying to tamper with the 'keystone' of the act, rendering it ineffective. Most people recognized that the operations of boiler rooms were damaging the reputation of the

Ontario financial community all across North America and must be halted. With little more debate, the new Securities Act became law, to come into force on 1 December 1945.[70]

III

The market for junior mining stocks in Canada continued to boom. Buyers showed little interest in the underlying value of properties, aiming instead for quick trading profits.[71] The situation provided a heaven-sent opportunity for Toronto's boiler-room operators, and American officials became more and more agitated. Canadians attending the annual conference of the U.S. National Association of Securities Administrators in St Louis near the end of 1944 heard many complaints. A survey of NASA members prior to the meeting produced such blunt criticisms of the situation in Toronto that the subject was discussed only in a closed session to avoid sparking an international incident. The OSC was allowing high-pressure salespeople to continue to operate, including those who had criminal records or were under investigation by the American authorities. In the United States, said one official, a single infraction could debar a person from registration for life: 'There are lots of jobs for ex-crooks, but we can't tolerate having them in the securities business.' Grumbling was heard that the OSC had failed to cooperate in the detection and prosecution of offenders selling by telephone across the border. Several of the Americans expressed amazement at the OSC's refusal to ban the 300 to 400 per cent margins between option and sale prices common on mining shares. Asked one official, 'Do you mean to say that people can take markups like that in Canada without going to jail?'[72]

In the spring of 1945 the bulletin of the Pennsylvania Securities Commission recorded that sales of speculative shares had become an increasing problem over the past three years, which had led to the issuing of thirty-eight cease-and-desist orders against Canadian brokers; nine such orders were recorded in February and March 1945 alone, provoking the complaint, 'These offerings have become a greater racket than anything ever experienced before the days of legislation covering the sales of securities.' J.T. Callahan, special counsel at the SEC's New York office, was instructed to warn Toronto dealers to stop violating American law. In the twelve months following November 1944 he sent letters to fifty-nine brokers, twelve investment advisory services, twenty prospecting syndicates selling units, and one hundred and fifty officers and directors of mining companies, advising them to cease their activities.[73]

Redmond and Company, for instance, was warned against bombarding school teachers in Nebraska with circulars followed up by telephone calls touting Pensive Yellowknife Mines. Unrepentant, the firm complained that this was 'a malicious and meddlesome piece of work instigated by Mr. Callaghan [sic] of the Securities and Exchange Commission, and is a typical instance of the type of operations carried on against Canadian brokers for a number of years.' E.M. McLean and Company also claimed that it had done nothing wrong: any orders received from U.S. residents had come unsolicited as a result of advertisements placed in Canadian publications. Allegations like that in *Time* magazine that 'Many of the promoted properties do not even exist' were simply libellous. 'A great deal of unpleasant publicity is being directed at this province in which all mining activity is referred to as "rackets," but nothing is said of the thousands of dollars now being made by citizens of the United States and this country as the result of sound mining development and spectacular values established by diamond drilling now taking place.'[74]

The failure of the Conservative government to crack down on Toronto brokers became an issue during the provincial election campaign in mid-1945. The deep-dyed Liberal *Toronto Daily Star* quoted BC superintendent DeBeck's grumbles about the laxity of the OSC in 'granting easier and easier terms until practically any issue will pass.'[75] New Brunswick attorney general E.R. McLenty chimed in that it was 'the general impression that Toronto is the headquarters for the financial underworld.' At its annual convention, representatives of the 250 members of the Investment Dealers Association of Canada expressed concern; incoming president A.S. Torrey told the *Financial Post* that Quebec brokers were becoming increasingly worried that funds for legitimate mining development were being diverted elsewhere. Even the governor of the Bank of Canada weighed in with a statement that problems did exist which needed to be dealt with by tighter enforcement.

The Montreal *Gazette* picked up the issue and interviewed a number of U.S. officials. New York's attorney general expressed the opinion that 90 per cent of American investment in Canadian stocks was being lost, and his assistant, Max Furman, complained that the Ontario government was not doing enough to restrain illegal sales. Furman alleged that 'staggering' amounts of money were being drained away, mostly by people who had set up shop in Canada after being banned in New York. New Jersey's attorney general agreed that there were probably more American shysters in Toronto than in New York itself. Pennsylvania's securities commissioner said he had already issued cease-and-desist orders against forty-five different Canadian mining stocks and brokers and had passed on their names to Blackwell. He added that if the OSC had provided evidence that a Philadelphia broker was 'running wild' north of the border, registration would have been cancelled at once: 'Why can't we get the same cooperation from Ontario?'

Premier George Drew, once safely re-elected with a large majority, sought to brush the whole issue aside. He called in a reporter from the sympathetic Toronto *Globe and Mail* for a statement, claiming that in the heat of the election campaign the *Star* had stooped to reproducing 'carefully calculated misrepresentations' aimed to 'convey the impression that fraud in the sale of securities is rampant in Ontario.' Such irresponsible reports were 'nothing less than sabotage of plans for postwar development in northern Ontario.'[76]

Drew's bluster could not obscure the fact that the increasing glare of bad publicity had revived demands in the United States for changes to the Extradition Treaty. The *New York Times* carried several stories during May of 1945. Edward Cashion of the SEC said he had been investigating the 'Toronto gold rush' but was powerless to prosecute salespeople who were defrauding Americans of as much as $1 million a week. SEC staff in Philadelphia (where the agency had been relocated during the Second World War) insisted that despite restraining orders from state regulators, an effective treaty was the only real solution.[77] The *Philadelphia Inquirer* ran a series of articles on the problem, co-authored by the Pennsylvania securities commissioner, that culminated in an editorial entitled 'Stop This Canadian Gold Swindle' and warned that 'Toronto ... has become a veritable nest of get-rich-quick Wallingfords.'[78] Republished as a flyer, this piece was adorned with a cartoon of a dim-witted John Q. Sucker answering a telephone call about a 'Get-rich-quick Canadian gold mine swindle' and was offered free to newspapers across North America for republication.[79]

Appointed by the National Association of Securities Administrators to chair a special committee to inquire into the sale of Canadian mining shares using 'lurid sales literature with a minimum of factual information,' the Michigan securities commissioner complained that the problem of Toronto brokers selling unregistered securities in his state had grown progressively worse during the past two and one-half years.

Attorney General Blackwell, however, continued to insist that he was doing all he could under the present law. The issuing of a cease-and-desist order by American authorities was not sufficient grounds for him to suspend or cancel a broker's registration in Ontario. If evidence of fraud or misrepresentation was forwarded, then the OSC would be ready to investigate, but no such material had been received since he took over as acting commissioner. Meantime, he must be bound by the current Securities Act: 'I am not the law in the province of Ontario but merely the person charged with its administration.'[80]

Blackwell was particularly annoyed by what he saw as a carefully orchestrated campaign by the SEC to force Canada to ratify a new extradition treaty covering securities offences. On a visit to Toronto in mid-1945 Callahan was 'pretty cagey' and did not say much, but he made it clear that he believed only the passage of a treaty would really clear up the situation.[81] The attorney general reiterated that he had so far received no evidence of fraud or misrepresentation from the Americans: 'What we do receive is [sic] cease-and-desist orders having to do with Canadian brokers who have not complied with the registration provisions of the Securities and Exchange Commission and the different states ... We have, however, refused to permit American officials to come here and examine into [sic] the affairs of Canadian brokers under the investigation powers contained in our statutes.' Blackwell insisted that at present he could only compel brokers to cooperate by threatening to cancel their registration.[82]

He was especially irritated because the campaign for a revised treaty had been renewed without any intergovernmental consultation. Ottawa might be in a position to make securities offences under the Criminal Code extraditable, but he echoed the reservations of his Liberal predecessor that the federal government possessed jurisdiction to do the same for violations of the provincial Securities Act: 'it seems extremely doubtful to me that the Dominion would have the power to include in such a treaty extradition regarding what might be termed as technical offences against provincial or state statutes in the United States or even technical offences under the S.E.C.'[83]

In June 1945 the embassy in Washington reported that resentment against Canadian stock swindlers was assuming 'rather alarming proportions.' A few days later the matter was raised in Congress.[84] The State Department had already swung into action and delivered to Ottawa a revised draft of a protocol concerning securities offences to be attached to the treaty. The Canadians were unconvinced that the new text was much of an improvement over the old one, but Justice Department officials concluded that it should probably be accepted. Blackwell's claim that Ottawa had no jurisdiction to make an agreement which rendered offences against provincial law extraditable was rejected. If the federal government had the power to provide for extradition, then it could surely define the types of offences to be covered by a treaty. Moreover, it was argued that securities frauds were really criminal acts but had been dealt with provincially because of the difficulty in obtaining convictions under the federal Criminal Code. Ontario's new Securities Act depended upon full disclosure, so that it was much closer philosophically to American legislation than previously. The United States was seeking assistance in enforcing a type of regulation now becoming 'in vogue' in Canada itself: 'We cannot maintain proper international relations with the United States if we permit persons in this country to initiate transactions which involved breaches of US law designed to prevent frauds in the sale of securities.'[85]

Officials from both countries quickly approved the treaty amendment, which provided that no person could be extradited for dealing in securities in the ordinary course of business according to the law. Only if an act involved fraud as defined in Canada or if an offence against U.S. law was knowingly committed could the treaty be invoked. Extradition would not be sought of those indicted prior to the ratification of the new agreement. Officials at External Affairs predicted that securities dealers and provincial regulators were still likely to oppose the agreement, but they recommended that the cabinet approve the protocol. This was done in early September and on 3 October 1945 the document was signed by both countries.[86]

The Canadian financial community at once launched a powerful lobby to prevent Parliament from ratifying the protocol. The stock exchanges, the Prospectors and Developers Association, and the unlisted brokers in the Ontario Securities Dealers Association led the charge. The TSE again retained Arthur Slaght as counsel and appointed Liberal senator Peter Campbell to assist him as special counsel in making its case. In addition, several provincial governments remained opposed because they had not been consulted, even though the treaty seemed to trench upon their jurisdiction. At a meeting of an interprovincial committee on the mining industry, the securities regulators from Ontario, Quebec, Alberta, and British Columbia passed a resolution condemning the agreement as a surrender of Canadian sovereignty and a danger to the future development of mining.[87]

The government therefore referred the matter to the House of Commons Standing Committee on External Affairs, which conducted extensive hearings in November 1945. John Read, the legal adviser to External Affairs, led off with an explanation of the decision by Canada to abandon the principle of dual criminality for securities offences. He argued that political arrangements and the legal systems in the two countries were so similar that fears of persecution by American authorities were not realistic. Objections that acts by an innocent person which were legal in Canada might become grounds for an extradition request were pooh-poohed by the Justice Department: 'This objection is more apparent than real because it is definitely provided that he must do so willfully and knowingly, and before it could be alleged that he knew what the laws of the United States are some action would have to be taken by the US authorities to ensure that he did know what these laws were. Any danger from this source might be quite easily overcome by providing that ... any extradition proceedings must be approved by the Minister before they are instituted.'[88]

Arthur Slaght, however, insisted that the treaty would 'bring about a radical and disastrous change in the entire fiscal policy between Canada and the United States which had prevailed for fifty years.' American officials had only to mail copies of the relevant laws to all the brokers in Canada to turn them into 'knowing' lawbreakers. Joseph Sedgwick, representing the Prospectors and Developers Association, admitted that half the mining companies licensed by the OSC sold shares in the United States without registering there. How could a junior mining company be expected to do so when it cost up to $60,000 to gain approval from the SEC? After the changes 'it will be absolutely physically impossible for any speculative mining venture to qualify either with the SEC or any state of the union. The cost is prohibitive. The difficulties are too great ... We will have our choice of either cheating on the law and taking the risk of going to jail or doing without American capital in its entirety.'[89]

Appearing for the Ontario Securities Dealers Association, lawyer Ralph Salter claimed that 'no reputable businessman or engineer or professional man would dare to act as a director or officer of a mining company that was in the promotional or developmental stage.' He pointed out that American state officials were often less than frank about their demands that Canadian companies register before selling shares. The New Mexico authorities had admitted to the OSDA that no Canadian gold mines would be licensed to sell shares unless they had also undertaken the expensive and time-consuming process of gaining SEC approval. Many other states simply kept applicants dangling until they lost interest in securing registration.[90]

A near-hysterical diatribe against the treaty came from the Toronto *Globe and Mail*'s mining editor, Sidney Norman. He blamed the SEC for the recent 'vicious, organized publicity attack' upon Canadian security dealers, based upon evidence collected by its 'spy or snooper or detective' in Toronto, whose task was to 'furnish the bullets for the SEC to shoot in its publicity campaign.'[91] These arrogant demands for extraterritorial application of U.S. law came not from the American people, who cherished their freedom, said Norman: 'I am not afraid ... to say to you that this protocol has been drafted and requested by the Security [*sic*] Exchange Commission, the most execrated and distinctive super-bureaucracy ever created to stifle free enterprise.' Canada, he said, should reject the convention out of hand.[92]

The Americans, however, remained confident that with a Liberal majority on the House of Commons committee and in Parliament, ratification was a foregone conclusion. J.T. Callahan, who held a watching brief for the SEC, reported to his superiors that 'responsible Canadians' believed passage of the agreement was only a matter of time. Surprisingly, however, the committee unanimously recommended that the government ought to reconsider not just the protocol but the entire treaty. In explaining the committee's decision to the House of Commons, Conservative Rodney Adamson, the only member to speak, noted all the concerns about blocking the flow of American capital into Canada, the abandonment of the principle of dual criminality, the fear that the treaty was creating extraditable offences which were not truly criminal but merely technical, and finally, the failure to secure the consent of the provincial governments where their jurisdiction was involved. Adamson reported cryptically to diplomat Lester B. Pearson that he, though a member of the Opposition, had written the committee report: '[T]here were quite extraordinary circumstances existing. Owing to the human element these phenomena still exist ... [T]he real story is not contained in the written evidence.' Whatever that meant, the government was forced to accept that if there was to be a treaty, negotiations would have to start all over again with the United States and the provinces.[93]

American irritation about the Canadian brokerage community was unabated. In January 1946, for instance, the *Saturday Evening Post* carried a story about the continued efforts of the SEC and the Better Business Bureau to stem the flood of worthless mining shares across the border. Since 1942 state regulators had acted against 335 different Canadians peddling stock, but these activities showed no signs of abating as 'smooth-voiced promoters' from Toronto continued to produce letters, wires, and telephones calls designed to trap the unwary. The SEC was convinced that Canada was more interested in keeping up the flow of American funds than in cracking down on the shysters.[94] There was no sign that 'the Canadian problem' would disappear in the near future.

2

Self-Regulation

Reliance upon the principle of 'full, true and plain disclosure' by promoters, dealers, and insiders lay at the heart of Ontario's 1945 Securities Act. Yet the new legislation also gave the Ontario Securities Commission a mandate to review the registration of every dealer and salesman to ensure that it was in the 'public interest.' That task occupied much of the time of the commission during 1946, as a good many of the shadier characters were deprived of their licences. At the same time OSC officials convinced themselves that the most effective means to stamp out abuses was to rely upon self-regulation. Various elements within the financial community would be required to police their own members, leaving the OSC free to cope with the most serious problems and to stiffen the resolve of the insiders only when it seemed absolutely necessary.

I

To oversee the clean-up of the securities business, the government of Ontario appointed a new chair of the Ontario Securities Commission. The person chosen was Charles McTague, a former judge of the Ontario Supreme Court who had recently headed up Canada's National War Labour Board. While applauding his selection, the *Financial Post* noted that McTague would have a challenging task.[1] No longer did salespeople search for gullible investors as they had in the past: 'They did not go out any more. They did not go to the farmer's back door; they did not go to the retired school teacher and take her last dime. That era was over. But the next thing was the flamboyant literature and the use of the telephone.' Protests about high-pressure sales campaigns by Toronto boiler rooms showed how serious the problem still was. At the November 1945 conference of the National Association of Securities Administrators, California's commissioner of corporations complained that sales of unregistered Canadian shares were still 'epidemic' in his state. The newly appointed McTague could only reply that he welcomed constructive criticism and advice from his fellow regulators as he was still learning his job; he promised that he would attack the boiler rooms vigorously.[2]

McTague's most pressing task was to set up a procedure to conduct the review of registrations. He directed the OSC's registrar, E.H. Anundson, to examine the dossier of every broker and salesperson. In any case where the registrar recommended against renewal, the licensee could appeal to the chair. Aggrieved parties were also entitled to apply to a judge of the Supreme Court of Ontario for relief from misinterpretations of points of law and procedure. The decisions of the chair might also be appealed to the full commission, now reinforced by two part-time members, H.C. Rickaby and Oswald E. Lennox,[3] who would sit with McTague when he heard appeals against his own decisions.

McTague initially intended that the review of registrations should take place behind closed doors, only the names of those refused being released without reasons given. As he put it, 'It was not felt that it would be healthy or altogether in the spirit of charity to hand out details of convictions and misconduct. The commission felt that it did not desire to place these men under additional handicaps if they sought to reestablish themselves in other occupations.' He soon learned, however, that a spirit of charity was misplaced amongst the denizens of the boiler room, since 'the commission had not found its policy appreciated or well received by some of the parties.' Brokers whose registration was cancelled released 'misleading statements with respect to the reasons. In some cases more or less organized attempts have been made to discredit the commission.' The press, meanwhile, published conjectures, sometimes 'entirely erroneous,' about the rationale for OSC decisions.

When McTague ordered the cancellation of the registration of H.R. Bain and Company, Rupert Bain launched a fierce counter-attack. Though a frequent cause of complaints to the OSC, he argued that he had been responsible for promoting mining companies which had produced $25 million worth of ore and paid $8 million in dividends. Yet the cancellation had been ordered on the basis of complaints dating from as far back as fourteen years earlier, even though twenty-three of these thirty-one problems were 'trivial.' An average of only two complaints a year, some of them registered after a lapse of many months, was surely not surprising from buyers of highly speculative stocks. Some of the information on which the OSC had relied about unconscionable profits on a bond deal in the early 1930s Bain dismissed as plain wrong. Faced with this assault, McTague decided to release the reasons for a decision in every case where they existed in writing; the first set of these were handed to the press in March 1946.[4]

Complaints were heard that publicizing the OSC's decisions would simply create intense distrust amongst investors and damage the market for mining shares. John H. Roberts, who put out a tipsheet called the *Canadian Mining Reporter*, protested directly to the attorney general; Leslie Blackwell replied that only a few shady characters had anything to fear from a review which had widespread public support, and that a small group of people should not be permitted to impede efforts to raise capital for resource development. He noted that despite the existence of an appeal process, some of those who had been deregistered 'appeared to feel that they could do better by appealing by way of propaganda to the public than by appeal to the courts.'[5]

One of Blackwell's constituents protested that by cancelling the registration of his broker the OSC had destroyed the value of his stock and cost him $900. The attorney general responded that the problems had been brought about 'by a section of those engaged in the brokerage business which felt that it could obstruct the operation of the commission by organized propaganda.' McTague, said Blackwell, had originally been willing to handle the review privately, but he was not prepared to allow rumours to spread unchecked.[6]

The Securities Act provided no definition of the 'public interest' except to specify that previous OSC decisions need not be treated as binding precedents. In one of the very first cases appealed to the full commission, the decision noted the difficulty of a precise definition of the concept but announced an intention to rely upon a broad interpretation. Salesman Ivan Israel was an American citizen who had failed to establish permanent residence in Canada and had fallen afoul of immigration officials. Not only did he have a previous conviction in New York, but he had been warned several times by the OSC and compelled to make restitution to customers. In the public interest Israel's licence was therefore cancelled, a decision upheld by a judge of the Supreme Court on appeal.[7]

The OSC had also to work out a number of procedural principles.

Were registrants to be treated as innocent unless proven guilty of misconduct? In the case of William Dykes, McTague concluded that each individual was merely being given an opportunity to present evidence to show cause why a licence cancellation should not take place.[8] Should the OSC operate as though it were a court of law? J.K. Gamble tried to hide behind his son, acting as a front, but lost his registration despite the lack of direct evidence of wrongdoing: 'we do not believe that acting as an administrative tribunal we are bound by the strict rules of evidence as they apply in criminal cases. We are a licensing body and must primarily be guided by what we believe is the public interest. We believe we are entitled to be guided not only by the actual evidence before us, but on our appraisal of the character of the applicant and his suitability to solicit funds from the public in a capacity that more than verges on a fiduciary relationship. We must bring to bear our general knowledge of the conditions that prevail in the market and on the street.'[9]

H.A. Morton challenged this position, appealing to the courts on the grounds that there were no clear reasons for refusing him registration. His case was heard by Ontario chief justice R.S. Robertson, who noted that Morton had received a fair hearing at which evidence of earlier misconduct had been presented. The judge held that while the OSC was bound to follow the principles of natural justice, it was also responsible for protecting the public interest. No specific charge or complaint need be filed to bring about an investigation, and indeed, the commission had been specifically directed to review all current registrations and not to be bound by its previous decisions. Registrants possessed no vested interests that had to be weighed in the balance against the public interest. The chief justice noted that the OSC possessed very wide discretion in defining the public interest, and that the court ought not to substitute its judgment for the commission's. He therefore upheld the refusal to grant Morton a licence.[10]

Would the commission allow offenders to escape punishment if they repaid their victims, as had often happened previously? Said McTague, 'An impression seems to have grown up among brokers and salesmen generally that if restitution has been made to complainants in questionable transactions, such a degree of respectability and honourable dealing has been evidenced that the broker or salesman is entitled to approbation rather than discipline and in no circumstances should cancellation be ordered. We do not accept any such philosophy.' The OSC was not an arbitrator of private rights, a task properly left to the courts, and to permit restitution was to 'constitute ourselves a benevolent collection agency.' W.E. Davison tried to represent himself as generous in compensating a ninety-two-year-old Port Hope, Ontario, woman who had in fact suffered 'most callous and unscrupulous treatment' at his hands, for which he richly deserved to lose his licence.[11]

Another common ploy was to try to shift the blame onto other people, particularly in the case of those accused of false advertising. G.F. Cockburn and Company committed a glaring offence against the Securities Act by issuing a circular claiming that a stock issue was 'approved' by the OSC. Cockburn blamed the mistake on the 'writer' who had composed the text. When M.F. Burrows was caught running misleading advertisements even during the period when his registration was under review by the OSC in the spring of 1946, he pretended that he had telephoned the information to the newspaper and that there had not been enough time to proof-read the final text. These excuses were summarily dismissed since the OSC had long since established the principle that brokers were responsible for any material which appeared with a licensee's name attached to it.[12]

Of course, most of the cases that came before Charles McTague did not involve issues of regulatory philosophy but merely concerned frauds or misrepresentations. Jack Rosen wanted to be registered as a securities salesman, claiming that a military injury had rendered it impossible for him to continue work as a garment presser. But it turned out that he had supplied misleading information about his conviction for bookmaking some years earlier and had concealed a charge of theft for trying to cash a coupon from a stolen bond won in a gambling game. His application was rejected as unlikely to serve the public interest, 'if the standard of trading is to be raised to any appreciable degree.'[13] J.W. Armstrong had persuaded the Connertys, mother and daughter, that they ought to sell their blue-chip stocks, such as Bell Telephone and Imperial Oil. When they suggested investing in Victory bonds, he had the gall to denigrate these as a good, safe investment. Instead he put their money into speculative oils and mines which proved worthless, all as part of 'a deliberate, persistent and unfortunately successful plan to victimize these people.' The OSC could not find a single 'favourable instance' in Armstrong's record, nor had he made any 'constructive effort' to promote mining development but preferred to leave his customers holding the bag.[14]

When Rupert Bain was threatened with the cancellation of his registration on the grounds that his telephone salesmen had frequently

made misrepresentations, he insisted that he had done everything possible to control his salesmen by warning them against such misconduct. The OSC rejected this excuse summarily: 'Nothing could be
further from the point.' 'The proposition that a firm cannot control its
salesmen is tantamount to holding that the sale of securities cannot be
regulated.' H.R. Bain and Company had become a major embarrassment to the OSC because its telephone marketing extended not only
across Canada but into the United States. Bain and his partner, R.S.
Newling, had frequently promised to correct these problems then
failed to act.

> The activities of this company outside the province had [sic] done more to
> discredit Ontario, than the operation of any other brokers which have
> come to our notice during the current review of registrations. The attitude
> of its responsible officers goes to the very root of administrative law. They
> apparently gave their undertaking to discontinue unlicensed activities as
> a matter of routine without any serious intention of implementing it.
> Their present attitude appears to be that by warning their salesmen they
> had done all that was required ...
> It is a matter of common knowledge that United States interests look
> with disfavour upon the manner in which sales are solicited by Canadian
> firms. It is reasonable to expect a high standard of trading from a com-
> pany of long standing and which has enjoyed some measure of success.

The registration of H.R. Bain and Company was accordingly cancelled, though Bain Newling and Company, the partnership that held a
TSE seat, was allowed to continue operating. In an effort to avoid the
unfavourable publicity attracted by the licence cancellation, Rupert
Bain tried to claim that he had simply decided to allow the registration
of the former firm to lapse in the spring of 1946, vainly insisting that
the OSC had not really uncovered evidence of any real wrongdoing
and that he had simply made up his own mind to concentrate his operations in Bain, Newling and Company.[15]

By the fall of 1946 Bain was applying for reregistration because the
salesmen at Bain, Newling and Company were prohibited from marketing over-the-counter mining shares during the hours when the
Toronto Stock Exchange was open for trading, so its most lucrative
business was in decline. Despite Bain's notoriety, the OSC concluded
that it could not simply refuse to hear the application and that a licence
cancellation should not be an absolute bar to reregistration. In light of

Bain's success in promoting worthwhile ventures like the Pickle Crow gold mine, the commission voted to regard the lapse of Bain's registration as an extended suspension and to allow him to resume business in hopes that this would have a salutary effect upon his conduct.[16]

A.E. DePalma was another notorious character who created a great deal of ill will amongst American regulators. Having fled New York in 1937 after an indictment for stock fraud, he applied for registration with the OSC, stating that he had lived in Ontario continuously for thirty-six years. As a salesman he persuaded two sisters in Kingsville, Ontario, retired schoolteachers, to sell their government bonds and blue-chip stocks in the early 1940s and buy highly speculative mining stocks. By making partial restitution, DePalma had succeeded in regaining his licence in the early 1940s, but the OSC considered his swindling 'about the worst example of ruthlessness and high pressure which has come to our attention' and cancelled his licence in 1946. Ironically, the result was a flurry of protest letters to Attorney General Leslie Blackwell from DePalma customers all across the United States who had bought shares of Peg Tantalum Mines and were angry that the regulatory crackdown would reduce the value of their stock to nothing.[17]

In 1947 DePalma applied to be relicensed as a broker, arguing that deregistration had made it difficult for him to raise funds for mining projects. He claimed to have handed over his old business to Robert Mitchell and Company, but the OSC noted that the only shares marketed by Mitchell were underwritten and promoted by DePalma, who admitted that he prepared all its promotional literature. Circulars for the Tantalum Mining and Refining Corporation bore all the hallmarks of DePalma's style, such as exaggerated estimates of 'future market potential' for the ore. He was not granted a new licence.[18]

At the same time the OSC secured approval from the attorney general to commence an investigation into Mitchell and Company, which soon revealed that it was a front for DePalma. Mitchell and DePalma had an oral agreement by which the former was guaranteed against any losses incurred marketing the latter's promotions, which had netted Mitchell $75,000 during the first year. Mitchell and Company was a telephone boiler room where three former DePalma salesmen had racked up 7,400 long-distance calls during a period of thirteen months. The firm was put out of business and the three salesmen suspended for six months.[19]

T. Earle Reid and Company was another boiler room deregistered in the spring of 1947. Reid apparently shared the notion prevalent on Bay

Street that if there were no records of telephone calls to private residences, the OSC would leave his salesmen alone. He agreed to surrender his brokerage registration, but McTague cancelled the licences of all the employees of the firm, noting, 'People who undertake the operation of boiler-rooms must be assumed to be willing to stake their registrations. Salesmen who participate should realize they take a similar risk.'[20]

Four of Reid's salesmen attempted to overturn this decision, first with an unsuccessful appeal to the full OSC, which they then carried to the Ontario Supreme Court. Their lawyers argued that they had not been represented at Reid's hearing, so that any evidence obtained from him should not be used against them. This suit produced a key decision concerning the authority of the chair in the OSC's licence review proceedings. Chief Justice Robertson held that McTague acted in a purely administrative capacity when making such decisions and reiterated that he had wide discretion to act in the 'public interest' under the 1945 Securities Act. Each of the salesmen had been heard by McTague, who had then used his administrative authority to cancel their registrations.

The salesmen also contended that no evidence had been presented to the full OSC that they personally had violated the Securities Act, yet the other two members of the board had joined the chair in upholding his original decision. The chief justice found that the other two members of the board were automatically entitled to consider all the evidence obtained from their former employer, Reid, since McTague himself would obviously possess this information. Roberston noted that section 45(3) of the Securities Act specifically held that the OSC 'shall not be bound by the technical rules of evidence,' which was designed to allow them to 'obtain information in any way they think best.' About the operations of Reid and Company the judge was unsparing, citing the commission's finding: 'This brokerage house undertook specialized concentrated telephone operations- in other words [it was] a boiler room. These salesmen are all specialists in telephone selling. It seems to be a prevalent idea on sections of Bay Street that because the Act makes telephoning to a private residence an offence, a boiler room can be operated as long as there is no proof of telephoning to a private residence.' The OSC had a duty to protect the public interest and in this case had quite properly decided to cancel the registrations of all those involved.[21]

When 31 March 1946 rolled around and all current registrations expired, the OSC's review had already deprived thirteen brokers and thirteen salesmen of their licences. Since a sizeable number of cases were still to be dealt with, the provincial government amended the Securities Act to provide that all current registrations should continue until the commission had rendered a decision about them. Charles McTague announced that telephoning outside Ontario for the purpose of selling securities was now banned, although he remained doubtful that the province had jurisdiction to do so, since the only way that the rule could be enforced was through cancellation of registration, a clumsy tool.[22]

McTague made clear it to the financial community that he intended to stay the course and use his authority under the new Securities Act as fully as possible. At the annual meeting of the Prospectors and Developers Association in March 1946, he reminded his audience that full, true, and plain disclosure was now the OSC's guiding philosophy. Mining brokers who took excessive profits by selling overpriced shares to gullible customers could expect to face disciplinary action. In June he told the staider members of the Investment Dealers Association that they too had an important stake in maintaining public confidence in securities markets. Once an investor was burned by some shyster, it was unlikely that anyone would be allowed to lay their hands on that person's money in future. The SEC was forced to scrutinize Canadian issues for sale in the United States so closely on account of 'wholesale and deliberate violations of their securities laws by a small coterie of Bay Street security dealers.' As a result, even IDA members trying to sell blue-chip issues were forced to advertise that they were not offering these securities for sale in the United States. If the situation were allowed to get any worse, the free flow of capital might be interfered with.[23]

Gradually the OSC's efforts seemed to bear fruit. At the meeting of the National Association of Securities Administrators in New York in the autumn of 1946, McTague received an unexpected tribute for his efforts from both the outgoing president and his successor. SEC officials told the *Financial Post* that the OSC was now doing a good job. Off the record, however, some American officials expressed concern that there were still brokers operating in Toronto who deserved to be put out of business. The SEC's chief counsel once again raised the issue of a revised extradition treaty between the two countries, noting that he still had numerous secret indictments against Canadians that he wished to proceed with once the accused could be brought to trial on American soil.[24]

Looking back on his efforts some years later, McTague observed that he had come to the OSC at a critical moment. The problem with the old Security Frauds Prevention Act was that it did not 'have any kind of particular philosophy behind it, beyond this, that it did put in the hands of the Commissioner ... broad and almost bureaucratic powers with respect to who might be registered and whether an issue would be qualified or not, and there was not anything back of it beyond putting the administration of the whole securities business into the hands of one man.' The OSC therefore possessed arbitrary powers and was not required to give reasons for its actions, so 'there was a tendency to say that there was a violation of the act, or of what the Commissioner thought was the right thing to do, ... but if you made restitution it was forgiven.' To McTague it did not seem right that a prospectus could simply be rejected without any avenue of appeal: 'Frankly, I do not like that kind of legislation, because I do not think that one man in any province is good enough for that. I certainly would be the first to admit that I could not do it, and I would not want to do it.'

The new legislation that he had been brought in to administer marked a considerable shift: 'The basic philosophy back of the 1945 act was quite similar to that behind the Securities and Exchange Act in the United States, namely full, frank and plain disclosure was made compulsory in respect of a prospectus, and the one-man commissioner was changed to a board of commissioners under a chairman.' The assumption was that purchasers ought to be able to make themselves fully familiar with any issue offered before a transaction became final and to have the right of rescission if full disclosure was not made. Administratively, the rules of the game were laid down in 'fairly definite terms' and the 'arbitrary power' of the commission reined in.[25]

In the three years after the new act came into force, 132 hearings were held, which resulted in the cancellation of the licences of 47 brokers and 38 salespeople. During the same period there were 116 prosecutions for breaches of the Securities Act or of the Criminal Code, leading to 98 convictions on charges such as telephoning a private residence, employing unlicensed salesmen, theft, or obtaining money by false pretences. The punishments included fines and jail terms of up to seven years.[26]

II

Soon after his arrival at the OSC, Charles McTague concluded that further reforms were necessary. The commission was still in a state of internal disorganization as a result of the reassignment of Roy White-head in 1944, followed swiftly by the death of his successor, W.A. Brant, which had left it without a full-time head for more than a year. On taking over in the autumn of 1945, McTague completed a restructuring begun by Brant, recruiting new staff including several war veterans.

Early on, McTague said later, he learned that the financial community consisted of three very distinct elements. The bond dealers and underwriters of blue-chip industrial issues were members of the Investment Dealers Association, founded in 1916, and they created few regulatory problems. Though the Toronto Stock Exchange generally managed its own affairs fairly competently, sudden and inexplicable fluctuations in the prices of the penny mining shares that still composed a large proportion of the TSE's listings indicated that some of its members needed close supervision. Far and away the most serious problems were created by the non-member brokers, promoters and dealers of over-the-counter stocks accustomed to taking down stock from a company treasury under option, paying 5 cents a share or less, and using high-pressure tactics to market the stock for as much as 90 cents. McTague became convinced that something must be done to clean up this 'jungle.'[27]

In a speech to the annual dinner of the TSE in May 1946, he floated what he admitted was a trial balloon of his own devising. Since each of the three groups faced a different set of problems best understood by their own members, why not create three separate self-regulatory organizations to assume primary responsibility for discipline under the general supervision of the OSC? Members of the IDA and the TSE expressed general approval of the proposal, though some noted that they operated in more than one of the three spheres. Stockbroking firms handled bonds (often having a partnership that belonged to the TSE and an incorporated affiliate in the IDA), while some exchange members also functioned as promoters and dealers in over-the-counter shares. Who would be required to belong to which organization? What would happen if these bodies found themselves at cross-purposes about what types of regulation were required? In particular, there were doubts about whether some denizens of the jungle were either willing or able to bend their efforts towards reform. In any case, everyone declared that a great deal of consultation would be required before any new legislation was introduced.[28]

Why did McTague suggest such a significant reform after only six months at the head of the OSC? He had had nothing to do with the drafting of the 1945 Securities Act and therefore felt free to propose changes. Moreover, he had agreed to accept his position only at the personal urging of Premier George Drew and had stipulated that he might resign after just one year in office.[29] He seems to have aimed to make his mark in a short period of time before departing the scene.

Attorney General Leslie Blackwell and Premier Drew felt that McTague's plan was worth a test. By end of 1946 each element of the financial community was considering a proposal to grant it statutory powers to impose discipline. Giving such authority to the Ontario branch of the Investment Dealers Association of Canada and to the TSE did not pose many problems, and the drafting of this new legislation proceeded smoothly.[30] However, drawing together the gaggle of people handling over-the-counter stocks proved more difficult. A committee was struck, chaired by broker Cecil W. Tom and including representatives of the OSC and the TSE. At a meeting in January 1947 about 150 mining promoters, broker-dealers, and salesmen approved the principle of self-regulation. Over the next couple of months plans for a new Broker Dealers Association of Ontario were discussed.[31]

OSC lawyer William Wismer prepared the bills, which finally made their way through the legislature's fall session in 1947, giving recognition to the IDA and TSE and creating the BDA, each being granted certain powers under the Securities Act.[32] Starting from scratch, the Broker Dealers Association faced the most challenging task. Of the nine governors appointed by order-in-council, who met for the first time at the National Club on 25 February 1948, three were chosen from firms that belonged to the TSE but also acted as promotional houses for unlisted shares, and one person represented the salespeople employed by BDA members. The board chose Arthur White as its chair. Wismer, who had drafted the legislation, moved over to become the full-time secretary and general counsel of the BDA.[33] Meanwhile, the association's lawyer, Ralph Salter, struggled to draft statutory regulations acceptable to the OSC that would permit the BDA to exercise its responsibility to discipline members for unethical conduct, and a set of rules was finally worked out to take effect on 3 April 1948.[34]

The BDA's first priority was to enroll all non-member brokers and begin collecting fees.[35] A Membership Committee was established to undertake the vetting of applicants. Information on prospective members had to be gathered by interviewing them where necessary and attempting to ascertain whether some people might be fronting for other undesirables. Much of the board's time was devoted to considering recommendations from the Membership Committee. After dealing with the brokers themselves, the board ruled that all salespeople employed by BDA members must be enrolled by 30 September 1948.[36]

Gradually a division of responsibilities between the OSC and the BDA was worked out which recognized the commission's ultimate authority. When the OSC intended to cancel a registration, it was agreed that advance notice would be passed along privately, so that BDA membership might be rescinded before the announcement of the decision. Salespeople who got into trouble with the OSC would only be considered for readmission to the BDA if they could persuade a member to employ them and take responsibility for their future conduct and if the OSC agreed to reregister them.[37]

Before long the BDA board recognized that a separate Discipline Committee was required. Harry Knight, its chair, was given authority to appoint panels of members as required to hear cases such as that of Reginald H. Mortimer, a salesman who had relieved an eighty-year-old Mennonite farmer in Elmira, Ontario, of $13,000 worth of cash and gilt-edged bonds in exchange for shares in a couple of speculative mining companies. The OSC immediately cancelled Mortimer's registration but agreed to allow the association to consider the case before announcing the decision. Mortimer was turfed out of the BDA. In mid-July the board approved the first fines imposed upon members for unethical conduct. During ten months in 1948 thirteen cases were dealt with and six members fined $650 for such offences as calling a private residence, promising to repurchase a stock within thirty days, and selling bonds to an aged woman at an unconscionable price.[38]

The BDA also concerned itself with the financial ability of its members to meet their obligations to customers, taking over from the OSC the responsibility of seeing that their books were audited. An Audit Committee was quickly established to be advised by the association's own auditor, R.H.B. Hector. The board fixed the modest sum of $5,000 as the minimum free capital required to be maintained at all times. The annual audit date was set at 30 November, and each member would also be subject to a surprise audit at least once annually.[39]

The BDA also made efforts to improve the public image of the over-the-counter market. A dinner was held for financial reporters in May 1948, with the aim of persuading them not to use words like 'stock salesman' or 'broker' in headlines about swindles pulled off by people who did not belong to the BDA. William Wismer offered to send a membership list to the Toronto newspapers; the *Financial Post*, the *Globe and Mail*, and the *Telegram* agreed to cooperate, but the *Daily Star* (with the largest circulation) refused to go along, though its editor did promise to record whether the perpetrators were licensed or not.[40]

Charles McTague stayed on at the OSC long enough to preside over the review of registrations and the start of the self-regulatory activity that was his brainchild, but in June 1948 he decided to leave and return to the practice of law. Oswald Lennox, a member of the commission since 1945 who had been promoted to the position of vice-chair a few months earlier, was the obvious candidate to succeed McTague.[41] At the outset Lennox expressed the same faith in self-regulation as his predecessor. As he put it later, 'I thought the best policy was to feel my way along and see, instead of getting out on a limb and having to back water.' The commission, after all, possessed statutory authority over everybody dealing in securities, but 'with the investment dealers and the stock exchange itself, it is essentially an overriding jurisdiction. If they are handling their affairs properly, they have the machinery to do so.' Even for the more unruly broker-dealers, self-discipline was 'an excellent principle.' When the BDA decided to ask the OSC to refrain from publicizing disciplinary actions against its members in the autumn of 1948, Lennox proved surprisingly amenable. He agreed to discontinue all adverse publicity about the securities industry until further notice.[42]

When E.M. McLean and Company got into financial difficulties because the firm's accountant had incurred losses on his own trading unknown to management, Lennox left it to the BDA to sort the problem out. The board quickly approved a rule banning officers, partners, and employees from having trading accounts without permission of their employers. L.V. Trottier and Company asked the OSC to overrule the association's refusal to grant it a brokerage licence, but Lennox declared that he would exercise his overriding authority only in the most exceptional circumstances and he sustained the board's decision.[43] The relations between the two agencies grew close enough that the BDA even contemplated asking the OSC to second its staff to conduct investigations, though the government eventually concluded that doing so would not be appropriate.[44]

The high point was reached at the start of 1949. Lennox decided that the OSC ought to start publishing a monthly *Bulletin* to record the commission's key decisions, so that brokers and lawyers could refer to them. The first issues of the new *Bulletin* carried an article by Lennox entitled 'The Operation of the Ontario Securities Commission,' followed by one on 'Securities Legislation,' which together summed up the current official philosophy. He argued that regulation of the securities business had originally stemmed from 'an insistent demand from the public as a whole.' The provinces had passed Security Frauds Prevention Acts because of

> broad popular demand for them, and they were extremely necessary. In Ontario they were brought about by the actions of many unscrupulous operators who used the financial hysteria of the lush 20's as a smoke-screen for their nefarious schemes. They were absolutely unprincipled. They bucketed in the true sense of the word – simply betting against the customer. It never seemed to occur to this particular group to put money into a company treasury – their own pockets were wide and deep enough for any money coming in from the public.
>
> The operations of these unprincipled gangsters could best be summarized in the words, 'Never give a sucker a chance.' Their deals had all the finesse of the proverbial sale of the Brooklyn Bridge. Smooth talk, flamboyant literature, fantastic promises were their stock in trade.

'No wonder there was a demand for restrictive legislation.'

During the 1930s and early 1940s, said Lennox, the OSC had made efforts to plug up the gaps in the fraud legislation by passing regulations to ban practices such as calling upon private residences. Unfortunately, restitution had been relied upon too frequently. 'Hundreds of thousands of dollars were returned to gullible purchasers because it was thought that they had been misinformed. There was no yardstick for such reversals; they depended upon the best judgement of the man in charge. Little priority was given to prosecutions for failure to observe the securities laws, and, undoubtedly, those in charge were frequently placed in the position of compounding a felony.' Even honest promoters had sometimes found the rules unclear: 'It was difficult to follow any particular precedent, there being so many special cases and so much was dependent upon individual judgement. Assuredly the opinions and decisions were given in all honesty, but legitimate business can be stifled, if not hamstrung, unless it has a firm background upon which to base its commitments.'[45] Another disadvantage of this ad hoc approach was that it engendered 'an attitude on the part of regulators that every promotional issue is a snare and a delusion ... If the basic concept of the administrative authorities is that the public should never risk capital but only embark on "sure things," there is good reason to believe that [mining] exploration and primary development would either cease or become the sole right of the big companies.'[46]

These problems had led to the shift to full, true, and plain disclosure in the 1945 Securities Act. Now 'the public can participate and enter into these speculations with eyes wide open and with full knowledge of *all* material facts where a prospectus of the type required under our type of securities regulation is required.' 'Gone,' said Lennox, 'if it ever existed here in Ontario, is the concept of the individual who is all knowledgeable, who knows what is good for the public and what is not good for the public.'[47] The 1947 changes had added self-regulation, and since then complaints from the public had fallen to an all-time low. He had nothing but good things to say about the disciplinary work of organizations such as the BDA: 'Who could be more jealous of their good name or more insistent upon fair practice than the group as a whole?' Cooperation between the OSC and the self-governing organizations had created a regulatory system both 'realistic and practical.' Lennox concluded his primer with the firm conclusion, 'There are undoubtedly still some refinements to be made, but one thing is certain – here in Ontario the trend is well away from bureaucracy and moving solidly towards self-government by distributing groups.'[48]

By the time that the members of the Broker Dealers Association read those heartening words, however, the whole notion of self-regulation was coming under increasingly critical scrutiny. The American authorities were once more growing acutely unhappy about high-pressure sales of unregistered securities by Toronto brokers. When the BDA was just getting off the ground in the spring of 1948, Charles McTague had called in chair Arthur White to warn that the OSC would refuse to license people intending to sell 'almost solely' in the United States, 'because the Crown would not be party to a broker registered under the securities laws of the province of Ontario violating the securities laws of a friendly country on a wholesale basis.' Each case would be considered on its merits, but if 'the illegal selling of securities in the United States had been on a wholesale basis,' registrations would be cancelled.[49]

Yet the old practices continued. W.F. Bradley admitted that his firm, Canadian Securities, was devoting its entire efforts to selling one issue, Trans-Canada Mines, with 95 per cent of its calls going to the United States. Shares taken down under options for 14 cents were being marketed at 35 cents while trading over the counter in Toronto for between 6 and 9 cents. In cancelling Bradley's licence, McTague noted that local brokers might sell shares to Americans on occasion, but 'registration surely cannot be obtained in Ontario practically entirely for the purpose of selling securities in the United States, not qualified there and by methods contrary to the laws of that country and various states ... We do not deem it to be in the public interest that we should license brokers and dealers for the purpose of permitting them to violate the laws of another country on a wholesale basis.' G.F. Cockburn and Company caused a flood of complaints, not only from individual investors but from state and provincial securities administrators across the continent. The firm's mailing list contained no less than 300,000 names, and 93,000 pieces of mail had been sent to Americans during January 1948 alone. McTague insisted, 'Ontario registration ... must not be used purely as a subterfuge for the purpose of violating the securities law of another country with impunity.'[50]

American officials were particularly offended by the exaggerated claims made in much of the promotional material. O.E. Lennox admitted that the OSC had had little luck in following up protests from investors about misleading advertisements. All that could be done was to send the complainants a questionnaire asking if they had actually received the prospectus and whether or not they had examined it with care. Many aggrieved losers must have shared the feelings of the person who had returned this form with the comment, 'It is bad enough being defrauded without being deluged with blankety-blank questions.'[51]

In September 1948 complaints that First Securities had been offering Quesabe Mines stock in the United States led the BDA to order a temporary end to all mailings across the border until the situation could be studied. Eventually the board decided that material from all members who did not belong to some other organization such as the IDA or the TSE should be vetted. William Wismer was sent off to the annual conference of the National Association of Securities Administrators to try to convince the Americans that a clean-up was underway. He arranged for half a dozen state regulators to visit Toronto in the fall of 1948 for discussions with the board about the sale of unregistered shares in the United States.[52]

Early in 1949 the BDA declared a sixty-day 'armistice' or moratorium on all mailings across the border. O.E. Lennox was impressed; he thought that the ban demonstrated the efficacy of self-regulation.

Before long, however, he learned that some board members had tipped off their friends, who had hastened to send out circulars before the deadline. That explained why the U.S. postal service in Buffalo, New York, was complaining about a flood of mailings from Toronto brokerages, and post offices as far away as Virginia were reporting that they were swamped.[53]

Lennox began to lose faith in self-regulation by the BDA. When the OSC made complaints about wholesale mailings to the United States by C.D. Wilson and Company in February 1949, the board found Wilson guilty of unethical conduct only with 'great reluctance' and fined him just $100. Lennox later observed that it had been over-optimistic to expect the inhabitants of the Bay Street jungle to change their spots overnight: 'I might as well be very candid and say that at one time there were about two hundred broker-dealers registered with the commission, and a very large percentage of that association from its inception thought that the information [sic, formation] of that association was nothing but an organization to facilitate them in their extravagant methods; that they thought it was a protection and they looked to their board of governors for protection in accomplishing what they had in mind.'[54]

At a meeting of the National Association of Securities Administrators, Lennox was deluged with complaints from his American counterparts. In July 1949 a diplomat from the Canadian embassy was summoned to the Securities and Exchange Commission in Washington and warned that nearly 10 million pieces of mail from Toronto brokers had entered the United States in recent months, netting up to $10 million from unwary investors. Lennox concluded that he would have to crack down. On 6 September 1949 he addressed a letter to all BDA members announcing that the OSC would assume full regulatory authority over complaints about brokers selling shares in the United States.

> It was perhaps too much to hope that this organization, to which these powers were temporarily delegated, could in so short a time cultivate within the circle of its membership the necessary function of self-discipline ... It is felt that this responsibility can best be discharged by the commission until others demonstrate more convincingly their ability to do so ...
>
> Until such time as a more favourable climate has developed it is deemed best that the full machinery of the commission should be used to ensure compliance with the spirit as well as the letter of the law.

It is generally recognized that the powers of supervision and investigation delegated to the association were in the nature of an experiment. It is now conceded that the facilities at the disposal of the association were not equal to the task.[55]

Arthur White and William Wismer of the BDA prepared a memorandum setting forth what Lennox had told them the OSC was prepared to tolerate as far as marketing shares in the United States was concerned. Each governor was deputed to call in a different group of BDA members, read this document aloud, and require everybody present to initial a copy.[56] At the same time the BDA board took another tack. One of the governors was acquainted with a New York securities lawyer, Hobart L. Brinsmade, who pointed out that under the SEC's regulation A an American company was permitted to sell a maximum of $300,000 worth of securities annually without undergoing the elaborate registration process but merely by filing a letter of notification with the agency's regional office. If the SEC could be persuaded to extend the rule to cover Canadian issues, it might permit the raising of capital without violating U.S. law.

Brinsmade first proposed the idea to the BDA board in the spring of 1949.[57] He then approached the SEC, where he received enough encouragement that it was decided to set up a meeting in Washington at which both the BDA and the OSC would be represented. O.E. Lennox agreed to accompany the BDA representatives, but he recalled, 'I did not speak unless I was spoken to for the simple reason that feeling between the BDA and the Ontario Securities Commission at that time was not very good, and if anything had happened to upset the success of the meeting it would have been all the worse, so I did not make myself vulnerable.' The Americans quickly launched into a strong attack on the failure of Ontario to clean up its brokerage business and drive out people selling illegally in the United States. What was really needed, said the SEC officials, was an extradition treaty between the two countries which had real teeth.[58]

III

Self-regulation by the BDA also failed to limit the highly inflated prices that members routinely charged for low-cost shares obtained under options. When the association was formed, Charles McTague suggested that broker-dealers ought to reveal the spread between takedown and selling prices to buyers as part of full, true, and plain disclosure. Such an idea was, of course, anathema to BDA members. Instead, vice-chair Cecil Tom suggested that if brokers operated on a 'fifty-fifty basis,' taking a markup of no more than 100 per cent, they 'would probably keep themselves out of trouble.' As a result, the BDA's Quote Committee normally authorized brokers to start selling a stock at double the takedown price.[59]

In the spring of 1949 the OSC discovered a BDA member marketing shares obtained under option for 5 cents apiece for between 55 and 60 cents each, and it insisted that the association create a Price Spreads Committee to which members must disclose the takedown and offering prices of any new issue and get their 'deal priced right.' If the spread seemed too great, the member was to be asked to justify it. The board rejected establishing a straight percentage markup and instead fixed a maximum offering price in each case. Under pressure from the OSC a sliding scale of markups was established geared to the option price. The maximum was normally permitted only 'if the underwriters had gone firm for a very large amount of money' placed in the company treasury.[60]

In the autumn of 1949 Junior Golds Securities Corporation, controlled by former BDA governor Sidney Davidge, undertook a high-pressure marketing campaign for shares in Yukeno Lead and Silver Mines in the United States, despite Lennox's recent warning that this could lead to the cancellation of registration. Salesmen got busy 'overreaching,' loading up gullible buyers with more and more shares until their financial resources were exhausted. One American customer, apparently of dubious mental competence, was persuaded to put up all his liquid assets by playing upon a vision in which he saw gold being discovered by the company, even though Yukeno was not a gold property. The price was pushed steadily upwards at no benefit to the company treasury since the amount paid by Junior Golds remained fixed by options at 15 cents apiece.[61]

When the OSC uncovered this operation, a hearing was held at which the salesman who had dealt with the unfortunate American offered only the lame excuse that he believed the man had been joking about his delusion. Junior Golds registration as a brokerage was promptly cancelled, but the BDA rushed to support Davidge's appeal against the order.[62] Lennox refused to be swayed. He called the Yukeno promotion 'the most glaring example of a treasury being sabotaged for the vendor's interest which has come to the notice of the commission in recent years.' 'The public was misled from every possible angle,' added the decision confirming the cancellation. Those words were particularly apt because the commission itself, though committed to full, true, and plain disclosure, felt that it had to omit the most damning facts about the case from the decision published in the *Bulletin* in the spring of 1950. Lennox tried to pretend that he had taken this decision to avoid discrediting the issuer, Yukeno, but he eventually admitted, 'The case was so glaring that we did not dare publish the details of it in the bulletin because that goes to outside jurisdictions, so in order to demonstrate our findings in case of an appeal to a judge of the Supreme Court we had prepared a schedule to our decision but we did not publish the schedule for obvious reasons.' In other words, he was concerned about the way that this story would play south of the border, since it only confirmed what the Americans had been saying about lax securities regulation in Ontario.[63]

By this time Lennox's patience with the antics of the members of the Broker Dealers Association was pretty well exhausted. He had tried to be tolerant about the problems faced by the governors: 'At first it was only natural that these people had a lot of domestic troubles, and they gave the commission a great deal of trouble. I would say for the first year – or the first year and a half – they possibly retarded securities administration. In short, they went to the commission and wanted the commission to give everything, and they did not want to give anything.' The board had done 'absolutely nothing constructive.' The 'armistice' on mailings to the United States in early 1949, which many members had evaded because they were tipped off in advance, said Lennox, 'putting it in common language – was nothing but a straight double-cross.' Asked if the BDA had not at least done something to clean up fraudulent promotions, he snapped, 'I do not give the original board an ounce of credit; I give them a lot of discredit.'[64]

As a result, the BDA had no luck in trying to persuade the OSC to drop two other rules that were much disliked: the ban on calls to private residences and the requirement that share buyers receive a copy of the prospectus for issues in primary distribution. Salespeople unanimously favoured ending the telephone ban, and brokers hoped to convince the OSC to permit them to send a prospectus only on demand. When the BDA tried to gain Lennox's support for ending the ban on telephoning in the summer of 1949, they got nowhere; he not only refused to consider the idea but took the opportunity to criticize the

BDA severely for not policing brokers better. Lobbying the government directly produced no results.[65]

When he first took over at the OSC in 1948, Lennox had believed that the BDA was simply split into insiders and outsiders scrambling to gain an advantage over one another. Eventually, however, he concluded that there were reputable brokers who were justifiably unhappy with the way the association's affairs were being run. Some members complained privately to Lennox that as soon as a broker encountered any financial difficulties, the news would leak out from the board, and before long the troubled firm would be approached with a takeover proposition.[66]

Evidence soon surfaced to support his contention that the present board 'did not have the respect of their members – at least a very substantial portion of them.' In November 1949 A.V. Conroy requested that the Nominating Committee should include 'a representative of his group' when the slate of BDA governors for 1950 was being drawn up. The board first tried to ignore this request, and chair Arthur White even threatened to call for a vote of confidence from members at a special general meeting on 15 November. Soon it became clear that the election of governors for 1950 would be a real contest between rival factions.[67]

The pressure for change came principally from firms that belonged to both the Broker Dealers Association and the Toronto Stock Exchange, tired of the constant glare of the bad publicity that the BDA seemed to attract. Early in December they stepped up the pressure as the chair of the TSE's Managing Committee, A.L.A. Richardson, met with Attorney General Dana Porter and proposed that some people be permitted to drop their BDA membership and become directly registered with the OSC as broker-dealers. Porter accepted the idea, and Lennox eventually agreed.[68] E.H. Pooler (whose firm also belonged to the Toronto Stock Exchange) was promised that if he quit the BDA, he and the other 'rebels' (as Lennox called them) would be granted independent registration. Since Pooler was himself a BDA governor and the chair of the Membership Committee, it was a serious blow to the association when he announced his intentions to his fellow governors at their meeting on 4 January 1950. Pooler was roundly criticized by the others, but he 'proceeded to defend his action in obtaining such recognition for his firm,' before handing in his resignation and stamping out of the room. He was quickly replaced by Marshal Stearns.

Thoroughly unnerved, the board hastily approached Porter and the new premier, Leslie Frost, to lobby against any further direct registrations. Lennox, however, refused to back down, knowing that the attorney general was behind him.[69]

In the BDA boardroom strong criticism was directed at two other founding members of the board, R.S. Lampard and Irving Picard, who also belonged to firms that held seats on the TSE. Both men offered to resign, but it was decided that they should serve out their terms.[70] At a stormy general meeting of members a resolution was passed objecting to the OSC registering anybody who was not a BDA member. Tempers flared and the Discipline Committee had to deal with two members involved in 'a fight which occurred shortly after the commencement of the Association's Buffet Supper in the Crystal Ballroom of the King Edward Hotel, Toronto, on Saturday evening, January 14, 1950.' H.H. Gillespie was fined $100 for 'unethical conduct' while E.A. Glass was let off.[71]

When the election of governors took place, there remained only three nominees from TSE member firms, so Harry Knight, John Rogers, and Marshal Stearns were acclaimed. However, a dozen people vied for the five spots reserved for non-member brokers, and the one seat set aside for a salesman was also contested. When the ballots were counted, there had been a considerable change in the nine-member board.[72] Arthur White agreed to serve again as chair, but the bruising nature of the recent battle was evident in his warning to the other governors that it was imperative that 'members remained loyal to each other and did not talk about confidential matters improperly outside board meetings.'[73]

As the sorry tale of the misconduct by Junior Golds Securities was being unravelled by the OSC, Lennox held firm in his resolve to shake up the BDA once and for all. Over the next few months he allowed thirty-three members to leave the association and secure direct registration from the commission. 'I thought they really needed a good dose of medicine and they got it,' he reported with satisfaction.[74] The BDA governors were left scrambling to replace the membership fees they had lost from the defectors, part of which they had hoped to use on a publicity campaign to glorify their works.

Publicly, the association put on a brave face. In a pamphlet issued at the beginning of March 1950 the foreword applauded the BDA as a body that was 'hardly two years old and still coping with a burden of reponsibility which was long ago smoothed out by such other organizations as the Toronto Stock Exchange and the Investment Dealers Association.' The BDA was not 'a police force cracking a disciplinary whip' but a trade association to help its members and to punish them only as a last resort. Discipline was really the OSC's task, and the BDA had been created to reduce the dangers of paternalism and government regulation. Raising capital for untried companies was vital to the Canadian economy, and the broker-dealers who did so required a good deal of freedom of action.[75]

In reality, however, the BDA found itself increasingly under the gun. In an address to the securities bar O.E. Lennox pulled no punches. Prior to 1945 'Ontario was content to adopt only one type of control, namely control over the dealer, which was and still is exercised by means of licensing, investigation, prosecution, cancellation of registration for cause and prosecuting unlicensed persons. Licensing ... is pretty much a hit-and-miss proposition, and unless the process is supported by a well-directed, organized industry, it merely serves to eliminate individuals who are definitely undesirable ... So far, the BDA, which has the largest membership has not been effective in ridding the industry of individuals lacking the necessary qualifications from the standpoint of good business.'[76]

3

Moose Pastures

'The Canadian problem' created by the high-pressure marketing of speculative stocks in the United States showed no signs of abating during the early 1950s. In fact, the advent of the atomic age only made matters worse. Uranium stocks became just as hot sellers as gold and silver shares, while the Cold War created a demand for other exotic metals like titanium and beryllium that might lie beneath the Precambrian Shield in Canada. Rocky, fir-clad hills and marshy lowlands, otherwise fit only to be 'moose pastures,' were touted as potential mother lodes. The 'stockees' at the promotional houses on Bay Street remained as busy as ever seeking out gullible 'suckers' and greedy 'mooches' to purchase whatever shares a boiler room had on the shelf; next month or next year there would be a new issue to sell.[1]

The 1951 *Annual Report* of the Securities and Exchange Commission painted a grim picture. There were daily telephone calls and visits from people who had been swindled, and during the previous year no less than 4,488 letters of complaint had been received from people approached to purchase Canadian stocks not registered in the United States.

The sales pattern is uniform and simple, though apparently convincing to many United States investors. The victim is first solicited by mail, told of the great money-making possibilities of the mine or oil well involved, and asked merely to send his name and address on a prepaid postcard. Within a few days he receives a telephone call ..., in which he is promised large and immediate profits if he invests at once. The salesman usually tells the victim that oil, gold or uranium (depending on the promotion) has just been discovered in large quantities, and he is being let in 'on the ground floor.' The victims are almost always inexperienced in investment matters and persons who can ill afford the inevitable loss of their savings.

Over the previous two years the SEC had collected evidence about more than two hundred such promotions, and in virtually every case the securities had proven to be worthless.[2]

I

Canada's ambassador in Washington, Hume Wrong, became concerned that the failure to crack down on the boiler rooms in Toronto might seriously affect relations with the United States. By mid-1949 newspaper articles critical of Ontario's regulatory laxity were beginning to appear. SEC officials were complaining that since O.E. Lennox had replaced Charles McTague at the Ontario Securities Commission a year earlier, cooperation between the two agencies had almost ceased. In the autumn Wrong reported that the mounting irritation now posed a threat to the 'general spirit' of relations between the two countries. If nothing were done, new American investment in Canada might begin to dry up.[3]

Yet Lennox showed little inclination to move to eliminate the Toronto boiler rooms. When an OSC investigation into Consolidated Astoria Mines revealed that at least twenty-five brokers were receiving secret kickbacks for touting this stock, Lennox decided to lay no charges but to leave it to the self-regulatory organizations to discipline their members behind closed doors. He admitted that his decision was taken because 'the damage resulting to the industry as a whole would be disastrous at a time when the United States press was conducting a smear campaign against Ontario promotional issues.'[4]

Since the Canadians refused to act decisively, the Americans decided to use the post office to try to control the advertising literature and payments flowing across the border. The SEC would investigate complaints from investors about fraud or misrepresentation, and when enough evidence had been collected, it would seek an indictment from a grand jury. The indictments themselves remained secret but formed the basis for mail bans imposed *ex parte* (without the accused being represented). Between July 1949 and August 1950 the U.S. post office issued seventy fraud orders against a dozen different Toronto firms. Mail directed to them was seized and returned to the sender.[5]

Affected brokerages quickly countered by creating up to half a dozen new addresses, provoking an additional nineteen fictitious name orders. In the spring of 1950 the Americans sought the assistance of the government of Canada. J.T. Callahan of the SEC was sent to Toronto to compile a list of the names of the worst offenders, and the Canadian postal service was persuaded to seize and open letters enclosing advertisements and circulars that contained alleged misrepresentations. The postmaster general cancelled the privileges of twelve broker-dealers on suspicion that the mails were being used for fraudulent purposes. Incoming letters were impounded and returned to their senders stamped 'Fraudulent – Mail to this address returned by order of the Post Master General.'

The mail ban affected some eighty individuals who were marketing shares in about a dozen oil and gold promotions. The Broker Dealers Association complained that the Canadian authorities were simply acting as a cat's-paw for the SEC and sought to enlist the support of the Conservative opposition in Parliament. Soon the party leader, none other than George Drew, was braying about the 'Star Chamber' methods adopted by the federal Liberals in denying people the use of the mails without permitting them to defend themselves. Why was the OSC not taking action if fraud or misrepresentation was involved, asked Toronto MP Donald Fleming?[6]

Eventually the wrangling in Parliament died away as many brokers agreed in writing to cease sending out 'offensive' literature and not to make 'improper' use of the mails in future. The federal government, meanwhile, decided that no further suspensions should be imposed without hearing from those affected, and it promised to amend the Post Office Act to permit appeals to the courts in future.[7]

The OSC played no role. Lennox complained that the mail ban had been bungled from start to finish. Callahan of the SEC had been gulled by one of two contending factions in the BDA seeking a way to pay off old scores, so 'some of the worst offenders operating in Toronto ... were left out of the ban.' Nobody at the post office had ever bothered to consult or notify him, with the result that certain people had been deprived of their OSC registration while other serious troublemakers went scot-free. 'I think the mail ban was not worth the paper it was written on,' grumbled Lennox, 'because it merely disrupted everything.'[8]

The failure of the mail ban to cure the problem convinced the SEC that the only real solution was a new extradition treaty covering violations of securities law. After a visit to Washington in June 1950, the

BDA's executive secretary, William Wismer, reported that Milton Kroll, the commission's director of enforcement, was intent upon seeing the treaty revised. Kroll said that he might consider swallowing the 'bitter bill' of a non-retroactive agreement, which would mean that all outstanding indictments were quashed. Still, he admitted that he was having problems in getting the people at the State Department even to focus on the need for treaty revision, as 'they were so busy with the Communists and perverts that now it was hard to get anything done.'[9]

That autumn the Canadian embassy was handed a sixty-two-page report from the SEC detailing cases of fraudulent or illegal share-selling. Since the start of 1949, 6,300 complaints had been received. Over the past decade investigative files had been opened on 335 promotions, 90 of them since mid-1948. The activities of notorious characters like A.E. DePalma were fully rehearsed. And the problem showed no signs of diminishing: the U.S. post office claimed that a check at border points over a recent two-week period indicated a flow of $750,000 into Canada for share purchases.[10]

A new extradition treaty did not rank high among the Canadian government's priorities, however. After a parliamentary committee had recommended against ratification of the revisions agreed to in 1945, all the momentum had evaporated. Low-level interdepartmental committees considered the problem in 1946 and 1947 and recommended doing nothing.[11] The abandonment of the principle of 'dual criminality' in securities offences might open the way for the extradition of Canadians who had committed no offence against domestic laws. One diplomat observed, 'The proposition has such far-reaching effects that I am surprised that the original treaty got beyond draft form. It would have the effect of making Canadians completely subservient to American securities regulation and indeed involves derogation of our sovereignty. I must confess I have considerable sympathy with the various protesting groups.'[12]

Meanwhile, rumours reached Lennox towards the end of 1950 that more mass mailings were planned. Promoter Frank Kaftel was reported to be going to send twelve to fifteen million pieces across the border (though he insisted that he had no such plans). Lennox therefore addressed a letter to BDA members warning them to desist, though he did not dare publish it in the OSC *Bulletin* for fear that the SEC would get wind of what he was doing. He also got in touch directly with two of the larger mailers and persuaded them to hold up for sixty days until the pressure abated. Yet the early months of 1951 saw a blizzard of mail emanating from Toronto, and the rumblings from Washington intensified. Before long, Milton Kroll was asking to come to Ottawa for consultations or else the SEC would unleash a hostile publicity campaign.[13]

The OSC finally stepped up its investigations. Many complaints had been received about high-pressure selling by Norwitt Corporation. Hundreds of circulars had been mailed out; over the past six months only 9 per cent of its mailings and telephone calls had been directed to Ontario addresses. Both Norwitt and Regional Securities were running advertisements for Sweet Grass Oils headed 'Bought, Sold and Quoted,' though no genuine market for this stock existed. Regional was also operating outside its authorized premises in an effort to conceal the extent of its activities. Lennox cancelled the registration of both firms.[14]

E.A. Glass was hauled before the OSC over his campaign for a uranium stock. The company had been described as 'now shipping uranium' because it had forwarded a bulk ore sample required by the Atomic Energy Control Board.[15] Other tipsheets made tantalizing mention of 'secret' prospects, but they not disclose whether the broker actually had the issue for sale or was merely trying to arrange a deal. Market letters padded with irrelevant material were common: the 'writer' employed by one house produced a two-page letter on an unsuccessful oil promotion which concluded by touting a cobalt claim. Sent to the BDA for vetting, this effort was rejected as unsatisfactory, whereupon it metamorphosed into a three-pager on the mineral prospect which nevertheless managed to omit any useful technical data. Large print and superlatives often set in expensive coloured type were common: even the BDA proved unable to stomach the claim that western Canada was 'THE WORLD'S LAST MAJOR OIL FRONTIER.'[16]

In the spring of 1951 the OSC finally pressured the BDA into drawing up stricter guidelines on advertising. Previously, single words, phrases, or paragraphs held to be objectionable or illegal had been altered without changing the framework of the document. Now the aim was literature not only omitting 'doubtful superlatives and exaggerated statements, but with the essential characteristics which determine whether or not it can be termed *responsible* in the true sense of the word.'[17]

Every registrant was required by the OSC to have a single address. Yet in May 1951 the U.S. post office was still intercepting mail to A.N. Richmond and Company's offices variously directed to 'Account Executive; Braun J., Book Dept.; Desk One; Dept. 24; Dover, Miss, Billings Dept.; and Reservation Dept.' When this case came before the BDA board, one of Richmond's salesmen, governor Jerome Henley, withdrew from the meeting, and the board then fined the firm $500 for unethical conduct, warning that any repeat offences would lead to more drastic disciplinary action. Henley thereupon resumed his seat at the board table to hear the next discipline case.[18]

In the spring of 1951 Lennox warned the new chair of the BDA, John Rogers, that if he got wind of any plans for mass mailings, he would crack down as hard as possible on a broker for any other minor infractions. Lennox pointed out to William Wismer that continuing adverse publicity about Toronto boiler rooms 'has fully demonstrated that serious mistake your association is making in allowing such generous price spreads.'

> Your present policy is part and parcel of a vicious circle, as these generous spreads render it possible for broker-dealers to resort to extravagant and unwarranted sales methods which would be out of the question if their profits were kept within reasonable bounds.
>
> Surely it is time that your association realized that something constructive must be done along these and other lines to gain public confidence and to combat current adverse publicity.

The BDA board reluctantly agreed to consider reducing the approved spreads, 'provided it was feasible,' but a couple of weeks later the governors concluded that spreads were 'not too far out of line under present conditions.'[19]

Nonetheless, Lennox agreed to end the experiment of allowing the more reputable broker-dealers to leave the BDA and seek direct registration with the OSC. These firms had to apply to the commission for approval of markups on option shares. Not only was the OSC soon swamped with work, but the regulators discovered how difficult it was to tell whether a stock was really trading freely or simply being nursed along by market support, without which the price would collapse. Lennox therefore advised the BDA that it might approach all its former members and press them to resume their places when their registrations expired on 31 March 1951. Self-regulation would be given another chance.[20]

The Americans remained very unhappy. On a visit to Ottawa in February 1951, Ambassador Hume Wrong reported that action on an extradition treaty was urgently needed. After his return to Washington he submitted a formal despatch arguing that Canada had better stop resisting 'strenuous' American efforts to reopen the discussions. The State Department had made it clear that it considered fraudulent sales of Canadian securities a growing problem, and there was increasing difficulty in restraining the SEC from launching a publicity campaign.[21]

It was already too late. Claiming that it had been fending off pressure from the press and Congress for months on the pretext of consulting the Canadians, the SEC decided to bring matters to a head. In January brokers in the United States were ordered to make no purchases of any securities, listed or unlisted, that were subject to option or underwriting agreements or had been in primary distribution during the previous year unless the issue had received regulatory approval in Washington. Commission officials claimed that 'the Canadian problem' had become sufficiently serious that such orders might assist in the illegal distribution of shares in the United States. Before long, Toronto firms with wire connections to New York were reporting a 50 per cent drop in the volume of orders flowing north. Members of the Toronto Stock Exchange began to get upset, and the Managing Committee called upon the TSE representatives on the BDA board to report on what steps were being taken to control the 'business conduct' of broker-dealers who sold in the United States. TSE chair A.L.A. Richardson was despatched to see Lennox at the OSC to discover what might be done.[22]

The SEC began leaking information to the press. In March 1951 the St Louis Star-Times ran a fortnight-long series of articles condemning Canadian share-pushing.[23] SEC chair Harry A. McDonald described the fifty-five Toronto boiler rooms, whose salespeople started working the long-distance phones at six o'clock each evening, seeking buyers for their 'beautifully engraved invitations to the poorhouse.' The stories contained lengthy accounts of the exploits of crooks like A.E. DePalma. Three BDA members were said to be fronting for DePalma, while three of the governors of the association belonged to firms currently subject to fraud orders issued by the U.S. post office. Before long, these articles were republished as a pamphlet entitled Suckers in Swindle-Land.[24]

The BDA's executive secretary, William Wismer, could only respond that the failure to register securities was just a technical violation of American law. He did his best to put on a brave face by telling the press, 'I'm the first to admit that Americans are greater gamblers and speculators than Canadians. Isn't it better to channel these funds into speculative enterprise for the development of Canada than into horseracing, for example?' O.E. Lennox was hardly more persuasive in his insistence that the problem arose simply because Canadians and Americans had different definitions of fraud. Asked about the need for an effective extradition treaty between Canada and the United States, he did admit that if an agreement was ever going to be reached, 'this is the time for it.'[25]

The SEC also fed information to radio broadcaster Ned Brooks, whose *Sunoco-3-Star-Extra* program was widely syndicated. Brooks ranted about the 'confidence game' played by Toronto brokers who leased some moose pasture in order to peddle uranium shares to a sucker list of Americans. He named BDA member C.R. Jenner for pushing 5-cent shares in Orbit Uranium Developments at a price of 45 cents from his 'dingy' one-room office.[26] The BDA's American lawyer, who dropped in to see the SEC's Milton Kroll, received a tirade. If the Canadians 'wanted to "indulge in economic warfare with the United States," ... for his part he was prefect[ly] willing for the United States to wage such warfare, since he was convinced the United States would win that kind of war, as the Canadians could not get along without the United States.' Kroll made clear that a satisfactory extradition treaty was a precondition for any real improvement in the situation.[27]

The External Affairs Department concluded that the time had come to ask for authority to reopen negotiations on an extradition treaty with the United States. Under-Secretary Arnold Heeney wrote, 'This appears to loom up as a "very hot" issue, and I feel that it is imperative that the memorandum should go up to cabinet at once.'[28] Justice Department officials were much less enthusiastic. The Americans were simply 'putting the heat on,' and negotiations would only provide the SEC with the opportunity of 'placing in a questionable limelight' the activities of Canadian brokers and dealers, most of whom were perfectly reputable. In the overheated atmosphere generated by the press and radio campaign, Canada might find itself bulldozed into permitting the United States to interfere in its domestic affairs: 'Unwarranted concessions should not be allowed to aggravate matters instead of providing an effective solution.'[29]

J.P. Erichsen-Brown of External Affairs argued that during the depression of the 1930s the United States had adopted a paternalistic approach and enacted 'very strict regulations governing the sale of securities.' In Canada the authorities preferred 'not to try to prevent the public from investing in an enterprise which was essentially speculative if the public, in fact, wanted to speculate.' In 'a young country with vast undeveloped resources' like Canada, 'venture capital is essential, and laws which permit the public to invest in speculative mines a necessary corollary.' As a result, investors were accorded less protection than in the United States, so that it was difficult to work out a single approach to securities offences to be embodied in an extradition treaty. In the 1940s Canada had been prepared to bow to American pressure and abandon the principle of dual criminality, but that had aroused opposition amongst reputable elements in the financial community, who succeeded in having the treaty shelved. Yet 'the fringe group in Toronto' was continuing to promote sales of Canadian stocks in the United States through fraudulent misrepresentation that ignored American law. The only solution was to harmonize the laws of the two countries and restore dual criminality.[30]

Lester Pearson, the minister of external affairs, began to hear from respected voices within the financial world, who agreed that the time had come to seek a settlement. By the end of March even the Broker Dealers Association bent under the pressure from Washington; executive secretary William Wismer wrote to the president of the TSE to announce that his board had finally concluded that it should be possible to reach agreement with the Americans on dealing with securities fraud. On 4 April 1951 the cabinet approved reopening negotiations and authorized Pearson to invite officials from Ontario to join in discussions to commence on 1 May.[31]

In preparation for the meeting with the Americans, representatives of the federal departments of External Affairs, Justice, Finance, and the Post Office and the Bank of Canada gathered to plan their strategy. The government of Ontario was so embarrassed about the situation that it proved reluctant to take a public role; the press was told only that federal officials were privately briefed by provincial ones. In fact, both Lennox of the OSC and C.R. Magone of the attorney general's staff were closely grilled. Lennox repeated the claim that the Americans always exaggerated the extent of the problems, though he did admit that between fifty and sixty new issues each year created difficulties. He emphasized the obstacles he faced in collecting evidence of wrongdoing; if a new treaty could be worked out on the basis of dual criminality, it would make his task easier. Magone contended that the Americans had not made the fullest possible use of the arrangements that already existed between the OSC and the SEC, but he too admitted that perhaps a new treaty was required to avoid further blackening of Canada's reputation.[32]

The American minister to Ottawa was backed up at the negotiations by Kroll and Commissioner Richard McEntire of the SEC, who did most of the talking. He contended that the public outcry in the United States against fraudulent Canadian share-pushing was already interfering with the free flow of capital between the two countries. A broader definition of fraud needed to be written into a treaty. If that could be worked out, then the obstacles that currently stood in the way of effective cooperation between the SEC and the OSC would largely disappear. As long as speculators who had lost their money to Canadian brokers were deprived of their day in court, it was hard to convince them that they had not been defrauded. During a second day of meetings an agreement in principle was hammered out. The Americans reluctantly consented to restore dual criminality for securities offences; mail fraud and fraudulent misrepresentation would be specifically enumerated as grounds for extradition.[33]

The agreement required the Canadian government to make a minor amendment to section 209 of the Criminal Code in order to broaden the offence of mail fraud to include material posted on either side of the border. This amendment was introduced to Parliament by Justice Minister Stuart Garson early in June. He was ready to concede that stock-pushing rackets had become a blot upon the country's reputation in the United States: 'This whole business is a scandal and a disgrace, and any Canadian who supports it should be ashamed of himself.' The new provisions concerning mail fraud came into force on 30 June, and Ottawa waited to see whether the administration in Washington was willing to accept the wording of the revised convention.[34]

II

During the summer and fall of 1951 a strong spotlight was focused upon the activities of Toronto's boiler-room operators. Responding to a number of complaints about the southwestern Ontario city of Windsor, the provincial legislature decided to create a Select Committee on the Administration of Justice. Attorney General Dana Porter became the chair, and Opposition Leader E.B. Jolliffe also joined the seven-member body.[35] This committee actually devoted most of its attention to securities fraud, collecting several thousand pages of testimony. The principal witness was O.E. Lennox of the Ontario Securities Commission. No crusading regulator, Lennox came across as a defensive bureaucrat: 'A Securities Commission does not impose its own pet ideas on the public. The Securities Commission canvasses the interests of the Ontario promoter, prospector and distributor to find out what the highest standards are which are acceptable to the better part of all those industries and tries to enforce those standards throughout the industry and to get rid of the ones who will not live up to those standards.' Investors themselves were much to blame, for they had grown accustomed to blue-sky regulation in the other provinces and the American states, where governments approved all securities before they were marketed. 'To my mind,' said Lennox, 'that form of legislation has been creating a false sense of security in the minds of the public.' The problem was that 'We only hear from the losers.' They wanted restitution, but he opposed the resumption of 'the most vicious practice there ever was, which did more to undermine securities administration in this province than any other thing.'[36]

Lennox tried to insist that self-regulation was 'an excellent principle, and I have every confidence that it is going to work out in this case.' Yet his grievances about the antics of the Broker Dealers Association became clear as he recounted his discovery that some of its governors had tipped off their friends about the proposed 'armistice' on mailings to the United States in 1949 so that they could beat the deadline. This 'double-cross' was all too typical of the original BDA board, whose members looked to it to protect them against regulatory interference while they continued their 'extravagant methods.' As a result, Lennox had permitted thirty-three members of the association to resign during 1950 to show the board that it must turn over a new leaf and take its disciplinary responsibilities seriously. He believed that it was this 'move which really brought the association into line.'[37]

He was particularly irritated by the claim that allowing the more reputable people to leave the BDA had only made matters worse and led to demands for a new extradition treaty. 'I cannot imagine any criticism being more unfair, but it is typical of the situation I have had to combat since I have taken office.' At the meeting in Washington in the fall of 1949, the Americans had made it clear that they were determined upon a new extradition treaty. It was the BDA's continuing failure to control mass mailings and high-pressure selling that had led him to permit some of its members to resign the following year. Lennox even tabled a sworn statement to this effect with the committee, repeating his complaint that 'I have been subject to similar tactics from that association. It is not typical of the present board, but it is typical of the board as it was constituted back in 1949.'[38]

Since every broker-dealer had now been compelled to rejoin the association, the BDA's membership numbered 135. Approximately 35 operated outside Toronto and created few problems, while another 20 were small firms that undertook little primary distribution. Of the remainder about half continued to cause trouble. Typical of these three dozen or so firms was John F. Burgess and Company, whose premises had recently been raided, leading to the discovery of an expatriate American salesman attempting to destroy his identification in a washroom, followed by his flight across the border to avoid arrest. Among four hundred registered salesmen, about fifty were probably engaged in high-pressure selling, and Lennox expressed suspicion that most of the problem firms were fronts controlled by a half-dozen or so big promoters to peddle their wares.[39]

Committee members wanted to know why Toronto brokers had such a bad reputation in the United States. At first Lennox temporized: 'I am afraid it is beyond me. I do not know what the reason is. It is a thing which goes back over many years. It is a situation I found on my doorstep; it is nothing new.' But when pressed about whether telephone selling was the root of the problem, he finally conceded, 'Oh, undoubtedly.' Still, he insisted that he was trying as hard as he could to clean things up: 'I have knocked down one after the other, and the full commission has upheld my rulings. The trouble is when you knock one down another crops up.' The Americans paid no attention to the fact that he had undertaken three times as many disciplinary actions as any other commissioner in the OSC's history, one hundred informal investigations and forty-two formal ones having been launched during the past year alone.[40]

Towards the SEC Lennox displayed a rather dismissive attitude. Every critical story about the OSC, he said, dredged up the name of A.E. DePalma, whose registration had been cancelled in 1946. Canadian brokers were certainly tempted to ignore American rules because qualifying an issue for sale in the United States was both expensive and time-consuming, and on top of that, registration was required with individual state commissions. 'The people I deal with in the SEC,' said Lennox, 'are a fine bunch of men, the very best ... But I think the whole gist of the thing is they do not want Ontario securities sold in the United States.'[41]

He believed that the SEC was exaggerating current problems. 'I think what you hear is that we are flooded with complaints from the United States. That is not a fact. We are not flooded with complaints; we are flooded with enquiries.' The muckraking articles in the *St Louis Star-Times* had claimed that Americans were being swindled out of $52 million annually for worthless Canadian shares. If that were true, each of fifty-odd Toronto brokers would be taking in an average of $1 million, but Lennox thought that no more than about $9 million worth of Canadian issues was being sold south of the border. He had tried to explain the costs and delays of the registration process; every year he put the case at the annual meeting of the National Association of Securities Administrators. The past spring he had travelled to Washington for further discussions but had come away convinced that the Americans were determined upon treaty changes first, 'so we are stymied.'[42]

Charles McTague followed Lennox to the witness chair. Securities regulation had not been very effective when he took over at the OSC in 1945. Offenders had frequently been permitted to avoid punishment by making restitution, but the only way that the commission could compel repayment was by threatening deregistration, and when compensation was paid, other penalties were dropped. The new Securities Act, however, embodied a regulatory philosophy much like that of the American SEC, requiring companies with shares in primary distribution to make full disclosure of all material facts to investors. McTague said that he much preferred this approach, which 'tended to lay down rules in fairly definite terms ... I mean that the tendency was to take away the arbitrary power which existed in the 1937 act.' He also recounted how he had hit upon the idea of establishing a trio of self-regulatory organizations. He insisted that insiders were likely to be much more effective than a bunch of government officials. Certainly problems persisted. McTague claimed that he had tried to impose a ban on brokers telephoning customers outside Ontario, but he contended that a provincial statute was a poor way to regulate interprovincial and international communication and trading, which fell primarily under federal jurisdiction. Threats to cancel the registration of brokers who made little or no effort to sell in Ontario were simply not efficacious.[43]

McTague's testimony had its greatest impact because he appeared as special counsel to the BDA. In the spring of 1949, scarcely one year after leaving the OSC, he had taken the surprising decision to accept a $5,000 annual retainer from the association.[44] The BDA certainly reaped a large return on this investment because of McTague's reputation. For instance, he rejected Lennox's claim that as many as three dozen broker-dealers were causing trouble, insisting that when he had headed the OSC, he had never been able to arrive at any such firm numbers. Opposition Leader E.B. Jolliffe pressed him on specifics: what about the BDA member who had brazenly issued sales literature to customers in the United States admitting that he did not comply with the restrictive rules there? This broker claimed to meet all the OSC's rules and invited people to consult the BDA regarding his 'integrity and reliability,' noting that members of his firm were active in the Toronto Board of Trade. 'What has that to do with the right to sell securities in the United States?' asked Jolliffe pointedly. 'It is just a lot of blarney ... If he is a responsible businessman he does not have to say that sort of thing.' McTague could only reply feebly that he wasn't in a position to discuss individual cases, but in general his appearance did a good deal to bolster the public image of the BDA.[45]

He also echoed Lennox's criticisms of the Americans. The SEC contended that it sought only disclosure, but 'I would take that *cum grano salis* from my experience down there.' Washington often tried to go behind all manner of statements in a draft prospectus and demand changes. Applicants could count upon delays of sixty days or more in qualifying an issue. In fact, the SEC seemed to have made up its mind not to accept any Canadian junior mining issues barring the most exceptional circumstances.[46]

McTague recalled that when he headed the OSC, dealings with American officials had often been difficult. Several times he had invited the SEC to send evidence regarding alleged offences, but nothing had arrived. Grand juries preferred secret indictments whose contents could not be communicated. Some states had pretty strange definitions of what constituted fraudulent conduct; Michigan, for instance, made it a fraud to do anything not permitted under its regulations, present or future. Like Lennox, McTague claimed that the Americans had developed a fixation about extradition as the only effective means of regulation, but he was not convinced that this was an appropriate remedy: 'it was a horrible kind of business putting people who could hardly be said to be in the field of crime, by the longest stretch of the imagination, into difficulty.'[47]

William Wismer, the executive secretary of the BDA, was also called to testify, and he too did his best to strike a positive note. He listed the growing range of responsibilities undertaken by the association over the past three years. Many of the problems, he claimed, were created by newcomers to the securities business who resorted to unscrupulous methods in a desperate struggle to secure a profitable clientele. Such brokers might poach salesmen and customers from one another or use mass mailings, even though the response rate might be as low as one in a hundred, while the orders received typically involved only about 250 shares priced between 35 and 40 cents. These tyros often dissipated their capital in short order and became vulnerable to takeovers by shady types in search of a front. Such problems kept the BDA's Discipline Committee busy, and Wismer detailed the number of fines and suspensions handed out each year.[48]

He sought to dispel the notion that the BDA was nothing but a den of thieves by arguing that comparisons with the Investment Dealers Association were unfair, since it had existed for over thirty years and had had plenty of time to do its 'housekeeping' and remove the bad actors. By contrast, the BDA was only now hitting full stride. Wismer had to admit, however, that the figures supplied by Lennox were correct. Amongst the 164 brokers and 282 salesmen who belonged to the association, more than one-third had undergone disciplinary scrutiny. At least 35 firms had encountered problems with the American authorities and been subject to postal-fraud or fictitious-name orders. As a result, Washington had resumed the pressure for an effective extradition treaty. Still, he contended that the worst was over. Lennox had permitted many BDA members to resign and seek direct registration with the OSC, and some insiders had doubted that the association could survive, but by the beginning of 1951 this experiment had been ended and membership was recovering.[49]

O.E. Lennox did not believe that there was any need for the committee even to hear the American side of things, but the members decided otherwise. Proceedings were adjourned to allow the SEC to prepare a submission, which came in the form of an eight-thousand-word letter from Richard McEntire, the SEC member who had assumed primary responsibility for relations with Canada.[50] He opted to put his views in writing so as to avoid charges that the United States was interfering in internal Canadian affairs. Yet he left no doubt that the issue had given rise to 'very real misunderstandings' and created a 'tender spot' in the relations between the two countries. Toronto brokers continued to make all kinds of fraudulent claims about mining promotions. McEntire pointed out, for instance, that one promoter had claimed a prospect was 'adjacent' to a genuine mineral find though the distance between the two had been at least seventeen hundred miles. The breathless report that Geiger counters were 'working' on a uranium claim had proved sufficient to take in some unsophisticated investors. 'There appears to be no limitation to the ingenuity employed by some of these telephone salesmen,' wrote McEntire. 'And indeed the gullibility displayed by some of our investors is equally unlimited.'

He was insistent that the sheer volume of complaints made it clear that the problems did not stem simply from unhappy losers trying to recoup by blaming brokers. He denied that the SEC was using the outcry to try to cut off investment in Canada altogether. The Securities Act of 1933 did not interfere with the ordinary course of securities trading, nor did it prohibit Americans from placing unsolicited orders. McEntire bluntly rejected claims that American regulations were unduly arduous to comply with. Since 1933, $59 billion worth of securities had been registered with the SEC, $1.1 billion of those by Canadians, including $285 million worth of industrial stocks and $120 million of oils and mines. Complaints about the expense and delay of the process were much exaggerated: a recent study showed that just .5 per cent of the funds raised by an issue went to meet the cost of a flotation outside compensation to the distributors. Filings were normally responded to within ten days of receipt, and once any changes demanded by the SEC's letter of comment had been made, registration was legally required within twenty days.

Much had been said about the problems created by differing state laws, but American issuers coped with these complexities every day. Registration was only required where a security was actually going to be marketed, and few Canadian brokers aimed at nationwide distribution. Moreover, some states, like New Jersey, had no registration requirements at all, while others demanded only the licensing of brokers making an offering. In any event, said McEntire, these excuses cut no ice. There was 'nothing ruthless or unreasonable' about attempting to enforce the law of the land. After all, these complaints came from people who chose to do business in the United States: 'I know of no American securities regulator who would provide any comfort, active or passive, to a resident of this country who, because he disliked your securities laws, proposed to offer securities in Canada without complying with the regulations imposed in each and every province in which his offering was effected.'

So far Canadian regulators had failed to control these abuses. Particularly galling to the Americans were the share-pushers who had been indicted in the United States but had fled across the border, where they continued to operate with impunity. A.E. DePalma, for instance, had jumped bail of $50,000. While the OSC might point out that he had lost his licence in 1946, the SEC believed him to have been the the moving spirit behind Palamino Gold Mines just the previous year. As a result, the Americans had concluded that a revised extradition treaty was the only effective remedy, so that prosecutions could proceed where evidence and witnesses were at hand. 'No honest person can be harmed by such a revision ...,' said McEntire. 'We fail to see how any valid objections can be made to our proposals.' He concluded that he had no interest in 'blame-placing or recrimination' but wanted only to see the proper tools in place to deal with these problems.

Recalled by the committee to discuss McEntire's letter, O.E. Lennox tried to be as diplomatic as possible, insisting that he didn't want to rehash the SEC's complaints in detail. Yet he remained dismissive about most of the specifics. One of the six cases cited by McEntire, he believed, was simply an attempt to recoup money lost on a bad investment, while another was more in the nature of an enquiry than a complaint. The use of the word 'adjacent' by the promoters of Indigo Consolidated Gold Mines in the Northwest Territories about Noranda's mine in northwestern Quebec had been reported to the OSC, but the SEC had never supplied any formal evidence. If DePalma was still in business on Bay Street, it was because he was using fronts who perjured themselves in sworn declarations to the effect that he did not control 5 per cent of the stock in a public company and was not an officer or director or sold shares to the public. Those people who signed false prospectuses were guilty of offences much more important than DePalma himself, who was little more than a 'clown.' Not one of the six cases, said Lennox, had resulted in a suspension or the cancellation of a registration by the OSC.[51]

He became increasingly testy as he described the OSC's efforts to get the Americans to produce evidence: 'We are doing our best, and we do not like to keep pestering them to return these documents, but we are responsible for the evidence on file in this commission and we have to keep after them until we get it. I have been put on the defensive about things about which there are no positive charges against us.' Under questioning by E.B. Jolliffe, Lennox did admit that there had been some embarrassing slip-ups. One BDA member slapped with a mail-fraud order in the United States had been permitted by the OSC to reregister under a new name, which implied that Ontario was conniving at the evasion of American laws. Lennox countered loftily, 'I do not think the Ontario Securities Commission has to operate for the benefit of the SEC.' That was not the point, responded Jolliffe. How could it be in the public interest to assist somebody in violating the laws of another country? Lennox argued that the broker in question had claimed he needed to reincorporate in order to secure limited liability, but Jolliffe retorted that this could hardly be convincing once a fraud order had been issued. Lennox was forced to agree.[52]

Charles McTague did his best to bolster Lennox's arguments that things were not nearly as bad as the SEC was claiming. He thought that the Americans were unnecessarily impeding the flow of vitally needed capital across the border: 'I am saying the financing which comes from Bay Street is a very important factor in connection with the development of the natural resources of this country. If you do not have that type of financing, then all you are going to have is control by the big interests or people who are fortunate enough to get in on that basis in the beginning, and then have sufficient capital to be able to carry it through.' Weren't some people in the securities business always complaining that regulation was hampering the development of Ontario's natural resources, he was asked? McTague admitted,

[C]ertainly many people who have been associated with the mining industry over the years have the very definite viewpoint that any act which tends to interfere or restrict their activities in getting money and so on is holding back the development of natural resources ... There is no doubt about this, that where you have government regulations which you have under the Securities Act, you are placing a certain amount of restraint around the investment of capital, but my view is that you have a duty to do that because it is not only the promotion of development of natural resources by risk capital, but also there must be certain rules ... [I]t is not like buying a horse that has a spavin or like having a bull that can- not perform. All you buy is the ownership in an equity and that leads to a lot of temptations.

Yet the only thing to do was to try to raise ethical standards through a continuing program of education and self-regulation.[53]

Yet when William Wismer of the BDA was asked what he believed was needed to bring renegade brokers firmly under control, he gave a devastatingly frank answer which must have distressed his employers: 'There is a way around it, but if I were to mention it, it would send a cold chill down the spine of Bay Street, I am afraid ... If the Ontario Securities Commission were given the discretion to refuse an acceptance for filing, if in the public interest any officer, director, promoter, underwriter or anyone in any way, directly or indirectly connected with the company was objectionable, it might go a very long way.' This comment was too much for McTague, who leapt in to try to save the day: 'I think it is very objectionable. You put in the hands of somebody who is arbitrary power to act in an arbitrary fashion, and you say it should not hurt the man who is above-board and so on, but it puts some human being in the position of giving judgement with respect to who is above-board in respect of those things without any rules.' Attorney General Dana Porter agreed: 'The other great difficulty is that when you give an administrator ... discretionary powers he may suspect quite unjustifiably certain persons without any evidence at all ... That remedy depends upon the personality of the man who is administering it ... I think if you give the administrator too much power without any appeal or without any recourse at all, that you are simply placing in the hands of a dictator the destinies of a lot of people who might be alright. That is a matter of which I would be afraid.'[54]

After hearing so much from regulators, the members of the committee were interested in getting the views of one of the promoters whose livelihood came from marketing speculative mining shares. Louis Cadesky, one of the founding governors of the BDA, described his methods: grubstaking prospectors, acquiring properties, and if a property proved sufficiently promising to raise more money, incorporating a public company. He would take a large block of vendor shares for his troubles and seek out a broker-dealer willing to underwrite the stock and market it to his clientele. Any profits, he claimed, came his way only if the flotation succeeded and a public market for the shares developed.

Cadesky insisted that mass mailings were necessary largely because the OSC banned securities marketers from calling on the private homes of strangers. The only way to maintain a sizeable customer list was to mail out hundreds of circulars, enclosing 'qualifying cards' to be filled out and returned. These cards then permitted salespeople to get in touch. As for telephone campaigns, said the promoter, customers had to express an interest and receive a prospectus before any sale could be finalized. If buyers developed doubts, most sensible brokers would not insist on going through with a trade. Obstreperous clients sometimes tried to blackmail brokers in order to get their money back by threatening to report them to the OSC or the SEC, and it was better to pay them off than face such complications. People who complained about their losses on speculative stocks were just sore losers: 'All in all I think the public is getting a fair run for its money. They cannot all win.' Cadesky brushed off criticisms by the likes of Richard McEntire. The BDA had been pressing the SEC for detailed information about the supposed wrongdoings of Toronto brokers for several years past without result. The recent decision of the OSC to compile a monthly *Bulletin* recording its disciplinary actions was only playing into the hands of Washington officials: 'Why put wood on the fire? That is where they get their propaganda.'[55]

After a brief re-examination of Lennox, the parliamentarians adjourned to meet in about ten days time. But before the committee could convene again, it was snuffed out of existence by the calling of a provincial general election for 22 November 1951. As a result, the committee never produced any report or recommendations, despite the 3,945 pages of evidence collected.[56]

There was no sign that 'the Canadian problem' was diminishing. In September the *Financial Post* supplied details of a swindle that had netted over half a million dollars. The promoters set up in business as broker-dealers at a cost of just $1,500, while a printing firm (controlled by the same people) agreed to prepare and finance all of the brokerage's mailings. A 3-million-share oil company was incorporated, with one-third of the stock being granted to the insiders as vendors of drilling rights in an area where small discoveries were common though production on a commercial scale was unlikely. Half the company's stock was optioned to the promoters, a block of 250,000 shares at 10 cents apiece and the remaining 1,250,000 at 15 cents. These shares were sold for whatever they would bring by salesmen who made scores of long-distance calls to the United States. Investors were lured in by telling them that no money need be sent until oil had actually been found. Following an oil strike, 1,479,000 of the optioned shares were marketed during a four-month period for $540,000 (or an average price of 37 cents), of which the company treasury received just $197,000. After paying the telephone bills, $10,000 for commissions, $20,000 for organizational expenses, and $125,000 in overhead (including the printing costs), the brokerage earned $85,000. As the treasury stock was sold, the vendor shares were freed from escrow on a one-for-one basis and became available for sale to the public too. These shares (which had cost just 1.8 cents apiece) were also marketed at an average price of 20 cents, with the proceeds going directly to the insiders. Over-all receipts totalled $750,822.65, netting the promoters a profit of $533,322.65, before the OSC deprived the brokerage of its registration and stopped the operation after just a few months.[57]

III

While such embarrassing revelations continued, officials in Washing-ton and Ottawa were settling the final form of the new extradition agreement covering securities offences. In September Canada's deputy minister of justice sent a letter to the deputy attorney general of each province, noting a recent 'outbreak of high-pressure selling across the border, chiefly from Toronto, by unscrupulous persons whose repre-sentations can only be described as fraudulent.' The resulting publicity, 'damaging to the reputation of Canada,' had led the government to conclude that a new treaty on the basis of dual criminality ought to be signed. F.P. Varcoe therefore forwarded the text of two new sections to be added to the Extradition Treaty. Section 11 (a) would create a new extraditable offence of 'obtaining property, money or valuable securi-ties by false pretences.' The words echoed the prohibition in section 17 (a) of the U.S. Securities Act of 1933 and that in section 444A of the Canadian Criminal Code. The treaty provision thus rested once more upon the principle of dual criminality. Section 11 (b) banned 'making use of the mails in connection with schemes devised or intended to deceive or defraud the public.' Here, too, the changes in the Canadian Criminal Code introduced in the summer of 1951, following discus-sions with the Americans, had added section 209 (c), which made the 'posting' of such misleading material a crime that also mirrored the provisions of American law.

Justice Department officials were confident that these 'slight modifi-cations' to Canadian law would be sufficient to permit the extradition of unscrupulous promoters who sold shares in the United States by mail or by telephone using misleading representations, actions that gave rise to 'much adverse publicity and cause great harm to sound Canadian investments.' The new rules were based upon 'sound logic and good international practice' and should work to the advantage of those honestly attempting to market securities in the United States. Ratification was 'exceptionally urgent ... because ... considerable harm is resulting from the press campaign being waged in the United States on an extensive scale. 'Varcoe's letter also noted that the text had 'already been cleared informally with officials of the province of Ontario which is chiefly affected.' The restoration of the principle of dual criminality (along with Ottawa's unchallenged jurisdiction over criminal law) made it difficult to raise objections, and all the provinces gave their assent.[58]

Word of the agreement did, however, bring nervous enquiries from leading figures in the financial community, such as the president of the Toronto Stock Exchange and the head of the Investment Dealers Association. Arthur Slaght pointed out that many American states had extremely broad definitions as to what constituted fraud and elected prosecutors eager to make a name for themselves by going after Canadian brokers. Yet the revelations before the Ontario legislative committee had finally convinced the more reputable elements in the financial community that such an arrangement would be to their advantage; no longer did they wish to be tarred with the same brush as boiler-room operators in Toronto. After consulting the Americans, federal officials agreed to let the TSE's legal counsel, Liberal senator Salter Hayden, examine the text. F.P. Varcoe argued that 'the concession to the United States is at a minimum, and we hope that your clients will agree that it would be in the best interests of our responsible brokers and security issuers that a limited extradition of this type should be provided.'[59]

Though the proposed agreement still left some brokers nervous about the possibility of being extradited to the United States for offences that were not considered serious in Canada, the restoration of the principle of dual criminality made it difficult to object. The directors of the Montreal Stock Exchange and the Montreal Curb Exchange journeyed to Toronto to consult with their counterparts at the TSE; they considered a formal opinion by lawyer J.J. Robinette that the agreement now met the terms of the objections registered in 1945 and conformed to current Canadian law. As a result, the exchanges decided to accept the proposed arrangement.[60] The board of the Broker Dealers Association dithered about how it should respond. Eventually, however, the governors concluded that little was to be gained from open opposition to the agreement.[61]

On 26 October 1951 the ministers of external affairs and justice signed the new convention to be attached to the Extradition Treaty. At a press conference Prime Minister Louis St Laurent noted that, strictly speaking, the government was only required to table the documents in the House of Commons since no legislative changes were necessary, but he promised to release the text once the U.S. Senate had ratified it and to provide an opportunity for discussion in Parliament in view of the controversy that had occurred in 1945.[62]

While waiting for the treaty to be finalized, the Americans moved in another way to increase protection for investors against the depredations of Canadian share-pushers. The SEC began to issue a 'Canadian Restricted List,' naming companies whose shares were believed to be marketed illegally. To counter 'serious concern' about 'the flood of literature from Canada' offering unregistered issues, this list would be distributed regularly to all the members of the National Association of Securities Dealers in the United States.[63]

The U.S. Senate approved the new extradition convention on 1 April 1952. The Americans then expected Canada to move swiftly to bring the convention into force. When there was no immediate action in Ottawa, Richard McEntire of the SEC reminded the embassy in Washington that speed was essential. Already he had had to dissuade the *Wall Street Journal* from running an article condemning Canada's foot-dragging. The SEC began enquiring almost daily as to when Parliament would take up the matter. Ambassador Hume Wrong advised that steps to show that those who swindled Americans would be brought to book were sorely needed in order to restore Canada's good name in the United States.[64]

In mid-May the treaty was finally laid before Parliament's Standing Committee on External Affairs. Justice Minister Stuart Garson explained the reasons for the agreement, taking care to emphasize that the principle of dual criminality had been fully restored. Tabling endorsements from the major stock exchanges and the Investment Dealers Association, he reported that most brokers were eager to see the convention pass as soon as possible. His deputy, F.P. Varcoe, stressed that Ontario and the other provinces had been canvassed and had expressed no objection to the changes. G.M. Murray from Cariboo, British Columbia, seemed to speak for other members of the committee in urging speedy passage: 'Everybody knows that Bay Street is infested with illicit operators.' American anger was only hurting Canada by restricting the flow of funds into mining development. The committee quickly approved the convention.[65]

Within a week it came before the full House of Commons. All seemed to go smoothly until Conservative MP Donald Fleming brought up a remark made by Varcoe before the committee to the effect that the convention covered only mail fraud, not the use of the telephone in selling shares. Alarm bells rang in Washington, and Milton

Kroll of the SEC hurried round to the embassy. The deputy minister of justice explained that the legal situation was complicated. The protocol expressly made 'use of the mails' to commit fraud an extraditable offence, but solicitation by telephone and by telegraph were not specifically mentioned. Neither was solicitation alone a fraudulent act under the Canadian Criminal Code: for an offence to have been committed, somebody must actually receive a payment. If the payment was received in Canada, it *might* be held that no offence had been committed in the United States, so the recipient would not be extraditable, while if the fraud was completed in the United States, it could be found that the misrepresentations had been made in that country alone. Privately, Varcoe admitted that he had avoided raising these problems explicitly before the parliamentary committee for fear that there would be a long debate, or worse, an adjournment.[66]

Other Canadian officials were inclined to dismiss these concerns as a tempest in a teapot. At External Affairs the view was that 'the SEC people have been making rather heavy weather of this question' only because the press had gotten hold of it. The lawyers at Justice eventually satisfied themselves that if the telephone was used and if money was fraudulently obtained from an American, then an extraditable offence would have been committed. After consultations, External Affairs drew up a carefully worded despatch: 'If a specific case should arise involving the use of the telephone or telegraph, and the United States authorities should conclude upon the evidence that an offence has been committed in the United States, they should not be apprehensive that a Canadian judge would take a different view.' The embassy was instructed to call in Richard McEntire of the SEC and read this opinion to him with the advice that he could telephone Varcoe if he sought further assurances.[67]

Even so, there were still a few more bumps in the road. In the Banking and Commerce Committee Senator W.B. Farris of British Columbia proposed a change that would have left anybody accused of securities fraud to be tried only before the Canadian courts, since Farris alleged that once the SEC had secured an extradition, public pressure might lead to individuals being handed over to the state courts for further punishment. In the end, however, the Senate committee voted to approve the convention by a margin of eleven to eight, and by early July 1952 the new agreement had become law in both countries. The Americans believed that they finally had the necessary tools to proceed against anyone who was fraudulently selling securities from across the border. In the *Bulletin* of the Ontario Securities Commission O.E. Lennox reminded his readers that this was just part of the process of turning over a new leaf: 'Canada's phenomenal postwar expansion and consequent upsurge in corporate financing has attracted many who have shown little regard for the high standard of trading established by brokerage houses of many years.' Times had changed, and membership in the Broker Dealers Association was now down to 150 as a result of tighter discipline. The *Financial Post* reported that with the treaty law in place, the telephones in Toronto's boiler rooms had fallen silent because brokers and salesmen were fearful of finding themselves in front of American judges if they persisted in trying to market unregistered shares.[68]

The members of the BDA watched the debate over the ratification of the new treaty intently. Their aim was now to secure the cancellation of all outstanding indictments, as well as any postal-fraud or fictitious-name orders, before the new rules took effect. Doing so was not made any easier because of continuing complaints about misconduct by broker-dealers. For instance, Malvern Trading Corporation continued to market a highly speculative oil issue through a blizzard of mail and telephone calls to the United States. The OSC found that '[i]n this promotional house the matter was placed on a higher plane. When a salesman had sold and re-loaded a customer to the best of his ability, the account was taken away from him and handed to a super-salesman in order to add the finishing touches.'[69]

Charles McTague tried to persuade Ottawa to extract a promise from Washington to drop all the indictments as a condition of Canada's approving the treaty. In May 1952 he requested a meeting with External Affairs Minister Lester Pearson and also interviewed Justice Minister Stuart Garson. McTague reported to the BDA board that Pearson seemed to grasp the fairness of having all outstanding indictments cancelled and had promised to have the embassy raise this issue informally with the Americans. As the date for final ratification neared, the lawyer continued to press for a commitment 'wiping out' any retroactive charges, but the State Department stuck to the strict letter of the law, claiming that there was no impediment to applying for extradition for any offence dating as far back as the original treaty.[70] Although all the old indictments appeared to have lapsed, the Americans bluntly refused to put any commitment not to prosecute in writing. If a really 'malodorous' case from years past was suddenly uncovered, a public outcry might force the SEC to take action whether it really wanted to or not. The State Department could not be placed in the position of having given any advance assurances of immunity from prosecution to the Canadians. The best that could be obtained was a statement that the Americans had no plans to 'dredge up' old cases.[71]

With the new convention finally in effect, Lester Pearson expressed a willingness to write to Charles McTague stating that 'the matter is closed.' The acting under-secretary of state for external affairs, Escott Reid, was much more nervous about putting anything on paper, 'so that we will not become involved to the extent of making any definite commitments to him on behalf of the Canadian or the United States governments.' Reid persuaded Pearson that he should send only a very brief note declaring, 'As far as we have been able to ascertain there is no disposition on the part of the United States authorities to dredge up old cases.' Astute as he was, McTague reported to the BDA that this was no firm commitment but merely the 'language of diplomacy.' Still, he concluded that in the present circumstances, 'I think we just have to take our chances on relying on what is contained in the language, cautious as it is.'[72]

Once the treaty became law, BDA members hoped that the SEC would agree to simplified short-form registration for small Canadian issues being sold in the United States. The draft wording for a new regulation D was released in September 1952. In order to make enforcement simpler, applicants might sell up to $300,000 worth of an issue annually, provided that they did not market such securities inside and outside the United States at the same time. The most serious problem for the broker-dealers was that any person who had been the subject of an indictment or injunction barring the sale of securities in the United States during the past five years would be ineligible to use regulation D.[73]

Charles McTague insisted that the BDA had always assumed everyone would be allowed to make a fresh start after the treaty; otherwise no broker-dealer would be prepared to register in Washington. He did succeed in arranging a meeting with Justice Minister Garson in February 1953, at which he pointed out that the new rules could only succeed if 'the past is completely wiped out.' He contended that the American proposal represented an 'unwarranted interference' in the regulation of securities in Canada, a 'breach of faith' which might lead to reconsideration of the treaty.[74]

When these complaints were forwarded to the SEC, Richard McEntire's response was that the Americans were willing to forgive and forget technical offences but not to overlook cases where brokers had been involved in clearly fraudulent operations. Since the latter would involve only a handful of Toronto boiler rooms, Canadian interests were not going to be served by pressing for changes in the rules which might jeopardize the goodwill of regulators and investors in the United States in order to please a few shady characters. McEntire even offered to provide confidential assurances that past conduct would not necessarily constitute a bar to the offering of securities under the new rules. Meanwhile, the SEC moved ahead and promulgated regulation D on 6 March 1953.[75]

The BDA was greatly disappointed. Asked by the SEC how many brokers might register, the association had originally estimated that between 65 and 75 of its 125 members would apply immediately and over 100 would become licensed eventually. Fears about being hauled before the American courts for past activities put paid to any such notion. In the spring of 1953 there were warnings from Washington that at least a dozen BDA members had illegally been carrying out extensive mailings, while four firms were currently conducting telephone campaigns. One of the broker-dealers involved was a member of the BDA board.[76]

To placate the Americans the BDA adopted a formal policy in March 1953 declaring it unethical for BDA members to market shares in violation of American law. They might send letters and other general information, but were warned that making specific offerings or soliciting orders would render them ineligible for future registration with the SEC. At the same time O.E. Lennox backed up this notice by issuing a warning to licensees that they risked suspension if they traded in the United States without registering with the SEC. This directive was carefully couched to imply that the OSC had no intention of interfering in relations between reputable Toronto brokers and their long-standing customers; only share-pushing operators who sought customers through mail and telephone campaigns need be concerned.[77]

Eventually the SEC issued rules modifying regulation D so that 'technical' violations of American law by applicants could be overlooked; only indictments and injunctions where fraud was alleged would be considered. Stuart Garson forwarded this news to C.P. McTague, noting that most of the brokers subject to such orders had already ceased business, so that few BDA members would still be liable to face charges in the United States. That, wrote the justice minister, seemed a fair outcome: 'Having regard to the public relations problems involved as between the two nations, it would seem that the general interest of Canada would not be served by changes which would jeopardize the goodwill of the United States investors and financial institutions in order to protect those who in the past have been guilty of fraudulent operations in this country.'[78]

McTague, however, reiterated the criticisms of American practices raised before the Ontario legislative committee. 'The SEC are very fond of labelling people as being guilty of fraudulent operations when they have not been before any court and even in some cases where the SEC has undertaken to establish some proof of fraud to the Ontario Securities Commission without success. That is the proposition that I fear in connection with the successful operation of Regulation D. The label "guilty of fraudulent operations" is the typical propaganda weapon of the bureaucrat.' During McTague's time at the OSC, Washington had failed to supply evidence of any fraud upon which he could act, and Lennox had had the same experience. To date, the SEC seemed disposed to act fairly and had not sought to open up cases retroactively. Regulation D might operate successfully, but McTague repeated, 'I still want to be on record as entertaining a good deal of fear that methods are likely to be employed to unfairly prevent people who enjoy registration in this jurisdiction from trading under the Regulations.' Garson had had enough. He squelched the BDA counsel pretty effectively by replying that if, as McTague claimed, he knew of no serious misconduct by Canadian brokers, then 'It seems to follow from this, that if the American authorities agree with your statement of fact, no problems at all will arise with regard to fraudulent operations which you contend have never taken place.' No more was heard from McTague.[79]

By early 1954 only five Toronto firms were reported to be making use of regulation D; others continued to sell illegally in the United States while waiting to see what the authorities would do. The SEC was still insisting upon a formal hearing before licensing anyone against whom there had been allegations of fraudulent misrepresentation by U.S. residents. The Americans could not simply ignore evidence of past wrongdoing, for fear that congressional investigators might discover what was going on. Eventually, however, the SEC agreed that as of June 1954 Canadian brokers who had no recent violations on their records would be approved, with the exception of those with secret indictments outstanding, who would have to await their fate.[80]

By that time, however, few broker-dealers were seeking to qualify further Canadian issues under regulation D, though some forty stocks had already been approved. The rate of economic growth was slowing, and successful promotions became more difficult. Membership in the BDA continued to decline from 139 in 1951 to 116 in 1952, 103 in 1953, and only 80 in 1954. As usual in such circumstances, the mining community blamed its problems on over-strict regulation. Promoter John R. Strathy sounded a familiar note in demanding that the OSC be abolished on the grounds that no new publicly financed mine had come into production since the 1947 Securities Act had been in force. Confining rules were the cause: 'Registration inhibits the development of a country's mineral resources.' While some mining investors inevitably lost money, Strathy complained, 'Surely we are making too great a sacrifice, when, in order to save a few widows' mites from some unscrupulous stock salesman (and no person is more opposed to them than the writer) we so retard the development of a great industry that we endanger our economic future.'[81]

Most American state regulators still refused to open their markets to Canadian securities, notwithstanding regulation D. Only in the 'free' states of Delaware, Maryland, the District of Columbia, Nevada, New Jersey, and New York could foreign brokers sell legally without local registration. Outside Pennsylvania and New York, which had made arrangements for full cooperation with the OSC to police trading, efforts to distribute shares were greeted with threats of injunctions. Moreover, regulation D had some serious flaws. Sharp-eyed American promoters realized that companies incorporated in the United States could also acquire mining claims in Canada and thus qualify to distribute stock under the relatively relaxed requirements of regulation D. No genuine mineral prospects need be demonstrated, but these scams were all lumped together as part of·'the Canadian problem.'[82]

By the fall of 1954 Lennox concluded that he should no longer insist upon Ontario brokers obeying his order of March 1953 to comply with American rules because so many states were refusing point-blank to register Canadian issues. The November OSC *Bulletin* carried a 'Statement of Policy,' designed 'to demonstrate beyond any reasonable doubt that the plan adopted as the solution to the so-called [Canadian] problem has proved a dismal failure from any point of view, including the interests of residents of the United States interested in speculative Canadian mining issues.' Despite regulation D, federal and state regulators continued to place serious obstacles in the way of Canadians seeking to register issues. The entire field was thus left to American-based promotions, and the OSC was bearing the blame for a 'Canadian problem' that was none of its fault. In future it would be left to individual brokers to decide how to conduct their business in the United States.[83]

Despite the failure of regulation D to reduce illegal sales of Canadian stocks in the United States, the Americans were confident that the new extradition convention covering securities fraud would enable them to prosecute serious offenders. Following the OSC order to comply with American regulations in March 1953, half a dozen Toronto boiler rooms shifted their operations to Montreal. T.M. Parker Incorporated began promoting Falgar Mining heavily in Michigan, using sales literature that included a doctored aerial photograph which showed the company's claim as immediately adjacent to the producing mines of the International Nickel Company and Falconbridge, which were one mile north of the actual location. In October 1954 the Canadian embassy in Washington received a demand for delivery of Parker salesmen Walter H. Link and Harry H. Green; the indictments charged the two men with defrauding seventeen Michigan residents by mail and by telephone. The case for handing them over to the Americans seemed open and shut: the chief justice of Quebec's Superior Court observed that the evidence submitted to him showed they had been 'neck-deep' in a 'nefarious' share-pushing scheme by a boiler room.[84]

J.T. Callahan, who prepared the case for the SEC, told his OSC counterparts confidently, 'It's our baby. We will take care of it.' Thus it was a profound shock when the application for extradition was denied. Judge W.B. Scott pointed out that the treaty principle of dual criminality required that the actions complained of be offences in both countries. Canada's Criminal Code had recently been amended to extend the ban on mail fraud, but it still did not cover use of the telephone. Because the charges combined the offences of mail and telephone fraud, Scott held that the application failed to meet the treaty test of dual criminality, even though fraud and false pretences were also prohibited under both Canadian and Michigan law. The judge therefore refused to order the delivery of the accused.[85]

The assumption in Ottawa was that the Supreme Court would rectify the situation by overturning Scott's decision. Justice Department officials were in no doubt that he had erred in law; grounds for extradition could be established simply by demonstrating that the actions complained of would have been crimes if they had occurred in Canada. Unfortunately, when leave to appeal was sought in March 1955, the Supreme Court unanimously refused on the grounds that Scott's finding was not a 'judgment' that could be appealed. The Americans were left angry and frustrated because Canadian swindlers had been let off the hook yet again; the SEC insisted that it had presented all the evidence necessary, and 'that if extradition could not be obtained in this case it never would be in any future case.'[86]

Before long, American politicians took up the issue. In April 1955 Senator Alexander Wiley wrote directly to the Canadian ambassador to suggest that further changes in the Extradition Treaty were urgently required to make it effective, a proposal that he soon repeated on the Senate floor. The Canadian financial community became worried that Wiley's Senate Foreign Relations Committee might start another investigation of Canadian share-selling in the United States, which would undoubtedly generate further unfavourable publicity. The diplomats in Washington reported that enquiries had again started to pour in about Canadian laxity concerning securities fraud: 'In some ways this is the softest single spot in Canadian-United States relations as far as people on this side of the border are concerned.'[87]

What could Canada do? The Department of Justice considered the idea of a reference case in which the Supreme Court would be asked to answer one or more questions concerning the validity of the extradition convention. The problem was that such answers would only be advisory and, in any case, would not affect the judge's refusal to hand over Link and Green to the Americans. The only other suggestion was that Canada's Extradition Act might be amended to permit appeals against decisions refusing to grant delivery of accused persons. Perhaps this change would be sufficient to head off further criticism by Senator Wiley.[88]

Wiley was not easily diverted, however. In June 1955 he inserted in the *Congressional Record* a lengthy memorandum prepared by the SEC, detailing the problems it had encountered in trying to prosecute violators of American laws because of a lack of cooperation from provincial regulators. In light of the unsatisfactory situation, said Wiley, the commission was considering methods of cutting off the flow of Canadian securities. Senator J.W. Fulbright introduced a bill making it illegal to use American mail or telephone service to violate securities laws. People in other countries who refused to submit to SEC jurisdiction following a warning might find it unlawful to send messages into the United States.[89]

Feeling the political pressure, U.S. attorney general Herbert Brownell suggested privately to Ambassador Arnold Heeney that perhaps the time had come to take another look at the Extradition Treaty. Would it be best to refer the problem to the Joint U.S.-Canadian Committee on Economic Affairs, where cabinet members from the two countries could discuss it behind closed doors? That would allow the administration to head off any rash action by telling both the SEC and the Congress that the problem of fraudulent share-selling had already been raised between the two countries at the highest level. When E.A. Ritchie of External Affairs visited Washington to plan for the meeting of the Joint Committee of Ministers, SEC chair J. Sinclair Armstrong insisted on seeing him. Ritchie was summoned to a 'seance' with Armstrong and three other commissioners, sat at a table like an erring schoolboy, and made to listen to the reading of a nine-page document. This 'Statement of Securities and Exchange Commission Regarding Illegal Sales of Canadian Securities' rehearsed the history of illegal share-selling as far back as the Second World War, noting that the problem had peaked in 1949–51, when over one thousand injunctions and indictments had been registered by American authorities. Since 1950 the SEC had received no less than 12,627 complaints about illegal offerings made from Canada, so that the existing remedies were clearly ineffective and action was urgently needed. In 1955 the SEC had already uncovered twenty-six more illegal offerings by at least sixteen brokers.[90]

Though the Joint Committee of Ministers does not appear to have discussed extradition, the Eisenhower administration made it clear that the imbroglio created by the *Link and Green* decision must be resolved. American legal scholars insisted that the judge in the *Link and Green* case had seriously misinterpreted the principle of dual criminality.[91] When Attorney General Brownell visited Toronto in the autumn of 1955, he told Justice Minister Garson privately that Ottawa ought to frame a reference case for Canada's Supreme Court so the decision could be overturned and the extradition convention reinvigorated. Canadian ambassador Arnold Heeney remained concerned about congressional criticism: 'We may at any time be faced with an embarrassing situation.' The clear consensus within the bureaucracy was that the judge had been plainly wrong, so that a reference case was required to restore the effectiveness of the extradition convention. As a result, the federal cabinet held several discussions of the matter during December 1955, but the ministers were faced with a political problem because there had recently been criticism concerning the administration of justice in the province of Quebec over the notorious Coffin murder case. Not wanting to antagonize Premier Maurice Duplessis any further, the cabinet put the idea of a reference on hold at least until after the provincial election in June 1956.[92]

When O.E. Lennox of the OSC visited Washington during April 1956, he tried to placate the Americans by pointing out that Walter Link and Harry Green had pleaded guilty and been convicted in Quebec court, the former having been fined $2,000 and given two months in jail and the latter fined $500 plus two months in jail for fraud.[93] Washington officials could, of course, respond that the offenders would likely have received much more severe punishment if extradited and convicted in the United States. Attorney General Brownell brought the matter up again with the Canadian ambassador in August 1956, and a few weeks later an official from the American embassy in Ottawa again raised the idea of a reference to the Supreme Court in an effort to overturn Judge Scott's ruling. Ambassador Heeney thought that the Canadians owed it to the Americans to suggest some action to prevent the extradition convention from becoming a complete nullity, but he could not convince his own colleagues. One diplomat wrote, 'I see nothing but trouble ahead if the Canadian government embarks on the negotiation of another extradition treaty with the US designed to deal further with securities fraud.' With Premier Maurice Duplessis's Union Nationale government safely re-elected in 1956, any enthusiasm amongst the federal Liberal ministers for a controversial reference case concerning the *Link and Green* decision evaporated. No more was heard about revising the Extradition Treaty's provisions concerning securities offences.[94]

The operations of Toronto boiler rooms illegally marketing worthless shares in plots of 'moose pastures' were fully revealed by the Ontario legislature's hearings in 1951. By that time, though, 'the Canadian problem' was assumed to be on the verge of solution because the governments in Washington and Ottawa had at long last reached agreement in principle on the revision of the Extradition Treaty between the two countries to cover securities fraud. The spotlight focused upon this problem by the hearings made it increasingly difficult for people in the Canadian financial community to resist such changes any longer. By the autumn the new extradition convention was signed, and it came into force in mid-1952. But the belief that the problem was solved was proven unfounded at the first serious test, when a request for extradition was refused by the Canadian courts in the *Link and Green* case. Fly-by-night brokers could evidently continue to peddle stock over the telephone without much risk of finding themselves having to answer to the American courts. Nor did Canadians make use of the SEC's new regulation D, which was intended to simplify the process of registering speculative share issues in the United States. Indeed, Canadians complained that they were bearing the blame for the actions of Americans, who were exploiting a loophole in these rules. Regulators in Washington and the various state capitals were left fuming as Toronto's boiler-room operators continued their depredations.

4

Regulating the Stock Exchange

The number of shares handled on the Toronto Stock Exchange re-mained severely depressed during the early part of the Second World War, and by 1942 seat prices had declined to just $12,000. Yet as victory by the Allies became increasingly likely, the pace of trading began to pick up. In April 1945 more shares changed hands than during the entire twelve months of 1942. By the time of the 1946 annual meeting the exchange's president could report a new record for yearly trading of 440 million shares; along with a record number of listings, this surge drove the cost of a membership up to $63,000.[1]

The return of good times, however, brought with it a recurrence of some of the abuses that had earned stock exchanges so much criticism during the early 1930s. The Standard Stock and Mining Exchange had been a well-known haven for manipulators and speculators until the Ontario Securities Commission forced it to amalgamate with the Toronto Stock Exchange in 1934.[2] In 1945 the TSE's listing standards, though admittedly 'relatively lenient and somewhat elastic,' remained unchanged from the time of the merger with the Standard a decade earlier.[3] For both mining and industrial companies the key benchmark was having a minimum of 1 million shares issued, at least 300,000 of them in the hands of no less than one hundred different individuals. Industrial companies were not required to disclose either their assets or their earnings, while mining ventures needed only a favourably located property with some indication of an ore body from surface exploration and enough funds to carry out a modest drilling program, $50,000 being considered quite adequate. The good reputation of cor-porate officers and directors and a record of previous active trading in the over-the-counter market were counted positive benefits. Only in

1945 was a Listing Committee created to vet applications, but no changes were made in these formal requirements. Moreover, promoters were aware that the TSE often did not adhere to its published standards. For instance, mining companies sometimes got listings even if they had only half the required amount of cash in the treasury, and it was suggested that $30,000 was a sufficient sum to finance exploratory work to discover whether a property had realistic prospects or not. A listing on the TSE was no guarantee of the soundness of a company or its securities.[4]

I

When the market for Canadian mining shares heated up in the mid-1940s, manipulators hastened to take advantage of these relatively relaxed rules. Among the most notorious was Samuel Ciglen, a lawyer and mining promoter who would have many run-ins with securities regulators over the next decade. Ciglen had some claims that he sold to Beaulieu Yellowknife Gold Mines for 1 million vendor shares (900,000 escrowed, 100,000 free for sale) plus a reported cash payment of $50,000. Instead of the cash, however, he was actually given 400,000 treasury shares, which permitted him to gain the release of another 400,000 vendor shares from escrow. He and his associates therefore controlled 900,000 free shares, which had cost them only about $30,000, or 3 cents apiece. In addition, an underwriting and option agreement permitted the insiders to take down another 400,000 shares at 12.5 cents with options on an additional 1,599,995 shares at prices ranging between 15 cents and $2.00. They began to market these shares to the public over the counter at an average price of about 30 cents apiece.

When the company commenced a program of diamond drilling on its claims, the drill holes were deliberately arranged in a close or 'pinpoint' pattern where high ore values were already known to exist, a fact that was disclosed in the prospectus in such a way that it was only likely to be discerned through careful study by a mining expert. In November 1945 Beaulieu Yellowknife was granted a listing on the Toronto Stock Exchange, and by March 1946 the share price had reached 78 cents. Sam Ciglen thereupon engaged the services of a 'market expert' to dispose of an additional 950,000 shares, on which he was granted options at prices ranging from 65 cents to $2.50. During March, accounts opened at two different brokers in the name of Ciglen's secretary were used to feed out another 120,000 shares at prices as high as $1.44. Rumours caused the price to slump in early April, and the insiders bought heavily to push prices back up to $2.07. Needing more funds to pay for his purchases, Ciglen made a deal with another operator, John Van Allen, to take 300,000 shares at an average cost of $1.37. Rather than marketing these shares as he was supposed to do, Van Allen double-crossed the others by simply selling them to the two brokerage accounts run by the syndicate at an average price of $2.00 apiece.

In early May the *Northern Miner* published a highly critical report on the company and the price began to slip once more. In an effort to reverse the slide, Ciglen again bought heavily, running the price up to $2.64 by 16 May. To do so he borrowed so much from his brokers, Harold A. Prescott and Company, that the TSE's auditors became concerned that the firm might not receive sufficient funds to meet its clearings on Monday, 20 May, and ordered the purchases to cease. Indebted to Prescott and Company to the tune of $830,000, Ciglen was trapped, and seeking funds, Prescott turned to another mining promoter, L.J. Brooks, who agreed to take 314,000 shares for $1.15. At that point the OSC intervened, ordering the exchange to investigate whether or not its own rules had been broken, at the same time beginning its own inquiry into the entire affair.[5]

As the OSC investigators unravelled the story during the summer and fall of 1946, the key question became whether or not the price of Beaulieu Yellowknife shares had been illegally manipulated. The conclusion was that Ciglen had created an artificial market but had not used fraudulent methods. There had been no conspiracy to inflate prices, which was prohibited under section 444 of the Canadian Criminal Code, so there existed no grounds for prosecution. Apparently the only regulation that might have been broken was the Toronto Stock Exchange's rule that nobody should make a short sale at a price lower than that at which the last board lot had traded. Yet this rule was almost never enforced since customers often failed to disclose short sales.[6]

The OSC sought to have the exchange revise its rules on short selling to prevent any recurrence, but the Managing Committee of the TSE pointed out that there was not even clear evidence of the rule violations.[7] The commission decided that no prosecutions were possible under the circumstances, and its report was finally released to the public early in 1947. In the end the Beaulieu Yellowknife affair petered out, leaving the OSC rather frustrated that it could not do more about the insiders who had manipulated share prices. For its part, however, the TSE could point out that there appeared to have been no serious rule violations by its own members. Privately, exchange officials claimed that the OSC staff members who had handled the investigation were not fully familiar with the way in which the brokerage business worked.[8]

Sam Ciglen was not the only promoter to take advantage of the laxness of the Toronto Stock Exchange's rules concerning such matters as listing requirements, disclosure by prospectus, and self-dealing. Lee R. Brooks believed that Eldona Gold Mines was sufficiently promising that he committed himself to put up $890,000 under option and underwriting agreements at an average share price of 50 cents apiece. Favourable drilling results in the summer of 1947 led him to acquire additional options to take down stock at between 35 and 60 cents. Trading volume rose rapidly as he engineered a primary distribution of the issue on the floor of the TSE; altogether 14 million shares traded between 15 August and 30 September as each of Eldona's 3.5 million shares changed hands an average of four times.

Brooks followed the conventional pattern of selling off shares in anticipation of takedowns under his option agreements, then buying back sufficient stock to stabilize the price. Broker Rupert Bain became particularly impressed with Eldona's prospects and arranged to buy large blocks of stock from Brooks, which he then marketed to his customers. Sensational news from the mine led share prices to rise from 32 cents to $2.60 starting on 26 August. Less favourable reports on 9 September helped to bring about a collapse to just $1.00 the following day. The OSC ordered an investigation.[9]

Brooks insisted that the break had occurred as a result of malicious rumours circulated by short sellers. In particular he complained about one salesman, Louis Chesler at the Draper Dobie brokerage, alleging that he was part of a concerted plan to profit by wrecking the promotion. As usual, the precise origins of the rumours proved almost impossible to establish; the OSC investigators found that they were 'based in the main on wishful thinking bordering on hysteria.' Nor, the commission noted, should one forget 'the important part that rumour and gossip always play in any market operation in which the public is heavily participating.' Short selling there undoubtedly had been, but without any evidence of an organized raid.

What the investigation did uncover was that Brooks's own trading operation had been so extensive that at least ninety-nine transactions covering 132,100 shares were wash sales, in which he had acted as both buyer and seller. Feeding stock into the market using no less than twenty-three different brokers, a dozen of whom had direct telephone lines to his office, he bought 2.7 million shares and sold 2.5 million during a six-week period. Spreading this business around not only helped to generate more interest among customers but also allowed his friends to earn commissions and made it possible to conceal his own actions from floor traders as the price was pushed up. Many of the transactions were actually carried out by 'jitney' brokers who had no customers but only acted for other exchange members on the trading floor, so that the activities of those who were known to be directly interested in Eldona could not easily be discovered. Brooks and his brokers insisted that the wash trades had happened inadvertently because they did not know the identity of the buyer or the seller, rather than as part of any scheme of price manipulation.

The OSC investigators concluded that the rapid run-up in Eldona had occurred as a result of the 'unusual speculative ardour of the general public' following the spectacular assay results in August, assisted by Brooks's own heavy buying designed to punish short sellers. The bad news in September had simply destroyed the confidence of investors. Brooks had certainly aimed at supporting the market price of Eldona, but again there was no evidence of an illegal conspiracy. As in the Beaulieu Yellowknife affair, the lack of real legal sanctions against such operations became crystal clear. In the United States, where the primary distribution of shares from the company treasury through an exchange was unknown, such an operation would have been unlawful. Because Brooks, like Ciglen, had acted on his own and not advised anyone about his wash trading, the OSC recommended that no charges be laid. It did propose that the federal government be asked to amend the Criminal Code, deleting the requirement that someone manipulating share prices must 'conspire with any other person.' Section 444A, which was promptly passed by Parliament, made it an offence to create the false or misleading appearance of an active public market in any security.[10]

The TSE's own investigation of the case, which involved the distribution of a questionnaire to all members who had traded Eldona between mid-August and mid-September, revealed no conclusive evidence of serious violations of exchange rules. Several members were called before the board to explain why they had lent Eldona shares directly to others (which could have been used for short selling), rather than through the exchange's Stock Loan Department; they were warned that any repetition might lead to severe penalties. In most cases members' explanations of their actions were accepted as satisfactory. Nevertheless, the TSE's elected secretary was asked to resign for reasons never clearly stated.[11]

To the public the TSE could claim that the Eldona investigation, like that into Beaulieu Yellowknife, had uncovered no violations of the Criminal Code or of the Securities Act by its members and only minor breaches of exchange by-laws. Privately, however, brokers admitted that the TSE's rules, which required the disclosure of short sales and forbade them at prices below the last board lot traded on the exchange, were regularly being ignored. Moreover, the values of some listed shares were being manipulated by insiders. The price of mining shares in the course of primary distribution was often artificial, dependent upon the willingness of promoters and insiders to provide support. In the fall of 1947 the *Financial Post* observed, 'There is unquestionably a legitimate place for proper sponsorship of issues and for a degree of market management. That is in the public interest. But there are too many cases where this leads to gross abuse which is not in the public's or the profession's interest.'[12]

Despite these two well-documented instances of price manipulation of stocks listed on the TSE, Charles McTague of the OSC pressed ahead with his proposals to make the exchange a self-regulatory organization. He remained convinced that the exchange should receive statutory powers to discipline its own members, and in 1947 the Securities Act was amended so that primary responsibility now rested with the TSE's Managing Committee rather than upon more 'clumsy and inefficient' rules to be administered by the OSC.[13]

The oil gusher that blew in at Leduc, Alberta, in 1947, was soon followed by other major petroleum strikes in western Canada; then came the discovery of uranium in northern Ontario. These finds fuelled a bull market for Canadian resource stocks. The outbreak of the Korean War in 1950 added to inflationary pressure. On 3 April 1951 a record 6.7 million shares changed hands. At the TSE's annual meeting in May the president was able to report that eighty new listings had been granted in the past year, half being oil and gas producers. A year later the rising volume of trading had pushed up TSE seat prices to $90,000, the highest since the crash of 1929.[14]

In the autumn, however, came sudden price drops in half a dozen mining stocks. Rumours began to fly blaming these falls upon concerted short selling or bear raids, and the exchange started investigating to see if deliberate manipulation had been involved. Critics in the United States began to complain that investors in listed Canadian stocks were no more likely to get a fair shake than when dealing in notoriously volatile over-the-counter markets. The TSE responded defensively, contending that its rules provided just as much protection as elsewhere. Exchange manager Arthur Trebilcock insisted that bear raids were a 'practical impossibility.' His enquiries indicated that 'There had been very heavy marginal trading in some of these issues, and when the so-called insiders, who had sponsored them in the initial stages withdrew their support – either voluntarily or involuntarily, as apparently happened in some instances-bids were hard to find and values simply evaporated.' The sharp price declines had come about either as a result of profit-taking by speculators or because of sales necessitated by margin calls as the stocks dropped. While it was sad to see investors lose money, there was little that the exchange could do to control speculative crazes. Trebilcock admitted that the TSE did not have an 'up-tick' rule like that imposed by the SEC, which required short sales above the price of the last recorded board lot, but since 1948 customers' men were supposed to mark slips for short sales with the letter S to alert their floor traders, and the rules forbade any short sales at prices below the last trade. However, many of the stocks that had fallen fastest were interlisted with the Montreal Curb, which had no rules against short selling; any skullduggery must have occurred in Montreal.[15]

The *Financial Post* complained that the rules were not nearly so hard to evade as the exchange pretended. Members were only required to report their short positions biweekly, and the TSE published nothing but aggregate figures for each stock, making attacks harder to detect. People might not tell their brokers when they were selling short, or customers' men might 'forget' to mark a slip, so that the floor traders could not detect a short sale. Moreover, when speculative stocks were being actively bid upwards, professional traders who operated for their own accounts routinely took short positions in anticipation of a break. Since these short sales did not usually create severe falls and were 'covered' within a day or two, they rarely showed up in the official tallies. It was by no means impossible to force down the price of a stock, particularly if two traders acted in concert, one selling long stock at the current bid price, the other selling short and going lower each time in larger and larger blocks, thus applying constant downward pressure. Nevertheless, the paper reminded its readers that whenever there was a price break, the promoters almost invariably used bear raids as an alibi.[16]

Despite the controversy, the OSC was content to leave regulation to the TSE. Listings continued to rise in gratifying fashion; by the spring of 1953 there were 1,028 listed stocks, up 150 from a year earlier. The boom in mining stocks continued, spurred on by new discoveries of base-metal deposits in New Brunswick and uranium in northern Saskatchewan. The exchange board did finally move to require underwriting and option agreements for listed stocks to include 'escalator' clauses, so that insiders could not continue to take down very low priced stock even after market prices had moved sharply upward, benefiting themselves at the expense of a company treasury. Though it was assumed that underwriters were entitled to higher returns as a pay-off for the risk entailed in financing exploration, the exchange now took the right to include escalator clauses as a condition of listing.

With the renewed boom in resource stocks, the TSE imposed these escalators in eighteen instances during 1951. The following spring the Listing Committee fixed the maximum number of mining or oil shares that could be subject to options at 1 million covering a period of no more than eighteen months. By the beginning of 1953 the board was insisting that all future financing agreements must include escalator clauses on a sliding scale, so that the markup of market prices over takedown prices at the time of the underwriting would be no more than 25 per cent on shares trading between 10 and 50 cents, the percentage declining as the option price of the stock rose.[17] The market for Canadian mining and oil shares continued to roar along. By the spring of 1954 an all-time high of 107 seats on the TSE were active, 22 more than during the Second World War. With 1,040 stocks listed, total trading volume of 850 million shares in Toronto far outstripped the 520 million changing hands on the New York Stock Exchange, although the dollar volume of $1 billion was a mere fraction of New York's $14.2 billion.[18]

II

Red-hot markets for Canadian resource stocks made it all the easier for promoters to manipulate prices. Pontiac Petroleums was supposed to drill a number of oil wells in Israel, and in September 1953 it was listed on the TSE. Pontiac was a promotion of the notorious Frank Kaftel, who had lost his OSC registration in 1949 and transferred his base of operations to western Canada.[19] Since then the commission had done its best to prevent him from marketing any of his deals in Ontario,[20] but the exchange listing was obtained by concealing Kaftel's role. He struck a deal with securities adviser James L. Gillanders to switch customers out of established stocks and into Pontiac. Gillanders set up a secret boiler room, protected like a gambling den by a system of doors and buzzers; telephone calls were made across the United States, with the long-distance charges being split with the offices of Uneeda Taxi Cab in the same building. The TSE member firm of Rittenhouse and Company agreed to handle the insiders' accounts in the company's shares, though Roy Rittenhouse was well aware that Kaftel was behind Pontiac. Share prices rose steadily as the promoters made a special effort to end each trading day by placing an order higher than the last previous bid. Eventually Kaftel decided that he had milked this promotion as much as possible. On 8 December 1954 support for the stock was withdrawn and the entirely artificial market collapsed as the price fell from $2.90 to $1.00 within the space of five minutes when all bids evaporated. The TSE suspended the stock and the OSC started an inquiry.

Investigators who arrived to search the secret boiler room found only one long-time crony of Kaftel's, who emerged from hiding in the washroom after ninety minutes. Gillanders had fled to New Mexico some months earlier, taking all his business records with him, but the OSC concluded that Pontiac had been 'a Frank Kaftel deal' from start to finish. His role had been carefully concealed through the undisclosed management and sub-option arrangements. Since he was no longer registered or resident in Ontario, there was nothing that the commission could do about him directly, though the brokerage registration of Rittenhouse and Company was cancelled.

O.E. Lennox decided that the time had come to send a strong message to the TSE. He proposed to send a copy of his decision on the Pontiac case to every member, who would be required to initial a covering letter indicating that he had read it. In the end the governors persuaded Lennox to allow them to call a special members' meeting at which a shortened version of the decision was read and discussed. On 2 June 1955 representatives of all the 107 members listened glumly as this tale of fraud and deception was unfolded. Meanwhile, the ripples created by Pontiac widened. A questionnaire distributed to account holders by the exchange auditor revealed that Newling and Company and its affiliated broker-dealer, Berwick Securities, had both engaged in high-pressure telephone marketing. Complaints were received that over 12,000 Pontiac shares had been charged to customers without their knowledge or permission. The TSE governors insisted that Newling and Company be wound up, and its managers were advised that they would not be readmitted as directors or partners of any other exchange member.[21]

Another serious embarrassment for the exchange occurred during August of 1955. The price of Midcon Oil and Gas had soared from 42 cents to more than $2.00 during the previous month without any apparent reason. On 16 August the stock dropped from $2.02 to $1.25, and the following day it fluctuated between $1.20 and 80 cents. The exchange ordered an investigation, which uncovered that two men had traded thousands of Midcon shares through Scarr, Tinkham and Company but had failed to pay the brokerage over $670,000. Within a week the exchange auditor reported that the firm had a deficiency of free capital totalling $313,000, and when the partners could not come up with the money, its exchange membership was suspended on 24 August. Two days later the brokerage failed to meet its obligations to the clearing house and was declared in default, and on 29 August Charles Scarr and C.J. Tinkham forfeited their exchange seat and the OSC cancelled the firm's registration. Not since the aftermath of the stock-market crash of 1929, a quarter-century earlier, had the TSE been compelled to order an expulsion, the heaviest penalty that could be imposed upon a member who failed to pay debts.[22]

The exchange board took the unprecedented step of delaying all trading in Midcon at the opening on 29 August to sort out the situation. During the morning, stock originally consigned to Scarr, Tinkham was resold and outstanding buy and sell orders for 125,000 Midcon shares were balanced at an average price of 70 cents apiece. This simplified the work of the clearing house, though it left some members with losses on shares priced at more than 70 cents. When Midcon resumed trading in the afternoon, the market had quieted down and the stock stayed in the range of 65 to 75 cents. Three weeks later Scarr, Tinkham's seat was sold for $90,500 and the proceeds used by the exchange to pay off the losses incurred by members, but the other creditors had to await the outcome of a voluntary fund-raising operation amongst exchange brokers to recoup some of what was owing them.[23]

Shady operators soon hit upon new means of swindling investors. In the spring of 1956 the long-established Morrison Brass Corporation, listed on the TSE, was taken over and most of its directors replaced. Using proceeds from the sale of 1,250,000 additional shares at $4 apiece, the new board promptly approved the acquisition of three American brass companies. Broker Frank Lawson reported to TSE officials that he suspected a 'milking' operation by which Morrison would pay inflated prices for the acquisitions, at least half the money being siphoned off to the insiders. In the absence of profit and loss statements the exchange auditor could come to no firm conclusions about the true value of the acquisitions. Nor was it clear whether these deals had really been at arm's length and how much money had actually changed hands. In September the exchange stepped in and announced the suspension of Morrison Brass stock pending a full investigation.[24]

Before long it was learned that the newly issued stock was being marketed through a New York boiler room controlled by Morris Black and Sam Ciglen.[25] Those names raised all sorts of warning flags. Under the Securities Act, investigators could secure authority to freeze assets, seize documents, and require witnesses to appear and testify without the right to refuse to produce evidence or to answer questions on any grounds, including self-incrimination. Normally, such inquiries were ordered under section 21, after the provincial attorney general had been supplied with a sworn statement of probable cause to believe that there had been a violation of the law or that an offence had been committed under the Criminal Code. Lacking such evidence, resort could be had to section 23, which permitted an inquiry 'into any matter relating to a trade in securities,' even in the absence of any statement concerning probable illegalities. In 1951 the OSC was given authority to undertake such an investigation of Ciglen and Black's Torny Financial Corporation under section 23.

Ciglen and his associates promptly challenged the authority of the attorney general to authorize such an 'endless fishing expedition,' and they retained two distinguished counsel, Joseph Sedgwick and G. Arthur Martin, to fight the case. The lawyers argued that granting such unlimited powers to an investigator was improper, as if a search warrant had been issued with no restrictions. Appearing for the defendant (OSC investigator J.K. Marcus), Eric H. Silk contended that the attorney general might not be in a position to issue a more specific order since 'he does not know what "matter" he is interested in until he receives the report of the investigating officer.' The judge agreed: 'It might well be that the Attorney General when acting under s. 23 has not the slightest suspicion that any breach to either the Securities Act or the Criminal Code has been committed, but feels, nevertheless, that the trading of the person as to whom he makes the order must be carefully scrutinized, perhaps to determine whether an amendment or extension of the statutory provisions should be submitted to the legislature.' Sedgwick and Martin might be correct that the result could be an endless fishing expedition, but the law quite clearly 'granted such fiduciary power ... [to] a senior Cabinet Minister in charge of the administration of justice and responsible to the legislature for the discharge of his ministerial duties. It might well be of the essence of effective administration of regulations governing the trading of securities in the modern and very complicated financial structure, that there should be left to one responsible person the broadest discretion in determining what matters shall be investigated and considered, even if the exercise of this discretion might result in very confusing, embarrassing and harassing interference with the affairs of those engaged in such trade.' The application to block the investigation was therefore rejected out of hand.[26]

So sweeping was this judgment in fact that it was almost an embarrassment to the regulators. Eric Silk later recalled that on returning to the parliament buildings after receiving the decision, he had recommended to the attorney general that his powers under section 23 should be exercised only in the most exceptional circumstances, when an investigation seemed urgent but there was no information available to justify a sworn statement about probable illegalities. Nothing seems to have come of this investigation of the insiders at Torny Financial, but the regulators continued to keep a close eye upon both Black and Ciglen.[27]

Sam Ciglen proved particularly difficult to control since he doubled as both company promoter and lawyer. As one of a small number of rogue members of the 'securities bar,' he was in a position to supply his associates with legal opinions justifying their own activities and cloak his activities behind attorney-client privilege. In the spring of 1956 the OSC was forced to issue a formal warning to registrants engaged in the distribution of speculative mining shares, stating that the commission would henceforth differentiate between lawyers who were independent of their clients and those having a financial interest in a promotion, who might produce 'gratuitous and self-serving' advice on demand. Such an opinion, said O.E. Lennox, was 'less than worthless – it is dangerous in the extreme.' Without the payment of a fee for legal advice, not only did no attorney-client privilege exist, but the OSC would consider the relationship to be prima facie evidence that the recipient was not independent but subject to the dictates of lawyers themselves active in the promotional field.[28]

The Morrison Brass case also demonstrated that operators like Ciglen and Black had realized the advantages of spreading their activities over a number of jurisdictions, so that no single regulatory body had complete control over them. To conduct an investigation that covered three provinces and several American states and extended as far away as Switzerland proved extremely difficult. Once the OSC had ordered a formal investigation, Ontario residents could be subpoenaed to testify under oath, but other people refused to come to Toronto. As a result, some witness might offer only hearsay or guesses, and the outcome would be much less conclusive than had been hoped. Still, there was good reason to believe that as much as $2.5 million had been illegally diverted through Morrison Brass.[29]

The SEC was advised about the evidence of high-pressure selling of the stock in the United States; the Americans promised to investigate further and eventually agreed to lay charges against one brokerage firm. About the only concrete result of the Morrison Brass inquiry was a proposal to require all underwriting and option agreements to be made by persons who were registered with the OSC or similar bodies in other jurisdictions in order to prevent the use of fronts. Eventually the TSE, the Investment Dealers Association and the Broker Dealers Association, all endorsed the idea, and in December 1956 the OSC imposed such a rule for all listed companies.[30] When Morris Black attempted to secure this kind of registration with the OSC in 1958, the TSE advised the comission that it would not accept any underwriting proposal from him.[31]

With the Morrison Brass investigation already under way, more problems surfaced about another company controlled by Black and Ciglen. In October 1956 the American Stock Exchange in New York suspended trading in Great Sweet Grass Oils and announced that the Securities and Exchange Commission was commencing an investigation. Great Sweet Grass was also listed on the Toronto Stock Exchange, which decided not to take action since there was no evidence of wrongdoing.[32] The SEC inquiry soon uncovered a scheme similar to the Morrison Brass case: a large amount of stock in Great Sweet Grass had been issued to supposedly independent companies in exchange for oil and gas properties, the real aim being to divert the money raised by the sale of the shares in the United States through high-pressure methods.

As president of Great Sweet Grass, Ciglen divided 1,690,000 shares amongst thirty-three nominees, almost all of this stock then being turned over to three New York broker-dealers. In 1955 and 1956 one boiler room mounted an elaborate sales campaign using thirty sales-men with fifty telephones which cost $40,000 per week in long-distance charges. Altogether 1,569,150 shares were marketed at be-tween $3.65 and $5.65, netting $7,750,000. When another transaction worth $390,000 was included, the total take came to over $8 million to finance the purchase of properties that had really cost only $2 million, so that after commissions and expenses the underwriters realized a $5 million profit, which was paid over to Samuel Ciglen's law firm or to Torny Financial Corporation. In addition, Ciglen and his associates put together other side deals that returned $2,440,000 for properties worth no more than $1 million.

The nature of these transactions, along with false figures for oil reserves, had been disguised by untrue or misleading information in the company's annual reports and in filings with the SEC. As soon as the investigation in the United States was completed in April 1957, trading in Great Sweet Grass on the TSE was suspended.[33] Both Ciglen and Black were ultimately charged with conspiracy to conceal their profits in order to avoid income taxation in Canada. Ciglen was even-tually convicted and disbarred as a lawyer as a result. Meanwhile, the TSE kept a careful eye on the two men. In 1962 one exchange member was found to be involved in trading with Tormont Mines, another Ciglen-Black promotion, and was fined $10,000. When asked why Sam Ciglen, an experienced lawyer, so frequently ran afoul of the authori-ties, his counsel, Joseph Sedgwick, was alleged to have replied, 'With Sam, it's just a habit.'[34]

The problems with Morrison Brass and Great Sweet Grass Oils showed that the Toronto Stock Exchange could exert only limited con-trol over the internal affairs of listed companies. The governors did try to prevent any repetition by passing a by-law giving them authority to refuse to approve the issuance of treasury shares to acquire properties when there was reason to believe that the transaction was not being conducted at arm's length. Only if a statement by all the vendors who held more than a 5 per cent interest that the deal was acceptable was submitted for publication in the exchange's bulletin would such a transaction be allowed.[35]

More problems developed in 1957 over the Aconic Mining Corpora-tion, which hoped to exploit a deposit of iron-bearing sands on the lower St Lawrence, 750 miles east of Montreal. Aconic secured a listing on the TSE in January 1957 after announcing that it had signed a contract to supply ore concentrates to a German steelmaker. On 6 August the price of the stock suddenly dropped from $11 to $9, and within the space of an hour it had plummeted to just $1. The TSE ordered an investigation and on 20 September suspended trading in the stock. No irregularities on the part of members were uncovered, but a criminal investigation by the Toronto police revealed that an option on some Aconic shares had been granted to D'Arcy M. Doherty. A recent TSE president, Doherty not only sat on the exchange's board but was also a member of the Listing Committee; he was called before his fellow governors, accused of conduct detrimental to the exchange. Though he insisted that there had been no arrangement that he should receive the option before Aconic was granted a listing, a committee composed of five other past presidents recommended that he be punished and Doherty was suspended from the exchange for three months.[36]

The exchange governors were inclined to congratulate themselves on having acted to impose swift justice, but public reaction was far less favourable. First of all, it became clear that Doherty, Roadhouse and Company would be able to continue in business as usual since the firm owned two other TSE seats. The *Financial Post* described the exchange's announcement as 'scanty, brief and mean-spirited,' and it raised several pointed questions: Who had been responsible for granting the option to Doherty, and how many Aconic shares had been involved? Was the option ever exercised? At what prices had the shares in question been sold? Four months after the suspension of trading the TSE could only report that it was still investigating.[37] If investors were to have confidence in the stock exchange, said the paper, then trading and listing rules needed to be altered and the penalties for infractions must be much stiffer. Even the *Northern Miner* joined in the chorus, noting that during the past year no fewer than eleven listed issues had had to be suspended, as against only one during the previous year and none in 1955. The paper alleged that the Aconic affair had cost brokers in Toronto and Montreal at least $800,000, while the Great Sweet Grass Oils fiasco had revived the attacks upon speculative Canadian mining issues in the United States that had been common in the early 1950s.[38]

In the face of these criticisms, TSE chair James Strathy called a special meeting of members in January 1958 to hear the results of the Aconic investigation and to consider recommendations about new rules for listed companies. He was sympathetic to demands for reform, since he worked for Dominion Securities, an investment dealer whose business was heavily weighted towards staider bond and blue-chip flotations rather than speculative resource stocks. What the exchange must do, said Strathy, was to alter its rules to prevent the misuse of its facilities in future. The 'treasury lootings' of listed companies had resulted from handing over cash for assets of dubious value. The board had concluded that new regulations were required to block any repetition of such scams, and full disclosure was the most effective means of prevention. The TSE should therefore classify all listed companies as 'exempt' or 'non-exempt,' and the latter group, which was supposed to include those most vulnerable to such raids, would be required to file statements concerning any material change in corporate affairs. Each filing would then be considered by the exchange board.[39]

Exchange official Arthur Trebilcock laid out the kind of material changes in company affairs that would require a filing with the TSE. Any alterations in the nature of the business engaged in and any change among the officers and directors, as well as any shift known to the company in its beneficial ownership, must be reported. Issuing additional shares to purchase new holdings had to be disclosed, along with all acquisitions of mining or oil properties or of any interest in another company costing more than $25,000. If the exchange refused approval for the proposed changes and the company concerned persisted with them, its shares would be suspended from trading.[40]

These rules had been carefully crafted to meet objections about undue interference in the internal affairs of companies. Mining promoters, in particular, were always quick to complain about efforts to fix values upon their properties, citing the one-in-a-million chance that a mother lode might lie underneath an apparently worthless stretch of moose pasture. In addition, tighter rules created delays, increasing the danger of leaks about promising drilling results and making share flotations more difficult. If a stock was delisted, losses were almost inevitable. Yet it was hard to continue to resist demands for full, true, and plain disclosure. O.E. Lennox expressed approval of the rule changes, which he argued had rectified the TSE's most serious problems and 'should stand out as a landmark in the overall history of the exchange.'[41]

The TSE did not, however, follow the New York Stock Exchange and appoint a full-time salaried chief executive with independent authority to enforce its by-laws. In 1956 Arthur Trebilcock was awarded the title of president, but this seems to have been merely a recognition of his long years of service.[42] The chair of the exchange and the annually elected governors continued to exercise wide-ranging authority over day-to-day affairs. When Trebilock retired in 1958, the governors did not appoint a successor, but instead they recombined his title with that of the board's chair.[43]

Ontario attorney general Kelso Roberts began to press the governors to appoint 'a man of stature' as a full-time president. In 1960 the board commissioned a study of the role played by the presidents of the New York and American Stock Exchanges, and new by-laws were drafted to permit such an appointment and to define the respective responsibilities of the president and the chair. The exchange's act of incorporation was changed to allow the president to be a member of the board of governors though not a member of the stock exchange. Howard Graham, who had risen to the rank of general in the Canadian army and become chief of the general staff, was finally chosen to fill the post and began to participate in the governors' meetings at the start of 1961.[44]

Graham moved quickly to develop new policies to permit full authority over certain matters to be delegated to him and his staff. For instance, he would now be responsible for making recommendations on the key issue of persons seeking partnerships, directorships, and shareholdings in member firms. Listing applications would no longer be circulated in full; rather, summaries would be prepared for the board carrying recommendations. Filing statements detailing material changes in the affairs of listed companies would be summarized by staff and not distributed to the members of the Filing Statement Committee prior to its meetings in order to ensure the confidentiality of inside information and avert complaints about conflicts of interest on the part of brokers.[45]

In the autumn of 1961 the Floor Procedure Committee conducted extensive surveys that revealed serious problems. Members reported that professional floor trading (commonly called 'chiselling') was thought to dominate much of the action on the floor to the detriment of orders from brokerage customers. Chisellers frequently bought and sold stocks on price fluctuations as low as one-eighth of a point (12.5 cents) or deliberately traded against the orders filed by the public. When new issues were announced, they would form syndicates to buy up an entire offering and push up prices as a favour to promoters, then dump the stock on unsuspecting outsiders before the price declined.[46]

The authority of the TSE to discipline its own members also became an issue. 'Put' and 'call' options were first traded in Canada in 1958. Purchasing a call entitled one to buy a quantity of a particular stock at its current price any time within a specified period (30, 60, 90, or 180 days); a put allowed the sale of the stock at that price within a similar time. Since these options provided leverage (with the potential for sizeable profits and losses), most brokers were reluctant to permit such transactions unless they held either the stock involved or the necessary funds, or else the buyer supplied a guarantee (usually from a bank) that obligations would be met. However, no formal TSE rules governed puts and calls since they were only used by a few aggressive investors. John T. Lynch of Peterborough, Ontario, was one heavy speculator on U.S. stocks, hedging his bets by acquiring both puts and calls at the same time. He had a $200,000 guarantee from two banks in Peterborough, but in at least one case the local manager had not obtained approval from his head office or required the delivery of stock as collateral for the guarantee. In 1961 that bank began investigating to see if it held sufficient security, and it soon cancelled its guarantee once it became clear that Lynch had a potential liability of up to $5 million if he could not unwind his positions. Since Lynch had been dealing through the member firms of Doherty, Roadhouse and R.A. Daly and Company, the bank alerted the TSE.

Another large player in puts and calls was Lido Investments, a syndicate controlled by Morton Shulman, which often took the opposite side to Lynch in his transactions. In January 1960 Wilfred Posluns, who held a one-sixth interest in Lido, also acquired a 5 per cent interest in R.A. Daly and became one of its directors. In March 1961, after meeting with the Daly board and hearing from Posluns, the governors concluded that he had acted as Lynch's agent in the brokerage house at the same time as he was one of the principals of Lido, placing himself in a serious conflict of interest. Under a rarely used TSE rule that forbade 'any conduct, proceedings or method of business, which the board in their absolute discretion deem unbecoming a member of the exchange or inconsistent with just and equitable principles of trade, or detrimental to the interests of the exchange,' R.A. Daly and Company was slapped with the maximum possible fine of $5,000, and Posluns was denied the right to continue as shareholder, director, or officer of the firm.

The TSE board hoped to settle this matter with as little public fuss as possible. If Posluns agreed to resign from the Daly firm and sell his shares, its resolution would not even be formally communicated to other TSE members. Posluns, however, refused to go quietly and retained lawyer E.A. Goodman. A prominent Conservative, Goodman quickly set up a private meeting with Attorney General Kelso Roberts. The lawyer argued that Posluns had disclosed his interest in Lido when he purchased his shares in the Daly firm and that the TSE had been fully informed about the situation. Goodman pointed out that there was no appeal against such a decision taken by the exchange governors and hinted that he might make the situation public. The board stuck to its guns, giving Posluns just three days to make up his mind on pain of having the formal notice distributed, and when he failed to go, the Daly board severed all connections with him, while the firm's president announced that it would no longer engage in option trading.[47]

Rumours began to spread that Posluns had been treated especially harshly because of pervasive anti-Semitism on the part of the old-line Bay Street firms.[48] He sued the TSE and its chair, E.D. Scott, claiming that they had exceeded their authority by requiring Daly and Company to get rid of him. Posluns also alleged that the exchange had acted at the behest of its vice-chair, George Gardiner, a competitor in the business of put and call options, and he demanded over $2 million in damages. When the suit finally came to trial in 1964, however, Mr Justice Gale found that although bodies which had been granted quasi-judicial powers must act according to the principles of 'natural justice,' the exchange had been 'morally justified and legally empowered' to act as it did. Posluns appealed the decision, but the Ontario Court of Appeal unanimously rejected his claims.[49]

As soon as the news about the Posluns case broke, the TSE moved to impose formal rules governing puts and calls. With option trading expected to grow in the years ahead, one TSE member told the *Financial Post* that he believed that regulations were necessary to prevent matters from getting 'out of hand' and creating 'some dandy headaches.' A committee including representatives from the ten or so brokers handling the options had been studying the subject for some time, and its recommendations were hurriedly enacted. Purchases of puts and calls were placed on a strictly cash basis, and the seller of an option was henceforth required to provide funds or marginable securities equal to 50 per cent of the value of the shares covered by any option.[50]

Mining and oil stocks still accounted for as much as 40 per cent of the value of trading on the Toronto Stock Exchange, but Howard Graham was keen to improve the quality of the TSE's industrial listings. In particular, he sought to prevent companies from transferring from one category to another. The rules governing resource companies remained lenient: unlike industrials, their entire authorized share capital was listed whether all the stock had been issued or some remained in the company treasury. Even if dormant and suspended from trading, a mining company could be restored to listing merely by filing a statement of material changes rather than distributing a prospectus to intending purchasers of additional treasury stock. Graham believed that these rules were a positive temptation to loot mining company treasuries through the purchase of assets of dubious value, particularly if non-mining assets could be acquired. In 1961 Conaurium Mines, which had run out of gold at Porcupine, Ontario, sought to transform itself into a real-estate holding company, and other mining companies such as Lorado Uranium Mines were eager to use the cash in their treasuries to enter other lines of business. Graham persuaded the TSE board to approve new rules that required a mining or oil company which altered the nature of its business activities significantly to submit a statement, and if the Filing Statement Committee considered that oil and minerals had ceased to be its principal type of business activity, the firm would be reclassified as a non-exempt industrial. Only shares already outstanding or issued for specific purposes would then be listed, and companies would be required to submit a prospectus to the OSC in order to market additional treasury shares. Companies that operated in two different areas would be clearly designated as such by the exchange in order to alert investors.[51]

At the same time the TSE began to move towards the abolition of its Curb market. Created at the time of the merger with the Standard Stock and Mining Exchange in 1934, this section had always allowed certain industrials to be traded even if they could not, or did not choose to, meet regular listing standards. The size of the Curb had been frozen in the early 1950s, so that the number of stocks involved had gradually dwindled to about fifty (though some of them were blue chips such as Price Brothers and Canada and Dominion Sugar. The first step was to remove six inactive issues and approach the others to see if they would transfer to the regular list. The number continued to decline until mid-1962, when only nineteen stocks remained, of which just five had no listing on another exchange. At that point the board decided that the

Curb should cease to exist and that all the remaining companies must either meet the regular listing standards or be dropped altogether.[52]

As far as the Ontario Securities Commission was concerned, the Toronto Stock Exchange should be left to govern itself as much as possible. Despite revelations about the manipulation of the share prices of Beaulieu Yellowknife and Eldona Gold Mines in 1946–7, the plan to give the exchange statutory authority to discipline its own members was carried through the following year. Only when there were serious allegations of fraud or criminal activity did the OSC step in and take over the investigation of Pontiac Petroleums and Great Sweet Grass Oils during the 1950s. Otherwise the board of the exchange was pretty much left to shape its own course. Harry Bray, a long-time subordinate of O.E. Lennox at the OSC, summed up his attitude nicely: 'It would be difficult to deny ... that he [Lennox] felt he had little or no control over the activities of the Toronto Stock Exchange. It was not a power which he sought, nor one which I would have thought to recommend.'[53]

5

Fighting Fraud

Two or three times each year during the late 1950s Sam Wacker would launch another of his promotional scams. For instance, in the spring of 1956 a complaint was received from an investor in Michigan that the prospectus for Triton Uranium Mines contained falsehoods. As a result, the Broker Dealers Association called stock salesman Benjamin Posner on the carpet to find out who was behind Triton. Posner, who claimed the company was controlled by a Toronto police inspector, was given a ten-day suspension for unethical conduct for selling shares by means of a false prospectus. However, his boss at George Hogarth and Company let slip that Triton was really 'a Samuel Wacker deal.'[1] Since Wacker was not a BDA member, the association could not compel him to testify under oath, so the investigation was handed over to the Ontario Securities Commission. Armed with a formal order to start looking into Triton Uranium, the commission's investigators quickly unearthed enough evidence to seek authority to begin poking into 'the entire Wacker empire.' O.E. Lennox pointed out to the attorney general that the time for such an investigation now seemed ripe; 'since the brokerage industry has shown a marked improvement, its members are entitled to some protection against the inroads being made by a comparatively few fringe operators.' Yet frauds needed to be exposed because they could still do a lot of harm to the reputation of the Toronto brokerage community.[2]

I

Who was Joseph Samuel Wacker and how was he able to swindle hundreds of investors, mainly Americans, through the sale of worthless mining shares? A typical promotion began with a deal for the rights to a clutch of totally unproven mining claims costing a few hundred dollars. Next came a low-cost engineering study recommending some further exploration and development of the property. Work, such as mapping, line-cutting, or an aerial magnetometer survey, costing a few thousand dollars might then be commissioned. Meanwhile, Wacker would have his lawyer incorporate a public company to purchase the claims in exchange for stock. An underwriting and option agreement was drawn up and a prospectus filed with the OSC attaching an engineer's and an auditor's report. To that point there was little to distinguish such a promotion from scores of other speculative mining ventures.

One key to Wacker's system was a loyal coterie of employees, associates, and friends, ranging from lawyers and executives through railway conductors and janitors, all willing to act as fronts and lend him their names for a few hundred dollars. These nominees were ready to sign cheques and documents in blank, including prospectuses that were full of falsehoods and omitted vital facts. The undertaking being promoted would cover all expenses, payable to a fleet of other companies maintained by Wacker. Exorbitant rates would be charged, $2,000 being paid for work costing a quarter of that amount or $500 worth of claims being resold for as much as $10,000, in order to channel the money into Wacker's own pocket. One of these companies would purchase enough stock to provide the money for the initial underwriting, and some of this money would be used to finance the direct mail campaigns that were a key to Wacker's success. Upon his arrival in Canada in 1938 from the United States, he had established Feature Press News to produce and distribute promotional materials for brokers, and he relied upon its services to create interest among prospective buyers for his own promotions.

With everything in readiness, he would select one broker-dealer to market a stock by telephone to those who responded to his mailings. So successful was Wacker that the firm chosen would soon find certain salemen, alerted by the grapevine, seeking jobs. One of these people would report daily to him on current sales, while the broker-dealer himself handled only the formal communications with the nominal underwriter, requesting the release of shares and forwarding payments. With sales under way, the brokerage would remit funds (after deducting commissions and other expenses) to cover stock taken down under options and still leave a healthy profit. The money flowed into a bank account in the name of the chosen front, who would have signed blank cheques ahead of time so that Wacker could draw out the money, using inflated charges to make sure that only small sums accrued in the corporate treasury. Once a telephone campaign had begun to run its course, there would be a final reloading drive aimed at the current shareholders, which often netted another $30,000 or $40,000 to be siphoned off through property purchases or additional management fees. Though he carefully confined himself to relatively small deals, Wacker probably brought off at least three such promotions annually during the late 1950s, earning over $100,000 in good years, with one of his campaigns tapering off as a new one got under way. Behind all these fronts Wacker operated as 'an unseen puppet master.' He usually moved so fast and covered his tracks so well that the OSC eventually discovered that the surest guide to his activities was to watch the movement of certain salesmen as he shifted his operations between different broker-dealers.[3]

When the Triton Uranium scam surfaced in 1956, OSC lawyer Harry Bray devoted more than six months to trying to untangle the skein of interwoven Wacker companies. At the centre lay Josamer Management, which had received at least $48,000 raised by the sale of Triton Uranium shares; of this sum $23,000 was supposedly expended on mining properties and the remainder channelled to Wacker for his personal services. For preparing and distributing promotional material, Feature Press News got $69,000, of which Wacker took $48,000 for 'supervision'; another $35,000 was siphoned off for purchases of shares in Banton Mining and Operating Corporation. In addition, $14,000 had to be paid over for additional mining claims when Triton neglected to protect its interest in the original properties. Bray concluded that no such operation could have been mounted without some central decision-maker, and the fact that so much of the money had flowed to him for illusory services pinpointed 'the ringleader, Wacker.' On an earlier occasion Wacker had escaped prosecution when an associate and one of the key witnesses providentially disappeared, so the OSC was determined to bring him to court this time: 'Wacker is one of the remaining fringe operators who create serious trouble.' Instructions were issued 'not to overlook a single opportunity of discouraging Joseph Samuel Wacker and his subordinates ... from promoting and distributing fraudulent mining issues,' and in March 1957 the commission laid charges under the Securities Act of filing a false prospectus in the case of Triton Uranium.[4]

The charges were not enough to deter Wacker, however. By September there were complaints about the misleading claim that there was an active over-the-counter market in Landolac Mines stock, when in fact no bids at all were available. Called before the BDA, broker K.A. Wheeler revealed that while E.A. Robinson was the nominal promoter, Landolac was really another Wacker deal. Association chair Malcolm Moysey reminded Wheeler that broker-dealers had a responsibility to consider a promoter's reputation, and another board member enquired pointedly whether Wheeler thought it wise to work with somebody who could not obtain registration with the OSC and refused to allow his name to appear on a prospectus. The broker asked if the board was telling him to 'go off the Landolac deal,' but Moysey replied that it was up to each person to take his own decisions. Wheeler, however, got the message and promised to cease primary distribution of the stock, departing with a final warning from the BDA against acting as agent for parties who refused to disclose their true identity.[5]

This effort to block the sale of Landolac shares greatly annoyed Wacker. He had already informed the BDA's executive secretary that he did not control the company but was merely handling its advertising and publicity. When asked to appear before the board, he had refused to do so, claiming to be out of town. Now, however, he demanded to confront them charging that they had shown prejudice against him. Marching into their boardroom, he warned the BDA governors that 'they could be held legally responsible for uncomplimentary remarks concerning himself.' Moysey tried to silence him by replying that 'the board did not propose to be abused by him.' Wacker, however, repeated that Landolac was not his deal, but he added that by its meddling the association was aiming 'to hinder any ventures he was associated with.'[6]

The OSC's efforts to prosecute Wacker over the Triton Uranium promotion encountered a serious snag in the spring of 1958. In magistrate's court his lawyer, Patrick Hartt, appearing with Joseph Sedgwick and Arthur Martin, advanced the argument that the sections of the Securities Act imposing penalties for the making of false statements in prospectuses were unconstitutional because they trenched upon the provisions of the Criminal Code concerning fraud. Judge W.W. McKeown accepted this submission, ruling that this part of the province's securities legisation was *ultra vires*; he gave no reasons, remarking gruffly that the OSC seemed uninterested in the proceedings since it had not bothered to send counsel. The commission promptly launched an appeal, but the magistrate died soon afterward, so that the charges against Wacker could not be reinstated.[7]

Moreover, other alert members of the securities bar picked up the claim that certain key sections of the Securities Act actually dealt with matters covered in the Criminal Code, where the federal government alone had jurisdiction. Lyle Francis Smith had been charged with filing a false prospectus for Canadian All Metals Explorations. In January 1959 his lawyer sought an order from the Ontario Supreme Court barring proceedings against him under the Securities Act on the same grounds, which was granted. When consulted, Deputy Attorney General W.B. Common delivered an ominous opinion that the decision was probably right and that the government should immediately introduce amendments to the legislation to remove any conflict with the criminal law. The OSC staff was highly alarmed that a failure to appeal might be taken as a concession that the mandatory requirements and prohibitions in the legislation were in fact *ultra vires*, which might even cast doubt on prosecutions stretching all the way back to 1945. Eventually an appeal was authorized, and the Court of Appeal validated the distinction between fraud (covered by the Criminal Code) and regulation of markets (under the Securities Act). This decision was ultimately confirmed in 1961 by the Supreme Court of Canada, relying upon the Privy Council's thirty-year-old decision in *Lymburn v. Mayland*, which had granted the provinces constitutional authority to ensure that people registered in the securities business were 'honest and of good repute.'[8]

Undeterred by the OSC's attentions, Sam Wacker used his customary modus operandi in the Riobec Mines promotion. O.E. Lennox became determined to make a case that would stick: 'This type of operation by Wacker is an old story to the Commission.' 'Riobec was his deal from the outset, which would probably establish that the prospectus of Riobec was false.' Lennox warned the attorney general that 'there are positive indications of a major siphoning operation.' Wacker had arranged for the sale of some mining properties to Riobec in the spring of 1957, again using E.A. Robinson as a front. A prospectus was filed with the OSC in Robinson's name, and by the autumn W.S. Alvey of Anglo-Northern Securities was handling the public sale of the shares. As usual, various Wacker enterprises were generously rewarded out of the money coming in. Feature Press News printed all the promotional material distributed by Alvey; Wacker's Northland Drilling was paid at least $10,500 (and perhaps twice that amount) for aerial survey work actually performed by another concern for a mere $2,600. The use of magnetometer flights over mining claims located in Manitoba was particularly ingenious because it seemed almost impossible to establish that the bills had been padded.[9]

Evidence that the prospectus for Riobec Mines omitted material facts was not hard to come by, but Lennox was determined to put a more serious crimp in Wacker's activities by securing a criminal conviction for fraud. After another six months of labour by Harry Bray, in 1959 the commissioner proposed an investigation to cover fifteen people. Attorney General Kelso Roberts responded that it was unusual to issue such an order under the sweeping powers in section 23 of the Securities Act when so many different persons were involved. Still, he agreed to allow Lennox to go ahead if he felt that this was the only way in which the necessary information might be obtained. In the end, however, the Crown attorney concluded that the evidence procured was not sufficient to permit a successful criminal prosecution.[10]

Though frustrated, Lennox and Bray were still determined to prosecute Wacker for offences under the Securities Act. The OSC's case rested upon the fact that Wacker had paid for the mining claims which were transferred to Riobec, so that he was their beneficial owner, a material fact that should have been included in the prospectus. Wacker alone knew everything that was going on and was responsible for the primary distribution of the shares, which made him personally guilty of failure to make disclosure. Alvey of Anglo-Northern Securities would make an excellent witness in order to redeem himself for his misconduct in carefully failing to enquire into the identity of the real promoter. Success was vital to the OSC, Lennox told the attorney general, since 'Wacker's organization is the greatest local challenge to our administration, although its operations are not so complex as other major operations involving concurrent activities in other jurisdictions.'

At long last the OSC's efforts succeeded. When brought to trial, Wacker presented no defence (and hence did not have to testify), accepting the maximum permissible fine of $2,000 for his offence under the Securities Act. The Riobec matter finally concluded in 1962 with an OSC order depriving Wacker and his principal associates of all future exemptions from making prospectus filings under the Securities Act. This decision firmly stated the principle that the true identity of any promoter must be disclosed and could not be cloaked behind a front.[11]

Despite this hot pursuit by the OSC, Wacker kept up his string of swindles. His flair for marketing shares was particularly evident in the case of Mack Lake Mining Corporation, incorporated in 1959. People who responded to advertisements for Wacker's booklet on gold were sent forms to 'reserve' Mack Lake shares when issued and told that they should buy now since enough money had been raised to permit production to begin. The promotional material included photographs of a mine and mill ready to process gold ore at the property in the Northwest Territories. In a nice touch Wacker had everything printed in Toronto but mailed from Yellowknife to create the impression that the company's operations were centred there. In fact, the pictures had been taken in 1952, after which the equipment had been removed from the site and the workings left idle without any further efforts to delineate an ore body. Telephone selling in the United States and mail orders from Germany brought in over $455,000 by mid-1962, more than $80,000 of that being paid in commissions to three unregistered salesmen and over $240,000 to various Wacker-controlled undertakings. When the authorities finally closed in, the company treasury contained just $31.96. After his conviction for the Riobec scam, Wacker at long last fled back to the United States for good.[12]

II

To critics O.E. Lennox could point out that the authority of the OSC was rather narrower than people usually assumed. Companies making a primary distribution of shares from their treasuries to the public had to file prospectuses and other financial information in order to provide disclosure for purchasers. The commission's jurisdiction was rooted in the requirement to have these filings accepted before the sale of stock commenced. Refusal of registration was mandated in cases where there was falsehood or concealment involved, or where unconscionable considerations had been paid for properties acquired or for promotional services. There were, however, significant exceptions to the requirements for registration. For instance, companies listed on a recognized stock exchange were largely exempted from the OSC's control, since they were not regulated by the commission but by the exchange. Individuals required licences to sell securities, but companies were allowed to market their own securities to their shareholders. Though each of these exemptions seemed justifiable, there was growing concern by the mid-1950s that the Securities Act was 'riddled' with loopholes of which the unscrupulous might take advantage.[13]

There was considerable pressure for amendments to the act as a result of the revelations about Toronto's boiler rooms before the Ontario legislature's committee in 1951 (see chapter 3). In the spring of 1951 Saskatchewan's securities regulator, J.A. Young, told the press that over the past couple of years he had received more than two hundred complaints about 'shady operators' in Toronto.[14] Before the committee, Lennox tried to brush off these criticisms: 'The chap in Saskatchewan has not done very much ... I have never had any trouble with him in any way, shape or form until ... he made a statement to the press ... He talked about worthless Ontario securities and said that a widow in Saskatchewan had lost seven thousand dollars buying worthless stock. I telegraphed him, and said to send the particulars, ... but I got no reply.' Lennox added, 'I might as well be perfectly candid: I am satisfied the whole thing is a pure myth ... I can scarcely recall of [sic] any person in Saskatchewan in recent years buying any appreciable amount of Ontario securities, in any way, shape or form.' Lennox was equally critical of other provincial regulators, such as G.M. Blackstock of Alberta, who still relied upon the old blue-sky approach to shielding investors. Since 1945, Lennox told the committee, the OSC had abandoned this paternalistic attitude: 'I think Mr. Blackstock thinks he knows what is under the ground. I have nobody on our staff who does.'[15]

Nonetheless, in the autumn of 1951 Lennox did agree to convene a meeting of Canada's securities regulators to discuss their common problems. Yet he sought to confine the agenda to relatively narrow technical issues, such as the exact information to be contained in a prospectus. His counterparts in the other provinces, however, wanted a more wide-ranging discussion of how investors could be better protected against shysters.[16] The regulators gathered in Toronto in November.[17] Blackstock of Alberta pointed out that he had formulated a tough set of rules to control oil and gas promotions: funds paid into a corporate treasury were held in trust and used only for exploration, and all the vendor shares were placed in escrow, to be released only upon the successful completion of a drilling program. Why, he asked, didn't Ontario and the other provinces extend the same rules to mines? Lennox replied that such rules would simply end money-raising by fledgling public companies. Invited to address the conference, Arthur Trebilock of the Toronto Stock Exchange agreed that options were necessary because no underwriter would make a firm commitment to finance a costly exploration program on an untried prospect. In the end, all that was agreed upon was that the provincial regulators would recommend to their respective governments the adoption of Ontario's rules about mining promotions while endorsing Alberta's stricter rules regarding oil flotations.[18]

Reporting on this meeting to Attorney General Dana Porter, Lennox claimed, 'A spirit of harmony and cooperation was evident on all sides, which has been definitely lacking. It appears that for the first time in many years the other provinces appreciate the extent of the problem facing Ontario, and admitted freely that actual progress was being made along constructive lines.'[19] Nevertheless, in January 1952 the *Saturday Evening Post* dredged up and rehearsed all the embarrassing allegations about the operations of Toronto's boiler rooms in an article by the pseudonymous Marcus Verner, entitled 'I Sell Phony Stock to American Chumps.'[20] Some of the tales were plainly old hat, such as the swindles during the 1930s, while others were rehashes of the disciplinary cases of A.E. DePalma and Frank Kaftel. In a critique of the article for Premier Leslie Frost, Lennox dismissed as ludicrous the notion that as many as fifty boiler rooms were still operating in Toronto. Sensational stories could be concocted about any kind of illicit activity in order to sell magazines, provided that one started from the assumption 'that if there is a police force there should be no crime.'[21]

Lennox insisted that most of the criticisms of the OSC were unfounded. A memorandum entitled 'Solicitations in the United States by Mail and Telephone'[22] detailed recent efforts to control boiler rooms selling south of the border. During its twenty-year history the OSC's only real failure had been 'a lack of continuity'; clear records and policies had sometimes been lacking, but the establishment of its *Bulletin* had ended that difficulty. Blame for many of the problems should lie with the Broker Dealers Association, which had been 'founded on the excellent theory of self-discipline and self-government. Unfortunately, many of the rank and file of this newly-formed Association considered this an invitation to organized racketeering. They were sold on the idea that in due course the functions of the Commission would be only secondary and that in future all policies would largely be dictated by the Association.' The situation had improved recently, but 'There is still a great deal to be done by way of educating the rank and file. There are still many who bring discredit to the Association as a whole and will continue to bring discredit until they are eliminated or until the membership as a whole refused to further tolerate their actions.' Moreover, the Americans had only themselves to blame for many of the problems: some of the worst offenders were U.S. citizens who had moved to Canada following the passage of regulatory legislation in the mid-1930s, and another wave had come after 1945. Wide publicity about the riches of Canadian resources and the ready availability of capital made these investments highly attractive in the United States. Was the flow of foreign investment to be cut off entirely as a result? Too much was being expected of the OSC: 'The true function of a Securities Commission is not to devise regulations and policy, but to canvass the opinion of the organized industry and adopt the highest standards acceptable to the best element and to enforce these standards throughout.'

Lennox succeeded in convincing the Ontario government that no sweeping changes were required in the Securities Act, despite the revelations before the legislative committee and the grumbling from his counterparts in the other provinces. The Conservatives had been handily re-elected in the general election in November 1951, and Dana Porter retained his post as attorney general. Speaking to the legislature the following February, he complained that criticisms by the American press implied that most Canadian brokers were dishonest and that most stocks they sold in the United States were worthless. Figures for total sales as high as $50 million per year had been casually bandied about; Porter said that he preferred to accept the OSC's estimate of $10 million. Many of the offerings being marketed were perfectly sound. He was particularly coruscating about the *Saturday Evening Post* article. Why should anybody believe 'Marcus Verner's' slanders, when publicizing the reminiscences of this self-confessed 'crook' was simply aimed at selling magazines? The attorney general preferred to take note instead of an article by Fraser Robertson in Toronto's *Saturday Night* upholding Bay Street's good reputation.[23]

Porter doggedly defended the work of the OSC. Since 1947 the total number of registrants had fallen from 264 to 212, many of those put out of business being large mailers into the United States. Since 31 March 1951 just four new licences had been issued to broker-dealers. The attorney general even tried to turn the tables on American critics by claiming that fly-by-night brokers in the United States were now mailing literature into Ontario, using 'sucker' lists of purchased names.[24] Word for word he repeated the OSC's own defence: 'It is easy indeed to devise policies designed to embarrass and discourage the worst element, but the most difficult problem confronting any administration is to regulate trading and the persons engaged in it without retarding development and expansion by ill-conceived politicies. Many policies which may seem advisable in order to curb the activities of consistent offenders may eventually unduly hamper an honest and constructive endeavour to raise venture or independent capital.'[25]

Buyers of speculative mining and oil stocks knew full well that a 'gambling element' was involved: 'There are a great many people who desire to invest money in this sort of way, and for those who do that, if the venture is successful they might make a very large profit as a result of the transaction, but, of course, they always take the chance, and most people who invest in this sort of security know that they are taking the chance, of losing perhaps all the money that they put in. Nevertheless, if it were not for the fact that a great many people are prepared to take that risk, many of our natural resources in this country, particularly in the mining districts, would never have been developed at all.' Porter therefore proposed only two minor amendments to the Securities Act, designed to make the life of brokers less 'onerous.' Currently, if sales literature on a new promotion was sent out and a customer expressed interest, a broker must then send out a prospectus and a set of financial statements to the buyer before a sale could be completed. Often the recipient read the promotional material but paid little attention to the formal documents. The changes would permit brokers to send a summary of these documents, approved by the OSC, along with the literature. Only if an order was received (and this rule applied to unsolicited orders too) would the customer receive the full prospectus along with the confirmation of the sale, thus saving time and money.[26]

The only serious criticism of the government came from perennial gadfly Joseph Salsberg of the Labour Progressives (the renamed Communist Party). He twitted Porter about the 'untimely death' of the legislative committee in 1951. Surely the 'astounding revelations' at the summer-long inquiry had amply demonstrated the need for fundamental changes in the Securities Act. Yet the attorney general hadn't even mentioned the evidence given to the committee and had presented nothing more than housekeeping amendments. Members were left to ask, 'Is that all?' Couldn't the combined might of the OSC, the Attorney General's Department, and the police even find out the identity of 'Marcus Verner' and see whether or not his accusations had substance?[27] Porter blustered that if Salsberg had followed the committee proceedings carefully, he would know that nothing much of value had been suggested in the way of concrete changes to the Securities Act. Porter himself had chaired the committee, and the voters had endorsed the conduct of the government by re-electing him. Plenty of useful information had been collected, but the government had decided to recommend only these minor changes to the Securities Act for the time being. The house approved Porter's amendments without further debate.[28]

Even some members of the financial community were surprised that the government had gone out of its way to make it easier for broker-dealers to distribute speculative issues; the lawyer for the Investment Dealers Association complained to Porter that his members believed that the prospectus and financial statements which they were required to deliver were already pretty summary and could hardly be condensed further without sacrificing full disclosure. Investors might legitimately complain that they were not being given enough detail to make informed choices.[29] Lennox pointed out, however, that the new procedure was an alternative to be available for mining promotions but its adoption was not required. After negotiations with William Wismer, secretary of the BDA, agreement was finally reached on what must be contained in these summary statements. Broker-dealers had been apprehensive that all details of option and underwriting agreements would have to be included, so that potential buyers would be able to calculate the exact size of the markup between selling prices and option prices, which went straight into the pockets of the insiders. Wismer claimed that those who sought to extract exorbitant profits were a small and steadily dwindling band, and that it was unnecessary to compel this type of disclosure. After discussions, the old practices were left to continue, with investors remaining in the dark about the size of the markups.[30]

The temptation for fly-by-night operators to try to swindle unwary investors remained strong as markets for Canadian resource issues continued to roar ahead in the 1950s. On 3 April 1956, the Toronto Stock Exchange enjoyed the greatest trading volume in its history as 12,682,000 shares changed hands and the ticker ran forty-five minutes late. Stock in mining companies, particularly ones with 'uranium' in their names, was snapped up by eager investors. Until the end of 1956, for security reasons the U.S. government banned the release of figures for ore reserves and production levels by uranium producers. In the absence of reliable information, investors could only guess at the commercial viability of such companies. In fact, when the ban was lifted, only state-owned Eldorado Mining was actually producing ore in Canada, so that the other prospects were rank speculations. This situation was, of course, was tailor-made for fraudsters.[31]

Telephone selling continued to be a serious problem. The Securities Act imposed a firm ban on telephoning a private residence for the purpose of selling securities unless the person called was 'in the habit' of trading with the broker. Otherwise, a written 'qualifying card' signifying a person's interest in receiving information about a 'specific' issue had to be secured.[32] Thus broker-dealers undertook extensive mailings of 'lead getters' in an effort to persuade people to return the cards in order to expand their clientele and allow individuals to be telephoned with a sales pitch. Such campaigns, however, brought frequent complaints from the United States and other Canadian provinces, accusing Toronto brokers of marketing unregistered shares.

The Broker Dealers Association agitated persistently for the removal of the prohibition on calling private residences. The ratification of the changes to the Extradition Treaty that were supposed to permit those accused of violating U.S. law to be delivered to the Americans for trial created hopes that Ontario might change its rule. In 1954 the BDA lobbied for an amendments to permit such calls to other jurisdictions where they were not prohibited. After consulting his cabinet colleagues, however, Attorney General Dana Porter sent back discouraging news: 'He said that the Ministers were pretty unanimous on the proposition that selling securities over the telephone was objectionable.' The association's lawyer, Charles McTague, was deputed to take up the question personally with Premier Leslie Frost, but he had no better luck.[33]

After Kelso Roberts succeeded Porter as attorney general in 1955, McTague and William Wismer, the BDA's executive secretary, met with him to discuss the possibility of granting the OSC discretionary authority to enforce the prohibition only where it seemed necessary, but again nothing came of the idea. When mining-share markets began to sag in 1957, the BDA again petitioned Roberts, arguing that the bad old days of boiler rooms were long gone. No other businesses in Canada were forbidden to use telephone sales, and raising capital for resource development was a vital national priority. At the very least, the association wanted the ban on out-of-province calling abandoned as beyond the jurisdiction of the provincial government.[34]

The attorney general's response was that the other self-regulatory elements of the securities industry, the Toronto Stock Exchange and the Investment Dealers Association, would also have to be consulted. When Lennox called them together with the BDA representatives, he discovered that the more-conservative investment dealers were opposed to any change; they were afraid that broker-dealers would seize the opportunity to bombard people with calls about dubious securities. The BDA sought to meet these objections by proposing that each card should specify that a customer wished to receive information only about certain types of shares in which a particular firm customarily dealt. Lennox had little enthusiasm for this notion; he thought that it would be a nightmare to administer, and he reminded the attorney general that 'public confidence is at a very low level in view of a depressed market coupled with a series of raids on corporate treasuries in connection with listed issues.' That was quite enough to persuade Kelso Roberts; he minuted bluntly, 'No action. No need to change.'[35]

Between 1955 and 1958 the attorney general was asked to approve more than twenty formal OSC investigations of fraudulent promotions under section 21 of the Securities Act. Among the more notorious was the case of Gregory and Company, which lost its registration as a brokerage in Quebec in 1956, but attempted to continue the illegal distribution of shares in a number of mining companies from Toronto. In order to conceal this operation, instructions to the salesmen were passed on from Montreal by a voice known only as Susie, who accepted reports in code; commissions were paid out on street corners by a person also known only by his first name. When an apartment in suburban Toronto was raided, the salesmen found there tried to explain the records and sales pitches by inventing a fictional character called Meredith to shoulder the blame. Kenneth Gregory and his associates were found guilty of misconduct by the OSC.[36]

A group of crooks acquired hundreds of thousands of shares in Shoreland Mines. When they were driven out of the United States by an SEC investigation, they set up a boiler room in a Toronto apartment. They hit upon an ingenious ruse. In August 1958 a forged telegram bearing the name of a well-known Toronto investment dealer was despatched to a U.S. resident offering to buy 20,000 Shoreland shares for $3.75 on behalf of a New York brokerage. The intended mark did not, however, rush out as expected and seek to acquire thousands of shares of the penny stock for a quick resale profit, but instead replied to the dealer that he owned just 10,000 Shoreland. Once alerted, the OSC soon discovered that the swindlers had already succeeded in obtaining $19,000 from more gullible people. Three men were taken into custody but refused to identify themselves or to admit to any association. After being released, the trio fled to Buffalo, New York, to avoid prosecution.[37]

Albert Gould hoped to loot the treasury of Cabanga Developments by having it purchase $456,000 worth of non-existent gilt-edged securities and using the money to acquire control of the company. The fraud was to be concealed by a document forged in Cuba acknowledging receipt of the securities from Cabanga by a Panamanian corporation. Investigations in Cuba produced evidence sufficient to convict Gould of fraud in November 1959, and he was sentenced to six years in jail. Also charged with wash trading, he pleaded guilty, the first recorded conviction under section 325 of the Criminal Code. Gould's brother, Irving, was also successfully prosecuted for perjuring himself during the OSC's investigation.[38]

When the *Link and Green* case made it clear that the Extradition Treaty could not be used to control illegal marketing of Canadian stocks in the United States, the SEC began to send out warnings about the marketing of unregistered Canadian securities, and state regulators threatened to impose more cease-and-desist orders against Toronto broker-dealers. After discussions with the SEC staff at the annual meeting of the National Association of Securities Administrators in 1956, BDA president Earl M. Robertson reported that 'there appeared to be little possibility of ever arranging a satisfactory medium of marketing speculative securities in the United States.'[39]

In the spring of 1957 a commissioner and one of the senior staff from the SEC visited Toronto. BDA president Malcolm Moysey expressed hope that a reservoir of goodwill still existed in Washington, because 'Ontario was making a sincere effort to control the securities business.' Executive secretary J.W. Gemmell (who had replaced William Wismer) tried his best to convince the SEC people that whatever the Americans' view of unregistered selling, they should 'realize that responsible people in Ontario held an honest opinion even though it might be contrary to their outlook.' In a follow-up letter Gemmell suggested that personal cooperation could do more to reduce the number of complaints about Toronto broker-dealers operating in the United States than any number of official exchanges. He added, 'I may be over-optimistic but cannot help but be pleased that our informal exchange of information has had what seems to be a favourable result.' With the BDA directors, however, Gemmell was franker: for all the cordiality, 'he was satisfied that the SEC attitude was so narrow that its application could only result in the ruin of independent promotional financing.'[40] His gloomy predictions proved fairly accurate. When the National Association of Securities Administrators gathered for the annual conference in the autumn that year, he tried to arrange a private meeting with a SEC staffer but managed only a few minutes' conversation in a hotel lobby. The American official would say only that at the moment no BDA members were causing his agency any particular problems.[41]

O.E. Lennox also tried to appear cooperative with the SEC when it requested information on the activities of Toronto brokers, but he became concerned in 1958 when the Americans submitted several requests for the OSC to order the production of records by local firms. He thought that the SEC might be acting merely to deflect domestic criticism that it was not pursuing its investigations seriously enough, blaming its failings upon foreigners when necessary. Lennox therefore scrutinized such demands for assistance, but when it became clear that OSC registrants might be involved in illegal activities, he did feel justified in assisting.[42]

Yet Lennox remained highly defensive about criticisms concerning the illegal marketing of shares in the United States. In the spring of 1959 the Toronto manager of the large American brokerage house Merrill Lynch created a minor furor by telling a press conference that neither the TSE nor the OSC was doing enough to discipline stock promoters. He claimed to be spending a great deal of time placating investors who had lost money on speculative stocks and suggested that Canada needed a national regulatory body like the SEC. Lennox insisted that Americans, unlike local investors, didn't understand that junior mining shares were always a gamble. The OSC's aim was to promote mining, not to create ghost towns, yet the Americans wanted to burden Canadians with a national agency that possessed wide-ranging, even dictatorial, powers over companies and exchanges rather than relying upon cooperation. Lennox grumbled that this kind of criticism was in line with previous statements emanating from the United States aimed at discrediting speculative Canadian stocks.[43]

Toronto boiler rooms continued to operate. For instance, between October 1958 and February 1959 Armada Corporation received no less than seven orders by state regulators to cease and desist doing business. An OSC examination of the firm's books showed a significantly higher rate of order cancellations than in any other case during the past decade, suggesting that the salesmen had adopted the old ploy of sending out bogus confirmations in hopes of extracting payment. J.A. Wintrop Limited amassed a mailing list containing the names of 75,000 Americans. Wintrop claimed that he had only been telephoning people as a public-relations exercise to pass along information about shares that he had sold them previously. Yet a questionnaire sent to his customers revealed that his salesmen were really pushing new issues. His most recent oil promotion had not been marketed to a single Ontario resident, while many of those telephoned in the United States were complete strangers called at their private homes.[44]

With the number of abuses apparently on the increase, Lennox decided that the time had come to reverse his laisser-faire ruling of November 1954 allowing Toronto broker-dealers to be governed by their own discretion about American marketing. In cancelling Wintrop's regislatration, the OSC announced that in future it intended to punish any broker found guilty of illegal trading because it was undermining confidence in Canadian issues in the United States. In October 1959 Lennox arranged a meeting with the BDA board to point out the unwelcome attention that its members were attracting south of the border. At the start of the new year he warned that regulators in states as far apart as Rhode Island and New Mexico were on the warpath again, issuing cease-and-desist orders against brokers detected selling there. In the summer of 1960 Lennox pressed Malcolm Moysey for some action, but the BDA chair refused to take the problem seriously, merely suggesting to the board that members be advised by word of mouth that between 2 and 5 per cent of any mailing ought to go to addresses in Ontario.[45]

The Americans became more and more unhappy. Efforts by Moysey to mend fences at the annual meeting of the National Association of Securities Administrators proved a dismal failure. In closed session some state regulators 'expressed the view that all Canadian securities were worthless.' Postal-fraud orders began to be issued not by the full SEC but on the say-so of staff members alone. Still, many Toronto brokers refused to abandon the lucrative American market and instead began to take steps to evade the unwelcome attention of the regulators. Since 1951 all broker-dealers had been required to register names and addresses with the OSC, which assisted the U.S. post office in its practice of enforcing postal-fraud orders by seizing mail, stamping it 'Fraudulent,' and returning it to the sender. Now a number of them began sending out envelopes carrying unregistered or illegible return addresses. American state and federal agencies continued to bombard the OSC with complaints. The BDA fined a few offenders $250 or $500 for unethical conduct, but in other instances where the rules had been broken, the board argued that there had been no intention to deceive and let the offenders off with no more than a reprimand.[46]

The election of John F. Kennedy ended the relaxed regime that had prevailed at the SEC during the Eisenhower administration, a shift confirmed by the appointment of William L. Cary as its chair early in 1961. By then there were 246 companies on the SEC's Canadian Restricted List. Mail to 25 Toronto broker-dealers was being intercepted by the U.S. post office, and at least 34 were under cease-and-desist orders issued by state regulators. Staider elements in the Canadian financial community began to get nervous: what if the Americans took steps to restrict access to capital markets when the economy was still suffering the lingering after-effects of a recession? Why should more reputable brokerage firms, bond dealers, and investment bankers pay a price for the antics of rogues? As a result, the governors of the Toronto Stock Exchange reached the conclusion that the time had finally come to rein in broker-dealers who were ignoring registration requirements and continuing to use high-pressure methods to sell speculative stocks in the United States.

How could this be done? Thirty-four members of the stock exchange were also required to belong to the Broker Dealers Association because they handled over-the-counter issues in addition to trading listed stocks, but they were greatly outnumbered by the seventy-eight members of the association who did not hold exchange seats. The only weapon that the exchange could use was to force its members to withdraw from the BDA unless the illegal marketing of stocks in other jurisdictions was banned. O.E. Lennox was therefore sounded out about whether he would register the thirty-four TSE-affiliated firms directly with the OSC as broker-dealers should the exchange compel dual members to resign from the association. Lennox, of course, had already tried a similar experiment in 1949 when he had permitted the more reputable members of the BDA to resign in protest. On that occasion he had concluded that self-regulation through the BDA was more effective than direct control by the commission, and he eventually forced the secessionists to rejoin the association after only one year. Now, however, he expressed willingness to throw his weight behind a clean-up campaign in order to placate the Americans.[47]

On 28 March 1961 the TSE board approved a letter from chair E.D. Scott to exchange members who also belonged to the Broker Dealers Association expressing 'growing misgivings' about the illegal marketing of unqualified issues. Extravagant promotional literature and illegal telephone selling must be stopped. These problems had largely been ignored for the past few years, but now they risked bringing the reputation of the entire Canadian financial community into disrepute.

In a letter to BDA chair Malcolm Moysey, Scott threatened that if the BDA board did not move swiftly to ban such practices and perform the self-regulatory functions for which the organization had originally been created, the TSE would proclaim membership in the association undesirable and force its members to withdraw and seek direct registration as broker-dealers with the OSC.[48]

This ultimatum threw the BDA board into a turmoil. Since the TSE letter had been released to the press without any prior discussion, there was no opportunity for behind-the-scenes haggling. Nevertheless, some of the directors were prepared to fight. At a long and acrimonious meeting Moysey, who himself belonged to a TSE member firm, pointed out the adverse publicity certain to result if the BDA failed to take immediate action. Only after much discussion, however, did his view carry the day. It was agreed that executive secretary J.W. Gemmell should release to the press a notice to all BDA members, warning that they must immediately cease selling securities in any jurisdiction where they were unregistered. A general meeting of the association was promised in the near future to discuss a long-term solution.[49]

As Lennox put it, 'In short, the Association was on trial, and the Association knew it.' To demonstrate its willingness to turn over a new leaf, the BDA board promptly levied a $1,000 fine against Harald N. Hansen for attempting to deceive the U.S. post office. In cancelling Hansen's registration the OSC noted that this was his second offence within six months, since he had been found guilty of using an unregistered address the previous autumn and had then switched to envelopes with an illegible name. In an effort to extricate his members from their predicament, Malcolm Moysey hastened to Washington for discussions with the SEC. Not only did he discover that the patience of the Americans had been exhausted, but on his return Lennox advised him that if the membership of the BDA did not endorse a crackdown by its board, he was prepared to take even more drastic steps. The OSC would impose strict limits on the markups that brokers were allowed to add on to the takedown prices of stocks under options, which would cut sharply into profits. Lennox not only put this threat in writing but authorized Moysey to pass along the warning to the BDA members if he felt it necessary.[50]

The general meeting of the BDA proved to be a stormy, three-hour affair filled with recriminations. In the end, however, backed up by Lennox's threats, Moysey's proposal carried the day. The action of the board in banning members from marketing securities in any state or province where they were not registered was finally endorsed unanimously. The broker-dealers agreed that they must seek registration with the SEC and qualify any issues that they wished to sell in the United States. In the days following the decision, BDA board members reported rumours that telephone selling was continuing, and the association had to issue a further formal notice repeating its warning that such actions would be punished.[51]

All that broker-dealers could now hope for was that the Americans would be lenient and overlook previous accusations, injunctions, and stop orders, provided that Canadian firms promised to obey the rules in future. The SEC did undertake to provide guidance about securing the lifting of the postal-fraud orders, and eventually it even agreed to send two senior staff members to Toronto to explain the process. This was followed up by a further visit to Washington by Moysey and Gemmell, who held discussions with the new chair, Cary, and other officials to try to clarify exactly what requirements must be met. Eventually the BDA board drafted new rules of conduct to be added to the regulations under the Securities Act, though many broker-dealers held back from applying for registration in order to see if the SEC would be lenient about past offences.[52]

American disclosure rules proved stern medicine for the Canadian brokers to swallow. When the SEC eventually accepted the first two prospectuses for Ontario mines in the spring of 1962, the *Financial Post* reported upon the striking extent to which blunt statements had replaced the huckster's spiel. Rather than the usual impenetrable engineering report, Dolphin-Miller Mines presented a narrative about its property, arguing that further exploration was justified even though ore bodies in the area tended to be 'small, narrow and discontinuous.' The offering price of 50 cents was admitted to be five times the current trading value, 'with no developments whatsoever occurring at the property or elsewhere to justify the increase.' Exactly who would receive the proceeds of the issue were clearly set forth, but buyers were warned, 'None of the proceeds of the sale of shares will be refunded to purchasers if only a limited number of shares are sold.' The cover of the prospectus bore the ominous words 'There is no known present market in the shares of the capital stock of the company,' and the document made clear that shareholders could not expect to profit unless a commercial ore body was uncovered. All in all, said the *Post*, such forthrightness was enough to 'make any old-time stock promoters choke on their telephone pitch[es].'[53]

The new rules soon created a rift in the Broker Dealers Association, because some members felt that the board had given in too easily. At the annual elections in 1962 a slate of six people, none of them belonging to TSE member firms, stood against the nine incumbents. The half-dozen included a number of notorious characters who had previously been expelled, disciplined, or denied membership for falling afoul of the authorities; three of the dissidents were elected.[54]

Before long, O.E. Lennox discovered that some broker-dealers were up to their old tricks, though now the new rules made them more likely to prey upon fellow Canadians. In 1959 a women in another province had submitted a request for information about a particular security to A.C. MacPherson and Company, and the following year she received a card asking her to verify her address. But this mailing also sought permission to send her information about several mining issues, and when it was returned, MacPherson used it as a qualifying card and began telephoning to offer shares in a mining promotion. Lennox condemned this sleight of hand as 'the type of device which is undermining public confidence in speculative issues sponsored by local promotional houses,' and he ordered MacPherson's registration suspended for one month. The BDA, however, took up the case, pointing out that the card had been accompanied by an explanatory letter and that other members had done similar things without being penalized. Confirming MacPherson's suspension, Lennox complained, 'The people of Ontario are now being subjected to solicitations from promotional houses on a large scale, since offerings in the United States have been materially curbed by the action taken by the Broker Dealers Association in March of 1961.'[55]

Ignoring Lennox's choleric comments, the BDA board decided upon another effort to get the ban on calling at private residences lifted. Walter Cummings, one of the new board members, was insistent that the provincial government should be approached, so Charles McTague was again despatched to sound out the attorney general in the spring of 1962. Kelso Roberts stated forthrightly that he had no intention of changing the Securities Act, adding that the new premier, John Robarts, and the rest of the cabinet were of the same mind.[56]

Broker-dealer Gordon Jones insisted that he could use his private contacts within the government to persuade the ministers to relax the rules by alerting them about the need to raise capital to fund the development of Ontario resources. The BDA staff was put to work drawing up a brief demonstrating the vital role that the sale of speculative shares played in this process. When a draft of this document was laid before the board, however, the executive secretary pointed out 'that since some of the information had not previously been placed before the government, he hoped it would not be brought to the attention of the Ontario Securities Commission.' Eventually the BDA board seems to have realized that Lennox was guaranteed to learn about these amateurish political machinations, so they had better present a formal brief to the government rather than trying to go behind the regulator's back. All the ministers were sent a proposal for a number of changes in the Securities Act.[57]

At a general meeting of BDA members in July 1962 there were complaints that it had become impossible to market Canadian issues in the United States because of the attitude of the regulators there, but the association could not drop its ban on selling unregistered shares south of the border because the Toronto Stock Exchange would not abandon its threat to expel anyone found to have violated American laws.[58] Rather than any regulatory activity by the OSC, what had really curtailed illegal sales of unregistered stock by Toronto boiler rooms had been the TSE's action.[59]

O.E. Lennox died on the very last day of 1962, after an unprecedented fifteen-year term as chair of the OSC, but his record in controlling fraudulent promoters had been a decidedly mixed one. Despite active share markets, which had resulted in an increased number of filings and new regulatory problems, under him the size of the commission's staff had declined rather than increased. Harry Bray, who had joined the commission in 1951, recalled that the number of lawyers actually fell from five to two over the next decade, while fewer investigators were employed; only the chief auditor and his assistant were professionally trained in accountancy. Two people were attempting to handle the examination of all prospectuses. Yet when Howard Graham, the president of the Toronto Stock Exchange, told the Chamber of Commerce in 1961 that he considered the OSC understaffed, Lennox rejected the idea. He explain to the attorney general that while attempts had been made to add a small number of new lawyers and investigators, it did not seem 'an appropriate time to consider enlarging the staff to any major degree, as promotional mining activities are at a very low level, as the [Toronto Stock] Exchange well knows.' Nor did Lennox feel that any major changes were required to the Securities Act. In Bray's words, 'Indeed, during the last years of his life Mr. Lennox resisted most changes suggested in the way of legislation or administration.'[60]

6

Windfall

On 12 April 1964 the Texas Gulf Sulphur Company announced a huge discovery of zinc, copper, and silver in Kidd Township near Timmins, Ontario. Prospectors commenced a frantic staking rush to secure claims nearby. Mining promoters hastened to try to market shares in any junior mining company with a promising property as speculators scrambled to get in on the ground floor. During April and May alone, the Toronto Stock Exchange reported that $6 million had been raised through the primary distribution of stock in listed mines. Another classic Canadian mining-share boom was under way.

I

One of the cherished myths about Canadian mining was that most of the great finds had been made by lone prospectors pursuing hunches independently. For instance, the president of the Prospectors and Developers Association cited the example of the discovery of uranium in northern Ontario by Franc Joubin after the Second World War. 'The uranium industry, however, is merely one example of where prospectors have "dug" out discoveries. In the postwar years some 32 other orebodies have been discovered across Canada ... Individual prospectors or prospecting syndicates were identified with 19 of these discoveries ... The vital role of the prospector in Canada's mining history can be traced back to the turn of the century and/or even prior to that date.'[1] The reality of the modern industry was rather different: one study showed that 86 per cent of exploration in 1960 was actually financed by companies that already owned producing mines.[2]

A key geophysical fact about the Precambrian Shield in northern

Ontario was that its valuable copper-zinc-nickel ores lay in tabular deposits consisting of sulphides of these base metals, averaging about 25 per cent concentration. These 'massive sulphides' (often associated with precious metals as well) might be uncovered in three different ways. First of all, most sulphides were a thousandfold better as electrical conductors than the surrounding rock. Instruments measuring the distortion of an alternating electromagnetic field in a zone of high conductivity could indicate their presence. Secondly, pyrrhotite, an iron sulphide common in the base-metal deposits, could alter the earth's magnetic field, so that about half such deposits registered on a magnetometer. Finally, these sulphides had specific gravities between 30 and 100 per cent higher than the host rock, so when present in sizeable concentrations, they could produce an increase in the earth's gravitational attraction measurable by gravimeter. Scientific prospecting on the Precambrian Shield was rooted in these three methods.

Only after the Second World War did aerial surveys, economical for tracts over five miles square, become feasible. Airborne instruments could map conducting zones down to a depth of about two hundred feet, and magnetic surveys might be carried out simultaneously. Statistics indicated that between five hundred and one thousand geological conducting zones existed for every one related to a base or precious metal deposit, common graphite having a conductivity comparable to metallic sulphides. Experience also showed that the most promising zones were conductors less than half a mile in length and possessing magnetic properties, since larger bodies usually proved to be graphitic deposits or sulphides with no significant base-metal content. Once identified, such conductors could be subjected to further ground-level electromagnetic and magnetometer testing, while gravimeter surveys were possible only on the surface. A body with high conductivity and high specific gravity was almost certain to have the high sulphide content common to about 75 per cent of Canadian base-metal deposits. Taken together, these three methods of assessment could eliminate 90 per cent of conducting zones while delimiting 85 per cent of the potential ore bodies, even though these constituted just 1 per cent of the sulphide concentrations. Diamond drilling was then required to ascertain the presence of commercially valuable mineral desposits.[3]

Particularly around Timmins, the geological structures made prospecting difficult because the bedrock of the Precambrian Shield was covered with up to three hundred feet of overburden, so that there were few outcrops for prospectors to sample. Following the discovery

of gold at Porcupine in 1909–10, there had been relatively little prospecting done north of there because of the difficulty of discovering
mineralization through surface exploration.[4] In 1959 Texas Gulf Sulphur, a major American mineral producer, began a systematic program
using a specially equipped helicopter which revealed a number of
interesting 'anomalies' (or deviations from the norm) in the area that
might merit further exploration. During the next four years the company had drilled one or more holes in over fifty such anomalies without success.

Surface work created its own problems. Because the fertile soil of the
Clay Belt had led government to envisage agricultural development in
the region, much of the land in the Timmins area had been granted to
veterans of the Fenian Raids, the Boer War, and the First World War.
Though few farms were actually established, these grants carried with
them both the forest and the mineral rights and so were not freely open
to staking by prospectors but must be leased or purchased.[5] In the
autumn of 1963 Texas Gulf secured an option on lands owned by the
estate of Murray Hendrie through a veteran's land grant; geophysicist
Hugh Clayton soon reported that an electromagnetic ground survey
had produced the most promising reading he had ever seen for the
north half of lot 3 in Kidd Township. On 8 November 1963 a drill crew
began work on hole K55-1, and four days later geologist Kenneth
Darke needed only a quick look at the core to detect massive sulphides
with significant copper and zinc content.

He immediately decided to camouflage the site and move the rig. He
knew that the 'moccasin telegraph' was bound to pass along rumours
from his crew: 'Even if they don't know what is in the core they know
from the drilling when we hit massive sulphides, and if they say anything at all we are going to be dead anyway as far as the company is
concerned.' Darke's best hope was to persuade the drillers that only
graphite had been struck, so the rig was moved some distance away,
where, as anticipated, a barren hole was sunk. In order to keep the men
out of circulation as long as possible, they were then put to work on
other properties far from Timmins: 'We kept them well fed with steaks
and with beer ... so they wouldn't complain.' Not until Christmastime
did some of the crew get out to Kirkland Lake, Ontario. By that time
the drill core had been split in two lengthwise and samples dispatched
to an assayer in Salt Lake City, Utah; the report received in mid-
December indicated that over its six-hundred-foot length the core
graded at 1 per cent copper, 8 per cent zinc, and nearly four ounces of

silver for every ton of ore. Of course, the chance remained that the K55–1 bit might have angled 'down dip' like a sword into a narrow sheath, but if further drilling confirmed that there was an ore body of any size, then Texas Gulf had a real bonanza.[6]

Before undertaking further exploration, the company had to acquire rights to the adjacent lands from the Roberts estate, which owned the south half of lot 3 in Kidd Township as a result of a veteran's grant, and from a local lumber company, which controlled the south half of lot 4. At the end of March 1964 drilling resumed near K55-1 with excellent results. On 12 April a company press release described the rumours starting to spread as 'premature and possibly misleading,' but eventually it was decided to reveal the news after Texas Gulf's board met in New York on 16 April.[7]

The company's find was especially welcome to the band of mining brokers and promoters in Toronto, whose business had recently been in the doldrums. As usual, much of the blame had been laid upon over-strict regulation. When Ontario's mines minister expressed concern that mineral exploration had reached its lowest level since 1955, broadcaster Gordon Sinclair trumpeted, 'It seems to me that any schoolboy can tell him why. It's because the Securities Commission harasses, pursues, downgrades and abuses any promoter trying to get an unwilling public to take a chance on a new prospect.' Sinclair insisted that people were eager to speculate on mining shares, even though

> the public knows that in at least nine cases out of ten it will lose its shirt. Up until six or seven years ago the public was quite prepared to take that chance in the hope that the one winner in ten would pay off at a rate strong enough to make the other nine losers fade away. But the Securities Commission looked on all promoters as thieves, bandits, pirates, ace chisellers and con men, whose slogan was 'Never give a sucker an even break.' Mines Minister George Wardrope must know, that if anyone went out today to risk life, limb and liberty and found the richest mine in the history of the earth he would probably still be considered a bandit and a thief before he got it into production.

The *Canadian Magazine* recalled the good old days of the 1950s, when promoters had supposedly raised over $300 million annually for resource development. Then American brokers had started a 'smear campaign' against competition from Canadian stocks, and bureaucrats had seized the opportunity to crack down on the promoters. Even though hundreds of unemployed people were tramping the streets, few diamond drills were operating in northern Ontario because of the OSC: 'Possessing arbitrary powers and always under pressure to justify its existence, the Commission will investigate companies on the flimsiest of pretexts.'[8]

The Broker Dealers Association launched a lobbying campaign to have the restrictions on the marketing of speculative shares relaxed. Frederick Cass, the recently appointed attorney general, received a series of missives pointing out that the hundreds of people once employed by the BDA had dwindled over the past year to fewer than fifty firms with only a couple of salesmen each. The time had come for dramatic changes in both personnel and policies at the OSC to make the financing of speculative mining companies easier.[9]

Texas Gulf's find ended all the doomsaying. Among the mining promoters frantically manoeuvring to take advantage of this upsurge of public interest were George and Viola MacMillan. She was well known to the public as a woman in an almost exclusively male business, having become enamoured of prospecting during the 1920s and eventually secured her own licence. The couple set up MacMillan Securities in 1933 and scratched out a living as mining brokers and promoters. Viola MacMillan worked each summer in the bush with her husband; she was also responsible for rustling up the money to finance exploration. Interviewed by the *Financial Post* in 1938, she declared, 'Prospectors don't make mines. Somebody's got to have the nerve to put up the money and sell the stock. If a property comes through, well the prospector gets all the credit. If it doesn't, the broker gets all the blame. I don't think the public gives the brokers nearly enough credit for their part in mine making.'[10]

When the Prospectors and Developers Association was organized, Viola MacMillan became its secretary. In 1944 she replaced her husband as president, a post she would hold for the next twenty years. After the Second World War the couple helped to develop the Violamac base-metal mine near Slocan, British Columbia, and in the 1950s the Lake Cinch uranium mine in Saskatchewan. Having acquired the Kamkotia copper property near Timmins in 1959, the MacMillans successfully brought it into production. George MacMillan felt intense pride about their record: '[As] wildcatters, we have to deal – [unlike] ... these big mining companies, you understand, we have to go out and make our mines, [while] those fellows have mines, they can carry on ...

[We] have to get on finding mines and we have to take bigger gambles, and that is the reason we took this [Kamkotia] property, because I knew we could make ... $3 million out of it, and they said I could not make a cent.'[11]

As soon as Texas Gulf released its news, the MacMillans sped north to Timmins. Later on George grumbled a bit enviously that Kenneth Darke, backed up by the might of a major company, had been able to strike $2 billion worth of minerals with one drill hole, worth more than the $1.7 billion in gold produced in the entire Porcupine district over the previous fifty years. 'That also made us people feel a little silly after being around here for twenty-five, thirty, years and not being able to find that orebody. It also made us very anxious to find one.' Three local prospectors, John Larche, Donald McKinnon, and Fred Rousseau, had staked a claim surrounded on three sides by Texas Gulf lands just at the time of the announcement in New York. After an unsuccessful attempt to strike a deal with Noranda Mines, they began negotiations with the MacMillans. The haggling went on until 5:30 in the morning; by the end Viola was so keen that she reportedly shoved George, who was not as smitten, out into the hall of their hotel and struck an agreement with the three men on her own. She considered the lands 'strictly a location bet,' but though the price was high, she felt felt very lucky: 'Everybody was trying to buy. I hope I live through another experience like that night; it was wonderful ... We were all very happy; everybody was happy.'[12]

Now the financing had to be arranged. Viola MacMillan originally intended to put the property into a closely held syndicate, the Lucky Texas, because she thought the odds of success so great: 'I had going through my mind [that] I was so happy about Texas Gulf and finding an orebody – believe me, it is luck, not all brains, that finds a mine.' In the end, however, she transferred the claims to Windfall Oils and Mines, which the MacMillans had acquired in 1961 for $65,000. Not only was control firmly lodged in their hands, but George had appointed as directors of Windfall several personal friends and employees (including the handyman at the MacMillan country place), mere nominees who could be relied upon to sign documents and ask no questions. Equally useful was the fact that Windfall was already listed on the Toronto Stock Exchange, though it currently had no operations. To raise funds by selling additional shares, such shell companies had only to produce a filing statement listing material changes in their operations. Once approved by the exchange, primary distribution of additional shares from the company's treasury could proceed simultaneously with secondary trading in the stock.[13]

Nevertheless, a hitch occurred. Viola MacMillan had agreed to hand over $100,000 in cash plus 250,000 Windfall shares to Larche, McKinnon, and Rousseau for their claims, but she in turn wanted at least $200,000 together with 300,000 shares from the company treasury for the properties. The rules of the Toronto Stock Exchange, however, forbade promoters making a profit on such non-arm's-length deals, so the filing statement prepared by Windfall was rejected. This rebuff infuriated Viola MacMillan, who seemed to consider herself entitled to preferential treatment from the TSE since she held the best claims in Timmins apart from Texas Gulf Sulphur. 'The Stock Exchange,' she complained angrily, 'thinks they [sic] know more what to do in mining than we did.' The governors, however, stuck to the rules: 'You are going to meet their terms regardless of what your situation might be.' After several weeks of wrangling, she had to accept no more than the $100,000 she had paid out, together with a quarter-million shares.[14]

A consulting geologist was quickly retained and by 23 June had produced an encouraging report on Windfall's properties to accompany the filing statement for the TSE. Within a week a diamond-drilling crew started a hole, working around the clock. Geologist Fenton Scott thought very highly of the prospect: 'It, of the many properties in the area, seemed to be the only one with a real chance of coming up with a Texas Gulf deposit.' He added, 'If anybody was going to find a mine right away near Texas Gulf, this seemed to be the property that stood the best chance.'

On Friday, 3 July 1964, mining people from all over the north gathered for a golf tournament in Rouyn-Noranda, and throughout the weekend most of the talk was about Windfall. On Saturday afternoon the golfers got electrifying news: George MacMillan had suddenly stopped drilling. Visiting the claim, he found that the sludge of water and rock dust ground up by the drill bit and forced back to the surface had turned a blackish colour, indicating that the bit might have penetrated a sulphide deposit. MacMillan got down on his hands and knees and examined the core from about five hundred feet down; he could see that the bit had 'entered into a graphite zone, mineralization, and to me it looked very favourable.' Texas Gulf had taken care to make sure that nobody knew the exact geological structure of its find, but rumours had been flying around during the past few weeks. MacMillan said, 'I thought I had a similar zone to what they had.' Immediately he ordered the drill stopped, and four boxes of cores were bundled into the trunk of his car. Why cease work so abruptly? There was no core shack in which to store and examine the samples more closely, safe from prying eyes: 'As I had no facilities to handle it at the property, I had decided to take those four boxes away.'[15]

Mining people found George MacMillan's actions mystifying. Even if dark sludge was flowing from the drill rig, it could easily have been washed away or spread innocuously around the area. Prospector John Larche said, '[W]e felt that if George MacMillan had pulled a good hole, he could easily cover this up. He is smart enough in that game not to leave any evidence behind if he didn't want anybody to know about it.' Kenneth Darke contended that there was no need to stop drilling; core samples could perfectly well be examined in the open, as he had done at K55-1 because Texas Gulf had a rule that something significant had to be discovered before any unusual expense was incurred. 'I would say security would be a very poor reason to put up a core shack, if you haven't anything to guard to begin with ... There was no more interest in Windfall than forty other drills in the area.' A.G. Schlitt, who ran a geophysical survey company, confirmed, '[W]hen something important is found ... they usually accelerate the development program, but ... when it came to my knowledge the hole had been stopped I found it difficult to believe.' So the news caught everybody's attention.[16]

MacMillan did allow the foreman of the drilling crew, an old friend, a quick look at the cores, and both agreed that they looked very promising. Back in Timmins at the offices of Bradley Brothers, the drilling company, MacMillan and the foreman again discussed whether there might be a valuable find. The foreman immediately passed this news along to Edgar Bradley, who in turn told his partner R.F. Spencer. Meanwhile, MacMillan telephoned his wife and summoned her north. Having driven all night, she arrived in Timmins near dawn on Sunday, and they decided to visit the property. Together they examined more drill cores, before George nailed another four boxes of samples shut and put them in the car.[17]

The news that something was up spread like wildfire; some members of the drilling crew attended mass in Timmins on Sunday morning. Donald McKinnon, who had sold the Windfall claims, got a telephone call asking if he had any idea what was going on. He was well aware that the big mining companies retained 'detectives' whose task it was to keep an eye on all drilling, and he was sufficiently intrigued to rent a helicopter and fly over the site. From a helicopter a knowledgeable observer might be able to tell the angle at which the drill was aimed by looking at its stiff leg and to estimate the depth of a hole by counting the number of drill rods being used.[18]

Viola MacMillan remembered helicopters circling overhead.Though both of them were elated, she and her husband didn't give off much with strangers around: 'We are too long in the game to let anything like this excite you to the point that you go to tell people that you have got a big mine.' Yet she felt elated because the drill was producing black graphitic sludge and the core indicated the presence of mineral-bearing rhyolite breccia, rather than just barren granite, 'where we had ground in close proximity [to Texas Gulf's]. This was the idea: go in and look at the ground. To me, it was elephant country ... Porcupine is a wonderful country.' In the car on the way back to town she could control herself no longer, throwing her arms around one of the drillers riding with them and thanking him for finding her a mine.[19] That, after all, had been her objective in life: 'we were hoping all the time that we were working, we were carrying on the way we had been for thirty years, and we never had millions or anything like that. And I don't mind telling you we had a rough time bringing other mines into production.' With the eight boxes of samples in the trunk of their car, the MacMillans set off for Toronto on Sunday afternoon. Even though Wilbert Bradley hadn't heard anything directly from Edgar, his brother and partner in the drilling company, he had no doubt about what was going on: 'Well, that's the whole thing on fire to me. People not knowing, hearing that the drill stopped, and the rumour went out that there was mineralization.'[20]

II

On the afternoon of Sunday, 5 July salesman Irvine Jones of Housser and Company got a call from a friend in Noranda reporting that there were eighty feet of mineralized sulphides in the Windfall cores. Jones telephoned a couple of specially favoured clients the same evening and reached seven others on Monday morning between 7:30 and 10 o'clock. One was his former partner at Bradley Brothers, R.F. Spencer; all Jones told him was 'If he had his gambling shoes on he should get some [Windfall], and he gave me an order then for 10,000 shares.' A few minutes later Spencer doubled it. Jones also called Wilbert Bradley, who started off with an order for 10,000, though in the end he.went for

60,000 shares at over $1.00 each. Bradley, who had been in the game since 1937, was laconic about his plunge: '[W]ith the activity in Timmins ... you risk one, you try the next one.' But why put so much on the line? 'Well, you've got to take risks, so I said, "People are willing to pay that price with all the commotion that was going on in Timmins." I figured I could make a few cents.'[21]

After Texas Gulf's announcement in April everyone believed that another discovery nearby was likely, said Jones: 'You know the fantastic background of excitement there was stemming from the Texas Gulf thing.' 'I think many people in the industry were ... just waiting to see which one would come up with something.' If any company drilled into sulphides, it was going to set off 'a frenzy,' so he told his customers, 'I could predict ... an exciting opening' when trading started on the Toronto Stock Exchange at 10 o'clock. The stock had closed at 56 cents the previous Friday, but now Jones got word that so many buying orders for the stock were on hand, it would open at $1.01. He alone was seeking 57,000 Windfall shares, and he realized that anyone selling was almost certain to withdraw, if possible, until it was clear what would happen in the 'obviously fantastic, tumultuous excitement.'

During the first half-hour Jones bent all his efforts to seeing that his orders were executed. Asked if he had passed on his tip to others at Housser and Company, he responded sharply, 'There was already total frenzy on the floor. Did I wish to add to it before I got my clients filled up? Certainly not.' Only afterwards did he share his news with the firm. Jones was proud of his work that day: as the stock rocketed upward to $2, he advised customers to sell part of their holdings when it reached $1.50. He told them, 'If you continue lucky, sell a little more at $1.75 and be content with a top profit of double, which is substantially what happened, because, as I recall it, I had everybody out no higher than $2, and this based on just an ordinary old-fashioned approach to trading in speculative securities.' He did not advise his customers to re-enter the market. After all, Windfall had a promising property close to Texas Gulf's but no proven find.[22]

Irvine Jones was not the only broker with sizeable orders from people in northern Ontario. Vernon Oille, who worked for Noranda Explorations, made a big purchase right after talking to R.F. Spencer, telling his broker that word had it there were eighty-five feet of mineralization in the cores. Altogether, Timmins-area people bought 97,000 shares on Monday, which had a 'profound effect' upon the brokerage community. Donald McKinnon explained that speculators always kept watch on what drillers themselves were buying, following their lead on the chance that they might have inside information and sometimes even offering to pay for tips. J.W. Dennis of Davidson and Company heard from 'reliable sources' about 'very good mining people who have access to information,' and he paid close attention because such knowledgeable folk were 'usually the forerunners of heavy buying, and when I see them buying a stock, very very rarely are they wrong ... [T]ime and time in the past the mining people know what a thing runs or doesn't run, three to four days before the street even knows, before it is ever public.'[23]

At the eye of the storm were the MacMillans. During the previous three months Viola MacMillan had been preparing for this moment, buying and selling about 500,000 of the already outstanding shares of Windfall. This market action, accounting for 40 per cent of all the trading in the stock, was intended to 'groom' the market and arouse interest. By the time she reached the offices of MacMillan Prospecting on Monday, 6 July, calls were already flooding in. A.G. Schlitt visited her at 8:30 a.m. but got no detailed information about Windfall, though when he mentioned Kamkotia, she did admit that she might have a similarly important find. C.W. Stollery managed to get through during the morning, but she would say only, 'You don't suppose I drove all night for nothing.' He felt that was significant enough to send a message on the private wire to Bongard and Company's other branches, advising that Windfall might have hit something though he was unable to confirm any details; later on, A.V. Vance sent out another wire to the Bongard offices which also mentioned eighty-five feet of mineralization. From Timmins, McKinnon tried unsuccessfully to reach George MacMillan and also talked to his own prospecting partners to see if they had heard anything more.[24]

Meanwhile, Viola MacMillan was hurriedly making arrangements to dispose of the 800,000 treasury shares of Windfall under her control. T.A. Richardson and Company, the selling broker she had chosen for the Windfall deal, was asked to open new accounts in the names of Mrs V.R. MacMillan, MacMillan Prospecting, Airquest, and Consolidated Golden Arrow Mines. She had already told G.A. Hunter at Richardson's that she would release her first 100,000 shares into the market only if the TSE opened at 90 cents. She was soon reminded, however, that Moss, Lawson and Company, the designated broker for the underwriters, had a responsibility to maintain an orderly market, and she released another 65,000 shares. By the end of the day, in fact, Mac-

Millan-controlled accounts had disposed of a total of 433,900 shares, or over one-quarter of those traded that day. The stock's rapid rise to $2 also triggered the takedown clauses in the underwriting agreement when the price reached twice the highest level specified in the options, and the exchange therefore notified the underwriters that they must immediately take delivery of all 800,000 underwritten shares. Viola MacMillan later complained about the fact that the exchange had ordered the stock to open at nearly double its previous close without any consultation with her. As a result she suddenly faced the need to raise $490,000 to pay for these shares: 'I was furious about it.' Yet the profits went not to the company treasury but largely to insiders like the MacMillans, since takedown prices were fixed by the value at the time of the underwriting agreement rather than by current prices.[25]

The newspapers quickly picked up the Windfall story. Richard Roberts, the *Toronto Telegram's* financial reporter, called Viola MacMillan for comment on a rumour that there were sixty feet of mineralization in the drill core. She replied, 'Oh, it is better than that. But we have no assays, no assays at all, but it looks pretty good. We expect to be on target for the weekend.'[26] Officially, however, Windfall merely released a statement on Tuesday, 7 July, dictated by George MacMillan and rubber-stamped by the board of directors, saying that drill cores had been 'sampled' but no assays performed. Yet there was also a tantalizing reference to the fact that explorations had encountered geological structures similar to those found by Texas Gulf. Not surprisingly, the stock continued in strong demand. That day Viola MacMillan disposed of another 40,000 shares, though short selling and profit-taking prevented a further strong advance and turned prices downward late in the day. Trading remained quiet on Wednesday, 8 July, but the MacMillans bought back 16,500 shares of the first 100,000 Windfall shares traded. Viola MacMillan insisted, 'In fact, it was not my intention to be on the buy side at all.' If purchases had been made when the stock touched various low points in this period, it was a coincidence: 'This I don't understand either. Reflex, I suppose ... Certainly not to turn the market.'[27]

Trading surged again on Thursday, 9 July, when a favourable story appeared in the *Northern Miner*. James Scott, the assistant business editor of the *Globe and Mail*, overheard George MacMillan say, 'If you want to be poor all your life, don't buy Windfall.' Viola MacMillan remained firmly in charge of the Windfall deal, using a direct telephone line to Eric Watson, head trader for Moss, Lawson, and to the firm's other floor traders at the TSE; she often gave orders to sell and to buy without specifying which accounts the shares were to be taken from or allocated to. Trading was so hectic, said Watson, that 'Nobody knew whether they were coming or going half the time. You had to wait for a certain length of time to straighten yourself out, and you were very fortunate – as long as you had experienced people – that it came out right.' Sometimes, he said, she was hard to get hold of, but afterwards she would always say something like 'Well, you should have sold more stock.' Viola MacMillan seemed to have a keen feel for the market. As Watson put it, 'She is quite a confusing person to talk to, but very brilliant. I like her very much.' He admitted that as the broker for the underwriters, he had not had enough stock to sell to keep the market entirely orderly. During the 'fantastic' buying and selling that day, Viola MacMillan was able to dispose of another 333,200 shares.[28]

On Friday demand for Windfall shares was so strong that the TSE's Floor Procedure Committee delayed the stock's opening for half an hour while it tried to pair off the buy and sell orders and assess demand. Eventually Windfall opened at $3.25, up 75 cents overnight, and by the end of the day it had hit $4.00 as the MacMillans released another 53,400 shares, bringing their sales for the week to 811,200 shares worth a total of $1,388,000.

That same day Viola MacMillan telephoned Howard Graham, the president of the TSE, with a surprising request. For the properties she had turned over to Windfall she had received 250,000 shares, 90 per cent of which were placed in escrow until the exchange certified that the funds raised from the sale of the other treasury shares were being used for development. Now she wanted these 225,000 shares released from escrow immediately so that she might sell them directly into the market at a minimum price of $3 apiece. Graham told her that any such request would have to be referred to the Filing Statement Committee, which met at once. It was pointed out that there was no evidence that any new money had been spent on the property, and that the escrow had not lasted for the required minimum of six months. No arrangements had been made to underwrite this block of shares to ensure an orderly market, and so long as the company failed to disclose any further information, the insiders were at a distinct advantage. Committee members thought it a piece of ridiculous effrontery that Viola Mac-Millan should casually telephone a request for the right to dump this stock into a rising market. On both sides a feeling of antagonism was strengthened by the resentments that still lingered about her acrimonious wrangle with the exchange a few months earlier, when she had attempted to bend the TSE's rules by securing for herself a larger compensation for the Windfall properties than had been paid to the prospectors.[29]

Viola MacMillan's request had significant consequences. The heavy trading in Windfall shares had naturally benefited the TSE's members considerably. All week long one member firm after another had been putting out more or less cautious recommendations to buy Windfall.[30] Not only was there commission income flowing in, but many firms had house accounts run by their floor traders for their personal or collective benefit.[31] No firm had benefited more than T.A. Richardson and Company, which was handling the trading for the multitude of accounts controlled by Viola MacMillan; Marshal Stearns, a partner in T.A. Richardson, was the chair of the exchange board.[32] Despite the lack of information forthcoming from the company, the TSE had done nothing to require further disclosure, but on Friday afternoon the full board of governors met to consider the situation in the aftermath of Viola MacMillan's audacious demands. President Howard Graham was instructed to advise Windfall that it must make 'an up-to-date statement' for public release not later than 9:15 on the morning of Monday, 13 July, or face a suspension of trading.[33] When neither of the MacMillans responded to Graham's telephone calls that afternoon, he telegraphed this warning to each director of Windfall. Graham and Stearns were granted discretion to take whatever action they saw fit in light of the response to this ultimatum.[34]

The Ontario Securities Commission also entered the picture for the first time. Since the stock was listed, regulatory responsibility fell to the TSE, so that the commission had played no direct role. In the temporary absence of chair J.R. Kimber, OSC director John Campbell, who oversaw day-to-day administration, was the senior official. He had become acquainted with Viola MacMillan when he was invited to speak at the annual meeting of the Prospectors and Developers Association the previous spring, and he and his wife had become social friends of the MacMillans. When Campbell learned from Viola MacMillan that the TSE had declared its intention to suspend trading in Windfall on Monday unless the company released more information, he decided to take a hand. He felt that the exchange's demands were both unprecedented and ill-advised: had Texas Gulf been forced to disclose the results of its first successful hole the previous November, the company would never have been able to secure more land around

K55-1. And there was the principle involved: 'I thought it was very dangerous, because any broker on Bay Street that wants to get information on a mine, all they have to do is start a rumour and then the Toronto Stock Exchange would call in [company officials] and say, "Give us your assays of your core."'[35]

Campbell was much impressed by Viola MacMillan's success as a mining promoter (though he did say, somewhat ruefully, when asked if he had discussed Windfall with her: 'I have heard her speak. It is a questionable privilege. She will go on and on about the same thing for hours, so I imagine this was part of the discussion'). He insisted that he did not dislike what the TSE was trying to do so much as the way in which the governors went about it, an approach that was bound to be rejected: 'You just don't go to Viola MacMillan and say, "I want this" ... I mean you don't do that to Viola MacMillan.' He thought any decision on the release of information should have been left to the Windfall board, who supposedly represented all the shareholders.[36]

The OSC had little authority beyond keeping a 'parental eye' on the TSE's activities. Its only sanction was the 'atom bomb' of threatening to withdraw official recognition from the exchange, which would have thrown the financial world into chaos.[37] Nevertheless, after visiting the MacMillans at their weekend place north of Toronto on Saturday, Campbell went to the country home of former TSE chair George Gardiner to warn that the exchange's demands seemed unjustified; Gardiner told him to take his concerns to Graham. On Sunday Campbell did meet with Graham to argue that the MacMillans should not be forced into the position of having to deny rumours that they had no responsibility for starting. The exchange president replied that in view of the number of stories flying around, including tales that Viola MacMillan was still carrying the Windfall core samples around in the trunk of her car, and that Texas Gulf was mounting a takeover bid for the company, the price of the stock was clearly being affected and a statement must be made to clarify the situation. Campbell also telephoned Graham before the exchange opened on Monday morning. When Graham told Campbell that he was still determined to suspend trading in Windfall, they got into a nasty row. Campbell said that Graham had failed to take the public interest into account; the president responded that Campbell was overstepping the bounds of his authority. Petulantly, Campbell declared that he would not talk to Graham any further and hung up on him in mid-sentence.[38]

That same morning Graham finally received a letter from Windfall's corporate secretary, T.F.C. Cole, written three days earlier in response to the exchange's demand for more diclosure. The letter merely recapitulated the situation and was not felt to be a satisfactory response to the TSE's demands; before trading opened on Monday, however, the exchange received another letter advising that drilling would resume now that a core shack had been completed to deter the inquisitive. Graham and Stearns decided not to suspend the stock. Its price slid downward to $2.70, but then recovered strongly to close the day at $4.70, helped along by buying from insiders at key times as Viola MacMillan disposed of another 30,000 shares.[39]

Jack Kimber of the OSC had been absent on holidays for the previous two weeks, but at his return on Tuesday, 14 July, he found the brokerage community in an uproar. John Campbell admitted that he had had a serious quarrel with Howard Graham, imperilling the normally good relations with the TSE. Graham made it clear that his patience was nearing the breaking point. He had now been officially notified that all the options had been exercised and the underwritten shares disposed of, which meant that Windfall's stock was out of primary distribution, so it was much harder for the exchange to exercise control other than by suspending trading altogether.[40] Yet there had been no further disclosure, even though share prices had risen over eightfold during the past ten days. Kimber decided to try to calm the situation by convening a meeting at the OSC that very afternoon after the market closed for the day, to which both the MacMillans and officials of the exchange would be invited.[41]

Viola MacMillan had also worked herself into a high dudgeon. On Friday she protested bitterly to Windfall's corporate secretary about the exchange's interference in her private affairs, going so far as to say that she might welcome the threatened suspension of trading. T.F.C. Cole recorded her complaint that 'All the sales she had made in the last day or two were directed to slowing up the price rise. She could see an attempt to force the sale [of a block sufficient to] ... take control of the company away from her, and will feel better if she is off the Exchange.' On Monday Donald Lawson also endured a great diatribe against the TSE: 'She was a very determined woman, and I think she would [have] be[en] talking and pushing at anybody and everybody that might have had any hope of doing something.' When Viola MacMillan complained that the exchange was making it too difficult to secure capital, Lawson tried to point out that 'really she hadn't tried to do anything about raising money, because she hadn't really sat down seriously with any dealer about doing a financing agreement within the normal frame of release, but this rolled off like water.' After a couple of bruising (and losing) confrontations with officials of the TSE, she was convinced that they were pursuing a vendetta against her. Why were the MacMillans being asked to supply information not being demanded of anyone else? 'Why only us? Why [require disclosure only] on part of the drill hole?'[42]

To the gathering at the OSC, Howard Graham left no doubt that he 'thought the company officials were being ... a little ridiculous in not making the kind of statement that any reasonable company should make, and I said it on a number of occasions here at that meeting.' At once, Marshal Stearns recounted, Viola MacMillan launched into a tirade:

> She started out, as I remember, stating that they should have special consideration. She felt that the MacMillans had been in business for a great many years. The public knew them and had confidence in them and knew what they were doing, and [they] shouldn't be subject to arbitrary regulations; that she should not be made to give assays right away and report the hole if she didn't see fit ...
>
> Then there was talk about the little fellow. If the assays were bad the little fellow would be squeezed out on the first hole. I know I said ... that if the second hole was a dud also, I thought the shareholders would not thank her for holding back [news about] the first hole, but that didn't seem to register.

Undeterred, she turned to the conduct of T.A. Richardson and Company, to whom she had handed over 100,000 Windfall shares on 6 July, only to see more than a third of them 'short-circuited' into the hands of the firm's own brokers and traders. Both Richardson's and Doherty, Roadhouse and Company were heavily interested in mining stocks and could have been collaborating in some kind of market operation to depress the price of Windfall, one doing the heavy buying that pushed the stock up to $2.00 before the other sold it short. 'Was it a group that didn't care whether we had ore or not, that was just wanting to make money on the market? It was like a bush fire.' TSE vice-president W.L. Somerville listened to this rant with amazement, wondering how short sellers could cause the price of a stock to double in a single day. But at that point nobody seemed to want to tackle Viola MacMillan directly because 'it was rather asking for trouble to address any questions to her. In fact, I think perhaps I made a point of not doing so. This is a common complaint of promoters, however, ... about short selling.' Somerville's conclusion was that she seemed to have convinced herself that the TSE's threat to suspend trading in Windfall was designed to depress the stock and thus assist the short sellers amongst its members. On she went, unchecked: if short selling wasn't the problem, then perhaps brokers had been fronting for a takeover bid by Texas Gulf or Noranda, buying up the stock that the exchange had compelled her to release.[43]

Viola MacMillan became so wound up that she finally insisted that Kimber and Forbes McFarland, another Ontario Securities Commission member, should leave the room with her, so that she might expatiate upon the iniquities of T.A. Richardson and Company outside the presence of Marshal Stearns. In private, she alleged that many of the 100,000 shares which she had released on 6 July for $1.00 apiece had been held off the market by brokers until late in the day, when the price approached $2.00. If the OSC was looking for wrongdoing, it should be directing its attention not to the MacMillans but to the activities of the TSE and its members. In an effort to calm her down, Kimber said that he would be quite willing to investigate the exchange if she could supply evidence. Meanwhile, they had better get back to the meeting and talk about what disclosure Windfall was prepared to make.[44]

The discussion then turned to whether or not the TSE would insist upon the immediate release of assay results by Windfall as a condition of allowing trading to continue. George MacMillan was asked point-blank by M.H. Frohberg, the consulting geologist for the OSC and the TSE, whether the core samples had contained significant copper or zinc, but he refused to answer, repeating only that the geological stuctures seemed similar to those found by Texas Gulf. William Somerville observed wryly that 'one felt from the conversation that you were given plenty of opportunity to get the idea that there was quite a valuable find here, otherwise why would all this other activity be going on – [talk of] acquiring properties and so on?' OSC lawyer Harry Bray carefully noted down Viola MacMillan's exact words: 'Everybody knows we hit it.'[45] Yet her husband remained insistent that they couldn't be expected to make any statement until they had finished the drilling and analysed the entire core. Marshal Stearns said that a close look at what they had already must give a pretty good idea of whether there were valuable minerals or not, but George MacMillan replied blandly that he couldn't tell about the presence of gold without an assay. Whether every mining company should in future be compelled to publish its assay results immediately was raised; Forbes McFarland opposed making this a blanket policy but thought it should be required in this case to dispel the rumours.[46] Once more Viola MacMillan unloosed a broad hint, 'If they publish[ed] the results, it would set the whole [Timmins] camp on fire.'[47]

Back and forth the discussion went, until finally Jack Kimber proposed that the company should be given a maximum of ten days to complete the hole and release a full report on the findings. The MacMillans still resisted; Viola MacMillan remarked darkly that any such statement would be a stone around Kimber's neck. George MacMillan objected particularly strenuously to any reference to a fixed time limit, since he insisted that he must finish the drilling, inspect the entire core, and have it assayed before announcing anything. Finally, it was agreed that Windfall should be given a 'reasonable time' to complete the work.

Talk then turned to what ought to be said about the existing core samples. Kimber suggested that the release should include the statement that the samples were 'under guard,' but George MacMillan complained that 'it might encourage people to think we had an ore body or didn't have an ore body.' This issue seems to have been almost the only one on which the exchange representatives agreed with the MacMillans, because Stearns accepted that the words seemed to imply that something of value had already been found, though the company had refused to confirm it. By the end of the meeting, having faced down her antagonists, Viola MacMillan was in a buoyant mood, saying 'that it didn't make any difference what report we put out, that this thing would grow and grow ... She said that this was a pretty big fire, and it would not be put out by any statement.'[48]

She was right. That very day E.D. Scott sent out a wire to staff members at J.H. Crang and Company urging them to have their customers go long on Windfall stock because its price might go as high as $20 per share.The rumour mill was further fuelled on Wednesday, 15 July, by the news that Texas Gulf itself planned to move a drilling rig onto the lands it controlled to the east of the Windfall claims. Graham Ackerly explained the reasoning behind his highly positive story in the *Northern Miner* on Thursday, 16 July:

> We have the background, a tremendous orebody found in Kidd Township ... In the history of pre-Cambrian exploration whenever an orebody is found like that, it is quite logical to find satellite orebodies ...

174 Moose Pastures and Mergers

There was a very big factor that Texas Gulf has broken into a systematic exploration program to move a drill right onto the boundary, 2,000 feet east of the Windfall hole. That was a very big factor in my mind ... We had market action and the stock had gone up ...
Here was another impressive factor. There had been no punitive action [against the company], and the Ontario Securities Commission had moved into the picture.

Mines Minister George Wardrope was also consulted, and while non-committal, he did admit that he had talked to the MacMillans and gave the impression that he thought prospects were good. In Ackerly's mind, the minister's comment seemed to indicate a kind of official endorsement: 'It was at this point that we knew Mr. Wardrope had personal contact with Mr. and Mrs. MacMillan ... Mr. Wardrope['s role] certainly encouraged us to sell this thing hard.' With this kind of favourable publicity the price of Windfall stayed up. The *Financial Post* reported that old-timers were harking back to the boom of 1953–5, when the mere news that a core shack was being constructed on a claim was enough to send a stock shooting upward.[49]

With the price of Windfall as high as $4.70, George MacMillan showed that he was in no hurry to make more disclosure. He waited three days after the 14 July meeting before ordering Bradley Brothers to resume drilling, then directed them to use only one shift per day. Towards the end of that week both MacMillans went north, where they continued to project an aura of confidence. John Larche, who had sold them the Windfall claims, visited the site; they told him that there had been no assay yet, but Viola MacMillan repeated that the geology of the core appeared similar to that of Texas Gulf's find and talked a great deal about the problems of arranging another underwriting, so Larche came away convinced that the news must be good. On the weekend two reporters from the *Northern Miner* arranged to drive out with the MacMillans to look at the ground. Graham Ackerly recalled, 'George was very quiet, and she was almost hysterical.' She was clear enough on one point, however: 'She made some derogatory remarks about the Toronto Stock Exchange. She was continually referring to her position that she wanted to make a mine and wished people would leave her alone ... Well, the whole conversation was disjointed. It was almost irrational on her part. We all had that impression: that she was very excited ... She obviously had a secret and she was keeping it, and it was her intention to keep it.'

To reporter M.R. Brown she confided that she regretted not having kept the claims for the private Lucky Texas syndicate, rather than handing them over to a public company like Windfall, which he interpreted as a clear hint that the drill had hit had something highly valuable. On their return to Timmins the reporters hashed over what they had heard with a group of experienced mining men. Stock speculator Nedo Bragagnolo summed up the consensus, saying that the MacMillans 'have got to have something, otherwise they will be in jail. That was the favourite remark in Timmins: "[If] they haven't got anything they are all going to jail, so they have got to have something. Better buy it [Windfall stock]."'[50]

And buy it they did. On Monday, 20 July, the price went above $5 before closing at $4.75, a new high that many traders took as further confirmation of a valuable find. Up to that point Sydney Ezrin had been one of the sceptics, accumulating a large short postion, but now he heard people saying that there must have been a mine found or else the TSE and the OSC would surely have stepped in and suspended trading; Viola MacMillan must have satisfied the authorities that she had a discovery like Texas Gulf's which she was only waiting to announce. Ezrin therefore began to acquire a long position which ultimately totalled 67,000 shares of Windfall. Allan Fidler heard rumours of the drill core showing a find that might take the stock as high as $50: 'You could mortgage your wife and buy it if you believed that. If I had seen the core, and it showed that [reported mineralization] I would have bought as much as the brokers would have allowed me to buy.'[51]

Not until Friday, 24 July, did the drill bit reach down 870 feet, far deeper than any geological consultant had recommended. George MacMillan finally called a halt, but more time was occupied in splitting the cores before he delivered twenty-seven samples to an assay laboratory in Swastika, Ontario, without any request that they be handled speedily. He also told the analyst not to try to make a verbal report to him because he had had a number of unhappy experiences with telephone calls made by assay offices. Meanwhile, Viola MacMillan made a visit to Howard Graham at the Toronto Stock Exchange, where she again complained about various brokers selling Windfall short: 'She was so distressed that she just sat and talked for about two hours. I just listened, and she went on and ... she was terribly upset. I felt sorry for her.' When her friend Doris Drewe asked, 'Why don't you stop the rumours that are going around?' Viola MacMillan replied angrily, '"I didn't start the rumours; let the people who started them stop them."' ... And she said that the brokers were playing with the stock and selling it short.' On Saturday, 25 July, George MacMillan started up a second drill hole at the Windfall site, which only added to the gossip.[52]

Following the meeting on 14 July TSE chair Marshal Stearns had departed for a summer holiday. Two weeks later, when he returned to work on Monday, 27 July, there had still been no disclosure. He and Howard Graham concluded that effective regulatory control over the company must pass from the exchange to the OSC. The two men went to see Jack Kimber the following morning and were told that the Mac-Millans did not expect to report until 1 August. Stearns advised Kimber to apply pressure. Finally it was agreed that a statement would be issued by Windfall on 30 July after receipt of the assay results. Though the *Northern Miner* was now complaining that the stalling over Windfall had become intolerable, rumours persisted that the long-awaited results would show excellent values of both zinc and copper, which helped push the price of the shares up throughout that day. Moss, Lawson and Company, for instance, put out a wire stating that the MacMillans must have terrific results to report. Finally, the Windfall board met to receive the assay results: no significant mineral values whatever in the cores. A press release was hurriedly approved.[53]

Globe and Mail reporter James Scott got word that the Windfall insiders were all at the bar in the Royal York Hotel and he rushed down to interview them. He got nothing but a litany of complaints. Both Mac-Millans denounced the TSE for not allowing them to raise more money by making an additional distribution of shares. George MacMillan claimed that the OSC was at fault for ordering the cores stored away under guard, which had 'tied his hands' until the assay results were received from the laboratory in Swastika. Viola MacMillan added, 'Imagine them trying to tell us how to do our work or how to run a mining company.' Said Scott, 'They seemed to be trying to blame the Toronto Stock Exchange and the Ontario Securities Commission for the whole situation.' In a revealing aside, however, a friend of the Mac-Millans, Queen's University geology professor J.W. Ambrose, let slip to Scott that when George MacMillan had showed him the drill core away back on 6 July, 'I knew as soon as I saw it that it was nothing to get excited about [for] copper and zinc, but I didn't know about gold and silver.'[54]

Next morning the vultures swooped. The TSE delayed the opening of trading in Windfall for thirty minutes while the Floor Procedure Committee attempted to process a flood of sell orders. Eventually, nearly 85 per cent of the 240,000 shares traded that day went for the opening price of 80 cents apiece. After exactly four weeks the Windfall wonder had become a fiasco. Angry investors demanded to know why the stock had been allowed to trade for so long without the company being compelled to disclose that it had failed to find any valuable minerals. Rumours even began to circulate that the mafia had been behind the whole scam. Mining speculator Nedo Bragagnolo was one old hand who expressed cynicism about all the fuss: '[T]he way I look at that situation, I think it was just like a big merry-go-round, and I think it was the great avarice of the public [that created it] – they had three weeks to get out of the good situation and make lots of money – there was a most beautiful stock, and you could make lots of money, and [they] had a chance to get out and didn't.'[55]

III

Immediately, demands began to be heard for a formal investigation into the entire Windfall affair. In fact, the OSC had already applied to the attorney general for an order to investigate the promotion on 30 July, the very day that the company finally announced its drilling results. Three days earlier George MacMillan and a number of brokers and journalists had received forged telegrams from New York as part of an apparent effort to manipulate share prices. In an attempt to entrap the perpetrators, no immediate announcement about this inquiry was made.[56] After the price of Windfall shares collapsed on 31 July, however, pressure began to mount for a more wide-ranging investigation. Within a fortnight Premier John Robarts ordered the creation of a royal commission into the entire subject of mining finance and the regulation of securities markets, to be headed by Mr Justice Arthur Kelly of the Ontario Supreme Court.

By that time the OSC investigators were already interviewing their first witness, George MacMillan. Within days there was a startling revelation: Viola MacMillan's lawyer, Joseph Sedgwick, announced that his client had informed him that she had lent OSC director John Campbell five thousand shares of Windfall stock. What could this mean? To date, nobody had even hinted at official corruption. OSC counsel Harry Bray, who had made a routine enquiry about whether Viola MacMillan had given or lent shares in Windfall to any other person, seemed as stunned as anyone, blurting out, 'I might say it was not the intent of my question.'[57]

This bombshell was a forceful reminder that at the time of the Wind-fall affair the Ontario Securities Commission was still struggling to reorganize. J.R. Kimber had been appointed vice-chair in the spring of 1963; he was tapped to succeed O.E. Lennox as head of the commission the following year. When he took over, appeals from rulings by the OSC chair still went to the full three-member commission. Since the chair sat on these cases at both levels, some lawyers argued that the process violated the principle of natural justice. One lawyer even alleged that Lennox had disqualified himself from sitting on certain appeals because he was so convinced that his original findings had been correct that he was unable to review them impartially. In 1962 W. Glen How launched two suits against the commission in which he claimed that his clients had suffered as a result of these regulatory practices, apparently the first recorded effort to sue a securities regulator for damages.[58]

Defending these suits was made more difficult because a judge of the Alberta Supreme Court had recently invalidated similar procedures, holding that the chair of that province's Securities Commission lacked express authority to sit on a panel reconsidering his own findings. This decision had not been appealed, which made it likely that an Ontario court would view the precedent sympathetically. When Frederick Cass succeeded Kelso Roberts as attorney general of Ontario in October 1962, he decided that eliminating this apparent conflict of interest should have a high priority. As a result, the Securities Act was amended in 1963 to create the new position of director of the OSC, responsible for day-to-day administration and the initial decisions about registrations and cancellations. The full commission would be free to hear appeals and make policy. Not only would this change end criticisms of current procedures, but it permit more efficient handling of applications, registrations, and complaints.[59] The new appointee was a civil-service outsider, John Campbell, who had risen to a vice-presidency at the Hawker-Siddeley aircraft company. Taking over as director in November 1963, Campbell, who had legal training, set to work to clear up the backlog of applications from licence seekers and rejected registrants. First impressions were favourable. In January 1964 the attorney general expressed his pleasure that Campbell was off to a good start, a view echoed a few weeks later by Deputy Attorney General W.B. Common, who minuted on one of the director's decisions, 'He sounds thorough.'[60]

When Campbell joined the commission, he told his wife to sell all her stocks, and she did so despite incurring some losses. In April 1964 Violet Campbell was introduced to Viola MacMillan, who suggested that she buy some Windfall shares. She did so without informing her husband, but when the price declined, Violet Campbell admitted what she had done and the shares were sold at a loss of $2,000. On Thursday, 9 July, the Campbells joined the MacMillans for drinks at the Royal York Hotel. Violet Campbell became convinced that the MacMillans were over-optimistic about Windfall, and the following morning she telephoned her broker and sold 2,000 shares short at $3.25. By the time trading closed that afternoon at $4.00, Violet Campbell had already incurred a sizeable loss.[61]

When his wife confessed, John Campbell was furious, saying that something must be done at once. Violet Campbell was a silent partner in a popular Toronto restaurant but was not able to liquidate this investment, and the Campbells already had a sizeable overdraft on their joint bank account. He had taken a pay cut from $18,000 to $14,500 when he moved into the public service. To finance the construction of a pleasure boat they had pledged their automobile as security for a loan of $1,000, even though there were bills for more than that amount outstanding on their charge accounts at local department and jewellry stores.[62]

When John Campbell visited the MacMillans' country place on Saturday, 11 July, to discuss the TSE's demands that Windfall make immediate disclosure, he explained his personal predicament to Viola MacMillan and asked if she could help him cover his wife's ill-advised short sale. He received no response, but on Sunday Campbell met again for drinks with the MacMillans and asked Viola to lend him 5,000 Windfall shares, saying that they would be returned within a few days. As any well-prepared mining promoter might have done, she simply rummaged in her purse and handed him a 'street' certificate for the stock.[63]

Campbell had violated no OSC rules, because the commission lacked any formal code of conduct governing investments by its employees. When Jack Kimber was appointed to the OSC, he wrote to the deputy attorney general to report that O.E. Lennox had held some blue-chip stocks listed on the TSE, but because the OSC sometimes received advance information, he had been careful about the securities he invested in. Said Kimber, 'I think there would be no doubt that trading in any speculative issues should not take place. I might say that this is going to be a blow to my wife, who is always hopeful of making her fortune in some penny stock.' W.B. Common told his superiors that he couldn't see any problem with blue-chip investments, since such companies 'would have relatively no control by the Commission.' There the matter rested for the next six months, until Attorney General Frederick Cass finally raised it with Premier Robarts and reported to Kimber that he was concerned that problems could arise even with blue-chip investments. Yet Cass merely passed along Robarts's views to Kimber privately, and no formal rules were imposed.[64]

Because regulatory responsibility for listed stocks rested almost entirely in the hands of the TSE, it seemed most unlikely that the OSC would be directly involved with Windfall until Campbell projected himself into the affair at the very time that his wife decided to short its shares. On Monday, 13 July, he deposited the 5,000 shares that Viola MacMillan had lent him with his brokers, Tom and Barnt, with instructions to hold onto the actual certificate so that it could be returned to her in due course. He immediately instructed the broker to sell 1,000 of these Windfall shares into the still-rising market. The losses on his wife's short sale had already reached about $1,500, and Campbell apparently hoped that he would later be able to recoup some of his losses by buying the stock back at a lower price to return to Viola Mac-Millan.

Campbell was not present at the meeting on 14 August, where the MacMillans stonewalled successfully until granted a 'reasonable time' to finish drilling and conduct assays before the made any disclosure. Meanwhile, he continued to try to solve his private problems by selling 2,000 more of the borrowed Windfall shares on Wednesday, 15 July. On 22 July he disposed of another 3,000 shares of the still-rising stock for $4.50, making total sales of 6,000 shares over a ten-day period, by which time the losses on his wife's original short sale had reached $2,800.[65]

The Campbells continued to quarrel bitterly over her rash act. In his desperation John Campbell borrowed another 1,000 shares from his own broker, Tom and Barnt, which were also sold. He explained, 'We seemed to be going deeper in the hole on Windfall because the thing kept going up, and I just figured I had to keep going the way I was going and that was about it.' If the assay results were as good as rumours had it, then 'I was dead.' By late July, however, he had concluded that even Viola MacMillan did not expect very favourable results, though she still believed Windfall had an ore body which might be hit by drilling from a different angle. Campbell hoped that share prices would dip sharply, so that he could buy in, leaving him able to cover his short position with a large enough profit to buy 5,000 shares in order to retrieve the certificate and return it to the MacMillans.[66]

When the assay results revealing no commercial values were finally released on 30 July, Campbell was as dumbfounded as everyone else, having by then convinced himself that there must be a find which would justify a share price of at least $2.50. Neverthless, he was quick to take advantage of the sudden nosedive in Windfall share prices: on 31 July he ordered broker J.W. Gemmell to buy 3,000 shares at 70 cents apiece and Tom and Barnt to purchase 2,000 more shares. He exchanged his purchase for the original, borrowed, 5,000-share certificate and handed it back to Viola MacMillan on 6 August. By that time Campbell was in a most unhappy state: 'I was very confused at the time. I was drinking too much, I was fighting with my wife, and ... I just wasn't thinking straight. Let's face it.' Nevertheless, he was able to calculate that the collapse in the price of Windfall had left him with an overall profit of $29,145 on the transaction.[67]

When the attorney general learned what had happened, Campbell was immediately suspended. Interviewed by commission investigators during September, he insisted he had done nothing wrong. By arguing with Howard Graham that the TSE should not suspend trading in Windfall, he had been trying to protect the interests of all the shareholders. Had the exchange gone ahead with its plans for a suspension on 13 July, the price of the shares would almost certainly have fallen to somewhere between 50 cents and $1.00 immediately, allowing the Campbells a quick escape from their predicament with a sizeable profit. After Viola MacMillan lent him the 5,000 shares, he had still advised her that she must come to terms with the exchange, even though that might mean that his wife would suffer losses in unwinding her short position.[68]

When Mr Justice Arthur Kelly came to pronounce upon John Campbell's conduct in his royal commission report, however, he was unsparing. Campbell's involvement had originated because he thought that the TSE was being too demanding of the MacMillans, but this opinion stemmed from the misguided view that a listed company's directors had discretion to decide how much disclosure should be made. As a result, Campbell had interfered in a matter in which the OSC had no need to be involved, since there was no suggestion that the exchange board was acting improperly. Because of his personal friendship with the MacMillans, Campbell had insisted upon pursuing the matter, even to the point of insulting Howard Graham and undermining the friendly relationship between the exchange and the commission. Fortunately, Jack Kimber's return from holidays had averted any further damage and restored cooperation between the two bodies. Even more seriously, though, Campbell had borrowed 5,000 shares from Windfall's promoter (along with another 1,000 from his own broker) and traded them during a period when he was concerned with the company in his official capacity. All in all, said Kelly, John Campbell, had displayed a 'lamentable lack of any appreciation of his duties and responsibilities.'[69]

Although Campbell's misconduct did not become a matter of public knowledge at once, the senior staff at the OSC was hastily reorganized. Campbell's resignation was accepted near the end of September 1964. Harry Bray, who had joined the commission's legal staff in 1951, was tapped to take the director's job.[70] Campbell was ultimately charged with breach of trust but acquitted at his trial in 1967. This decision was appealed, and the Supreme Court of Canada eventually agreed there should be another trial, but this was never proceeded with.[71]

While the Campbell affair was unfolding, Mr Justice Kelly busied himself in rounding up staff for his royal commission, recruiting Patrick Hartt (who had once had the notorious stock promoter Samuel Ciglen as a client) as chief counsel. Advertisements solicited representations from interested parties. Eight hundred people who had invested in Windfall shares (half being gainers, half losers) were sent questionnaires, nearly 80 per cent of which were returned and analysed. In an unusual arrangement, the OSC investigation continued in parallel with the royal commission, taking private testimony under oath from all the leading participants in the affair. This evidence was collected over the next eleven months and frequently referred to when the key individuals repeated their stories in public. Between February and June 1965 there were forty-four days of public hearings conducted by Kelly, at which 144 witnesses testified.[72]

Naturally, the conduct of the MacMillans was the central focus of the inquiry. Could George MacMillan simply have made a mistake by believing that the drill cores contained valuable minerals when he stopped the drilling on Saturday, 4 July, and set off the entire chain of events? Kenneth Darke, who had overseen the work at K55-1, pointed out that if the core was dirty or greasy, it only had to be cleaned off with a solvent, and even gasoline would do. Then any knowledgeable person should be able to assess the copper content within half of 1 per cent and make a pretty good guess as to the amount of zinc present. Though not a trained geologist, George MacMillan was a seasoned mining man who had handled lots of copper and zinc from the Kamkotia ore body and would definitely have recognized if there had been similar heavy mineralization. When shown a sample of the Windfall core, M.H. Frohberg, the OSC's consulting geologist, said that if a client had sent it to him, one look would have told him there were negligible levels of copper or zinc. Dr B.S.W. Buffam was equally categorical: 'I could tell visually that there were no economic amounts of either [copper or zinc] ... minerals in the core, and couldn't tell whether there was gold present.' He added that it was normally possible to feel silver by rubbing the core carefully. After seeing the samples, another geologist, Fenton Scott, said, 'There is nothing in the core that I saw here which led me to expect that there was a mine in the immediate vicinity.' Nobody would make a fuss about the samples as they were 'obviously barren' and 'not worth a hoot.'[73]

MacMillan never did supply a convincing reason for stopping the work. Six weeks later all he would tell OSC lawyer Harry Bray was 'I just didn't want anybody to look at that core.' Bray: 'No particular reason, that is just how you felt: is that right?' MacMillan: 'That is right.' In the end he had to concede that he had not seen any evidence of zinc, copper, silver, or gold, though he continued to insist that only an assay could definitively establish the presence of the precious metals. All he would say was that the drill had penetrated just a few inches into a promising stratum that looked just like what Texas Gulf Sulphur had found. Though no commercial values were showing, he had decided to cease drilling and say nothing because 'if I had announced that no ore had been found and then drilled deeper and found something, which in my estimation at the time I have a fifty-fifty chance of doing, the roof would have fallen in on me. I would probably have been shot, because they would have said that I knew all the time that I had ore.'

Moreover, the mineral structure seemed to be trending northward onto lands owned by somebody else, 'and if we were to find an orebody and it would dip onto his property, it was obvious that we should have [control of] his ground before we knew too much about our ground as to whether we had an orebody or not.' Trying to acquire additional property without disclosing knowledge about a valuable mineral deposit could open the way for lawsuits. Better to stop working for the time being, remove the cores from the site to foil snoopers,

and do nothing about the routine business of splitting them and ordering an assay until the entire drill hole was completed. Finally, Mac-
Millan remarked cryptically that 'it is very simple not [sic] to find an
orebody when you have got one, even close to you – and when should
you, and what should you, tell your shareholders as this work kept
going?'[74]

OSC investigators soon uncovered some damning evidence. On the
morning of Monday, 6 July, George MacMillan had delivered two samples from the cores to the Technical Services Laboratory in Toronto, and
later that same day the assayers had reported negative results to Viola
MacMillan by telephone. Moreover, the MacMillans had summoned
Dr J.W. Ambrose, a geology professor from Queen's University, to their
home on the Sunday. After looking at the cores in the trunk of the Mac-
Millan car, Ambrose said that he could see no signs of valuable minerals, though he agreed to take away some pieces of the rock when he left
the next morning. After further analysis he still could find nothing, but
his attempts to communicate this news to George MacMillan by telephone on Wednesday, 8 July, were unsuccessful; Ambrose's calls were
not returned. Commission counsel Patrick Hartt nailed the situation
down: 'I put it to you, Dr. Ambrose, that at least by July 9th you had
formed the opinion ... that ... there were no commercial values of copper, zinc or silver in the Windfall core.' Ambrose: 'That is correct.'[75]

After listening to the evidence, Mr Justice Kelly was in no doubt. In
his report, delivered in September 1965, he concluded that what he had
heard from the MacMillans was a lot of guff. First, he punctured the
notion that a promising find had been concealed because of a desire to
acquire adjacent claims before their price increased. No negotiations
for these lands had ever been actively pursued, and in any case the
assay results would have reduced rather than raised the cost of the
lands, so such a suggestion need not be taken seriously. As an experienced prospector, MacMillan could readily have detected any copper
and zinc in the cores, and the lack of mineralization had been confirmed by Dr Ambrose as early as 6 July. '[T]he continued absence of
any categorical denial that the core had commercial minerals, despite
the release of statements by the Windfall company that assays had not
been made, was bound to reinforce the belief that a factual foundation
for the rumours existed. People having only a perfunctory knowledge
of mining and geology were aware that commercial values were accurately predictable within reasonable limits by visual examination.' 'It is
impossible to accept as a fact,' wrote Kelly, 'that George MacMillan

was unaware of the lack of value of the core,' so the press release he composed on 7 July was 'deliberately misleading.'

When asked about her own conversations with Ambrose, who had spent the night of 5–6 July at her home, Viola MacMillan claimed that she could not remember asking his opinion about whether or not the cores from Timmins contained signs of valuable minerals. She even pretended that she did not know that Ambrose was taking some samples back to his laboratory in Kingston for further study. Of a long-distance telephone call lasting eight minutes from the MacMillan home to Ambrose in Kingston on 14 July, Viola MacMillan denied all recollection. Kelly concluded that if she remained ignorant of the lack of mineralization, it was only by her own choice. Yet at the meeting at the OSC that same day both she and her husband had done their best to create the impression that something had been found and that drilling needed to be 'completed' before an announcement was made.[76]

The MacMillans even refused to concede that the failure to release information had been connected in any way to the sudden rise in the stock price.[77] Nobody could say whether they had deliberately started the rumours, but there was no doubt that they stood to gain substantially from their spread: 'Throughout, all their conduct was such as to heighten the element of suspense and promote a belief in the rumours.' Kelly explained,

> The urge to distribute the underwritten and optioned stock made it undesirable that any positive statement as to the actual value be made while the distribution was going on. To complete the sales of the Windfall company shares under option, and to avoid the waste of the period of market grooming which had preceded 6th July, it was necessary that the public be kept unaware of the negative results of the drilling ... [T]he conclusion cannot be avoided that the uncertainty as to the truth or falsity of the rumours was deliberately allowed to continue, and the elaborate security measures and the emphasis on the absence of assays were employed to perpetuate the belief that there was some factual basis for these rumours: the evasion of the issue of what was in the core gave support to the belief that the rumours were not pure fiction.[78]

Moreover, sales had been handled in ways that maximized the profits to the MacMillans personally. The Windfall shares were traded through a number of different personal and corporate brokerage accounts. Eric Watson, the head floor trader at Moss, Lawson, testified that Viola MacMillan had telephoned him buy or sell orders without indicating which account was to be credited or debited; only at the end of the trading day would that be sorted out. On 6 July sales of 169,500 shares at prices between $1.01 and $2 were allocated so that the proceeds from the higher-priced sales went to the accounts entirely controlled by the MacMillans, while the lower-priced shares were taken from companies that had substantial minority shareholdings.[79]

There were many advantages to one person directing such a large selling operation. Donald Lawson complained that Viola MacMillan had tried to control every aspect of the distribution. In a rising market most promoters simply wanted to get rid of their stock as fast as possible, but if somebody bid for 5,000 Windfall shares, his traders were supposed to consult her before accepting, even though that might mean that the order went elsewhere. She would never agree to allow the brokers to sell a block as large as 50,000 shares within a 10–cent price range. More important still, she might intervene to turn things around with strategic trades at times when the price seemed to be slipping. For instance, on 10 July Viola MacMillan had traded 244,000 shares between the various companies she controlled, even though her brokers pointed out that they could have been shifted privately just as well at a saving of $3,600 in commissions. She, however, insisted that the shares be handled on the floor, and when they were recorded on the tickertape, prices had suddenly leapt upward. Said Kelly, 'The arrangement can be looked at as nothing other than a skilfully managed piece of manipulation.'[80]

The same solicitude for the MacMillans' personal interests was evident in the handling of short sales. When one person controlled two or more companies that might profit from the sale of shares, payment of income taxes could be deferred if the size of the profit could only be calculated once shares were purchased to cover a short position. For instance, if Golden Shaft Mines bought and then sold shares, any profit would be taxable, but if MacMillan Prospecting made the sale and borrowed the shares from Golden Shaft to make delivery, there would be no taxable income for either company until MacMillan Prospecting was required to buy shares to return those borrowed. Only in August, after the price of Windfall stock had collapsed back to 73 cents, were the short positions unwound. By using such methods, the MacMillans were able to retain as working capital thousands of dollars that would otherwise have gone immediately to pay taxes.[81]

In addition, Viola MacMillan conducted the affairs of Windfall

Mines solely in her personal interest, even though she was neither an officer nor a director of the company. The members of the board were merely fronts who were not advised or consulted as to what was going on. Marjorie Humphrey, one of the directors, met Viola MacMillan on Monday, 6 July, the day that the rapid price rise began, but recalled that she had refused to say what had been found by the drill. Commission counsel Patrick Hartt remarked acerbically, 'Let's take the board of directors: they are there presumably to protect the shareholders ... What do we have here? We have the MacMillans and we have three nominees of the MacMillans. To start with, the whole concept of protection is gone. It doesn't function. Viola MacMillan calls the shot – [she's] not even a director. A fellow named Mills, one of the directors, he owns a farm [and] he works for them parttime. He doesn't do anything. Was at a meeting [but] doesn't recall what took place. He is a dummy director, but he was smart enough to buy some stock at the right time and sell it at the right time to make money.' In his report Kelly complained that the failure of the MacMillans to inform the board about what was going on 'offends every element of company law' and demonstrated the degree to which they regarded all of their companies as personal ventures to be conducted entirely as they saw fit.[82]

Kelly was also called upon to pronounce on the roles played by both the OSC and the TSE. About the commission he did not have a great deal to say. Exchange-listed stocks were outside its regulatory ambit, and the OSC had only become involved as a result of Campbell's initiative. In calling the meeting on 14 July, said Kelly, Jack Kimber might have acted unwisely, but he did so because of his wish to repair the rift created by Campbell's quarrel with Howard Graham. His desire to help out was understandable, even if the statement released by the OSC that the MacMillans would be permitted a 'reasonable time' to complete their drilling program only strengthened the belief that there had been a genuine find.[83]

The real problem had been the failure of the TSE to intervene more decisively. First of all, there was the comparative laxity of its rules and their enforcement. Resource companies were accorded special treatment: only the issued shares of industrials were approved for trading, while all of the authorized shares of mines were treated as though listed. Permission to undertake a primary distribution of additional shares was easy to come by, since it was granted simply on the strength of an engineer's recommendation for further work. Many listed mining companies found no commercial ore bodies, but this situation did not result in delisting; even after being suspended, dormant companies could resume trading by meeting conditions less arduous than starting from scratch. Shell companies could easily secure approval to resume primary distribution of unissued treasuty shares merely by filing a statement with the exchange concerning material changes. Operators such as the MacMillans frequently made use of these shells as vehicles for new promotions, and if they owned sizeable blocks of stock, they might dispose of them with no benefit to the company treasury. The exchange's underwriting and option rules were supposed to limit promotional profits, but during July 1964 the MacMillans had sold 953,100 Windfall shares in all, netting the corporate treasury only $490,000, while they and other insiders got another $1 million.[84]

The Toronto Stock Exchange was supposed to provide a free, continuous auction market to which all investors had equal access. Yet Kelly pointed out that at least 15 per cent of the TSE's floor traders had arrangements that granted them a share in the profits from their dealing, and one-third of the first 400,000 shares of Windfall that changed hands on Monday, 6 July, had been for the private accounts of brokers or their firms. Indeed, the extent of the own-account trading that went on during July 1964 was such as to create the impression that the TSE was not there to serve the public but 'for the personal convenience and profit of some of the persons associated with it.' Many brokers seemed to treat the exchange as 'a private gaming club maintained for their own benefit,' with insiders paying only one-fifth the commissions charged to others. Indeed, a study ordered by the exchange board the previous January showed that thirty-three members had partners or directors with minority interests worth less than $5,000 (twenty-four of whose interests were worth under $1,000), all of whom qualified for reduced commissions on their own trades.[85] Although the tickertape recorded prices and volume, there was nothing to indicate the extent of the in-and-out positions betting upon short-term market movements. Apologists for the exchange might try to defend this trading as increasing liquidity and price stability, but that was not its purpose (even if it did work that way sometimes), so that it could not be justified solely on such grounds. To investors a TSE listing was a stamp of approval, a guarantee of the soundness of a company, and the trading in its securities was seen as a true reflection of the supply and demand for the shares. Though the TSE's listing requirements for industrials seemed sound enough, speculative mines had been allowed to trade even when such activity might operate to the detriment of shareholders and other investors.

The rules had been tightened somewhat early in 1964, but once a listing was granted, companies that failed to discover a commercial ore body were still permitted to continue trading their stock for up to a year before the TSE imposed a suspension (followed by delisting after another year of inactivity). Pressure was strong not to raise the standards for speculative companies any higher, since in the past year alone, Montreal's Canadian Stock Exchange had granted nearly three dozen new listings to mines that could not meet TSE requirements.[86]

What responsibility did the Toronto Stock Exchange have when rumours began to fly? Once the stories were clearly affecting share prices, said Mr Justice Kelly, the governors were 'perfectly justified' in demanding disclosure. John Campbell had tried to argue that Windfall was in the same position as Texas Gulf Sulphur would have been if compelled to release the drilling results from K55-1 near the end of 1963. Kelly pointed out that the two situations were quite different: '[Where] somebody like Texas Gulf have [sic] a valuable find ... it was essential to the development of their find that they keep quiet until they got more property. I don't think anybody was hurt market-wise on that at all. Again, if Windfall had started out and said that they were going to drill and reported no results from any hole, no person would have been hurt market-wise ... A good indication as to whether notice should have been given right away depends on whether it is withheld for the purpose of the market or withheld for the purpose of the promoter.'

Lack of disclosure meant that trading in Windfall was driven almost entirely by rumour. Stock markets, of course, were always fuelled by gossip. In the absence of any definite information, members of the brokerage community could only pass along each new tale from Timmins, adding details and making the rumours more persuasive in the process. The longer the affair dragged on, the more convincing the stories came to seem. Some people had been highly critical of the press for its role in sustaining the furor. Kelly noted that the newspapers could hardly be expected to ignore the stories that were driving markets; nor could they be faulted for the fact that as more and more attention focused upon the company, the news reached less and less sophisticated readers, unfamiliar even with day-to-day financial reporting, which helped to draw in other share buyers.[87]

Many investors had suffered losses as a result of the MacMillans' refusal to admit that trading in Windfall shares was taking place on the basis of misinformation. The TSE governors should have acted much sooner than they did in insisting that the company issue a satisfactory release or face suspension from trading. The acceptance by the TSE and the OSC of a further temporizing statement had only served to reinforce the credibility of the rumours, and the refusal by the MacMillans to provide any more information for another two weeks made matters worse.[88]

IV

The royal commission was not directly charged with answering the most intriguing question about the Windfall affair: why had George and Viola MacMillan behaved as they did? Many people professed amazement that the woman who had been president of the Prospectors and Developers Association during the previous twenty years should have acted improperly.[89] Donald Lawson said he had readily agreed to act as underwriter for the MacMillans because they seemed highly reputable. Asked why he had purchased 5,000 Windfall shares on 9 July, broker-dealer Hugh Borthwick said, 'I ... started work in 1929 ... I have had a lot of experience watching tapes, and I kind of like the market action ... I didn't go by the rumours. Knowing the MacMillans, I figured they were honourable people, that is why I bought the stock, and the property being close, just north and slightly east of Texas Gulf.'[90]

Of course, some people insisted that they had always had their doubts about the couple. Albert Applegath, a customers' man at G.W. Nicholson and Company, was asked if he had ever tried to consult the MacMillans about Windfall. 'No, there would be no point discussing anything with these two people. They have, to my knowledge, never, on any occasion, told the truth to anybody in our industry ... This is a feeling prevailing on the 'street' for over twenty years.' All along the two of them 'have functioned in an area with brainless mystery being the most important factor of their operation.' When James Scott of the *Globe and Mail* was asked if he had ever been able to get any clear answer from either of the MacMillans about why disclosure had been delayed so long, he replied, 'Not really. You very seldom get a satisfactory answer from either George MacMillan or Viola – really not a satisfactory explanation, anyway.'[91]

Even those more kindly disposed admitted that dealing with Viola

MacMillan could be a chore. Throughout the inquiry people brought up her tendency to talk incessantly. When somebody remarked to John Campbell that she had once talked to Viola MacMillan during a train ride, he replied, 'You don't talk to Mrs MacMillan – you listen.' During the spring and summer of 1964 she seemed to be in a particularly agitated state. Broker Donald Lawson recalled that the dispute with the Toronto Stock Exchange even seemed to be affecting her marriage: Viola MacMillan 'was in such a state over this thing, so determined, that she was talking in terms of [how] this could result in the breaking up of the two of them.' She felt, Lawson observed, that in light of her record she ought to receive preferential treatment from the Toronto Stock Exchange: 'Well, she was the darling of Timmins.'[92]

Lawson was not the only person to comment upon Viola Mac-Millan's conviction that she was owed special handling. In April 1964 OSC lawyer C.J. Meinhardt reported on her proposal that members of the Prospectors and Developers Association be allowed to sell units in prospecting syndicates directly to the public. Who would regulate these activities, she was asked? In Meinhardt's words, 'On the tenor of the comments made by Mrs MacMillan it appears that the prospector and the Prospectors and Developers Association consists [sic] of special type of people who should be above the control, and who must be left alone in order to succeed.'[93]

The conduct of the inquiry did raise questions about how the Mac-Millans' legal rights ought to be protected. Both of them were compelled to testify in private before the OSC investigation, though they were allowed the advice of counsel.[94] When George MacMillan first told his story in August 1964, he displayed terrible forgetfulness about events just one month earlier. Then Viola MacMillan supplied her version of events. Forced by Harry Bray to admit that she had said, 'Everybody knows we hit it,' at the meeting at the OSC, she could only make the feeble claim that she hadn't really meant to suggest that Windfall had made a valuable discovery.[95]

Before the royal commission began its hearings, Mr Justice Kelly announced that all the questioning of witnesses would be done by commission counsel Patrick Hartt, but that if any allegations were made about illegal conduct, the parties concerned might request a witness to be examined about a specific issue or demand a cross-examination. In mid-March 1965, at the suggestion of their lawyer, Joseph Sedgwick, both George and Viola MacMillan made statements before the commission, but Hartt did not ask them any questions. On

29 March, when Richard Pearce of the *Northern Miner* testified, Sedgwick demanded the right to cross-examine on the grounds that he did not wish to have his questions put by the commission counsel. Kelly ruled that Sedgwick did not have the right to conduct the interrogation but must allow Hartt to do the questioning. The lawyer rejected this proposal, insisting that he should handle the examination himself, and at the same time he asked to be provided with transcripts for anyone who had given evidence to the OSC in order to prepare for their cross-examination before the commission. When the judge would not agree, Sedgwick asked the Ontario Court of Appeal to pronounce upon whether or not Kelly's ruling was correct. Within a week the court approved the judge's conduct to date, though it declined to rule upon any future eventuality.[96]

Six weeks later both the MacMillans were recalled by the commission to be examined by Sedgwick. His questioning of George MacMillan revealed little that was not already known, as the promoter tried his best to pass himself off as a bluff, hearty mining man, getting on with the dirty but necessary job of developing the country's natural resources. When asked why he had said to James Scott of the *Globe and Mail*, 'If you want to be poor all your life, don't buy Windfall,' MacMillan claimed he had only been joking. Sedgwick attempted to float the red herring that trading by the house accounts of TSE members had been the cause of all the gyrations of the market in Windfall. By then Kelly had had enough; he squelched this line of interrogation, remarking that he would like to wind up the affairs of the commission before it came time for him to retire from the bench.[97]

Viola MacMillan did not make a good impression when she testified. In answer to questions from Sedgwick, she put forward a number of implausible explanations. She had been as surprised as anybody when Windfall stock started to rise sharply and had felt that 'there should have been more stock go in the market to hold it from going up, but at that time I didn't know there was [*sic*] big pools operating. I had no idea there was such big pools operating, and whether they were pools or what. I didn't know what was going on.' Only later did she figure out that the rise had been orchestrated by large traders on the Toronto Stock Exchange, forcing her to exercise all the outstanding options and pay more than $490,000 into the company treasury. Her aim, she claimed, had been to keep the price down and sell more treasury stock to raise money for exploration, rather than see the profits go to these mysterious manipulators. Asked if she herself had not been responsible for the market action by hinting to various people that favourable assay results were on the way, she could only reply, 'I can't recall what was happening because that week, in fact that whole month, was a nightmare to me. I didn't know what was happening.'[98]

Under cross-examination by Patrick Hartt, Viola MacMillan was vague, forgetful, and unconvincing. When he asked her to explain exactly what George MacMillan had said to her about a certain matter, Joseph Sedgwick objected on the grounds that this evidence was hearsay. Mr Justice Kelly finally intervened: 'You must admit, Mr Sedgwick, that it is very difficult to come to a conclusion from many of the answers.' Sedgwick: 'I must agree. I have had my own troubles.' In fact, the answer most frequently proffered by Viola MacMillan to Hartt was 'I am sorry.' Sedgwick was eventually moved to remark, 'Don't keep saying that. Just be sorry once.' She was able to recall that at a gathering in the bar of the Royal York Hotel on 9 July, with Scott of the *Globe and Mail* and John and Violet Campbell, they had sat at a large round table, but since she was opposite her husband, she could not hear what he was saying because of the noise. Kelly observed acidly, 'This is one of the few areas [discussed] today in which you have had an accurate memory for details.'[99]

Skilled counsel that he was, Joseph Sedgwick tried to put the best face possible upon the MacMillans' conduct in a final summation that concluded the commission's hearings. The couple, he said, were highly respected promoters, and with Timmins 'athrob and aglow' following Texas Gulf's announcement in the spring of 1964, everyone naturally paid the closest attention to what they were up to. When orders for Windfall stock began to pour into brokerage offices from northern Ontario, the TSE decided on 6 July to increase the opening price of the stock by more than 40 cents over the previous close, adding 'tinder' to the gasoline. Viola MacMillan had released stock in an effort to maintain an orderly market, but many of the shares were snapped up by insiders on the exchange floor for their own profit. She did take down and sell all 800,000 shares under option, and was willing to sell another 225,000 shares into the market, but exchange officials refused to allow her to do so. What were the MacMillans supposed to do about rumours floated by others when neither the TSE nor the OSC proved able to quell this wave of speculation? Even if they had sold all 1,700,000 shares of Windfall in their hands, they probably could not have dampened the speculative surge and would simply have lost control of their promotion. This couple, he concluded, were 'honest, hard-working people of humble origins, who had striven all their lives to make a contribution to the Canadian economy.'[100]

Why did they act as they did? In the case of George MacMillan, it seems likely that he stopped the drilling on Saturday, 4 July, because he became convinced that he was encountering the same kind of rock as that in which Texas Gulf had made its fabulous find nearby. The very act of stopping work proved quite enough to uncork a flood of rumours that washed over northern Ontario within the next twenty-four hours, then spilled onto the floor of the Toronto Stock Exchange. Once share prices shot upward, it became harder and harder to go back, even though the geologist Ambrose had told MacMillan on Sunday afternoon that he could see no signs of valuable minerals in the core, a fact confirmed by an assay in Toronto the following day. But perhaps the drill bit was just about to enter the pay zone. If, as Mac-Millan said, he felt that he had a fifty-fifty chance of making a big strike, there was no hurry. Arthur White, a leading member of the Broker Dealers Association, once explained to the OSC's Campbell that timing was all-important: 'I am sure, if you consult your professional engineers, they will confirm that fact that one drill hole can change the destiny of a prospect, a new mine or even an old has-been mine.'[101] Now was the time to take advantage of the market action, let the rumours sell the stock, and fill the company treasury (not to speak of his personal bank account). Later on, work could be resumed at a more leisurely pace.

In some ways Viola MacMillan's conduct was even harder to explain. She might have shared her husband's initial optimism, but by Monday, 6 July, she too knew that the drill cores contained nothing of value, both from Professor Ambrose's remarks and from the report of the Toronto assayers on the small samples dispatched to them. Yet the market upsurge meant that the optioned stock was flying out the door, putting almost $500,000 into Windfall's treasury for future exploration during a single day of trading. And the increasing spread between the option prices (which averaged 53 cents) and the current market price meant that she and her husband personally benefited to the tune of $1 million. Still, as the one in charge of trading, she made no move to dispose of their personal holdings of Windfall shares, having almost 900,000 of them in the end as she had at the beginning. Why not try to push these out onto the market too at such a favourable moment, even if it meant depressing prices somewhat? The answer, it seems, is that Viola MacMillan wanted above all to believe she had a major mine, as rich and significant as Texas Gulf's discovery. And therefore she didn't want to dispose of the control block in the company, as her regret about not putting the property into the privately controlled Lucky Texas syndicate indicated. The money was important, but it wasn't as important as securing a place in Canadian mining history as the independent promoter who had brought out the biggest find in northern Ontario in years.

Rather than a cynical deceiver, she seems to have become an irrational convert who could throw her arms around one of the members of the drilling crew and thank him for finding her a mine. When lawyer Thomas Cole, Windfall's corporate secretary, talked with her on Friday, 10 July, she complained about having to sell so many shares obtained for between 40 and 70 cents apiece at prices like $1.80. Why was that a 'tremendous hardship,' Cole was asked? He could only recount his own response: '"You are making money. Why do you worry?" But this is not the way it is with the MacMillans; they are more interested in the mine ... I don't think the money aspect had that much appeal.' Her underwriter, Donald Lawson, had a feeling that Viola MacMillan was not really listening to him when he discussed how they might extend the financing agreement to raise more funds for the company: 'Nowhere in any later conversations did I ever feel I was making any impression. She had her mind made up and focussed on a certain idea, and it was like talking to a wall beyond that.'[102]

That wall seemed impenetrable. Early on, Viola MacMillan convinced herself that the members of the Toronto Stock Exchange were determined to do her in and prevent her from attaining her ambition. First of all, there was the refusal to allow her to grant herself twice as much money as she had had to pay the prospectors for the Windfall claims. She became convinced of the malice of the exchange governors. Then, when the share price zoomed upward in July, she got it into her head that in addition to profiting from trading for their own accounts, various pools of brokers were either trying to short the stock or else to buy up blocks as part of a takeover scheme. To Cole she complained at the end of the first week of hectic trading that 'all the sales she had made in the last day or so were directed to slowing up the price rise. She could see an attempt to force the sale ... and take the company away from her.'[103] The distribution of the treasury shares of Windfall orchestrated by Viola MacMillan had virtually ended by 14 July, and she sold little of her own stock during the next fortnight.

She seems by then to have been in a highly overwrought state as a result of her hopes for the mine and the stress of the promotion, intensified by the knowledge that for the time being the rising share price rested upon false rumours about the contents of the drill cores which she had to prop up with tantalizing hints. Jack Kimber later told an enquiring journalist about the meeting at the OSC on 14 July 'that while Mrs MacMillan did not say so in as many words, she gave the impression by her gestures and by what she said that she had core containing very high values. He said that one of the difficulties during the meeting was in following Mrs MacMillan, who jumped from subject to subject and it was almost impossible to communicate intelligently with her.' Of his two-hour automobile ride with the MacMillans out to the drill site on 19 July, Graham Ackerly of the *Northern Miner* recollected that, 'it was one of the weirdest conversations I have had in my life. I cannot give you an accurate description of it because the woman was on the verge of being hysterical, and she talked constantly. She was evasive and wouldn't answer questions.' Viola MacMillan herself realized that her behaviour during this period had been somewhat bizarre, for she told the royal commission, 'I am afraid that period between the sixth [of July] and right through until the end of November I wasn't too well, too good. I am sorry.' In the spring of 1965 she still appeared to retain the conviction that she and her husband had been on the brink of a big strike: 'If we had been lucky and found an orebody there, it would have been nothing. And I am not so sure when we get settled down and [have] had some time to ... do some honest-to-God work on that ground, and with some new theories, there may be something worthwhile yet. In my opinion, they [*sic*] are not ruled out at all.'[104]

So Viola MacMillan either believed or wanted very much to believe that she and her husband had been on the verge of a major discovery. In answer to her lawyer, Joseph Sedgwick, she insisted, 'We were not interested in making a market play; ... now it looks as if it was the intent to do ... this, but I assure you it was not ... To find a mine ... That is our history. No other thing in mind.'[105] George MacMillan seems to have shared this ambition (though he was a good deal more reticent about it): if he went on drilling deeper on the Windfall site, he was going to hit a deposit like that found by Texas Gulf. Once the stock price took off on 6 July, both of them succumbed to the temptation to say what was necessary to help distribute the optioned stock and coincidentally enrich themselves. After all, a bit of boasting and even the odd outright lie were hardly new to the history of mining promotion in

Canada, and the funds could easily be put to good use if the MacMillans were to bring a major mine into production.

Once the merry-go-round had started, however, it became increasingly difficult to get off. To admit that all the geologists and the assay results were negative about the first six hundred feet of drill cores would guarantee a sharp drop in the price of Windfall shares. At first Viola MacMillan resorted to obfuscation, then to straight-out lies. By Tuesday, 14 July, she was telling the assembled officials of the TSE and the OSC, 'Everybody knows we hit it.'[106] The deeper she got in, the harder it was to back out, so that in the end nothing could be done except to stall for a couple of weeks while drilling was completed in slow motion.then the negative results finally came in and disaster ensued.

Of course, the legal system was not designed to probe psychological complexities but to uncover whether or not laws had been broken. After the royal commission's report, with its stinging condemnation of their conduct, appeared in 1965, both the MacMillans were accused of fraud. Charges of wash trading against the couple resulted in George MacMillan, who had had little to do with the share dealings, being freed after a preliminary hearing, but the couple was committed to trial on the other charges. These cases dragged on for years. In 1968 Viola MacMillan was finally convicted of wash trading (not, ironically, in the shares of Windfall but of another of their companies, Consolidated Golden Arrow Mines). This conviction was upheld on appeal, and she eventually served eight weeks of a nine-month jail sentence.[107]

The trial of the two MacMillans for conspiring to affect the market price of Windfall shares and for fraudulently promoting the stock did not come on until early 1969. After hearing the evidence, the judge ordered their acquittal on the grounds that nothing they had said to the public had been other than factual, and that simply delaying the progress of the drilling was not a fraudulent act.[108] One of the brokers involved in handling Windfall shares was also charged with wash trading, but he too was acquitted.[109]

The Windfall affair proved to be the last hurrah for the old system of financing mining-exploration companies by the sale of speculative shares. Lack of disclosure, manipulation of stock prices by insiders – all this and more had been winked at by brokers and investors alike in the hope of striking it rich by getting in on the ground floor of the next great find. The royal commission report revealed just how little control the Toronto Stock Exchange and the Ontario Securities Commission actually exercised over the activities of promoters. Installed as director of the OSC as a result of John Campbell's dismissal, Harry Bray observed, 'While I am unable at the present time to point with pride to our overall record in the last several years, primarily I suggest as a result of lack of staff, the policy of enforcement had largely driven the smalltime confidence man from the securities field. By the same virtue, the inroads of the sophisticated and unscrupulous promoter has resulted, I suggest, from our ability to effectually enforce the legislation that we have.' He promised in future to remain 'strongly enforcement minded.'[110] More important, however, the revelations had convinced many politicians, investors, and regulators that wide-ranging changes in securities legislation were necessary. The pressures for reform were mounting.

Rupert Bain (r.) built Graydon Hall by promoting mining shares, but his sales methods led to many run-ins with the Ontario Securities Commission during the 1940s.

Charles P. McTague was appointed chair of the Ontario Securities Commission in 1945 to administer the new Securities Act requiring 'full, true and plain disclosure.'

Members of the Broker Dealers Association of Ontario at their annual dinner, 1954.

Bustle on the trading floor of the Toronto Stock Exchange during the 1955 bull market in Canadian resource stocks.

Toronto conference of securities regulators, 1951, with O.E. Lennox at centre of head table, Charles McTague at right end with Viola MacMillan of the Prospectors and Developers Association to his left, opposite Arthur J. Trebilcock of the Toronto Stock Exchange with Milton Kroll of the Securities and Exchange Commission on his right.

Touring the moose pastures: brokers and promoters visit mining country in the 1950s, with Samuel Ciglen in second row left (behind man with dark fedora and sunglasses) and Morris Black, second to Ciglen's left.

O.E. Lennox in his office at the Ontario Securities Commission shortly before his death in 1962 after an unequalled fifteen years as chair.

Toronto Stock Exchange governors in their Georgian-style boardroom, 1961, with new president Howard Graham at the right of chair Eric D. Scott and future chair Marshal Stearns third from right.

President Howard Graham telephones in front of a poster of the Toronto Stock Exchange trading floor in 1964 as the market for mining shares heats up.

Annual meeting of the Prospectors and Developers Association, 1967, promotes the myth of the independent prospector.

Watching share prices at the offices of Davidson and Company, 21 April 1964, after the Texas Gulf Sulphur discovery.

The Windfall bubble bursts on 31 July 1964 as the floor post at the Toronto Stock Exchange shows no prices for 'WDM.'

Viola and George MacMillan leave court on 3 December 1965 with lawyer Gordon Langille (r.) during fraud trial concerning Windfall.

Angry shareholders of Prudential Finance gather in a church on 9 January 1967 following the company's bankruptcy.

C. Powell Morgan arrives at hearing into the collapse of Atlantic Acceptance on 17 January 1966.

J.R. Kimber became chair of the Ontario Securities Commission in 1964 and oversaw the development of the new Securities Act of 1966, before leaving to serve as president of the Toronto Stock Exchange between 1967 and 1976.

Harry Bray was appointed director of the Ontario Securities Commission in the aftermath of the Windfall affair; he later became vice-chair and a key figure in regulatory policy.

Lawyer James Baillie was appointed to head the Ontario Securities Commission to bring in the new Securities Act of 1978.

PART II

7

Challenges

By the early 1960s the Ontario Securities Commission found itself facing new kinds of regulatory problems. Previously, much of the commission's efforts had been devoted to policing stock promoters, most of whom trafficked in the shares of speculative resource companies. Now, however, the regulators became concerned about the continuing operations of corporations, particularly when the activities of management might lead to investors being defrauded. Financial-service companies created a particular challenge because their assets consisted primarily of changing portfolios of loans, advances, and other paper. Not only did these inventories turn over rapidly, but these items could be difficult to value accurately. Moreover, flows of capital through such enterprises offered dishonest executives opportunities to divert funds into deals not conducted at arm's length. In the absence of suspicions about fraudulent activities, the OSC had little authority to oversee continuing corporate activities once a primary distribution of securities had been complete. The cases of Prudential Finance and Atlantic Acceptance provided vivid evidence of the problems that might arise and the losses that investors could incur.

I

The Prudential Finance Corporation had been established in 1928 to provide consumer credit and sales financing, but by the 1960s it was not a flourishing operation. The management of the London, Ontario, company, headed by Aubrey H. Rafuse, did not display great business acumen. For instance, one board member recalled,

Somebody up in Kitchener conceived the bright idea of buying up a lot of used television sets and taking them down to Newfoundland and selling them there, which was supposed to be a terrific market ... Apparently Rafuse financed this and gave them the money to buy all these sets ... They got the sets down there and they had a very good sale of them apparently, and the chap who had done this, I think it was a father and son combination, they built a hotel in Newfoundland and told Rafuse to go look for his money ... There was nothing he could do; he had no lien on things in Newfoundland. He knew that they were down in Newfoundland yet he had nothing to protect the company's loan on it.[1]

By June of 1961 the Bank of Montreal, which had lent the company over $1 million secured by its receivables, concluded that up to half its loans were bad debts and installed an employee in the company's offices to seek their liquidation. Near the end of that year Prudential passed into new hands. On the whole, Aubrey Rafuse was relieved. Afterwards, said his son, he 'broke down and cried ... His life's work had been sold, he felt, for a pittance. He had always hoped to leave a flourishing business to his sons. Yet he remarked, "Well, boys, I guess half a loaf is better than none."'[2] By the time of Rafuse's death in August 1962 the bank estimated that as much as $900,000 of the company's $1 million in receivables might have to be written off.

The company had been acquired by Joseph Benoit Brien, a self-trained accountant who had recently joined Prudential as general manager. Despite the firm's shaky condition, he agreed to pay Rafuse $200,000 over the next six years at the rate of $3,000 per month. What attracted Brien was the opportunity to raise money from the public, assisted by the inevitable confusion between the finance company and the long-established Prudential insurance group. In November 1962 Prudential Finance began running advertisements offering to pay 8 per cent interest on an issue of notes, which attracted many buyers since other financial institutions paid much lower rates. After eighteen months under Brien's control, Prudential had raised $8.2 million, other financial institutions were becoming increasingly concerned about the competition for funds from these so-called ten-per-centers.[3]

Issuers of notes with a term of less than one year were not required to register with the OSC or to disclose their financial condition to investors by prospectus. But the commission had suddenly become aware that such companies could create problems. In the autumn of 1962 Gulf Intercontinental Finance Corporation opened a storefront outlet, and in just six weeks it had sold $750,000 worth of short-term notes bearing high rates of interest. When the OSC started to investigate the Montreal-based company, it was quickly discovered to be a front for several well-known racketeers from Florida, who had put up only a negligible sum to establish it and had siphoned off nearly $300,000 before its bank accounts were frozen. Charges were laid against the perpetrators, but not before large sums of money had been lost.[4]

In February 1963 Prudential began marketing five-year debentures paying 7½ per cent annual interest to its current note holders to encourage them to lengthen the terms of their investments. Since these people already held the company's securities, no prospectus had to be distributed to them. Prudential also started offering deposit accounts paying 5½ per cent interest. Altogether eight thousand individuals became note holders; most people were entirely unaware that their investments or deposits enjoyed none of the protections offered by more closely regulated banks and trust companies.

As a result, the OSC finally ordered an examination of Prudential's books in early 1963. The most worrisome fact was that funds borrowed for less than one year were being lent out again for much longer periods. Because no provision had been made for the repayment of the notes as they fell due, a rush of redemptions or withdrawals from deposit accounts could easily create a crisis. J.R. Kimber, the acting head of the OSC, reported that, while 'we have no evidence of any fraudulent intent on the part of the operators of the company, it would seem from a review of their financial situation that their liquid position is very delicate.' Moreover, 'Apart from the danger inherent in the lack of liquidity in these companies, there is also the danger that this [kind of] vehicle can very easily be used for fraudulent purposes.'[5]

How should the regulators respond? One solution was simply to ban the sale of such notes, but a bit of delving by the OSC revealed that dealings in short-term commercial paper worth at least $5 billion took place annually in Ontario alone, a trade that had 'caused so little concern that the [securities] administrators were not aware of it previously.' Requiring all note sellers to issue prospectuses would seriously interfere with these transactions, and in any event, it seemed unnecessary for the bankers, investment dealers, and corporate treasurers who purchased the vast majority of the notes. At their semi-annual gathering in Toronto in February 1963, securities regulators from across Canada discussed other methods of amending securities legislation to control the ten-per-centers. Perhaps some buyers could be defined as 'sophisticated' investors, permitted to purchase short-term paper without receiving a prospectus, so that institutions such as pension or trust funds might receive permanent authority to purchase (but not resell) such notes. On the other hand, sellers might be forbidden from approaching 'individuals' or 'natural persons' without supplying a prospectus, or limitations could be imposed upon the amount of any issue that an individual was permitted to buy. Possibly, sales of exempt issues without a prospectus should be limited to corporate entities or those already registered as sophisticated investors.[6]

After consultations with the Investment Dealers Association and securities lawyers, the OSC recommended that the Ontario government amend the Securities Act by adopting a combination of these approaches. Restrictions should apply only to the sale of notes in denominations of less than $50,000, leaving sophisticated buyers and sellers to deal in larger sums in the exempt market. The OSC would be given authority to vet all advertisements for notes to be marketed to the general public. At the same time the Deposits Regulation Act could be changed to impose more stringent standards upon deposit-taking borrowers. Henceforth they would be required to set aside cash or short-term securities equal in value to 60 per cent of the sums being solicited to ensure that they could be redeemed if necessary, the aim being to end such deposit-taking by the ten-per-centers altogether.[7]

After the legislation was amended, the key question then became when the new rules would be proclaimed into law. The OSC investigation had revealed that Prudential Finance was already in a most precarious financial situation. If this fact was disclosed through a prospectus, the situation would likely become critical as depositors would hasten to withdraw their money. Fortunately for the company, one of its long-standing directors was C.C. Carrothers, senior partner in the London, Ontario, law firm of Carrothers, Robarts, Betts, Menzies and McLennan, to which Premier John Robarts belonged. This connection ensured Prudential a respectful hearing from the government, and an approach was immediately made to Attorney General Frederick Cass to convince him that it would be 'most embarrassing' for the revised laws to come into force before the end of May 1963. Cass promised to get in touch with Prudential president Joseph Brien to assure him that there would be no proclamation at least until 1 June. OSC officials eventually recommended 15 June, but Cass decided upon 1 July, the assumption being that the legislation could take effect then 'without adversely affecting any of the companies which will be required to change their plans and way of business to conform with the acts.'[8]

Prudential got busy preparing a prospectus to disclose its situation to potential investors. The draft submitted to the regulators aroused grave concerns, but the OSC reluctantly agreed to accept it. 'Though the staff of the commission recognized that the company's financial position was such that it would have difficulty in continuing in business successfully, the staff also recognized that if the company's prospectus was not accepted the 8,000 noteholders then tied into the company would suffer financial loss. In these circumstances the commission staff were persuaded that the company, if properly managed, might be able to overcome its financial difficulties and thereby avoid severe loss to its existing noteholders. Accordingly, the prospectus was accepted for filing on June 20th, 1963.'[9]

This gamble seemed to pay off. Prudential Finance continued to accept some deposits, but the stringent reserve requirements imposed by the revised Deposits Regulation Act caused this type of business to decline. With some prodding from the OSC, the company ceased taking deposits altogether in January 1964, giving account holders the option of withdrawing their money or accepting its notes. Prudential did continue to raise money by selling notes, and at the end of 1963 it had $13.9 million worth of short-term paper outstanding, an increase of $5.7 million over the previous twelve months. Efforts continued to persuade note holders to convert their investments into the five-year debentures covered by the prospectus. Joseph Brien expanded aggressively. Prudential's head office was moved from London to Toronto, and to the seventeen branches that had been set up by the end of 1962 were added seven more in 1963–4. The funds taken in were channelled to a small fleet of other companies that Brien personally controlled: the Independent Businessman's Credit Corporation, Triangle Management, Robco Publications, and Rambo Developments. The group's business began to swing away from consumer lending into real-estate development. In 1965 Prudential acquired control of O'Brien Gold Mines and also purchased all the shares of North American General Insurance, having previously taken over Wentworth Insurance.

The OSC continued to keep an eye on Prudential. In July 1964 the prospectus required by the new legislation expired and was not renewed, so that the company was once again confined to raising money from its current security holders, at least in Ontario, though similar restrictions did not apply in all the other provinces. The com-

mission insisted, moreover, that Prudential should deliver a prospectus-like document to all investors. In October 1965 the company
advised the OSC that it had discontinued selling securities to its own
note holders, but the commission remained concerned because this
commitment was not legally binding. After a further inquiry and hearing, the OSC revoked Prudential's statutory exemption to sell securities to its current investors without prospectus on 31 March, 1966,
though such sales did continue in other provinces.[10]

When the OSC finally secured a financial statement for 1965 from
the company, it showed an income of $3.5 million, though more than
half of this had not been received in cash but as stock dividends from
its subsidiaries or as mere bookkeeping entries for fees supposedly
owed by them. In August 1966 Jack Kimber reported to Attorney General Arthur Wishart that he suspected Prudential was insolvent. The
directors ought to declare bankruptcy, but on the basis of past experience, it was unlikely that they would do so. Kimber, however, did not
recommend any investigation under the Securities Act because there
was no evidence of wrongdoing. No securities had been sold to the
public in Ontario for some time, and future sales were blocked. If the
provincial government wished to intervene, the only thing that might
be done was to have the provincial secretary order an inquiry with the
intent to dissolve the company. Nothing resulted.[11]

On 1 November 1966 the interest payments due to Prudential's note
and debenture holders failed to arrive, and the company did not make
the required payment into its sinking fund. Metropolitan Trust Company, as trustee for the debenture holders, demanded an up-to-date set
of accounts from Brien, and the unaudited statement proved alarming
enough that assistance was at once sought from the OSC. By 14 November it was learned that the Ontario superintendent of insurance
was concerned about the financial stability of Wentworth Insurance.
Two days later the OSC ordered B.C. Howard to commence an investigation into Prudential Finance and its associated companies.

More disturbing information was uncovered almost at once. The
OSC auditors found that Prudential had borrowed $1.9 million from
the treasury of O'Brien Gold Mines on the security of the finance company's notes. The Toronto Stock Exchange had not been notified of this
transaction as required, and on 17 November trading in O'Brien Gold
stock was suspended. A check of O'Brien's brokerage accounts then
showed that 24,000 shares of Dominion Glass had gone missing from
its treasury, and the mining company's assets were frozen to prevent

any further dissipation. On 24 November a formal order to investigate the Prudential group was issued. Documents began to be seized and witnesses interviewed. At the end of the month Joseph Brien was arrested and charged with six criminal offences over O'Brien Gold, two of forgery, two of uttering, one of theft, and one for delivering false and deceptive statements to Metropolitan Trust; he was released on $10,000 bail.[12]

As the news of Prudential Finance's apparent insolvency spread among its 8,500 note and debenture holders (3,500 of whom lived in Ontario), complaints mounted. Attorney General Arthur Wishart responded that a recent dispute over the election of the board of directors had led the government to conclude that 'the affair had involved a dispute between competing businessmen, and that the government should not take part in such a matter for the benefit of either side.' It was up to corporate officers and directors to 'make their own business decisions where the government has no authority to interfere.' This refusal to accept any responsibility earned criticism from the Liberal government in Ottawa. Wishart reiterated, 'It surely is not the proper role of government to invade the field of corporate management.' He went on 'to emphasize again that securities legislation cannot guarantee an investor against loss. There is risk in every investment and the size of the return to the investor depands substantially on the size of the risk.'[13]

Ontario's new department of Financial and Commercial Affairs had by then assumed oversight of the OSC. In January 1967 the minister, H.L. Rowntree, announced that the accountants Clarkson, Gordon would be retained to assist the commission in the investigation. Liberal MPP James Trotter observed that the retention of an outside accounting firm only showed how 'weak and ineffective' the OSC was, since it must have plenty of staff of its own to handle such a task. New Democratic Party leader Donald MacDonald condemned the government as 'unbelievably casual' for not bringing in legislation to prevent such abuses sooner. Behind the scenes there was finger pointing: Jack Kimber of the OSC complained to Rowntree, 'While not wishing to criticize any other branch of the government, there has not been as vigorous enforcement of the requirements of the Corporations Act. In fact, the penalty provisions of the act are too lenient and the limitations for bringing proceedings under the act also make enforcement difficult.'[14] The government tried to deflect further criticisms by pushing through legislation in just three days during February 1967 creating a new

Ontario Deposit Insurance Corporation Act, which required all provincially incorporated loan and trust companies to contribute to a fund that would cover up to $20,000 in losses by each depositor in the event of a failure.[15]

During the early months of 1967 a five-person investigative team interviewed one hundred and thiry-three people and ploughed through reams of documents. The picture that emerged was far blacker than anticipated. Early in March Clarkson, Gordon rendered its report, which made clear that the Prudential's affairs had been rife with fraud and misconduct. With the connivance of a small group of insiders, Joseph Brien had been systematically looting the money raised by the company for years. By February 1963 its board consisted of Brien and three other employees, along with two outside directors, C.C. Carrothers and R.C. Fuller, but the directors had surrendered all control of Prudential's financial affairs to Brien, so he could use its treasury 'as he pleased without let or hindrance.' Prudential had already advanced $3.8 million to the Independent Businessman's Credit Corporation (which Brien personally controlled), money that was then lent to other Brien-controlled companies, and by the end of 1963 another $655,000 had been passed along the same way. None of the insiders expressed any concerns. Carrothers recalled, 'Mr. Brien was supposed to have access to unlimited money. That's what we were told when he took over the company: he was a very wealthy man. And this IBCC had access to all sorts of money.' Had the directors not seen the financial statements, which showed that as early as 1961 up to half of Prudential's accounts receivable were already in arrears? 'I'm positive we were getting statements from Mr. Brien's office showing arrears, but they were never anything like that,' said Carrothers.

OSC investigator B.C. Howard pressed him: how as director and corporate treasurer could he be 'completely unaware' that employees in the London offices of Prudential had known for years that the company was in trouble as a result of uncollectable debts totalling up to $1 million? Carrothers refused to budge: 'I can't see there was any reason for me to have doubts about the thing at all.' After all, Aubrey Rafuse continued to buy up Prudential's common shares whenever he could, and his wife had held onto the preferred shares after his death, so they were optimistic about the company's prospects. Fellow director Ross Fuller also continued to buy stock, 'which he certainly wouldn't have done had there been any suspicion of this.' Yet at the time the prospectus was being prepared in 1963, the Bank of Montreal had presented Prudential with a confirmation that read 'notes pledged as collateral, $994,000.00, E/W [estimated worth], $100,000.00.' Didn't that mean that the company's receivables were almost valueless? Carrothers could only reply, 'Of course, I never saw that ... They never drew that to our attention. That's a sad story.'[16]

In fact, all along, the revenues from Prudential's consumer loan and sales financing business had barely been sufficient to cover salaries and operating expenses. No money had been set aside to cover the cost of additional borrowing or of bad debts and investment losses which had been aggravated by careless management and over-rapid expansion. In its final report the OSC was unsparing: Brien and his senior employees had known perfectly well that the company was insolvent by early 1963, but they had 'determined to keep Prudential Finance in the business of raising money from the public by the sale of short-term notes, and put forward to the commission an "acceptable" financial statement knowing it to be false and misleading.' Thus even the prospectus that had been approved so reluctantly by the OSC in June 1963 was based upon a tissue of lies.[17]

Prudential had simply accepted the book value of the Independent Businessman's Credit Corporation, assets consisting of shares in and amounts owing to it from other Brien-controlled companies, without making any effort to arrive at a true valuation. 'In no case was the fair value of assets acquired from a non-arm's length vendor determined by disinterested parties.'[18] In fact, IBCC's books overvalued its holdings by at least $910,000. Combined with an under-provision of $500,000 to cover the cost of bad consumer loans and sales finance receivables, the prospectus concealed the fact that Prudential was in serious difficulties and probably insolvent. The true nature of the transactions and written agreements between the two companies was not fully disclosed, and while the prospectus stated that Prudential's investment decisions were subject to approval by the board of directors, the minute books showed that such approval was rarely sought or obtained.

How had any hint of these problems slipped past the lawyers at Carrothers, Robarts, Betts, Menzies and McLennan in London, who had done the preliminary work, and at Tory, Arnold, DesLauriers and Binnington in Toronto, who had overseen the final preparation of the 1963 prospectus? With all the concern amongst securities regulators over such finance companies that had led to the legislative changes, had everybody not been exceptionally careful? W.J. DesLauriers argued that there had been due diligence. The 'watchful eye' being directed at the ten-per-centers by the OSC had certainly had an effect. In his words, the paradoxical result was 'with the lights, maybe incorrectly, that we thought were glaring on this company at that time, the publicity ... had a disarming effect on intentional misstatements in the prospectus or intentional leaving out of information.' Rather than being asleep at the switch over Prudential, DesLauriers claimed that he had sought to 'take more care than usual to make sure they did nothing wrong, because at this time the question of whether this type of borrowing should be permitted was being debated in the public and another company [Gulf Intercontinental] had just got into difficulty ... and this company could not afford to get into that situation.' Lawyers were entitled to accept statements from company officers and auditors at face value unless they had reason to suspect otherwise, and like Carrothers, DesLauriers insisted that there had been no grounds for suspicion.

Wasn't there a larger question about full, true, and plain disclosure: why was Prudential Finance permitted to continue to solicit new investment, even though it 'did not have a ghost of a chance of paying off its obligations to existing noteholders?' DesLauriers agreed, then hastily retreated: 'I think this was everybody's feeling, including that of the Securities Commission, that it would be improvident if this company was going to experience what was known as a run on the bank ... I think everybody's efforts were to see it was done properly within the law. Suspicions that might have been there were allayed because of what I call the glare of publicity on the company. I am not offering it as a reason why we should have to be less vigilant, but as to why we should have been less suspicious.'[19] Understandable or not, if full disclosure had been made, Prudential would immediately have been barred from selling additional securities to the public and would almost certainly have gone into liquidation. With the acceptance of the prospectus, an unspoken compact amongst crooks, lawyers, regulators, and investors was in place which put off the day of reckoning for another three years.

In 1964 Prudential had begun to advance funds to Triangle Management, another Brien-controlled company, which had no independent financial resources and an authorized share capital of just $3. Triangle then lent the money to IBCC and other companies among the thirteen subsidiaries in the group. To make IBCC look more solid, shares in Prudential purchased by it for $233,686 were resold to Triangle Management for $1.2 million in exchange for a promissory note due in 1968. Since it had no assets, Triangle had no means of paying off this loan, but the paper profit of $976,314 on the deal, along with the failure to write off a loss of $225,900 on a loan to Robco Publications, allowed IBCC to show a surplus rather than a sizeable deficit, so no questions would be asked.

The following year Prudential acquired control of O'Brien Gold Mines. The OSC had been concerned about this diversification, which appeared to be paid for with the sale of part of Prudential's consumer-finance operations. Buying the mining company seemed to reduce liquidity at a time when Prudential still had outstanding a large number of short-term notes, payable either on demand or over the next three years. At the time Jack Kimber pointed out to Attorney General Arthur Wishart that the commission had been watching Prudential's affairs with the intention of preventing it from distributing further securities to the public if it seemed to be in serious difficulties, but Brien had forestalled such an order by ceasing to raise funds through sales to the public. Kimber remained hopeful that Prudential might be able to work its way out of its problems, though he admitted privately that the situation was likely to become worse before it got better.[20]

In fact, by 1966 the cash and securities in the treasury of O'Brien Gold had begun to be siphoned illegally to Prudential on the strength of a forged banking resolution giving Brien sole authority to act. At the same time as the mining company was acquired, he had also purchased control of the federally chartered North American General Insurance Company, after previously securing provincially incorporated Wentworth Insurance. Before long, an acute shortage of funds led him to begin transferring cash from North American, both directly to Prudential and via Wentworth. These complex transactions were recorded as purchases of notes from Prudential, as exchanges for marketable securities, or as accounts receivable. Such cash transfers as well as the appropriation of the securities from North American eventually rendered it insolvent, while at the same time Prudential's investment of $915,545 in the insurer became worthless. In order to conceal this fact, false returns were filed with the federal superintendent of insurance and the same thing was done for Wentworth with the Ontario insurance regulator. On its own books Prudential recorded the payment of inflated finders' fees and management charges, as well as notional profits by its subsidiaries totalling $4.2 million, in order to conceal its real situation. The credit of the subsidiaries was used without regard to the interests of any other creditor of the various companies, and the cash flow and securities of one company not wholly owned were appropriated despite the existence of minority shareholders.

By the end Brien had created a vast jumble of paper through which the credit of each company had been used to secure mortgages and guarantee obligations for the others. John Jonak, one of the insiders whom the OSC considered deeply implicated in the swindle, would later claim that 'even today I am still confused as far as the relationship is concerned, because I never got a true picture of whole setup.' Jonak also made the apt observation 'If Mr. Brien would have been able to be president, secretary and treasurer in one person, I think he would have done that.'[21] Shares of the few profitable operating companies had been pledged for further loans. The real estate of some subsidiaries was used as collateral for mortgages and the money passed along to Prudential. Brien and the other insiders knew perfectly well that Prudential's thirteen subsidiaries were a serious drain since only five of them operated profitably. After unravelling the mess, Clarkson, Gordon's accountants observed, 'It is scarcely credible that some of these operations were continued and more money poured into keep them operating. The companies were used in a series of complicated transactions, many of which were designed to cover up the fact that they were incapable of paying their borrowings from Prudential Finance.'[22]

Within the Prudential group nobody had ever raised any questions. Regular board meetings were not held and documents waiving them were not secured. Carrothers and Fuller, the two outside directors, were absent from some meetings, and their attendance declined as time passed. No formal approvals were ever sought for loans given to other companies in the Brien group, and Brien himself did not abstain from voting on non-arm's length transactions. In fact, he 'treated the company and other associated companies as his personal property, and as long as his employees cooperated, he was free to do whatever he wished.'[23] Said the OSC's final report, 'The conclusion is irresistible that the financial statements in the Prudential Finance prospectus [of 1963] were an instrument of fraud by means of which, together with the false prospectus, the commission was deceived and members of the public were defrauded of some twenty million dollars between June, 1963 and November, 1966.'[24]

When the investigation finally revealed the full extent of the problems at Prudential, Jack Kimber was defensive about the OSC's role in failing to step in sooner. After all, the law had been changed in 1963 to require the company to file a prospectus. Even the best laws, he pointed out, could always be broken and could not 'wholly protect fools from their own folly or the knavery of others.' Kimber also complained that plenty of notes had legally been sold in other provinces after Ontario banned their distribution, but no other province had commenced an investigation. The OSC already had 'sufficient problems' to deal with, but 'again, however, as is often the case the burden of ferreting out the facts is left to Ontario.'[25]

Yet the undeniable fact was Prudential Finance was based in Ontario, and its prospectus of June 1963 had been approved by the OSC. Once the commission's interim report recommending that charges be laid was released, demands began to be heard for compensation from angry people who had lost money and wanted the provincial government to make them whole again. H.E. Langford, who had by then succeeded Kimber at the OSC, reported that Prudential had over 5,100 creditors who together were owed $23.5 million. Of these over 3,100 were Ontario residents who were out $14,750,000.[26] A Prudential Creditors Association sprang to life, and at a meeting in September 1967 four hundred people met and agreed to wire the leaders of the three political parties in the forthcoming provincial election asking what compensation each would promise. The association retained New Democratic Party MPP James Renwick as its legal adviser, and a meeting was arranged at the OSC on the eve of the commission's final report on the whole debacle in October.[27]

Safely re-elected, the Conservative government finally released excerpts from the OSC report in January 1968, though information required for the prosecution of Brien and the other Prudential insiders was kept confidential. Financial and Commercial Affairs Minister Leslie Rowntree noted the creditors' continuing campaign for reimbursement but refused to budge: 'It is a recognized principle that securities legislation cannot guarantee an investor against loss ... Normally, a high percentage of return reflects a high degree of risk.' NDP leader Donald MacDonald kept up the campaign, arguing that the OSC had known in 1963 that Prudential was being so poorly managed that its bankers had cut off its credit, yet the securities regulator had approved a prospectus which permitted Brien to try to gamble his company out of bankruptcy by victimizing additional investors. The commission staff attempted to claim that the terrible state of the company had only become clear after its default in 1966, and that Brien had done everything he could to maintain a good image and conceal his fraudulent activities. B.C. Howard, who had headed the OSC investigation, grumbled that investors had been only too happy to accept Prudential's generous interest payments. In fact, many had become debenture holders by buying notes and then agreeing to have them converted into longer-term debt. Even after the prospectus lapsed in 1964, some people had bought debentures, though they had never held the notes: 'They did not complaint [sic] to the Commission.'[28]

The Prudential Creditors Association continued to urge the creation of a royal commission to look into the whole affair, but the government stubbornly resisted. When the OSC was asked to support such an inquiry, Langford refused to help. He had no desire to see the agency's embarrassing role in the Prudential affair rehearsed once more. He argued that since the creditors had turned to opposition politicians for support, it would be wrong for him to do anything: 'The last thing the Commission desired was to involve itself in any way in a political controversy.'[29]

In October 1968 Joseph Brien was sentenced to four years in penitentiary on two counts of fraud and one of theft. By that time four of his close associates had already been found guilty of unlawful trading under the Securities Act, but had received suspended sentences and paid only small fines. After the investigation was complete, Brien and the other insiders escaped further charges under the Securities Act on the technical grounds that the minister of financial and commercial affairs (rather than the attorney general) was the one who ought to have signed the required consent to prosecute. The OSC had warned of this outcome, but the minister had ignored its advice and the time for relaying charges had elapsed. When the Prudential Creditors Association renewed its demands for reimbursement one last time in the autumn of 1969, most people could hardly recall the sequence of events.

Nevertheless, Leslie Rowntree felt the necessity to make another defence of the OSC's actions when tabling the full text of the commission's final report in September. The minister was careful to lay the entire responsibility for approving the Prudential prospectus of June 1963 upon Jack Kimber: 'While the risks involved appeared to be adequately disclosed in the prospectus, he was mindful of the consequences of refusal. It was clear that the company, having embarked on an acquisition program, was not generating profits. However, to refuse the prospectus would doom the company to failure and the approximately 8,000 individuals involved to virtually certain loss because of the lack of liquidity.' Rowntree tried to blunt criticism from the opposition parties that the government had failed to act. Ministers must rely upon advice received from the commission: 'It seems strange to me that those who most strenuously urge that the Commission should operate without political interference, as the facts I have presented so clearly demonstrate that it did in the present case, should now attack the minister involved.'[30] The OSC could not be sued, and an effort by holders of Prudential Finance securities to claim damages for breaches of trust and contract, deceit, and negligence on account of the prospectuses and other documents filed with the OSC was ultimately rejected by the courts in 1971.[31]

With that the sordid and unhappy story of Prudential Finance finally dragged to a close. The amendments to the Securities Act in 1963 had reduced the flow of funds into the ten-per-centers, yet the OSC's failure to crack down on Prudential had allowed Joseph Brien and his cronies to continue their depredations for another three years. For the commission, however, the passage of time was a blessing since it helped to mute criticism of the ill-advised decision to accept the company's original prospectus, but it also greatly increased the losses suffered by Prudential's investors. In 1968 law professor John Willis, a part-time member of the commission, claimed that heading the OSC was 'the hottest seat in the Civil Service' because angry investors who believed they had been swindled aimed their fire in that direction.[32] In truth, however, the commission got off lightly despite its failure to take a firm stand in the case of Prudential. By the time the reasons for the company's collapse were fully revealed to the public at the end of 1966, new problems had arisen to occupy the attention of the regulators, and only the note holders who had been swindled continued to fight for compensation.

II

Even before Prudential Finance finally slid into bankruptcy, the OSC had received a further demonstration of the new challenges created by companies in the financial-services sector. On 14 June 1965 Atlantic Acceptance, a much larger finance company with 130 loan offices across Canada and possessing nearly $155 million in assets, defaulted on a short-term note for $5 million. Atlantic's failure undermined the British Mortgage and Trust Company of London, Ontario, so that it had to be bailed out with an Ontario government guarantee, and by mid-August the receivers were reporting that Atlantic's subsidiaries were also in default to the tune of $32 million. Atlantic shares, which had been worth about $20 in early June, rapidly slumped to $7.25 on the TSE, and trading was suspended in mid-July when the stock had sunk to $1.65. An OSC investigation was launched as soon as the initial default occurred, but at the end of July a royal commission headed by Mr Justice Samuel Hughes was appointed to try to unravel the situation. The affairs of Atlantic Acceptance and its interlocked associates proved so complex, however, that the final report of this commission would not be delivered for more than four years.[33]

The company had been founded in Hamilton, Ontario, in 1953 to finance consumer purchases of televisions and used cars, but it emerged from obscurity in 1955 after the Wall Street investment banking firm of Lambert and Company was persuaded to invest $300,000. A great coup occurred in 1959 when, as a result of the Lambert connection, the pension funds of United States Steel and the Carnegie Foundation were persuaded to lend the company $3 million, followed by a similar investment by the Ford Foundation in 1961. With this seal of approval Atlantic Acceptance was able to sell shares and borrow heavily in both Canada and the United States. President C. Powell Morgan, a chartered accountant by training, used his skills to inspire 'unbounded confidence' on the part of his board of directors, 'nourished by the gratifying results' of steadily increasing profits. When the default occurred, Morgan claimed that all the difficulties stemmed from the restrictions on U.S. dollar lending imposed by President Lyndon Johnson in February 1965. Yet as the lawyers and accountants delved about, they soon discovered evidence of serious fraud, and Morgan was forced to resign. The highly reputable auditors whom the American investors insisted must be retained had been successfully kept in the dark. The royal commission's eventual conclusion was that, 'From the earliest days ... the activities of C.P. Morgan, prosecuted with considerable energy and ingenuity as they were, have been shown to be dishonest.'

'Morgan let no grass grow under his feet after he had taken over full-time management of Atlantic Acceptance at the end of 1958.' Dubious accounting practices had been used from the outset to enable the finance company to survive and attract the favourable attention from Lambert and Company. Once the American funds had been induced to invest, Morgan quickly moved to create subsidiaries, Commodore

Sales Acceptance, its subsidiary Commodore Factors, and Adelaide Acceptance. These companies were run personally by Morgan and granted large loans from Atlantic, a fact concealed from its board by him and his fellow accountants, William L. Walton and Harry Wagman. 'The Trio,' as they called themselves, undertook a raft of deals, 'mostly dishonest and undertaken at the expense of Atlantic Acceptance.' An associated firm, Aurora Leasing, also made large loans at Morgan's direction to other companies in which he and his friends held interests. In addition, British Mortgage and Trust, which was headed by Wilfrid P. Gregory, an Atlantic director and close Morgan associate, lent about $12 million to various individuals and companies in the same orbit. By 1966 the investigators calculated that Atlantic's losses would likely total between $50 and $65 million, while British Mortgage was out $6.5 to $7 million. When the royal commission report was finally rendered, the losses had mounted to at least $70 million, together with $2.2 million paid out for such services as auditors, receivers, and liquidators. Shareholders' equity had been completely wiped out, while the senior creditors were expected to recoup no more than 75 or 80 cents on the dollar for their lendings.

Where had all the money gone? As in the case of Prudential Finance, proper provision had never been made for bad debts in order to inflate profits, so that 16 per cent of Atlantic's receivables, or more than $21 million was simply swallowed up. Morgan had amassed a personal fortune of $2 million by the time of the collapse, and he and his associates had stashed more funds in offshore tax havens. But the real problem was that by 1965 over one-third of the $155 million owing to Atlantic was formally booked to the satellite enterprises controlled by Morgan. Mr Justice Hughes expressed amazement at the manner in which the huge sums passed through them had simply been frittered away: 'examples abound of great ingenuity in devising methods of purloining Atlantic money only to invest it in business venture of astonishing folly, operated either by incompetents or thieves. Millions of dollars were lent ... only to be spent in operating businesses which never had any chance of success ... Having once begun on a lending policy which was unsound in every sense, except that of yielding hidden and dishonest profits to him and his fellow-conspirators, Morgan was caught in a current from which there was no escape until it finally swept him into the abyss.' Only because Morgan died in the midst of the investigation did he escape the lengthy jail term to which he would almost certainly have been sentenced.[34]

The royal commission investigation did turn up a couple of instances in which Morgan and his associates were linked with the sort of shady promoters that the Ontario Securities Commision was more accustomed to dealing with. The Trio had used Atlantic funds to acquire control of Commodore Business Machines and Analogue Controls as a means to extract secret and dishonest profits for themselves. In the autumn of 1964 Frank Kaftel, 'a notoriously fraudulent stock promoter with established connections in the world of organized crime,' was introduced to Morgan, and his services were retained to market shares in those two companies. Kaftel, having departed Canada for Paris following the stink over Pontiac Petroleums in the mid-1950s, made a deal with Morgan that the newsletter of his Luxembourg-based International Financial Advisory Service would hype Commodore Business Machines stock in exchange for $25,000 during every week that at least 35,000 shares of stock were sold. The extravagant praises of Commodore sung by IFAS up to June 1965 may have netted Kaftel as much as $370,000. This arrangement provoked Commissioner Hughes to a lyrical flight of fancy, with the claim that Kaftel's appearance cast upon the scene 'that lurid and wavering half-light generally associated with a coming storm.'

C.P. Morgan also used Atlantic funds to acquire a large block of stock in Analogue Controls, the market for which was being manipulated by the brokerage firm of Barrett, Goodfellow and Company along with the Rush brothers. After the Toronto Stock Exchange suspended trading in Analogue shares in May 1964, R.A. Goodfellow joined with David Rush ('a well-known stock market tout') and Myer (Michael) Rush ('a self-described stock promoter but, in fact, a professional criminal with wide, indeed perilous, connections in the field of organized crime') to secure Kaftel's services to market Analogue shares in Europe. When Atlantic collapsed in June, 1965, Kaftel was left with over 22,000 unsaleable shares of Analogue on his hands, and the smell of scandal finally led the Luxembourg authorities to deport him in the spring of 1966. Goodfellow was eventually expelled from the TSE that summer for his role in handling the stock of Analogue. The OSC, however, bore little responsibililty for dealing with these operations except to supply the royal commission with details from the dossier that had been collected on Kaftel since he first fell afoul of the regulators back in 1949.[35]

Atlantic Acceptance also invested heavily in the Racan Photo-Copy Corporation. Elias Rabbiah announced in October 1962 that his company had developed a low-cost, plain-paper copier at a time when Xerox alone had a reliable machine that did not use specially treated sheets. He filed a prospectus for the company and swiftly made an offering to the public. By May 1963 Racan shares had hit $26 in over-the-counter trading. At that point the Racan copier was shown at a public demonstration in New York but immediately broke down, leading to bad notices that lowered share prices. At a meeting in Toronto in July, shareholders were told that fifty copies of a document had just been made, but when a member of the audience asked to operate the copier, he was refused and the prototype was hastily spirited away while the lights were out. At least one of these copies was later discovered to have been made on treated, rather than plain, stock. Again Racan share prices collapsed, and in August 1963 the OSC ordered an investigation to discover whether the prospectus had been accurate. Meanwhile, Morgan had sunk about $1,250,000 of Atlantic Acceptance money into Racan.[36]

The final stage of the Racan saga began on the very day that Atlantic Acceptance defaulted on its $5 million note. Between January and June 1965 the price of the Racan shares had risen from 50 cents to $8, and on 2 June the company launched a new publicity campaign for its copier. On 14 June fifty-eight New York brokerage houses received orders to buy over 127,000 shares of Racan at about $10. With only a small float of the stock, such a buying spree would send prices shooting upward. Though all the orders were accompanied by certified cheques, only eighteen firms attempted to execute them before making enquiries at the Royal Bank of Canada, which revealed that the cheques had been forged using a rubber stamp. Rumours began to circulate that Rabbiah had engineered this fraud in an effort to inflate the price and make a killing, and after the sensational publicity Racan shares quickly sank back to $2.50.

The OSC investigation into the company's affairs had been dragging along since August 1963, but after almost two years its pace suddenly picked up. In March 1966 a Racan employee revealed that the photocopier used in the demonstration in New York was actually made by another company and its nameplate altered. Rabbiah had kept his one prototype taped up so that nobody could examine its internal workings and as late as April 1965 and refused to allow even the his associates to examine it. In fact, he never appears to have developed a workable copier. The Racan prospectus misrepresented the financial position of the company, since documents shown to the auditors had been falsified to conceal the loans from Atlantic that were channelled to Rabbiah. Altogether he probably took at least $1 million out of the company for his personal use.

In June 1966 Elias Rabbiah was charged with fraud and conspiracy and held in a Toronto jail, unable initially to raise bail. Finally freed on $100,000 bail, he made an abortive attempt to flee from Canada and eventually escaped in September 1966. From New York he issued a series of statements through his lawyers exculpating himself. These claims were later dismissed by Mr Justice Hughes as 'a farrago of libellous nonsense ... as worthless as might be expected from the manner of their transmission.' Like so many of Morgan's investments, Racan was eventually revealed to be, in Hughes's words, one of those 'business ventures of astonishing folly, operated by incompetents or thieves.'[37]

The irony of the Atlantic Acceptance affair was that, in the end, the biggest losers turned out to be well-heeled banks and pension funds, precisely the kind of sophisticated investors that were hardly supposed to need much protection from regulatory tribunals like the Ontario Securities Commission. Shot through with fraud and deception, the operations of C.P. Morgan and his associates had taken in not only the regulators but a whole host of accountants, bankers, lawyers, and pension fund administrators before the entire house of cards collapsed. Jack Kimber pointed out to Justice Hughes that the Ford Foundation probably had a larger staff of expert advisers overseeing the investments it made (including the one in Atlantic Acceptance) than most provincial securities commissions. Many of the Canadian purchasers of the company's notes had applied for exemptions under the Securities Act to permit them to buy the notes without the required disclosure, so that it was hard to sympathize much with them. Kimber therefore concluded that Atlantic was probably not the surest guide as to how securities regulations should be rewritten for better investor protection.[38]

Nevertheless, Atlantic's collapse in the summer of 1965 provided dramatic evidence that the OSC had little authority to intervene in internal corporate affairs. Kimber reminded the attorney general that the commission's responsibility was simply to accept a prospectus for filing, and that it could only halt trading in a company's shares during their primary distribution to the public if that prospectus was discovered to contain falsehoods. When problems arose in the secondary trading of a security, the OSC could investigate to see if offences against the Securities Act or the Criminal Code had been committed.

Once Atlantic defaulted, inquiries revealed that the company had little or no equity left and the shares were essentially worthless, but the OSC then could do little except stand by and watch as shares prices dropped from $20 to under $2.[39]

The new challenges that faced the Ontario Securities Commission during the early 1960s stemmed from the fact that its authority was severely bounded. The principle of full, true, and plain disclosure applied to companies making a primary distribution of their shares from the treasury for sale to the public. A prospectus was supposed to review all the material facts in order to inform investors, but once the shares had been sold, the OSC had quite limited powers to oversee ongoing corporate activities. Dishonest managers might use the required annual reports and financial statements to conceal their activities unless the directors and accountants intervened. As a result, frauds might be difficult to detect until long after they had occurred. In the case of Prudential Finance, the commission had made matters worse by turning a blind eye to a situation already known to be serious, while there was little cause to intervene in the affairs of Atlantic Acceptance until it was already too late.

8

Disclosure

Even before the Windfall affair in the summer of 1964, while the swindles at Prudential Finance and Atlantic Acceptance remained hidden from view, other concerns had arisen regarding the lack of disclosure about the operations of public companies. A growing wave of corporate mergers in Canada had already led the Ontario government to commission a task force to look into possible changes in securities legislation to protect investors. When the royal commission on Windfall was established, it too was directed to consider regulatory changes. The default by Atlantic Acceptance in mid-1965, along with the reports of the two investigative bodies, seemed to confirm that the most effective means of regulation was to require much fuller disclosure.[1] As a result a new Ontario Securities Act was prepared and passed into law in 1966.

I

Mergers and acquisitions became an increasingly significant feature of the Canadian corporate landscape during the early 1960s. These takeovers raised new questions for securities regulators. Were rules required to ensure that the shareholders of public companies involved in such transactions got fair treatment? Should limitations be imposed on corporate insiders to prevent them from using privileged information to their own profit on these deals? Near the end of 1959, for instance, the directors of Canada and Dominion Sugar had received a takeover bid from Tate and Lyle; they recommended acceptance of the offer to C&D shareholders, but without disclosing any detailed financial information about the state of the company. Even at C&D's annual meeting demands for fuller disclosure were resisted with the support of board members, who now represented the interests of Tate and Lyle. About the same time St Lawrence Cement made an offer directly to the stockholders of Standard Paving and Materials, bypassing its board but providing no details about St Lawrence's earnings. The contrast between the disclosure rules in Canada and the United States was highlighted by Macmillan Bloedel's acquisition of the Powell River forest products company through an exchange of stock, where corporate information was fully set forth in accordance with the SEC's rules.[2]

Angry complaints about insiders profiting unduly from takeovers were heard during the summer of 1961. Ventures Limited owned 56 per cent of Falconbridge Mines, while McIntyre-Porcupine Mines, in turn, had a 25 per cent interest in Ventures. Rumours began to circulate that Ventures would be folded into the two active companies and wound up, and between 17 July and 1 August its shares rose on the Toronto Stock Exchange from $47.50 to $63. On 27 July the board of Ventures issued a statement that none of the three companies had so far considered 'any concrete proposal,' but only four days later a complex merger was suddenly announced.[3] Since share prices commonly advanced when news of a deal leaked out and then fell back once it was completed or dropped, there were charges that insiders had misled the public. The TSE suspended the listing of Ventures and ordered an analysis of all trading in the stock since 24 July, though the company insisted that negotiations had simply stalled over the valuation of its assets before an agreement had suddenly been arrived at. The exchange investigation uncovered no evidence of any significant trades by officers or directors of any of the three companies during the previous five weeks, and the outcry gradually faded away.[4]

In the spring of 1962 Levy Industries made a successful offer of $20 per share for a control block in Russell Steel, but minority shareholders protested that they had had no chance to tender their stock, which soon slipped to $15.[5] Such offers were normally made only to the directors, executives, and large shareholders of target companies, which obviously placed them in a privileged position. Trading on the basis of this kind of inside information had technically been illegal in the United States since the 1930s, and in 1960 Britain promulgated takeover rules that required any offer to be made to all stockholders, the shares to be taken up pro rata if more stock than required was tendered. Canada, however, had no such regulations. As the Ontario Securities Commission J.R. Kimber observed, 'There is nothing in our legislation which prohibits an officer of a company from distributing inside information. Nor is there anything improper in a person receiving such information from acting thereon.'[6]

In August 1962 Shell Oil made an offer for all the shares of Canadian Oil Companies at $39. Though the stock was trading around $35 on the TSE, COC's president, Harold Rea, rejected the offer as inadequate and advised his shareholders to hold out for more. Heavy trading carried COC up to $47 per share by 25 September, when Shell improved its offer to $52.50 plus a warrant conditional upon at least half the outstanding stock being tendered. The deal was done, but within a few weeks rumours began to circulate that the brokerage house of G.H. Rennie and Company had been privy to inside information in acquiring 303,000 shares of COC, earning a profit of up to $900,000 after the stock was resold to Shell. The press, led by the *Toronto Daily Star*, took up the case, partly on the nationalistic grounds that the only integrated oil company under Canadian control was being taken over by a multinational and partly on account of a growing concern about corporate concentration as a result of such mergers.[7]

OSC chair O.E. Lennox therefore requested Attorney General Frederick Cass to order a formal investigation, even though it was not clear that there had been any violations of securities legislation or the Criminal Code. Jack Kimber pointed out that the proposed inquiry was most unusual in that it 'really could not lead to any definite action but was simply the amassing of information.' Moreover, Shell was a foreign-based firm, and persons residing outside Ontario could simply refuse to testify. In light of the outcry orchestrated by the *Star*, however, Cass agreed to issue an order.[8]

The OSC investigation did uncover some suspicious information. T.J. Anderson, the president of Rennie and Company, and his partner Richard Wookey had apparently bet so heavily on the takeover because Wookey was a personal friend of V.F. Grafstrom, the president of Shell Investments, the holding company that made the formal offer for COC. As a result of conversations with Graftstrom, Wookey had become convinced that Shell would follow up its initial bid with another, more generous offer, though both men insisted that Grafstrom had disclosed nothing confidential. Wookey personally acquired almost 70,000 shares of COC stock on margin, while Anderson had nearly 8,000. In addition, they bought more than 300,000 shares in the name of the brokerage, a commitment they managed to conceal from their other partners. So much of the firm's money was tied up in COC stock that the auditors for the TSE discovered that Rennie and Company temporarily lacked the required minimum free capital. The exchange governors quickly fined the brokerage $15,000 and suspended it from doing business for the month of November 1962.[9]

Alistair Dow of the *Toronto Daily Star* learned that Wookey and Anderson had actively tried to deceive officials of the TSE about their firm's true situation. When the exchange auditor first learned of the capital deficiency on 9 October, Anderson panicked and claimed that he had a binding promise from Shell to purchase all of Rennie and Company's COC shares. Wookey then appealed to his friend Grafstrom, who agreed to write him a letter containing such a commitment, falsely dated to make it appear to have been in place for some time. Grafstrom insisted that this letter had been intended only for Anderson's eyes, but the very next day it was shown to the exchange auditor. The TSE then demanded that the letter be formally produced, but Graftstrom refused to permit this and got in touch with exchange president Howard Graham, so the letter was hastily withdrawn on 13 October. With Rennie and Company clearly in violation of exchange rules, the governors imposed the heavy fine and suspension. Wookey and Anderson admitted that they had acted under 'extreme stress and panic,' but they claimed, less convincingly, that they had subsequently realized their actions were wrong and withdrawn the letter because their consciences would not permit them to sustain the deception. Wookey was subsequently sued by two of his disgruntled partners in the brokerage house, with whom he made a large settlement.[10]

While Wookey and Anderson's conduct seemed highly dubious, there was no evidence that they had done anything unlawful. Disseminating insider information was perfectly legal, and Grafstrom could have told anybody he pleased about his plans. A leak of this sort might be contrary to accepted business morality, but Grafstrom's only responsibilities were to his employer, Shell, and its shareholders. In fact, he seems to have revealed nothing to Wookey, who drew his conclusions about Shell's determination to consummate the takeover largely from the fact that his friend Grafstrom had made a visit to corporate headquarters in Holland. Wookey, of course, was under no obligation to COC and recommended his own customers to purchase its stock to their profit. He was not even the most aggressive operator since an Amsterdam bank had acquired an even larger block of shares. Jack Kimber pointed out that while the circumstances that had led to the original investigation order certainly appeared 'very suspicious,' plausible explanations existed for everything. Since the TSE had already severely punished Rennie and Company, the OSC decided not to take action against Wookey and Anderson over the deceptive letter. After the *Star* raised a further outcry, however, the commission felt obliged to reconsider. In the end the conclusion was that since both men had been in the securities business for some time and possessed exemplary records and their brokerage firm had already been heavily penalized, their OSC registration should not be cancelled.[11]

The only immediate result of the furor over Shell's acquisition of Canadian Oil Companies was that the stock exchange got together with the Investment Dealers Association and the Trust Companies Association to develop a voluntary code of conduct for takeovers. By January 1963 a draft had been developed and submitted to all members for study. Meanwhile, the Provincial Secretary's Department was also considering imposing a version of the rules adopted in Britain, but Jack Kimber, who now headed the OSC following Lennox's death, pointed out that regulating takeovers would be difficult without also considering the conduct of corporate insiders. Eventually it was decided that the whole subject required more detailed study. In October 1963 Attorney General Frederick Cass announced the appointment of a committee chaired by Jack Kimber, consisting of Deputy Attorney General W.B. Common and lawyer R.A. Davies, with instructions to consider changes in the regulations concerning both takeovers and insider trading.[12]

Before long, however, broader concerns were raised regarding the amount of information available to investors about corporate operations. Shareholders were entitled to receive annual reports and financial statements, but certain companies still refused to disclose other important information. Ogilvy Flour Mills had an investment portfolio valued at $11 million whose makeup it refused to reveal. Though listed on the Toronto Stock Exchange, Ogilvy had not sought to raise funds from the public for a generation, so that neither the exchange nor the OSC had ever been in a position to compel the company to file a prospectus. A similar situation was known to exist in the case of both Coniagas Mines and Loblaw's supermarkets, but there was nothing that the OSC could do.[13] Thus in the autumn of 1963 the Kimber committee decided to recommend that it should conduct a more wide-ranging review of securities legislation, and that more members should be recruited. Corporation lawyer H.C.F. Mockridge was asked to join, along with two people from the financial community, C.W.

Goldring and T.A.M. Hutchison, while from inside the civil service came H.I. Macdonald and J.S. Yoerger. TSE president Howard Graham was also approached, but he subsequently withdrew on the grounds that he might find himself in a conflict of interest if the committee ultimately recommended significant changes in the role of the exchange.[14]

While this body awaited submissions from the financial and legal world, the report of the federal Royal Commission on Banking and Finance in February 1964 also called for changes.[15] Chaired by Dana Porter, who was familiar with the problems of the securities industry from his term as attorney general of Ontario during the early 1950s, this commission concluded that Canada's stock exchanges lacked both the resources and the authority to protect investors properly. Even when they did choose to act, they 'occasionally find themselves in conflict with their members, and quite frequently encounter massive resistance from a public anxious to make a quick profit on speculative securities.' Many abuses stemmed from lax listing requirements, which led some people to believe that the exchanges were little more than gambling dens. The Toronto Stock Exchange, for instance, lacked fixed standards even for industrial issues, which did not have to have a solid earnings record, provided that they could satisfy the Listing Committee in other ways. Rules concerning disclosure of financial information, proxies, and trading by insiders were absent in Canada. When four hundred companies had been pressed to publish interim financial statements by the TSE, over half did not even bother to reply and only fifty had agreed to do so. 'We were told,' said the royal commission, 'that delistings for reasons other than voluntary choice or outright fraud were very infrequent, not amounting to half a dozen in recent years.' Recent efforts to adopt more stringent rules in Toronto had encountered resistance, not least because of competition for business from the Montreal Stock Exchange, which 'goes well beyond the point of a normal, healthy rivalry in some instances.'

The Porter commission found that exchange members created many of their own problems. A 1962 study of the MSE showed that 30 per cent of all transactions were for traders' own accounts.[16] 'Much more serious possibilities of abuse arise from the unique practice of some Canadian exchanges of permitting the primary distribution of shares through their facilities.' A promoter normally held the controlling interest in a junior mining company, so that conflicts of interest, wash trading, and treasury looting were real and obvious dangers. The trading of large blocks of stock by insiders meant that 'a true auction market no longer exists'; artificial share prices could often be sustained in hopes of attracting outside investors. The TSE's failure to require the automatic distribution of its filing statements about the material facts concerning primary distributions to share buyers was a 'serious weakness' that left investors with little information and no rights of rescission. The royal commission called upon the TSE to 'intensify its efforts to police the activities of primary distributors.' The ultimate goal should be to end this system altogether, so that 'all new issues should be sold off the exchanges under the direct supervision of the securities commission.'

Porter's report declared that equity investing was 'a field in which hanky-panky at the fringes is temptingly easy.' Nor was self-regulation a panacea. Organizations such as the Broker Dealers Association might have raised standards, but 'the present situation is still less than perfect.' Self-regulation, with all its limitations, was 'made particularly significant by the inadequacies of the understaffed securities administrations.' 'Unfortunately, moreover, securities administrators are all too often willing to pass the difficult problems on to the self-regulating associations.' Organizations such as the BDA had to be carefully supervised to ensure that they were neither too lenient nor too arbitrary, and appeals must be permitted against their decisions. Regulators must take a more active role and assume 'final responsibility' for the health of the securities business, but to make 'substantial improvements' they needed more resources, human and financial. Some provincial securities commissions even lacked staff capable of analysing corporate financial reports. All in all, the Porter commission suggested, plenty of changes were required to improve the functioning of Canada's capital markets.[17]

In May 1964 the Ontario legislature created a Select Committee on Mining, which held hearings and received submissions on subjects including the financing of mining exploration.[18] This committee heard testimony high critical of the status quo. For instance, the United Steelworkers union, citing E.K. Cork's study for the Porter Royal Commission on Banking and Finance,[19] pointed out that even the Ontario Mining Association had admitted that of 6,679 public mining companies chartered in Ontario between 1907 and 1953, only 348 had found producing mines and just 54 had ever paid dividends. Since a mere 40 per cent of the funds raised by the sale of junior mining shares were estimated to have gone into company treasuries, of the $850 million that Cork calculated had been put up by investors in Canada between

1953 and 1960, $510 million had been absorbed by sales costs and promotional profits, while just $150 million had actually been spent on exploration. 'Any system of development financing conducted in the atmosphere of a gambling casino must be extremely inefficient,' said the Steelworkers, proposing a much more stringent regulatory system modelled upon the SEC in the United States.[20]

The great discovery by Texas Gulf Sulphur near Timmins in April 1964 brought a further reminder of the differences between Canadian and American law as far as the use of inside information was concerned. In the immediate aftermath of the announcement a number of company officials had purchased its shares. The SEC eventually laid charges of insider trading against Texas Gulf and thirteen of its employees and directors for having benefited from their privileged knowledge about the discovery when trading in its shares or supplying tips to others. At a trial in the spring of 1966 most of the charges were dismissed, but many of these findings were later reversed on appeal.[21]

The submissions received by the Kimber committee from organizations such as the Toronto Stock Exchange were mostly prepared during the first half of 1964, before the sensational rise and decline of Windfall stock in July. As a result these documents exuded a sense of complacency soon to be overtaken by events. The TSE's brief, for instance, included the laughable claim that when wash trading occurred, the losers were typically its own members rather than the general public.[22] The revelations about Windfall made it increasingly difficult to defend the status quo. Appearing before the Kimber committee in the autumn of 1964, David Grenier, financial editor of the *Toronto Telegram*, noted, 'The Windfall affair raised a good number of questions as to how far the [stock] exchange, in its role as a self-policing institution, was able to achieve a proper regulation, or whether there was a prima facie case ... that the [Ontario Securities] Commission should have exercised a more immediate disciplinary effect on the company concerned.' Liberal politician Elmer Sopha was blunter: 'I don't believe in self-regulation, and I don't believe in self-policing; I don't believe in setting up what are in effect clubs and saying to people, "Well, we entrust to you the responsibility for being good and obeying the law, and seeing that the investor gets a fair shake ..." There is the test ... they don't work; the self-regulating body does not police itself and a good many innocent people get hurt and hurt in such a way that they can ill afford to sustain the losses. We have seen it time and time again.'[23]

The briefs and testimony before the Kimber committee did, however, reveal a growing consensus that wider disclosure about internal corporate affairs was desirable. The Toronto Society of Financial Analysts pointed out that a recent study of the companies which made up the TSE's 300 index showed that 108 of them failed to release figures for at least one of the following categories: sales, year-to-year comparisons, numbers on the source and application of new capital funds, and interim financial statements. The Canadian Institute of Chartered Accountants wanted all shareholders to be sent quarterly financial statements. The TSE itself agreed that fuller financial information ought to be available about all public companies, together with reports on important events such as a change of control, the sale or acquisition of assets, legal proceedings, and changes in investments.[24]

When the Kimber committee delivered its report early in 1965, it commenced with the observation that the knowledge possessed by participants in securities markets was often imperfect, so that the objective of regulation ought to be the reduction of such imperfections and the promotion of efficiency. British law, upon which subsequent American and Canadian statutes were based, had always emphasized disclosure, and tightening standards had produced 'significant improvements and developments in ... ethical standards.' Dissemination of such information would serve both companies and their shareholders equally. The committee therefore recommended that the Ontario Securities Commission should be granted authority to force compliance with stricter reporting standards in financial statements and prospectuses.[25]

A similar consensus existed about proxies. Ontario law contained no requirement that shareholders be permitted to vote against any resolution at an annual meeting or to appoint some person other than a board nominee to cast their votes. Proxy battles were almost unheard of since dissidents often had no choice except abstention, which merely played into the hands of management in most cases. Companies were not required to distribute explanatory circulars to their stockholders as they were in the United States, and the Canadian Bar Association pointed out that misleading information had sometimes been used in proxy fights. Both the CBA and the TSE therefore proposed that all companies incorporated in Ontario or listed on the exchange, as well as any with over one hundred shareholders with Ontario addresses, should be required to send out information to stockholders that would allow them to exercise their voting rights intelligently.[26] The committee agreed that new rules were required: 'Capital investors, both domestic and foreign, are demanding more adequate information as well as greater protection.' Choices should be permitted to shareholders in the case of nominations and other key issues. Solicitation of proxies about nominations and other major issues should be mandatory, and each request should be accompanied by an information circular.[27]

Concern about the use of inside information was one of the issues that had led to creation of the Kimber committee, but there proved to be less agreement about what new rules were required in this area. The TSE's brief revealed a division of opinion. Some members contended that trading by insiders might make for more liquid markets and provide more realistic prices. The majority, however, believed that disclosure of insider trading was necessary, and that a register open for public inspection should be created for monthly reporting of all trades by senior officers and those shareholders possessing an interest of 10 per cent or more in a public company.[28]

Most of the witnesses before the Kimber committee were unequivocal about the need to control insider trading. David Grenier of the *Telegram* argued that there was a widespread conviction that those with privileged information were skimming off the cream. The Canadian Bar Association's brief bluntly observed, 'The unfortunate fact is that insiders ... appear regularly to take advantage of this information ... The only inhibition against abuse is a remnant of social pressure or religious conviction. Some people seem to believe that taking advantage of insider information is like cheating at income tax – only bad when you are caught.' Speaking for the CBA, W.J. DesLauriers declared that the sale or purchase of a security on the basis of inside information which might materially affect its value ought to be banned. Still, the lawyers wanted only annual filings about insider dealings with the OSC, at least at first, on the rather feeble grounds that too frequent disclosure would only dampen the public appetite for such information.[29]

The Kimber report concluded that insider trading certainly took place, though its extent was unknown. If securities dealings were to operate upon the basis of the widest possible knowledge, then disclosure requirements provided the first line of defence. In addition, some statutory controls seemed necessary to ensure that insiders who profited from trades that materially affected the value of a security could be compelled to compensate those who suffered from their actions. The first step was a precise but flexible definition of an insider, and the committee proposed to include all directors and senior officers of a company as well as the five highest paid employees earning more than $20,000 per annum. Other employees might come to possess confidential information, but their policing ought to be left to management. Since substantial stockholders might receive such news, those who held more than 10 per cent of a company's shares should be considered insiders, following the same arbitrary standard established by the SEC. They ought to be required to report on any trades within ten days of the end of each month, the details to be published by the OSC. Insider trading, however, should not bring automatic sanctions unless wrongdoing or liability could be established. If a company failed to bring an action against some person, any other shareholder might apply to the Supreme Court for an order authorizing the OSC to commence an action for recovery of damages.[30]

On the matter of takeovers, which had originally spawned the creation of the committee, there proved to be little agreement in the financial community. In the press, people who sought to take over going concerns were often represented as predatory 'raiders,' and such deals aroused anger that insiders were extracting high prices for the sale of a control block of shares, premiums that were not available to other stockholders. Yet in the business world the general view was that takeovers could be advantageous to companies and shareholders alike, creating additional value by dislodging uninspired managers, installing more efficient organization, and supplying additional investment. The representatives of the Canadian Bar Association, for instance, told the Kimber committee that public companies ought not to be given protection against takeover bids, nor should insiders be supplied with additional legal weapons to repel them. Shareholders needed only the opportunity to pronounce upon mergers or amalgamations on the basis of full disclosure.[31]

In recent times there had been a number of controversial takeover offers in which bidders had attempted to conceal their identities. David Grenier of the *Telegram* argued that concealment always favoured buyers, who believed that secrecy might help to reduce the price demanded, while it did nothing for the ordinary shareholder. Yet the bar association and the Investment Dealers Association suggested that there was no need for cash bidders to reveal themselves; those offering securities should do so in order to allow the market to value their bids more accurately.[32] There was also disagreement on the question of how to handle a bid limited to a specified percentage of the outstanding stock, since it might benefit insiders unduly if offers were accepted on a first-come, first-served basis before other shareholders even had an opportunity to tender. The CBA argued that requiring shares to be taken on a pro rata basis from all tenderers would hamper bidders and might make takeovers more difficult. The IDA, however, felt that if more shares were offered than sought, equity required that they should be taken up pro rata.[33]

In dealing with takeovers, the Kimber report began by observing that despite the suspicions they aroused, mergers were not inherently harmful and might well be economically desirable. Yet a set of statutory rules was required to make vital information available to the shareholders of the target company without unduly impeding bidders or putting them at a disadvantage when faced with a hostile response. A takeover bid, then, should be defined as an offer that would leave the successful bidder controlling more than 20 per cent of the outstanding voting shares (including any owned beforehand). Cash bidders need not identify themselves. Each offer should include a circular, and the management of the target should have enough time to assess a bid and give advice to its shareholders if it wished to do so.

Such a system would require a set of time limits: offers must be tabled for at least seven days to permit targets to consider them, followed by a two-week period for management to pronounce and shareholders to decide whether or not to tender their stock. Bidders who raised their offers would be required to pay the higher price for all shares ultimately acquired. If an offer did not cover all the outstanding shares in a given class, then those tendered should be accepted pro rata to the desired level. If adopted, these rules would result in more open and efficient capital markets, which would not only increase public confidence but benefit investors since non-disclosure was more likely to be harmful.[34]

Having received the report of the Kimber committee, the Ontario government awaited the findings of the royal commission into the Windfall affair. The default by Atlantic Acceptance in June 1965 only seemed to emphasize the urgent need for tighter securities regulation. Kimber reported to the province's attorney general that while the public had lost up to $3 million over Windfall, the collapse of Atlantic was likely to cost its shareholders more than $50 million. He pointed out, however, that investors had misconceptions about the current legislation: the Securities Act was only a 'disclosure' statute, not a 'discretionary' law designed to permit the commission to assess the merits of any particular investment. Registration of any share offering that met cer-

tain specified criteria indicated no endorsement of its future soundness. Once a prospectus had been accepted for filing, the OSC had
neither the authority nor the resources to supervise internal corporate
affairs on a continuing basis. Though speculative mining ventures had
long created problems, Kimber observed that in recent years financial-
service companies had also become a particular cause of concern; they
operated on slim profit margins but with little equity beyond a constantly varying list of investments, which made it hard to assess their
true worth. A radical change in the OSC's mandate would be required
to permit continuing supervision over them.[35]

II

The Kimber committee had originally been established in 1963 to advise
the Ontario government on ways to deal with takeovers and insider
trading, but its mandate was subsequently extended to include a wider
review of securities legislation. The royal commission on the Windfall
affair was instructed not only to examine the conduct of the promoters,
George and Viola MacMillan, but also to consider the broader issues
raised by the financing of mineral exploration through the flotation of
public companies. As a result, Mr Justice Arthur Kelly's report on
Windfall, released in September 1965, dealt with a number of issues that
were also covered in the Kimber report, delivered a few months earlier.
On some subjects the two documents agreed, while on others they differed significantly.

Kelly began his analysis by arguing that current regulatory legislation, which had not been significantly amended since the end of the
Second World War, suffered from serious deficiencies. For one thing,
the Securities Act contained no statement of its purposes. Many investors clearly liked to gamble on speculative stocks, and the Ontario
Securities Commission was not supposed to prevent them from doing
so. Yet some people in the securities business exploited this urge by
using promotional techniques and hard-sell methods; the likelihood of
improper conduct was increased because of the incentives for dubious
behaviour. Wrote Kelly, 'The protection to which the investor is entitled is only from the use of improper methods in the merchandising of
securities.'

Yet the legislation seemed defective to Kelly even for those purposes. He argued that the OSC had carved out for itself a workable
sphere of control over the issuing of securities only by a 'self-con-

ferred' extension of its power to reject prospectuses. In the main the commission tried to follow its own precedents, but it sometimes exercised its discretion even though the legislation contained no fixed standards of reference against which to gauge whether or not a particular requirement was fair or appropriate. The result was an undesirable lack of clarity about what was required to register an issue. That fact was clear, since it was admitted that a person familiar only with the statute and the precedents upon which the commission relied, but without any experience of the working practices of the OSC, would not be able to make a successful filing.[36] Such an undesirable situation pointed up the inadequacy of the statutory regime under which the securities business operated.[37]

The relationship between the OSC and the TSE was a particular case in point. Kelly accepted that self-regulation under government supervision was theoretically superior to any alternative, since exchange members might know the best means to achieve any desired end. Yet in practice, he pointed out, the TSE's control over its members had proven to be feeble for three reasons. First, rule making had not kept pace with the ingenuity of evaders; second, the spirit of existing rules was often ignored; and finally, there had been a 'woeful' lack of supervision over the way things were actually done. During the Windfall frenzy some members had treated the TSE like 'a private gaming club maintained for their own benefit' and created the impression that the exchange existed 'for the personal convenience and profit of some of the persons associated with it.' For instance, testimony before Kelly had revealed that resort was frequently had to accomodation trades, by using a third party so as to avoid revealing that brokers were selling shares to their own customers. The TSE must accept some fairly drastic changes in its governing structures if public confidence was to be regained, and self-regulation must be subject to outside supervision if investors, members, and listed companies were to accept that the exchange had become a legitimate institution that aimed to serve the public.[38]

Kelly believed that if the Securities Act was to be rewritten, then the provincial government and the legislature ought to make clear its objectives. Because of the division of constitutional authority between the federal government and the provinces, the Criminal Code could provide protection only against certain types of fraudulent conduct such as misrepresentation and wash trading. Investor protection therefore required provincial legislation, and Kelly suggested that there were at least half a dozen potential aims worthy of consideration. To protect share buyers the act might regulate sales practices and seek to prevent market manipulation. There might be a ban upon the solicitation of sums beyond those required for specified purposes, and supervision to ensure that funds raised were actually used for these ends. More general public-policy objectives could include efforts to minimize interference with free markets and the requirement of full disclosure about the internal affairs of public companies. In any event, Kelly argued, a new act ought to identify its purposes clearly and specify the tasks to be performed by the OSC. Such legislation need not contain detailed provisions covering every conceivable matter, because it was necessary to allow flexibility to cope with changing circumstances, provided that statutory regulations were not designed to make policy, as often happened at present, but simply to implement it.[39]

Clearly, the exchange must be brought much more closely under the OSC's control. Whatever the theoretical virtues of self-regulation, Kelly approvingly cited former SEC chair William O. Douglas's observation that exchanges were private associations which operated like clubs and so should not be vested with responsibility for determining the public interest. In light of the abuses revealed by the Windfall inquiry, the legislature must decide how much external regulation was required. As agents, brokers must act in the interests of their customers, follow their instructions, and avoid conflicts of interest. Segregating these functions from those of brokers dealing on their own accounts would help to prevent such conflicts and at the same time put an end to the lower commission rates enjoyed by insiders, which acted as a postive incentive to engage in short-term in-and-out shifts, to the possible detriment of brokerage customers.

In addition, the OSC urgently needed the authority to compel the revision of a number of other exchange rules. While listing requirements seemed to operate reasonably well in the case of industrial companies, speculative mining promotions had largely escaped effective control. The argument that delisting dormant companies might harm their shareholders must be weighed against the many undesirable uses to which corporate shells had been put. At the present time the TSE had exempted up to four hundred companies even from the requirement to make filing statements about material changes, so that they were effectively freed from disclosure requirements before they raised additional capital. Unconfirmed rumours had plainly affected the price of Windfall shares, so the TSE had a duty to demand disclosure, and listed companies must accept that they could have no secrets from the public. In fact, listing requirements should be more, not less, stringent than the prospectus rules for unlisted issues. The OSC should have explicit authority to oversee the performance of any responsibilities delegated to the TSE.

Kelly knew that he must consider whether to recommend ending the current system which permitted listed companies to undertake the primary distribution of additional shares at the same time as secondary trading continued. He asked the commission staff: 'Isn't this one of the things we are going to have to make a finding on – as to whether the present wasteful way in financing is necessary, or whether there is an alternative? ... [A]ssuming the present system has to be maintained, can it be protected against this secondary profiteering?'[40] In other countries, stock exchanges were devoted entirely to secondary trading of securities, and even if the worst abuses associated with primary sales could be eliminated, the two activities did not mix comfortably. Although the mining industry's growth had unquestionably played a vital role in the economic development of Ontario, the fact that the odds of any given project succeeding were very low could not be ignored. Investors were still willing to put up sizeable amounts of money, especially in the aftermath of big discoveries like Texas Gulf Sulphur's, but the financing methods that had evolved channelled unduly large sums into the hands of promoters rather than supporting exploration and development.

The Kimber committee had devoted considerable time to considering this same question. It heard a forthright condemnation of current practices from the mining promoters at Pope and Company, who thought that primary distribution through the exchange was nothing but 'an invitation to promoters to rob the public.' The price of shares under option was inflated in order to draw in unwary unvestors until marketing was completed, but this support ceased once the 'legalized theft' had occurred. Nobody seemed to care very much about the subsequent falls in share prices unless they were too precipitous, in which case the exchange governors only clucked about the evils of promoters and threatened to cancel listings. The OSC might believe that the TSE supervised these flotations effectively, but no promoter considered that to be the case. In fact, Pope and Company even offered to accept a subpoena from the committee in order to present further chapter and verse concerning the evils of insider trading and price manipulation without fear of libel suits.[41]

Journalist David Grenier also argued to the Kimber committee that Canadians were ready enough to take risks by buying junior equities, but that was no reason to allow mining and oil operators to market securities with no intrinsic value through the TSE. How could a company's shares be in primary distribution at the same time as they were trading on the secondary market? In the aftermath of the Windfall affair, Grenier contended that the TSE governors could no longer be relied upon to deal with such problems: 'I think that asking the exchange to exercise a decision is a difficult issue, simply because the exchange must primarily represent the interest of its members. It is not a publicly-owned body and you can't expect it to behave like a publicly-owned body.' Thus the whole philosophy adopted in 1947 was fundamentally flawed: 'I do not think that a self-policing institution is in a position to represent the public interest. The public interest must be involved by a public regulatory body.'[42]

Most people were not prepared to accept such a stern conclusion. The Canadian Bar Association complained that it had not really had sufficient time to study the whole issue, so existing arrangements should continue 'at least for the present time.' Ending primary distribution through the exchange summarily would simply deprive investors of the protection that its rules did afford.[43] Not surprisingly, the TSE's brief to the Kimber committee defended current practices. Prepared well before the Windfall scandal broke, this document conceded that speculative oil and mining issues could create problems, but it argued that the exchange had imposed much tighter controls over such flotations in recent years. Since 1958, listed companies had been required to submit filing statements including the terms of all underwriting and option agreements before commencing a primary distribution. Underwriters had an obligation to maintain orderly markets, but rumours, tips, and genuine news might still provoke sharp price fluctuations, while penny stocks were particularly subject to price manipulation by wash trading. Against these problems must be weighed the value to Canada of the resource development funded in this fashion.[44]

By the time TSE chair Marshal Stearns led a delegation of exchange officials to testify in front of the Kimber committee in the autumn of 1964, Windfall had garnered the exchange bushels of bad publicity. On the issue of dormant companies, exchange president Howard Graham insisted that a real effort had been made to review all its listings during the past year. Though such shells numbered as many as two hundred, the TSE had come in for severe criticism from the investing public for trying to withdraw any listing, thus removing the last selling point for a stock. '[F]rom a practical point of view,' said Stearns, 'that company will be a completely dead duck, [and] it will surrender its charter in a very short time, because it is an asset to have a listed company.' Wasn't it better to allow a mining promoter to procure another prospect through a shell and try to raise the money to find a mine through a further primary distribution?

Who really benefited from this system in which dormant concerns were treated differently from applicants for new listings, asked committee member H.C.F. Mockridge? A shell did not have to demonstrate that its current properties had any real promise of being developed into a mine, and it might be a completely speculative vehicle to market shares. The real beneficiaries were the promoters and those investors who had already lost money speculating, as against other people who were prepared to put up additional money for the stock. If further work on a company's properties wasn't justified, there was no reason to allow promoters to raise additional funds for a new venture.[45]

Exchange governor J.E. Houston argued, however, that investors who purchased speculative shares wanted to gamble and were not interested in reading elaborate prospectuses. If that were really so, asked committee member Ian Macdonald, wouldn't it be better to treat that part of the securities business in the same way as horse racing, so that the players would know from the outset that they risked losing their entire stake, rather than mixing together trading in long-established blue-chip industrials with the primary distribution of penny mining stocks? Jack Kimber broached the idea of a separate stock exchange to trade only speculative shares. TSE vice-president W.L. Somerville's reply was that this solution might improve matters from a public-relations point of view, but it was not going remedy any of the underlying problems plaguing the marketing of speculative shares. On the contrary, with such an exchange dominated by mining promoters, the abuses were likely to be more widespread. Stearns added that the duplication of facilities was unlikely to produce any economies; better to allow the TSE to designate clearly which stocks were in the course of primary distribution, so that investors would know where they stood.[46]

After considering all the submissions, the Kimber committee concluded that the TSE's rules were the source of many of the problems. Promoters were eager to gain control of dormant shells with exchange listings because they could then obtain permission to engage in primary distribution to raise funds more easily than by meeting the requirements for a new listing. All that needed to be done was to submit a filing statement detailing new underwriting and option agreements without demonstrating that company properties contained any ore reserves. In preparation for such an operation, a promoter would normally work at 'conditioning the market' by buying up a number of the outstanding, low-priced shares. The results were fourfold: new interest was aroused in the stock by these bids; a price level was established at which additional stock might be disposed of; before the distribution of additional treasury shares began, the float of stock was reduced; and the promoter acquired additional inexpensive stock to feed into the market if the operation succeeded. Once a primary distribution began, the share price was normally fixed largely by buying and selling out of the 'box' controlled by the broker for the underwriter. Sometimes running a market would entail significant purchases by the insiders to induce increases or block declines. At all times promoters were entitled to sell any 'free' shares not subject to escrow agreements. No fixed maximums governed the prices at which stock could be sold on the exchange, though the rules did require options to be exercised when prices rose sharply.

The Kimber committee's analysis remorselessly exposed the failings of this system. First of all, price manipulation using strategic purchases and carefully orchestrated news leaks and rumours, if not cruder illegal methods such as wash trading, was positively encouraged. Since the assets of junior mines had no measurable value, tips about drilling results and finds on adjacent properties could all too easily be manufactured and spread around. The price and volume of trading recorded on the exchange tape simply facilitated such activities since nothing was revealed there about the amount of insider dealing. As a result, one party, the promoter, had a clear interest in undertaking such manipulation. Taken together with a lack of public knowledge about when primary distribution was actually taking place, the whole process ran contrary to accepted wisdom. The Kimber committee concluded, 'Most people regard a stock exchange as a place where the trading is confined to shares already issued and distributed, and where transactions are effected among bona fide sellers and buyers. There is no real disclosure of material facts made to the buyer of speculative securities in this type of primary distribution. For these reasons, primary distribution on the exchange is inconsistent with a free market.'

Piecemeal repairs could not overcome these flaws. Even if compa-

nies were required to file prospectuses, it would be virtually impossible to place them in the hands of buyers because of the almost
instantaneous execution of trades on the exchange. The current filing
statements might constitute partial disclosure, but they were not
widely distributed and purchasers did not receive them. Omissions
and misinformation contained in such statements were not subject to
the penalties that applied to prospectuses. Defenders of the current
system frequently referred to the quickness with which the Filing
Statement Committee could approve applications, but there was no
reason why full disclosure should be sacrificed when speed was
mainly in the interests of the promoter and issuer rather than the
investing public. Speedy approvals and the feverish trading that sometimes resulted conferred further advantages upon exchange members
and floor traders; they could watch and anticipate price changes much
more easily than outsiders, who depended upon the tape, which could
sometimes lag seriously behind events on the floor. Own-account trading by TSE members was not controlled, and floor traders were permitted wide latitude to trade for their personal or house accounts.

The committee's conclusions were blunt:

> The existing system of primary distribution thrives on the traffic in the
> dormant or inactive company (the shell company). There is no justifica-
> tion in the public interest for the trading in the control of these corporate
> shells which now takes place. The Exchange's rules applicable to these
> companies are not sufficiently strict; shell companies do not deserve the
> stamp of reputability attached to an Exchange listing. It is not possible to
> justify a listing system which has relatively high initial listing require-
> ments, yet permits a shell company to enter into financing arrangements
> through the facilities of the Exchange for the purpose of speculative
> exploration of unproven property and generating trading profits for pro-
> moters and underwriters. It should also be kept in mind that the old
> shareholders get an undeserved 'free ride' in these cases at the expense of
> the new shareholders.

Control of shells was cheap and easy to obtain, which made it all the
more difficult to exclude undesirable promoters. Such people and their
activities ensured that only a small percentage of the capital raised
went into exploration, so that the cost of raising funds was high and
the chance of creating a working mine was low. Confidence not only in
the TSE but in the entire Canadian financial community was impaired

as a result. If such methods had once been necessary to procure funds for mining and oil ventures, that time had long passed. What should be done? In other countries companies must be financed through private placements or over-the-counter flotations before qualifying for an exchange listing. In Britain a legal judgment in 1892 had held that the market-support techniques routinely employed in Canada involved the common-law offence of conspiracy to defraud if individuals agreed to purchase stock in an attempt to induce others to believe that there was a bona fide market for the shares. After the crash of 1929 American state laws and exchange rules had eliminated such distribution in order to create genuinely free markets for securities. The Kimber committee therefore recommended that Ontario should follow these precedents and outlaw primary distribution through the Toronto Stock Exchange. Speculative mining and oil companies would then have to be financed in the same way as industrials, while OSC and exchange regulations could be tightened up to ensure that all dormant companies were deprived of their listings. 'We have concluded that the alleged detriment to shareholders of such a delisting policy is to some extent illusory, and, in any event, of lesser importance than the reputation of the Toronto Stock Exchange and the financial community generally.'

Since the imperfections of the over-the-counter market were well known and in some cases even more serious than operations on the TSE, these changes could not simply be implemented overnight. The committee therefore recommended that the Ontario Securities Commission undertake a special study in collaboration with the exchange, the Investment Dealers Association, and the Broker Dealers Association to see what new rules would be required to govern new flotations. The anti-manipulation sanctions in section 325 of the Criminal Code, which were hardly ever applied, might have to be rewritten to make them more enforceable. While these studies were under way, all primary distribution on the TSE should be phased out during a two-year period. The Securities Act should be rewritten to provide the OSC with additional powers to regulate underwriters, optionees, and selling groups so that their activities could be effectively policed, and the commission would need more powers to compel the TSE to supervise listed companies more closely and delist shells promptly.[47]

After considering the evidence he had heard about Windfall, however, Mr Justice Kelly reached a different conclusion. He argued that while the TSE should be left to handle secondary trading in well-seasoned issues, mines, oils, or industrials, a separate exchange should be established for trading the stock of speculative ventures, so that investors could understand exactly what they were getting into.[48]

III

With the recommendations from both the Kimber committee and the Windfall royal commission in hand, the OSC staff began drafting a new Securities Act in the autumn of 1965. The main objective, in the words of OSC director Harry Bray, was to write a law that 'faithfully reproduces and indeed improves upon' the recommendations of the Kimber committee. Early in 1966 Jack Kimber reported to Attorney General Arthur Wishart that draft legislation was now ready.[49]

With the case of Prudential Finance in mind, the bill gave the OSC wider authority, so that instead of simply approving or disapproving applications for registration by a securities issuer, it would now be able to impose specific conditions. The commission's investigative powers would be left unchanged since these were needed to unravel complicated transactions. However, the rules for commission hearings should be set forth in more detail, confirming the right of applicants to have legal counsel who could cross-examine witnesses and to appeal its decisions. Commission staff could still summon witnesses to appear, but from now on only judges would have the power to find those who refused to testify in contempt.[50]

Private placements of securities, sold by agreement and not offered to the public, might be exempted altogether from the registration and prospectus requirements. To objections that this policy would not prevent the recurrence of the problems created by Atlantic Acceptance's dealings with the likes of the Ford Foundation, Jack Kimber's reply was that sizeable financial institutions had a responsibility to protect themselves against such risks. The changes to the Securities Act in 1963 already permitted such institutions to register as 'exempt purchasers' who did not need to receive prospectuses. Now it was proposed to make all purchases by institutions valued at over $100,000 automatically exempt from prospectus requirements. Consideration had been given to permitting individuals to claim a similar exemption, but it had been decided that this degree of sophistication could only be presumed about companies rather than about persons.[51]

Other proposed changes had frequently been discussed, such as the requirement that all underwriters of share issues be registered. The

Windfall affair had demonstrated conclusively that it was the promoters who really controlled the sale of stock during a primary distribution, and the commission was determined to gain direct authority over these people so as to exclude undesirables. Another change was the authorization of preliminary prospectuses. Under the current law, buyers for new issues were not supposed to be solicited until the OSC had accepted a completed prospectus for filing, but though the practice was technically illegal, brokers and underwriters frequently canvassed customers on an 'if, as, and when issued' basis in order to assess price and demand for a new flotation. Better to legitimize the status quo by permitting a preliminary document to be shown to those solicited, with a final prospectus going only to actual buyers. At the same time, share buyers should be granted the right to rescind a purchase up to forty-eight hours after a prospectus had been delivered. In fact, purchasers could even nullify a sale on the basis of untrue statements in a prospectus without having to show, as at present, that they had relied upon the document in making the investment. These provisions, Jack Kimber predicted, were certain to arouse a storm of protest from brokers, but they would not only ensure fuller disclosure and make the issuers of prospectuses more conscientious.[52]

The bill naturally contained new rules regarding takeovers, which closely followed the recommendations of the Kimber committee. Any bid for more than 20 per cent of a company's shares (including those already controlled by the bidder) should be open for a minimum period of twenty-one days, and shares tendered could not be taken up for another seven days in case a higher offer was received. Circulars must be issued to inform investors about the details of a bid, and the directors of a target company should make recommendations to their fellow shareholders about whether or not to accept; similar rules would apply to proxies, so that shareholders might make informed choices. Also adopted was the committee's recommendation that the identity of a cash bidder need not be revealed. Since takeovers were often advantageous for the shareholders of target companies, it was argued that nothing unnecessary should be done to discourage them, such as the publicity surrounding a failed bid.[53]

Insider trading was now to be regulated. Directors and officers, including the five highest paid employees, as well as persons holding more than 10 per cent of the stock were to be classed as corporate insiders. Whenever their shareholdings changed, these people would have ten days from the month-end to make a filing with the OSC disclosing their initial and final interests. Insiders who failed to file might be liable to compensate other investors who suffered losses as a result over the succeeding two years. The requirement that individuals disclose personal financial information proved controversial. Several provincial cabinet ministers quickly objected to the fact that all insiders must make an initial public declaration about their investments as an invasion of privacy. Jack Kimber responded that this disclosure was owed to other shareholders: nobody seeking a business partner would expect to refuse co-venturers details about the exact size of a personal interest. Likewise, individuals who held themselves out as officers or directors of a public company should be prepared to reveal the size of their stake in it. Their responsibilities included protecting the rights of investors, and the larger their personal interest, the more diligent they could be expected to be. In a speculative venture the identity of those with sizeable holdings could be especially important, and people ought not to be able to hide behind nominees. Since anyone might become a shareholder in a publicly traded company, this information ought to be generally available. Potential investors should be able to learn the current position of each insider.[54]

Finally, there was the thorny issue of whether or not to permit the primary distribution of treasury shares in a company through the stock exchange at the same time as secondary trading was occurring. Lawyer James Baillie, who headed the OSC's Timmins Area Inquiry established at the time of the Windfall affair, pointed out that any change carried its own risks: 'To me the chaos which would result if the distribution of all speculative mining companies was removed from the Exchange would be little short of catastrophic. Primary distribution unquestionably acts as a destabilizing influence which opens possibilities of manipulation on the Toronto Stock Exchange; off the Toronto Stock Exchange these factors would be magnified rather than lessened. With presently available facilities only the Toronto Stock Exchange can provide the pure white light of publicity which I feel to be needed as a disinfectant.' Baillie also rejected the idea that 'a secondary or subsidiary stock exchange would solve anything.' Better to give the OSC more authority to police trading in speculative shares on the TSE. When the exchange polled its own members in the autumn of 1965, eighty-six of ninety-seven responded, with sixty-one favouring the continuation of the present system, twenty-four wanting to shift distribution to over-the-counter markets, and only nine supporting the creation of a second exchange for speculative stocks alone.[55]

Like Baillie, Jack Kimber was not attracted by the idea of a separate exchange proposed by the Windfall royal commission. True, it might serve to warn investors and perhaps enhance the reputation of the TSE, but it could also create plenty of problems. The demand for tighter control came from brokers and investment dealers who specialized in industrial blue-chips, but 'A separation of the exchanges would remove the influence of the more conservative members and might delay the adoption of improved standards.' On an exchange designed to serve the promoters of speculative issues alone, the temptation to manipulate prices when making primary distributions would be even more irresistible. The present system, though flawed, did at least permit the small investor to participate in mining plays, and changes might put a serious crimp in financing for this important industry. Moreover, Kimber pointed out, Ontario was not alone among the provinces in permitting primary distribution of securities through exchange facilities. To ban the practice in Toronto might solve none of the problems, but simply propel them into other jurisdictions in the absence of some prior agreement with other governments. Better to give the OSC authority to approve all TSE by-laws and to make orders about practices deemed to be contrary to the public interest and force the exchange to comply. The draft bill did not recommend ending the current system.[56]

Rising in the legislature on 16 March 1966 to move first reading of the new Securities Act, Attorney General Wishart emphasized how closely it followed the recommendations of both the Kimber committee and the Windfall commission. The main thrust of the bill was to ensure fuller and more accurate disclosure for investors. Prospectuses would contain greater detail; public companies must make financial disclosure every six months; investors would have a chance to scrutinize proxies and takeover bids; insiders would have to reveal their dealings. The OSC was being given much more authority over the TSE. Primary distribution through the exchange was not banned, but Wishart promised that the problems which it created would continue to be closely studied.[57]

The *Financial Post* reported that opinion in the financial community was generally favourable towards the bill, but the opposition parties in the legislature were less complimentary. Liberal Vernon Singer charged that Ontario was simply lurching from one fiasco like Windfall to another like Atlantic Acceptance. The new act might be an improvement, but 'It is too little and too late.' Had it not been for the scandals, the government might have taken no action at all. Singer remarked scornfully that legislation 'failed to enter into the most sacred of Tory realms, the stock exchange,' or made any effort to 'end the archaic self-interest perpetuated in the Toronto Stock Exchange.' The OSC, he suggested, would be a far more effective regulator if freed from control by the government and allowed to report directly to the legislature.[58]

Fellow Liberal Elmer Sopha spoke for the miners and prospectors in his Sudbury riding, reminding everyone that he had been saying for years that the 'activities on Bay Street ... gave our country a bad name in foreign lands.' Why had nothing been done to prevent scams like Windfall, which had 'created such a furor and such a pang of anguish in this province among those who gambled for gold in the gigantic crap game on Bay Street?' The answer, of course, was that the Conservatives didn't want to do anything that 'interrupts or interferes with or disturbs the serenity of the private club that operates the Toronto Stock Exchange.' Wilfred Posluns, 'a Jew fighting city hall,' had found himself summarily booted off the exchange. Even the regulators, who were supposed to protect investors from those seeking to 'mulct them of their savings,' often targeted the wrong people, so that hard-working promoters were 'harried to bits, to distraction, by the securities commission.' Playing to his northern constituency, Sopha even had a kind word for promoters such as Louis 'Keneski' (Cadesky) and Sam 'Siglund' (Ciglen), who, he claimed, 'had created a lot of jobs. They took their chances.' Meanwhile the blue-chip brokers who controlled the exchange looked down on the over-the-counter traders, even though the professional traders were mostly 'floor chisellers' blessed with what 'amounts to a license to steal' from the public because they paid only one-fifth the regular commission rate. How many more people had to be hurt before the government got up the nerve to tackle the TSE and clean up this private club?[59]

For the New Democrats James Renwick echoed many of the same complaints. The number of scandals and corporate bankruptices suggested that something was seriously wrong with the TSE as a self-regulatory body. The government had better stop procrastinating and put an end to primary distribution on the floor by shifting it to a separate exchange for speculative undertakings. Renwick insisted that the bill did not provide the OSC with the necessary powers to control the TSE, since the ultimate sanction of withdrawing formal recognition would never be used because it would topple the financial world into chaos. The commission needed an entirely new mandate that would include specified regulatory powers, though it was essential that it continue to report to the legislature through a government minister so that parliamentarians could have their say.[60]

The attorney general took all of this in good part. Sopha's speech he dismissed as 'a demonstration of erudition obscured by a considerable amount of circumlocution,' in which the member was simply snorting and sniping rather than proposing any real alternatives. The government had shown its concern about these problems by appointing the Kimber committee away back in 1963, well before the Windfall affair. Wishart insisted that his opponents were wrong: the bill gave the OSC plenty of authority to control the TSE should it prove necessary. Yet it would be foolish to end primary distribution on the exchange without careful consideration of what might replace the current system. Second reading was then approved, and the bill sent off to committee, where interested parties would have ample opportunity to make their views known.[61]

When the Standing Committee on Legal Bills held its first meeting on this matter in May, there was a long list of groups such as the Canadian Institute of Chartered Accountants and the Canadian Bar Association ready to make submissions. Some organizations welcomed the legislation. The 425 members of the Toronto Society of Financial Analysts applauded the requirement for continuous disclosure of financial information, pointing out that American rules were already much stiffer. In an obvious reference to Atlantic Acceptance, the analysts observed that a number of Ontario companies had suddenly collapsed without investors having any hint of their difficulties because of the lack of such information. As its members depended on such data for their livelihood, the society pronounced itself generally 'most satisfied' with the bill.[62] Other people seized the opportunity to promote their pet projects. For instance, the Broker Dealers Association sought an end to the ban on salespeople calling private residences, as it had been doing for the past fifteen years. To that suggestion Jack Kimber's response was forthright: 'I certainly do not think that securities should be sold on a door-to-door basis.'[63]

The Toronto Stock Exchange's response to the bill was mixed. On insider trading and disclosure of financial information the exchange noted that the legislation accorded well with its brief to the Kimber committee. But the idea of regulating takeover bids by statute was rejected, the TSE preferring nothing more than the voluntary code of conduct that it had put forward in 1963.[64] On the central issue of primary distribution of stocks through the facilities of the exchange, its governors were relieved that the demands for an outright ban had fallen upon deaf ears. Yet chair Marshal Stearns remained strongly critical of any proposal to require each company to file a revised prospectus with the OSC before undertaking primary distribution. The excessive influence of rumour upon the price of speculative shares had often been condemned, but delays would only add to the uncertainty and make it more difficult for the exchange to ensure that markets remained orderly. Nor would the new requirements prevent treasury shares from being sold into a fluctuating market in which prices were not governed by supply and demand alone. Everyone admitted that the timing of an issue was critical for junior resource companies. If promoters were faced with the risk that the moment to raise large sums from investors might pass irrevocably while they awaited approval of a prospectus by the commission, they would no longer continue to rely upon public financing but would be forced to turn to already well-established mineral producers to fund exploration and development. All other ventures would be compelled to depend upon the over-the-counter market, where regulation was even feebler than on the exchange, leaving the OSC faced with an even greater challenge.

Stearns did admit that the complaints about present financing practices were sometimes justified, since comparatively small sums often went into a company's treasury, insiders had too many opportunities to profit from insider trading, and share purchasers were usually in the dark, without either the information contained in a prospectus or the right to rescind a deal for misrepresentation. He insisted, however, that the TSE was already preparing a revised set of rules which would ensure closer supervision of trading on its floor and provide stronger sanctions against wash trades. Unsavoury characters would no longer be permitted to promote their ventures through the exchange, and there would be controls to ensure that the funds raised were spent for the designated purposes. Underwriters would have to seek approval from the exchange by providing a filing statement and one of material facts that could be delivered to buyers, who would now have the right of rescission. The TSE would supervise trading to ensure that bona fide distribution occurred at arm's length and that trading by insiders was only designed to stabilize the market.[65]

The most serious criticisms of the bill came from an unexpected source, the Canadian Manufacturers Association. Though its members included most of the blue-chip companies that seemed unlikely to have much concern about the more speculative side of securities markets, H.J. Shurtleff, manager of the CMA's Legislation Department, prepared a ringing attack. His principal objection was to a lack of uniformity across the country if Ontario moved to change its rules without persuading the other provinces to follow suit. Some businesses would be compelled to disclose financial information that their competitors could conceal. Nor was there evidence that the intrusive rules to govern insider trading met a pressing need or promised benefits outweighing their detriments. Instead, new regulations on matters such as insider trading would simply confuse the roles of directors and shareholders, imposing obligations upon the latter even when they lacked legal responsibilities, and making it harder to recruit directors or to induce them to hold large interests in companies. Rather than targeting this 'most innocent' group, they should require all brokers and share owners to reveal their holdings.[66]

Shurtleff also produced a legal opinion from lawyer J.J. Robinette that cast doubt upon the constitutionality of key sections of the new act. An attempt was being made to regulate the conduct of insiders in companies incorporated in Ontario even if they lived elsewhere. How could the province claim the right to penalize the director of an Ontario company resident in Quebec when he used his inside knowledge to benefit from a trade in its shares conducted wholly in his home province? The new rules about proxies would require federally incorporated companies listed on the Toronto Stock Exchange to send notices to any shareholders whose last known address was in Ontario, a clear attempt to interfere with the relationship between these companies and their shareholders. As for takeover bids, the act would also require federal companies to send offering circulars to the address of any shareholder living in Ontario, another effort to control the activities by the management of such extra-provincial corporations. Robinette concluded ominously that this was not an 'exhaustive' opinion, but that there seemed to be enough doubts about provincial jurisdiction to justify a reference to the courts before the bill was passed.[67]

The government had no intention of following such a course. The Kimber committee had taken the precaution of consulting Mr Justice Bora Laskin of the Supreme Court of Ontario about the constitutionality of its recommendations, and Jack Kimber was quietly confident that the bill could withstand any challenge. Companies affected were those with clear connections to financial markets located in Ontario, because they either had a listing on the Toronto Stock Exchange or sold their securities to investors living in the province. Federal companies without an exchange listing that did not seek to raise money in Ontario would not fall under the new regulations. While uniformity might be desirable in theory, the federal government had left its Companies Act unaltered for a period of twenty-five years, despite repeated proposals for harmonization with the provinces. Even a reference case was certain to entail a considerable delay while any decision was appealed to the Supreme Court of Canada.

Kimber believed that the CMA's animus against the bill had originated with the head of the legal department of the Steel Company of Canada, who seemed to feel that the required level of disclosure might have an adverse effect upon his firm and wanted federal companies to be held to less-strict standards than provincial ones. Why this was so remained unclear since many large companies in Canada were already providing this kind of information, either voluntarily or because American law required it. The International Nickel Company, for instance, had to comply with SEC rules because its shares were listed on the New York Stock Exchange, and U.S. regulators had been seeking for some time to persuade other Canadian companies whose shares were marketed south of the border to make similar disclosure.[68] Kimber reported to the deputy attorney general that he had reason to believe that not all members of the CMA supported its brief, and that while they might quibble about details, most of them felt the new act was a step in the right direction.[69]

During May and June of 1966 the legislative committee held nine meetings to review the act clause by clause.[70] For the opposition parties the discussion was again dominated by Liberal Elmer Sopha and New Democrat James Renwick, Attorney General Wishart, backed up by the OSC's Jack Kimber, defended the proposals for the government. Few changes were actually made. The Investment Dealers Association challenged the mere possession of $100,000 as the mark of a 'sophisticated' investor who did not require regulatory protection. Kimber admitted that the definition was arbitrary but necessary; in the end the figure was simply reduced to $97,000, leaving $3,000 to cover the cost of commissions on a deal. The Broker Dealers Association and the Canadian Mutual Fund Association renewed their pitch to allow salespeople to call on private residences, but the attorney general declared that the ban reflected definite government policy and would only be changed after consideration by cabinet, so the proposed amendment was rejected.[71] J.J. Robinette expounded his doubts about the constitutionality of the provisions for disclosure and insider trading so far as they applied to non-Ontario companies, but to no effect. An effort by Renwick to impose the same standards as the SEC and require companies to reveal the remuneration paid to each chief executive officer was also turned back. A proposal by Liberal Vernon Singer to ban members of the Ontario Securities Commission from trading in securities altogether was rejected, as was a suggestion from the Canadian Bar Association that commissioners be given quasi-judicial appointments with fixed terms on the American model.

The only significant amendment concerned the vexed question of whether to permit the primary distribution of shares through the facilities of the Toronto Stock Exchange. The original bill would have allowed the practice to continue, but Renwick proposed a complicated amendment to section 58 which would have eliminated it altogether. Because of some confusion on the part of the government members of the committee, this amendment was adopted when two Conservatives voted in favour of the proposal. The attorney general was then left scrambling to arrive at a compromise, and in the end, the bill was further modified. Listed companies proposing a primary distribution must still file a statement of material facts with the TSE which had to be approved before selling might commence. However, share buyers would now have to be supplied with these statements and permitted a forty-eight-hour period in which they might rescind their purchases under a 'welsh' clause, in the same way as people who had received full prospectuses for over-the-counter stocks.[72]

When the bill returned to the legislature for third and final reading, the New Democrats took up the attack once more. James Renwick and Kenneth Bryden demanded that insider trading rules be further tightened along American lines so as to punish 'tippees' who received and acted upon tips. Otherwise what was to stop insiders from passing along confidential information to someone else who might make a killing but escape any punishment? The attorney general pooh-poohed that idea: nobody was going to give out inside information without getting something in return, and receiving such benefits was now illegal. Renwick repeated his condemnation of the government for its lax attitude towards the Toronto Stock Exchange and proposed a lengthy amendment to give the Ontario Securities Commission more control over it. Elmer Sopha endorsed the idea, repeating his assertion that the Posluns case showed that anti-Semitism was rife in the financial world. But Arthur Wishart pointed out that Renwick had failed to make his proposal at the committee stage, and the house voted down the change and passed the new Securities Act into law.[73]

Still left, of course, was the complex task of drafting the statutory regulations. Wishart had originally told the legislative committee that he hoped to have a draft of the regulations ready for its consideration, but he later admitted that the task had proven too complex, though he promised that all representations from interested parties would receive careful attention. Jack Kimber made clear, however, that while he would be glad to meet with various interest groups, they should not regard these negotiations as an opportunity to 'knock down' the principles of the new legislation. Nonetheless, W.L.S. Trivett, secretary of a special securities law committee of the Canadian Bar Association, announced that he was at work on another brief that 'would point out some unfortunate holes in the act. It isn't going to work, you know.'[74]

For his part, Jack Kimber was well satisfied. In a memorandum to the deputy attorney general he drew attention to a speech by the SEC's Manuel Cohen before the National Association of Securities Administrators in the United States, in which Cohen had remarked favourably upon Ontario's new Securities Act and observed that the SEC ought to catch up by imposing its own regulations regarding takeover bids. Following instructions from the cabinet, the OSC commenced a series of public hearings on the proposed regulations in the autumn of 1966. Kimber told Cohen that most of the meetings had consisted merely of informal discussions. The financial community seemed keen to make helpful suggestions that would allow the rules work well without imposing undue burdens, and nobody had raised major objections to the new disclosure requirements. 'I feel it is quite fair to say that the industry in Ontario has generally accepted the philosophy of our new act without any strong opposition.'[75]

The OSC director, Harry Bray, was also pleased with the changes: 'The Securities Act, 1966, represents a change in philosophy. Since the Security Frauds Prevention Act was passed in 1928 the legislation has required registration of people engaged in selling securities to the public ... The securities themselves were to be the subject of filings ... The Securities Act, 1966, enables a somewhat more flexible approach in that terms and conditions may have to be applied to registration.' 'The new approach is found in the concept, for the first time in Canadian law, that once a man has purchased he immediately becomes potentially a seller, and both the buyer and seller are entitled to a continuing quantity of information concerning securities that are publicly traded.' Required was 'a much more sophisticated and detailed disclosure' in a comprehensible narrative form that would cover not only financial information but primary distributions, takeover bids, proxies, and insider trading, so that investors might make informed decisions.

Criticisms of the act Bray largely dismissed. True, both the Kelly and the Kimber reports had recommended changes to the current system of primary distribution of listed stocks through the TSE because it 'encourages promoters to manipulate the price of stocks upward, whether by criminal means or some other market devices in order that they might make a maximum profit.' As a result, 'Much outcry has been raised because primary distribution was not totally removed from the Toronto Stock Exchange.' Yet requiring filing statements to be approved in advance and distributed to buyers would permit the OSC and the TSE to create a system 'designed to minimize the opportunities of profiting from manipulation.' The opposition parties had suggested that the act did not give the commission adequate power to supervise the operations of the exchange, but Bray thought that section 139 was 'disarmingly simply because of its breadth. It gives the commission complete power to direct the manner in which the stock exchange carries on business, to interpret or vary any bylaw, ruling, instruction or regulation of the stock exchange, to direct how trading is to be conducted and the standards of listing, and to generally supervise the activities of the exchange, where it appears to be in the public interest.' In fact, said Bray, 'the new act might almost be called, as [is] its American counterpart, The Securities and Exchange Act.'[76]

All that remained to be done before the new act came into force was the completion of an internal reorganization at the OSC. Kimber and Bray had been working away on changes ever since the latter's appointment to replace the disgraced John Campbell as director. Bray observed that 'with the resignation of Mr. Campbell in September, 1964 a low ebb had been reached. On my return to the Commission ... the first problem to deal with was morale.'[77] One year later Jack Kimber reminded Attorney General Arthur Wishart that although they had discussed a code of conduct regarding share ownership by the OSC staff, no formal rules had ever been issued. Prohibiting people from trading securities altogether not only might create hardships but seemed unnecessary since the commission possessed little or no information about many stocks. Perhaps the best way to deal with the problem would be that adopted by the SEC in Washington: staff must not

trade any issue about which the commission had confidential information on pain of disciplinary action.[78]

Nothing was done until the spring of 1966, when Kimber prepared a
draft set of rules based upon the American precedents. Again, matters
were allowed to slide, but in the autumn he pressed Wishart to
approve the rules. The commission staff was eager to have firm guidelines because 'The matter which highlighted this most significantly
was the difficulty that arose with the previous Director.' The OSC *Bulletin* finally set forth new rules in its October number, pointing out that
high standards must be maintained and conflicts of interest avoided in
order to ensure public confidence in the agency. As a result, nobody
was to be permited to use his or her official position for personal profit.
Employees and their immediate households were allowed to trade in
securities only for 'bona fide investment purposes.' Shares were not to
be purchased for at least sixty days following the filing of a prospectus
or the issuing of a ruling by the commission, and all transactions were
to be reported within five business days. Employees assigned to work
on the affairs of a securities issuer in which they held an interest must
declare that fact and might be reassigned as a result. All members of
the staff were to file a complete list of their holdings with the commission annually.[79]

In the spring of 1965 Bray pointed out that in the aftermath of the
Windfall affair the commission was now scrutinizing mining prospectuses with a new rigour, since 'the cost of raising money is out of all
proportion to the money spent in the ground.' Not only that, but as
the complaints showed, at long last the OSC was also casting a
sterner eye upon industrial and finance company promotions: 'No
doubt it has been disturbing to those engaged actively in the preparation and submission of filings to discover that the period of "anything goes," provided it is disclosed, is past. No doubt it is equally
disturbing to find a hardening of attitude to the promoter as opposed
to the risk which he, in fact, is taking. I suspect that it might properly
be said that we are taking an aggressive attitude towards mining, as
towards all filings, and I would hope that this aggressiveness is not
in any manner viewed as hostile.'[80] Tougher standards had been imposed once more lawyers joined the investigatory staff as higher salaries made recruiting easier. 'For the first time lawyers were hired specifically to review prospectuses.' Chartered accountants were now
being added where 'Previously, our so-called auditors were individuals who had had some accounting experience, preferably in the secu-

rities business. The net result ... was an increased professionalism in the commission staff.'[81]

In the summer of 1965 the management consultants Price, Waterhouse and Company were asked to undertake a full study of the OSC.[82] The shape of the 'basic organization' responsible for overseeing registration, auditing, and legal issues had not been altered since 1947. The staff of the chief auditor was responsible for reviewing the financial information in prospectuses as well as conducting routine audits of dealers and undertaking special inquiries, while the chief counsel was to check prospectuses for legal compliance. As a result of this division of responsibilities, no one person actually made recommendations to the director as to the acceptability of a new prospectus.

The consultants therefore proposed a thoroughgoing restructuring. Since the new Securities Act required the commission to take on the additional responsibilities of regulating insider trading and monitoring continuous financial reporting along with the supervision of takeover bids, the size of the staff should be increased from fifty-seven to seventy-nine. Four new operating sections should be created: registration to handle applications; filings to review prospectuses; investigation to conduct surveillance and enforcement; and administration to manage common needs. The four chiefs would report to the director, and the senior staff ought to be paid at rates competitive with private employment or else the OSC would be unable to carry out its functions or attract 'able young professional men.' Only by recruiting 'able and experienced' people would the commission become a desirable place for new recruits to work, gaining professional expertise even if they had to sacrifice something in earnings. The commission counsel should be a seasoned senior lawyer freed of operational duties to give legal opinions and advise the chair; the commission accountant should occupy a similar position on the financial side; and a research assistant, a 'young man of particular promise,' should be available to undertake special studies.

When the position of director had been created in 1963, the government had assumed that chairing the OSC would be a part-time position, and Jack Kimber was expected to continue to occupy himself part-time as a master of the Ontario Supreme Court. But the Windfall affair and the creation of the Kimber committee, along with the work generated by booming securities markets, required him to devote all his energies to the commission. In the autumn of 1964 the attorney general had therefore recommended that he be given a salary of $20,000 and $6,000 for heading up the committee.[83] A year later the commission proper still consisted only of Kimber with part-time assistance from the provincial mining commissioner, J.F. McFarland, though the act provided for as many as three other members. The Price, Waterhouse consultants recommended that from now on the OSC ought always to consist of five people, perhaps retirees from 'distinguished careers' in finance, accounting, and the law, who met at regular intervals.

These changes, it was hoped, would rectify some frequently heard complaints. Outsiders often protested about the lack of published rules, policies, and decisions beyond the decisions in the OSC's *Bulletin*. From time to time there had been grumbling that standards differed among the members of the commission's staff. Harry Bray admitted that such discontent 'might have had some justification. This should become increasingly less.'[84] Because the new Securities Act granted considerably greater discretion in rejecting prospectuses, it was all the more important that policy guidelines be made public and an internal manual of administrative procedures developed. The Price, Waterhouse consultants suggested that if the commission was able to provide a reasonably firm estimate of the time required to pass upon a typical prospectus, then applicants could know when a proposed issue might be offered to the public. The filings staff should prepare a single report on each application and end delays and overlaps as prospectuses moved between the present registry and audit sections. Once preliminary approval had been given to an offering, a final go-ahead on a sale price for shares might be granted in as little as twenty-four hours. Meanwhile, the rest of the audit staff should be transferred to investigations, where a strong group was required to ensure public confidence. The central administration should service the other sections and maintain a card file of all persons and companies, including the new reports on insider trading and continuous financial disclosure.

As soon as the report of the management consultants was received in January 1966, Kimber moved to begin implementing their recommendations. Within a month he reported to the deputy attorney general that he had transferred some of the director's responsibilities to the heads of the new registration and filing sections, who could now approve routine applications. Only problem cases need be referred to the director, who was empowered to refuse filings.[85] By the end of the year the the statutory regulations under the new Securities Act had been approved; both were to come into force on 1 May 1967. At the same time the OSC was transferred from the ministry of the attorney general to the new department of Financial and Commercial Affairs. The minister, H.L. Rowntree, praised the new act, saying that he was 'fed up with business being done under the table ... This bill will help ensure that business is done on top of the table.'[86]

Kimber reported to Rowntree that another part-time commissioner, law professor John Willis, had already been added but that two vacancies still remained. Since the commission counsel, accountant, and research assistant were supposed to report to specific commissioners on particular issues, they had not yet been appointed. Meanwhile, the filing staff was fully occupied reviewing prospectuses, and at least two and perhaps as many as four more people were required. So many vacancies remained in the vitally important investigation branch that some cases were receiving scant attention, since eight new appointees were still needed. With the rush of new work generated once insiders began to file their trading reports, the central administration staff would also have to be expanded.[87]

Meanwhile, other changes in the securities business were in the cards. Early in 1966 Howard Graham announced his intention to retire as president of the Toronto Stock Exchange, and the search for a successor got under way. The board was eager to secure someone well known and respected to shore up its reputation following the black eye it had received from Windfall. Various names were suggested: Ontario chief justice George Gale, Windfall commissioner Arthur Kelly, former federal Conservative finance minister Donald Fleming, or experienced corporate executives such as Trevor Moore of Imperial Oil and Harvey Cruikshank of Bell Telephone. When Graham stepped down on 30 June after the exchange's annual meeting, no replacement had yet been chosen.[88]

Not until November 1966 did the TSE governors come up with a promising runner. Jack Kimber wrote to the attorney general to say that he had been approached to take over at the exchange. Though the position did not seem as challenging as his present one, it would, after all, mean a lot more money after a number of years of sacrificing a corporation lawyer's paycheque for the responsibilities of public service. Would the cabinet mind if he took the job? The ministers raised no objections, and in January 1967 the TSE board voted to offer Kimber the presidency at an annual salary of $40,000. He took up his new post on 1 May the very day that Ontario's new Securities Act came into force.[89]

9

Decline of the Broker-Dealer

The new Securities Act that came into force in Ontario in 1967 relied principally upon greater disclosure about corporate affairs to protect investors. By that time the business of Toronto's broker-dealers who promoted speculative shares in the over-the-counter market had already entered a serious decline. The 1961 ban on marketing unregistered stocks in the United States, forced on the Broker Dealers Association by the Toronto Stock Exchange, quickly took a heavy toll, since up to three-quarters of the shares in speculative mining companies had been sold over the telephone to American buyers. A decade earlier the Broker Dealers Association had counted 179 members, but by 1963 only 66 firms remained in business. So precarious had the financial position of the BDA become by then that the governors were forced to reduce the annual retainer of their legal counsel and sublet the boardroom in an effort to balance the books.[1] These cutbacks proved to be but a portent of things to come.

I

Other Canadian provinces came to be almost as hostile as the Americans to the activities of Toronto boiler rooms. In 1963 the BDA's efforts to persuade officials to allow telephone solicitations without seeking registration from local regulators came to naught.[2] Before long, Manitoba laid charges against W. McKenzie Securities of Toronto on the basis of a complaint from a Shilo man. Having received both telephone calls and a tipsheet from the broker, he bought some stock in Canadian Gift Sales for about $5. When he proposed to sell the shares in February 1964 for just half what he had paid, he was persuaded to hold on, even though the company soon collapsed into bankruptcy; at the same time he was induced to buy 1,000 shares of Marimac Mines for 30 cents apiece. The brokers were charged with unlawfully trading since they were not registered under the Manitoba Securities Act.[3]

Found guilty, McKenzie Securities launched an appeal on the grounds that the firm was duly registered under Ontario law and had committed no acts within the jurisdiction of the province of Manitoba. Interprovincial trade fell solely under federal authority, so that the provinces could not regulate it. Seeking support from the BDA, the McKenzie people pointed out that a successful appeal would remove such marketing from provincial control entirely and open the way for Toronto broker-dealers to peddle shares from coast to coast without fear of provincial interference. After procuring a legal opinion from a Toronto firm, however, BDA executive secretary Michael Gee reported to the board that he thought there was less than a fifty-fifty chance of the appeal succeeding. The BDA declined to participate.[4]

When the case came before the Manitoba Court of Appeal in 1966, the prosecution argued that the decision of the Judicial Committee of the Privy Council in *Lymburn v. Mayland* (1932) had granted provinces constitutional authority to pass legislation 'to secure that persons who carry on the business of dealing in securities shall be honest and of good repute, and in this way to protect the public from being defrauded.' Manitoba's Securities Act did not purport to regulate conduct outside the province's jurisdiction but merely to control the conduct of securities traders within its own boundaries. McKenzie had repeatedly contacted the Shilo man both by mail and by telephone, and his purchases constituted trading securities in Manitoba. The conviction was unanimously sustained, and leave to appeal to the Supreme Court of Canada was subsequently denied.[5]

Meanwhile, the Ontario Securities Commission was doing its best to clamp down upon dishonest sales practices. A 1961 policy statement made clear that 'irresponsible use of material and reports prepared by interested parties specifically for use in promotional sendouts would not be tolerated.'[6] Nonetheless, in 1965 James Stewart put out a market letter claiming that Ganda Silver Mines had made 'an enormous gold discovery,' and he sought to create the impression that a commercial mine was in the offing by references to the construction of a pilot ore mill. Since the find was neither new nor enormous, Stewart was haled before the commission and warned that 'Practices verging on the deceitful or fraudulent will not be tolerated.'[7]

The OSC took a particularly stern view of mining exploration companies that simply purchased shares of other speculative promotions. The OSC's J.R. Kimber pointed out that many major mining companies raised additional capital to finance exploration, but they had other assets that gave some intrinsic value to their securities. In a 1965 decision the commission noted that ventures such as Rivalda Investment Corporation aimed only to engage in short-term speculations designed to profit from market fluctuations. Rivalda's success should rest upon the ability of its directors to assess the value of various mining properties, so that its prospectus ought to disclose their backgrounds in this field. In fact, only one Rivalda director had any such experience at all and that limited to a single property which had not yet reached production as a commercial mine. If the promoters retained qualified advisers to play the role of investment counsellor and a well-trained geologist who could supply independent, practical, and experienced advice, said the OSC, then Rivalda's stock might be marketed to the public.[8]

Promoters still went to great lengths to deceive the unwary. In 1966 Harry Bray waxed almost poetic in describing one such scheme:

> Raising capital for 'grass roots' development is difficult for at this point in time the purchaser is being asked to purchase an interest in a hope. That hope is that against substantial odds this property, or perhaps some future property, will prove to contain fabulous wealth. It is the kind of questing hope that has driven man over the horizon to seek new frontiers and into the atmospere to seek new worlds. The first men on the moon will no doubt bring back geological samples.
>
> The cause of complaint is that the word pictures painted on occasion make this hope appear suspiciously like reality. Indications become fact, and in the wilderness of rock, muskeg, water and forest the shimmering image of a mine appears.

G.D. Richmond Securities might claim that a knowledgeable and well-informed reader would not be deceived by its tipsheet, but it was clear that the real objective was to convince the unsophisticated that Goldmaster Mines would become a 'golden carrot.' The OSC had been trying for years to rein in such flights of fancy, forbidding not only outright misrepresentations but deceptions created by the omission of material facts. If shysters had previously been able to escape punishment because the commission was too caught up in major investigations into scams like Windfall or Atlantic Acceptance, said Bray, times had now changed: 'It is my conclusion that those who complain of what they suggest is both new and unique in enforcement and administration are those who took advantage of the weakened surveillance and enforcement ability rather than adopting a policy of enlightened self-interest through self-discipline during what has been the most difficult period in the Commission's history. The substantial strength of this stand and its lack of fundamental morality must have served to sabotage the constructive efforts made by the BDA executive and its permanent secretary.'[9]

From time to time there continued to be allegations that criminal elements had infiltrated the securities business. In 1965 the author of a tipsheet on speculative mining stocks reported to the Toronto police that he had been threatened with violence if he talked too much, and two detectives visited a meeting of the governors of the Broker Dealers Association to urge other people to come forward. The OSC promised to keep any information it secured confidential and not to use the revelations for disciplinary purposes. Fearing that the discussions at a public meeting were certain to leak out, the board directed secretary Michael Gee to write to BDA members asking them to come to see him so that he might brief them and request them to divulge any knowledge about such activities.[10]

An OSC investigation into the affairs of a dormant company called West Plains Oil Resources did reveal that shareholders had been offered an opportunity to convert their holdings into stock in two Nassau-based enterprises, Standard Mining and Oil Development and Essex Bank and Trust, upon payment of additional sums. The identities of the officers of these two shell companies could not be uncovered, but the post office boxes to which the money was sent were being cleared by Robert Webb and Michael Russ, the latter better known in the Toronto criminal courts as mobster Myer Rush. By the time the commission began investigating, however, they had fled Ontario, and only a single person could be subpoenaed to testify. The OSC was convinced that criminal types like Rush were behind the scam, but it was unable to demonstrate the connection beyond a doubt.[11]

Sometimes the OSC got anonymous telephone tips. Jack Kimber received a whole series of calls from a 'Mr Stewart,' alleging that Myer Rush had now switched his attentions to Victoria Algoma Mines. Calling from an apartment on Spadina Road in Toronto, salesmen were falsely representing themselves as employees of a member firm in the

TSE. The crooks had also sent a whole series of fake (or 'wooden') orders to buy the stock through members of the New York Stock Exchange backed up by forged certified cheques. All that the OSC could do was to issue a cease-trading order for Victoria Algoma because of misleading information about its properties in the prospectus.[12]

In 1967 Myer Rush was finally charged with conspiracy to defraud by selling shares in the deftly named De Veers Consolidated Mining Corporation. This case attracted great publicity when Rush was assaulted and beaten up in his home and then his room in a Toronto hotel was blown up. Jumping bail, he fled to Panama, but was eventually tracked down in Britain in June 1968. He was extradited to Canada on charges of having obtained cheques by false pretences and in 1969 was sentenced to ten years in jail.[13]

Yet Rush seems to have been unusual. Most criminals apparently preferred to stick to purveying commodities such as drugs and sex that did not require much effort to market.[14] Certainly, the cases investigated by the OSC mainly involved the familiar offences. Near the end of 1966, for instance, complaints about telephone selling in other provinces from Toronto revived. The BDA reissued its ban on members calling to places where they were not registered, and a formal notice was sent to all members making clear that this rule was intended to apply not just to the United States but to all parts of Canada. Summoned before the BDA board, Walter Cummings claimed to believe that the ban was to take effect only on 1 December; calls made since that date had been simply to collect unpaid accounts.[15] When the governors refused to accept such a lame excuse from someone who had until recently been a board member himself, Cummings hired a lawyer and challenged the disciplinary authority of the association. He staved off punishment for an entire year before agreeing to plead guilty, but when fined $500 and suspended for eight weeks by the BDA, he refused to accept the penalty. He tried to argue that the original 1961 ban on selling in other jurisdictions was 'apparently not on the books of the association.' Annoyed by all this foot-dragging, the OSC at long last issued a formal policy that shares could be marketed only by prospectus in the provinces where broker-dealers had complied with local requirements.[16]

The promoters of Wee-Gee Uranium also did their best to block any interference from the regulators. Claiming one of the largest finds in the world, Edward White took down 1 million shares at option prices ranging from 10 to 25 cents, selling them for between 65 cents and

$4.15. The OSC, however, stepped in and issued a blanket order in February 1968 suspending all trading in the stock on the grounds that there had been no genuine primary distribution. The commission complained that the shares were really being 'warehoused' with a group of White's confederates with the aim of reselling them for even higher prices on the basis of rumours about the exploration of claims in Quebec, where the company falsely claimed to be drilling.[17]

The Wee-Gee investigation was hampered by the fact that a sergeant in the Toronto police force, friendly with the promoters, kept interfering and trying to find out exactly what evidence the OSC had collected, even resorting to false pretences.[18] Eventually the commission concluded that it lacked sufficient evidence that the sales of Wee-Gee were really a 'secondary primary,'[19] and a judge held that the OSC had exceeded its authority in issuing the blanket cease-trading order, though seventeen insiders were still restrained from dealing in the stock. Edward White insisted that daily monitoring of the trading in Wee-Gee by all broker-dealers constituted harassment, and as he left the commission offices after a visit, he pointed at the staff member responsible and said menacingly, 'You are under wraps.' When the price of Wee-Gee shot up again in the summer of 1968, the commission imposed further cease-trading orders. At the same time the OSC persuaded the government to amend the Securities Act to grant it authority to ban trading in any stock altogether.[20]

The Wee-Gee insiders were so angry that they filed suit in the Supreme Court of Ontario for $5 million in damages, claiming that there was a conspiracy against them. Commissioner and law professor John Willis concluded that the OSC and its staff were in an exposed position. Legal tradition granted public servants protection for acts performed in their official capacities which lay within their jurisdiction, but the original blanket cease-trading order imposed on Wee-Gee was not covered because the OSC had been wrong in assuming that it possessed the authority to impose such a ban. Henry Langford, who had succeeded Jack Kimber as chair of the OSC in 1967, felt that the threat was sufficiently serious that he persuaded his minister to approve the hiring of renowned counsel J.J. Robinette to defend the case. Langford argued that 'it is of exceeding importance to the government that it be handled with efficiency and success. Any thought that members of government commissions could be successfully harassed in this way would render it exceedingly difficult to recruit candidates [to the OSC] in the future.'[21]

In addition to concerns about personal liability for negligent or malicious acts, there were fears that the Wee-Gee suit might be used to force the disclosure of internal OSC documents and communications, including information passed along by third parties. Should this demand succeed, it would certainly spawn a host of imitators amongst those disciplined by the commission. Robinette's defence therefore asserted the right of government to maintain secrecy, since it would be 'most inappropriate and dangerous if it were ever established that for the price of a writ and for the time it takes to raise frivolous allegations of conspiracy and malice, that a disgruntled person could force the complete disclosure of all material in the hands of the Commission relating to the matter.'[22] In the end, however, the Wee-Gee suit does not seem to have been pursued.

Meanwhile, membership in the BDA had entered a steep decline. In an effort to balance the books, even the boardroom sofa was sold off for $75. In 1970 the fees were increased to $1,000 ($400 for TSE members). By 1972 the small size of the association's membership made it difficult to keep the organization functioning without raising fees to levels certain to drive broker-dealers out of business. Fewer and fewer TSE members considered it worthwhile to belong to the association, so the board decided to reduce its size from nine to seven by cutting the number of seats reserved for TSE-member firms from three to one. A long-running OSC investigation into the affairs of W.D. Latimer and Company proved particularly debilitating because Latimer, a former BDA chair, acted as a dealer to all other brokers for many of the seven hundred over-the-counter issues traded by using its one hundred direct telephone connections to firms across Canada. In 1971 Latimer and one of its salesmen were charged with participating in a scheme to raise the price of shares in Santack Mines. The promoters had entered matching buy and sell orders through two different firms, but when Latimer's trader 'broke' the order between them, it concealed the manipulation. After the firm had stalled off the OSC by challenging the legality of its investigation for as long as possible, news of the charges finally became public in 1973, though it was two more years before Latimer received a three-month suspension.[23] By the time the Latimer hearing was held in 1975, the Broker Dealers Association was well on its way to oblivion. Only about fifteen broker-dealers continued to operate as the volume of trading in the over-the-counter market sagged sharply, and the organization gradually melted away to little more than a shadow of its former self.[24]

II

Parallelling the declining role of the broker-dealer during the 1960s and 1970s was a reduction in the number of junior mining promotions. Faced with the usual complaint that the drop-off in mining exploration was caused by over-strict regulation, Henry Langford decided to create a committee to look into the whole subject of mining-company finance in 1967. Commissioner D.S. Beatty, a former investment dealer, was tapped to head this body, which also included four other members of the OSC. The first step was to distribute an open letter requesting answers to a series of questions concerning the role of prospectors, the formation of mining-investment companies, the system of underwriting and options, and the granting and escrowing of vendor shares. In addition to considering the responses and briefs received, Beatty's committee held hearings in Toronto and travelled to Port Arthur, Sault Ste Marie, and Timmins in order to listen to testimony.[25]

The OSC staff also prepared its own submissions. Muriel Browne, who had long been responsible for examining all mining prospectuses, argued that the existing system, particularly the demand by vendors of every property to receive 750,000 shares, heavily favoured insiders. After all, junior mining companies were

> rarely more than a location bet – acquired at the cost of staking plus time – or from the original staker for $2[,000]–$6,000, on which a minimum program is recommended. Presupposing indifferent results and in an effort to hold the vendor shares, this program can be prolonged until a new property is staked to replace it – with another minimum program.
>
> Acquiring property by staking and/or option is good business, but if the moves are made chiefly for the purpose of protecting the vendor interest no real selection may be made, with the company and the public [the] losers.

Sellers of property often argued that they needed big blocks of stock to ensure control of the company, but 'This claim is at variance with the speed which freed [of escrow] vendor shares are offered for sale.'[26]

Most mining promoters, however, were fairly content with the status quo, and the Toronto Stock Exchange pronounced the current regulations satisfactory. President Jack Kimber admitted that the sharp criticisms of listed companies engaging in the primary distribution of additional shares through the exchange had sometimes been justified.

Yet he argued that new rules could be devised which would permit established companies with good track records that were willing to make prompt disclosure to continue to raise capital in this way.[27]

Beatty's report was delivered in the autumn of 1968. He began with a bow to the received wisdom that developing mineral resources in Canada was 'a part of the frontier economy, and as such it does not conform easily to the standards which more mature economies are able to impose. The leaders in this field are rugged individuals.' As a result, the current promotional system should not be tampered with, even though, as Beatty admitted, 'The view has been expressed to the committee that the main purpose in acquiring these properties is to enable the underwriter to sell stock to the public, rather than the purpose of selling stock to the public being to provide funds to develop a promising property.' Primary distribution of the shares of listed companies through the TSE should be allowed to continue, although the rules against price manipulation ought to be tightened up. Options should be limited in term and number to prevent promoters from dumping blocks of penny stock onto the market at a time when prices were rising. Meanwhile, the current system of granting vendor shares should not be changed; the only reform recommended was that 90 per cent of the vendor stock would no longer be escrowed but would belong to a different class with limited transferability of voting and special rights upon the winding up of the company. The Broker Dealers Association should draft a code of conduct to tighten discipline over its members and punish high-pressure selling. In response to persistent claims that prospectors and promoters could raise money only by going through the expensive and time-consuming red tape required by the OSC's prospectus requirements, Beatty proposed that individuals might be permitted to raise up to $100,000 for a project without producing an independent engineering report or an audited financial statement.[28]

These modest proposals produced little result. The Securities Act was amended in 1969 to permit a 'mining exploration company' to issue only a short and simplified prospectus when raising less than $100,000. Yet drafting the necessary regulations under the act proved devilishly difficult for the OSC. How did one define a genuine 'exploration' company to distinguish it from a mere promotional scheme? New regulations were eventually proclaimed law in the summer of 1970, but few people bothered to take advantage of them.[29]

Meanwhile, the promotion of speculative junior mining companies continued much as before, since the basic rules concerning options and underwritings, along with the escrowing of vendor stock, remained unchanged. A study prepared for the OSC during the summer of 1970 reported that in 20 per cent of cases the principal backer was also the incorporator of the company, and in 70 per cent of cases this individual became a director of the new venture. Eighty per cent of all promotions were handled by a single underwriter, who sold shares through registered dealers. Most of the shares were marketed at the maximum markup permitted. Broker-dealers took a commission of 25 per cent and underwriters between 15 and 25 per cent on a mining promotion. The OSC staff concluded that the main purpose of most promotions was still to sell shares, with little concern about whether or not a mine was discovered.[30]

The anaemic state of the market for junior mining shares led to continued complaints about over-strict regulation. Among the most vociferous critics of the OSC was J. Patrick Sheridan, who made a particularly outrageous speech to the 1972 annual convention of the Prospectors and Developers Association in which he singled out Jack Kimber and Harry Bray as the two people to blame for the depressed state of mining finance. Kimber's Toronto Stock Exchange required listed companies to make filings disclosing all material changes in their affairs, which emasculated the decision-making authority of corporate boards. But the principal villain was Bray, who had overseen the implementation of a triad of policies fatal to the flotation of junior mining promotions. First of all, companies could not exploit opportunities because they were not permitted to raise any more money than required for immediate exploration needs. Second, the OSC had developed a policy of refusing to allow junior mining companies to purchase shares of other like enterprises. Finally, the commission refused to free for sale escrowed shares granted to the vendors of claims, thus locking their investments in and impeding new ventures. Sheridan concluded his address with the inflammatory claim that Kimber and Bray were conspiring to prevent all future mining development in Ontario, and that one of them had even been heard to declare to a friend that there would be no more junior mining flotations in future.[31]

Harry Bray was so annoyed by Sheridan's charges that he prepared a long 'background paper' covering the entire history of the regulation of mining finance as far back as the Second World War.[32] Once upon a time freewheeling promoters had not hesitated to manipulate prices in order to market their stocks on the basis of the wildest rumours; the markups between option takedown values and selling prices had known no effective limits. Control positions changed hands on the TSE without restrictions, and professional traders could profit from going short when the inevitable declines in share prices occurred. Trading was normally suspended only when actual thefts from corporate treasuries were uncovered. Filing statements had been required only in 1958 after a series of treasury lootings. Despite the appointment of Howard Graham as president of the TSE 'to strengthen its image,' the Windfall affair had revealed that the rules still needed tightening significantly. Bray pointed out, 'It was not until the appointment of John Kimber in 1969 [sic, 1967] that the permanent staff attained substantial independence from the Board of Governors in fact as well as theory.' Then a surveillance staff had been created to keep an eye out for any unusual market activity and to intervene if necessary. Meanwhile, the members of the Broker Dealers Association remained 'merchandisers of paper who, operating within certain very broad rules, sold grossly inflated or misleading expectations through carefully designed mail or telephone campaigns.'

Bray devoted much of his paper to Sheridan's complaints that OSC regulation had actually interfered with mine development. 'In the atmosphere which then existed it cannot be questioned that it was not difficult for the legitimate promoter to obtain financing ... Unfortunately the amounts of money going to the company ... represented something less than one-third of the public subscriptions, with this amount being further reduced by the fees paid out of it to lawyers, accountants, engineers, professional secretaries and other administrative charges. In the majority of cases it is fair to conclude that little money was spent on the ground.' Bray argued that most promoters had little interest in establishing genuine exploration companies, preferring to market shares in companies owning nothing but 'moose pastures' with little apparent merit because they were 'more interested in selling paper than in producing a mine.' The number of broker-dealers had dwindled away, so that only nineteen now remained in business. Nothing that the commission could do, said Bray, was likely either to revive their business or to eliminate them entirely.

Promoters continued to play the tired tune that the depressed markets for mining shares were caused by over-regulation. Murray Watts demanded 'long overdue changes within the Ontario Securities Commission, or perhaps some other public body to take its place, since it long ago outlived whatever punitive usefulness it may once have possessed.' With Conservative-held seats in northern Ontario in danger, in

1973 the government announced consultations on revising OSC policies on the financing of junior mining and oil companies. Since escrowed vendor shares were now released only when there was substantial evidence that a commercial mine could be developed, few prospectors ever saw much return on such stock. In order to make raising money easier, proposed new policies would now permit the release of some shares if development work was being undertaken on the advice of a qualified engineer. Prospectors would thus realize some return even when no mine resulted.[33]

Still there remained a 'vocal segment' in both the Prospectors and Developers Association and the Broker Dealers Association who resented any interference with their activities. As one official of the Ministry of Natural Resources observed, 'Some of these may actually believe that a prospector is entitled to some sort of free ride at the public's expense, and that the only protection that should be offered the shareholder is "let the buyer beware."' After a 1974 investigation of Herbert and Company, which was promoting a whole stable of junior mining companies, the OSC complained that this operation still seemed to be run on the famous principle 'Never give a sucker an even break.' The OSC tried to send a warning: 'We will frown on prospectuses filed in the future which show a pattern of operation which can't help but be successful for the underwriter, but which may very well have little or no chance of being successful for the investors.'[34]

Nonetheless, a 1975 study concluded that the few remaining broker-dealers, many of whom operated as promoters and mining-company managers as well, continued to do business pretty much as usual, moving from one speculative venture to another on a 'one-shot' basis. Almost all of their profits seemed to come from the sale of the 75,000 vendor shares free from escrow. The face page of a prospectus for a junior mine was now required to disclose that there was no genuine resale market for its shares, but complaints to the OSC revealed that many buyers still had the impression that they could dispose of their stock if they wished. After the promoter withdrew support for an issue, the price collapsed and liquidation of the company was only a matter of time.[35]

Despite this dismal picture, the mining community continued to insist that the problems in raising funds for exploration and finding new mines stemmed from the regulations. In the spring of 1975 the Prospectors and Developers Association persuaded the new chair of the OSC, Arthur Pattillo, to order an elaborate set of hearings on how

the rules might be revised. As a sign of the degree to which the speculative junior mining sector had declined in economic importance, however, its self-appointed advocates received pretty rough handling from
the commissioners.[36] The OSC's counsel struck a sour note at the outset by pointing out that 80 per cent of the work of the investigation
branch concerned junior mining shares, leading people to wonder
whether any genuine markets existed for most of them.[37]

G.M. Webster set out the familiar complaints: 'I think the general
attitude of the mining fraternity is that the Ontario Securities Commission tends to be, or has tended to be, bureaucratic, autocratic and arrogant.' Promoters had shifted to Quebec and then to British Columbia
because the rules were now too restrictive in Ontario. Commissioner
R.M. Steiner, a retired investment dealer, responded that most promoters seemed interested only in mining people's pocketbooks rather than
exploring claims. Webster blustered that the difficulty was to identify
the fringe group who bent the rules, to separate the cats from the dogs.
'Not for me,' Pattillo shot back. 'I can tell the difference between a cat
and a dog.'[38]

Murray Watts trotted out the familiar gripe that it was impossible to
sell the stock of junior mines on the Toronto Stock Exchange any more.
Steiner, a former exchange governor, observed that the TSE had simply
told its members in 1961 that they had to stop running boiler rooms
selling unregistered shares in the United States by telephone or else
they would be kicked out. Faced with this threat, the Broker Dealers
Association had finally imposed discipline upon its own members; the
OSC had been happy to see the self-regulatory organizations functioning in the way that they were supposed to.

Watts then shifted into a recitation of the hallowed myths of Canadian mining history. Independent prospectors had once fanned out all
across Canada, but now they were all tied up in red tape by securities
regulators. In the good old days of the 1950s he had acted as prospector,
exploration manager, field geologist, pilot, even cook: 'these far-away
desposits could not have been developed by myself ... under today's
restrictive rules of the Commission with all its attendant excessive
costs.' It was no use relying on the established firms with producing
mines to find new ore bodies: 'They have never been other than follow-
ers.' All the problems stemmed from regulators listening to cry-babies
who had lost money. American investors 'would go in with the idea
that they were taking a long-shot bet,' but Canadians 'always wanted a
ten-cent clip, so that you are just not capable of maintaining it.'

Having listened to a great deal of grumbling from Watts over the years, the commissioners seized eagerly upon the chance to respond. Exactly which rules was he objecting to, asked vice-chair Harry Bray? When he received no specifics, Bray pointed out that the OSC had always been careful to consult the industry before issuing new policies, but 'Every time you come up and tell us something different.' When Watts complained about the recent requirement that all the vendor stock should be returned to the company treasury if a property was abandoned as barren, Arthur Pattillo snapped, 'Why should you get 750,000 shares you are entitled to keep, for a piece of moose pasture that you say is no good and that is not worth developing?' Watts blustered that he needed to control the company: 'I want to know that I have got the stock, that that is my stock and not somebody else's stock.' Pattillo counterpunched: 'I will tell you this, Mr. Watts, as long as I am Chairman of this Commission there is [sic] not going to be any further 750,000 shares handed out for a piece of moose pasture, and having an auditor set up a statement showing this land, which isn't worth a pinch of you-know what, as having a big value.' Only when he actually brought a valuable mine into production should a promoter reap a big profit. Watts tried once more: 'That sort of philosophy will wreck what is left of the business.' Pattillo was having none of it: did Watts want the OSC to have discretionary authority over who were to be allowed to keep their vendor stock, when all the briefs seemed to say that cut-and-dried rules for everyone were wanted?[39]

Geologist Michael Ogden did admit that there were fewer good mining prospects on offer than there had once been. Why then, asked Steiner, blame the regulators for killing junior mining in Ontario when the industry had simply run out of valuable claims? Hadn't the promoters moved to British Columbia because the economy there was booming and metal prices were high, so investors were keen to put up funds? Under questioning, Ogden conceded that the real problem was that prospectors were no longer being offered enough for their claims and broker-dealers were skimming off all the profits. As for the idea that buying a speculative mining stock was the same as purchasing a blue-chip, Ogden finally conceded, 'I would suggest that there cannot be an aftermarket ... To suggest that a penny promotion ... should try to maintain an aftermarket ... is a hopeless thing ... There is a distinct parallel between lottery ticket and this penny mining market.'[40]

Natural Resource People Canada, Incorporated, was a new organization composed of six hundred members of the Engineers Club of

Toronto who had connections to the mining business. W.S. Vaughan repeated the conventional wisdom that over-regulation by the OSC and the TSE was killing the mining industry. Once again the commissioners refused to take these criticisms lying down. Harry Bray replied, 'My philosophy has been ... not that there should [not] be a horse race, but that the horse race shouldn't be crooked and that's all ... That's the only philosophy I ever had ... That's all, okay?' Arthur Pattillo added that mining people had to take a share of any blame for the industry's problems, but so far every witness had claimed to be 'lilywhite': 'I could tell you if I wasn't sitting up in this position, if I was down below and cross-examining, there would be a lot of things coming out that I have been allowing to go [on], but I don't think anybody's fooled.' If investors were really as sophisticated as the witnesses were claiming, then there wouldn't have been a sharp nosedive in the stock market just last year. 'We wouldn't have had people thinking that all you did was buy, and that you never sold, and yet a lot of people would say that those were sophisticated people.' Share buyers should be told when they were putting their money into a highly speculative exploration company, and that there would be no buyers for their shares unless there was a material change, which would have to be reported.

The Natural Resource People trotted out a hardy perennial: the establishment of a separate stock exchange to handle speculative mining stocks. R.M. Steiner explained succinctly why he was having none of the idea: 'This market could be just the vehicle that the promoter needs; this was the great danger. That is why the Toronto Stock Exchange got a bellyfull of mining business: they were serving the promoter and not the mining business.' Anyway, said Pattillo, such an exchange would run an annual deficit of about $1 million, which would hardly help the brokerage community. When Vaughan replied feebly that at least there ought to be a new curb exchange at the TSE where untried stocks could be traded, Pattillo replied that this was quite unnnecessary since W.D. Latimer (who had just been severely disciplined by the OSC with a three-month suspension) 'runs his own stock exchange' by acting as a dealers' dealer in unlisted stocks.[41]

In a ruling concerning New Hiawatha Gold Mines in 1976, the OSC reiterated the same jaundiced view of the current state of junior mining promotions. Here was another case in which 750,000 vendor shares had been granted for a property that had cost only a few hundred dollars. Like other one-shot deals, the aim in this case was to raise only a small sum to undertake minimal exploration. The cost of marketing the shares was high, but the large markup between the option price and the selling price, plus the disposal of the 75,000 free vendor shares, had proven sufficient to earn a profit. The OSC decision went on, 'We have been told in public hearings that it is through the sale of these shares that the real profit is made ... The free shares are sold. The exploration programme in the vast majority of cases finds no indication of economic mineralization. Work is stopped. The company is allowed to die ... One is left with the impression ... that not only were the public asked to bear all the real financial risks, but indeed that they were not being asked to assume a risk – they had no chance at all. They rather than the property were being mined.'[42]

Like a spoilt child who suddenly receives a spanking for obnoxious behaviour, mining people seemed shocked by being chewed out in this way. After the 1975 hearings one mining executive wrote dolefully to the commission's director, Charles Salter, to say,

Generally speaking the OSC are [sic] doing their job, but both the public and management have a genuine FEAR of the OSC, and the image must be changed if we are to get more involved in mining and generating interest. It seems to me that more emphasis should be placed on advertising the OSC as a corporation designed to assist and promote mining ... The prospector needs encouragement ... As it stands today the moguls of the mining company [sic] are squeezing out the junior companies; this has to be rectified. The mining industry has been singled out as a whipping boy from [sic] all levels of government. Lotteries are a GAMBLE, and in a sense so is mining ... We need guidance, not an autocratic type of supervision: ... revise the regulations to enable us to tap a reservoir of speculative funds.[43]

With pressure still coming from a provincial government worried about holding on to Conservative seats in northern Ontario, the OSC again set about devising a friendlier policy for the financing of speculative junior mines. The idea was to find some way of rewarding genuine prospectors and encouraging the raising of funds for exploration without permitting the abuses of the past. In future, promoters and underwriters should operate at arm's length. The solution was to abandon the hallowed system of step-up options and to require the raising of at least $75,000 for the company treasury by selling shares to the public for no less than 20 cents apiece. If prospector and promoter were paid in stock not cash, they were to receive a special new class of up to 500,000 'promoters' shares' which would lapse after five years without diluting the equity of the company unless the other stockholders in the meantime had voted to convert them into common shares. The decision as to how much money might be raised from the public for a particular property would be taken by the OSC's new Exploration Advisory Committee, acting upon the advice of professional engineers. The commission noted that any people who were described in a prospectus as 'promoters' would have to disclose their track record in the mining business during the previous five years since 'On a raw property it is impossible to distinguish between a high-risk property and a property with no apparent merit.' To warn investors about what they might be getting into, these speculative companies would no longer be permitted to use the word 'mine' or 'mining' in their names unless they were actually producing minerals, but must be decribed as 'exploration' ventures.[44]

Despite the OSC's effort to be accommodating, the new policy received stern criticism. Mining engineers had no desire to play such a key role in deciding which properties ought to be allowed to raise further funds for exploration. The Prospectors and Developers Associaton insisted that cheap stock was easier to sell and demanded that the minimum price of shares be 15 cents and the amount of money to be raised only $50,000. In a joint brief with Natural Resource People Canada, the PDA claimed that the new rules were too restrictive and could never work. NRPC (which now claimed one thousand members) insisted that it could not find anyone with the 'slightest' desire to operate under the new policy, adding, 'Only a fly-by-night promoter conceivably could be interested in such a jerry-built arrangement.' The Broker Dealers Association took dead aim at the discretion granted to the Exploration Advisory Committee and predicted that the new rules would kill junior mining finance in Ontario altogether. At the PDA convention a few weeks before the new policy was due to come into force, people were seen wearing scornful buttons reading 'Away with Bray,' who was blamed for the new scheme.[45]

The OSC was highly defensive. Harry Bray pointed out that the new policy really did nothing to increase investor protection, though it did try to ensure that if a property failed to pan out, the promoter would acquire new ones rather than simply letting the company slip into liquidation. Arthur Pattillo repeated the claim that if mining development had shifted to other provinces, this was not the fault of the regulators but of the cavalier attitude of promoters towards the investing public. In a speech to the Prospectors and Developers Association meeting he rejected the notion that Harry Bray was the demon behind the new rules. Funds were there to be raised, he told his restive audience, but 'We want this money to be spent in the ground and not to take off on flights to the Bahamas.' The hullabaloo frightened the politicians, however. Premier William Davis hastily promised that a monitoring committee including industry and OSC representatives, chaired by the deputy minister of natural resources, J.K. Reynolds, would be set up to see what happened over the next year.[46]

Reynolds reported that the junior mining industry in Ontario remained in a depressed state. In recent years such companies had been spending only $1 million per year, or just 6 per cent of the total investment in mining development in Ontario, whereas in the early 1960s as much as four times that amount had been raised annually. Mining people, of course, blamed this sharp drop upon the overrestrictive policies of the OSC, but Reynolds pointed out that such an argument was unduly simplistic. Taxation changes, restrictions upon foreign ownership, and, most recently, wage and price controls had all had an impact. For the politicians the problem was that the public might come to believe that the government was favouring large (and sometimes foreign-controlled) corporations at the expense of the small operators in northern Ontario. The OSC, for its part, was firmly convinced that the regulations were necessary and justified, and would only change them if ordered to do so by the cabinet, which could be seen as unwarranted interference with a respected independent agency.

Reynolds did conclude that the OSC had been handling mining issues better in recent months since Dr G.C. McCartney, who had experience in the field, had been added. He suggested that the appointment of another person with some experience in mining finance might be wise, though he admitted that since mines constituted fewer than 10 per cent of the flotations handled by the commission, it should not devote too many resources to this area. The principal objections of the mining community to the new policy were to the creation of the special promoters' stock and the discretion given to technical experts to pronounce upon whether more money for development should be raised in each case. The latter complaint the deputy minister dismissed as more emotional than practical since it seemed improbable that a board of consultants would refuse an application from a group of reputable promoters. Still, there was provision for an appeal board, and if this were appointed, it might take the steam out of the issue. The OSC had also said that it might waive the five-year time limit on promoters' stock, but it had so far refused to specify in what circumstances. By doing so it would damp down the other major grievance.[47]

A 1977 study by the OSC's staff of 'who got what' indicated that the financing of junior mines had really changed very little. Forty per cent of the money raised still went to the company treasury, 11 per cent to the underwriter-promoter, and a whopping 48 per cent to the broker-dealer for marketing the stock. The beauty of the system for the insiders remained that they could go on insisting that a mining claim had a potential value and selling stock until it was conclusively proven otherwise. 'Involving the broker-dealers in the raising of funds for junior exploration is like sending the fox to feed the chickens.' The only way to really improve matters would be to require that some fixed percentage of the funds, say 70 per cent of the amount raised in the first year, should go to the company treasury and that two-thirds of that be spent on actual exploration.[48]

Such a proposal would have sparked a paroxysm of rage amongst broker-dealers and promoters. Instead the OSC simply opted for an 'Explanatory Note' in its *Bulletin* which provided an extended rationale for the changes made in 1976. It was pointed out that promoters still had the right to exercise a warrant (the so-called promoters' stock) to acquire up to 500,000 shares of common stock at a price one and a half times that which had been paid for the company's treasury stock, well below the market price of shares in any valuable mine. As a result, continuing companies could replace one-shot promotions, and commercially valuable deposits would be spun off into separate companies for development. The promised appeal process was put in place for those who felt ill-treated by the Exploration Advisory Committee.[49]

A report to the new OSC chair, James Baillie, who took over at the start of 1978, made it clear that the revised rules had not eliminated all the abuses. Since each deal now required 375,000 shares to be taken at 20 cents apiece, dealers frequently went short by overselling the quantities allotted them, claiming that cancellations and non-payment of orders were quite frequent, particularly with shares priced over $1. Unlike a normal market, where the shorts, who borrowed stock to sell, risked a price rise that would compel them to buy in at a loss to meet their commitments, the dealers completely controlled prices and could always reduce them before buying back stock to cover a short position.

Dealers were really acting as principals not agents, so they could profit on both the original sale and the buy-back, since they had only to stop supporting a stock to leave their customers with no recourse. Dormant companies had once again become a problem, since it was only during a primary distribution that shares had to be sold at the price announced in the prospectus. Lacking the chance to profit on the 75,000 vendor shares that were formerly granted free from escrow, dealers were now loading up on shares for prices as low as 3 cents once a primary distribution was complete and the company seemed to be going nowhere. Then they would push up the price again and dump the stock in the secondary market, where there were no restrictions on markups. A study of deals during the first fifteen months after the revised policy came into force showed that stock acquired for just $32,368 had been resold in this way for $2.5 million. As a result, most financiers were avoiding deals that involved the issuing of the special promoters' stock, which was locked up for five years, so that only about a half-dozen had used the new system.[50]

Critics of the OSC did succeed in gaining the ear of the minister of natural resources, Frank Miller, who represented a northern Ontario constituency, and in July 1978 his department published *Financing of the Junior Mining Company in Canada*. This report, which claimed to be 'an analytical study of the regulation of junior mining using modern economic technique,' had actually been commissioned by Natural Resource People Canada. The chapter on the 'Economics of Regulation' pointed out that junior mine financing had recently fallen to just 15 per cent of the levels common in the 1950s, as promoters had been deprived of access to the pools of capital available through the Toronto Stock Exchange. Promoters and broker-dealers had lost interest in such ventures once the use of shell companies was restricted and the number of shares available under step-up options had been sharply reduced. Then the 1976 rules had eliminated options entirely. Not only did the OSC need to relax the rules, but it should go back to the old policy of simply requiring disclosure, rather than trying to assess the relative merits of various properties. Not surprisingly, the main recommendation was that Natural Resource People Canada's pet project, a separate stock exchange for junior mines, should be given the go-ahead. Anticipating that he would be asked to comment upon this quasi-scientific and quasi-official document, which Frank Miller could be expected to do his best to promote, OSC chair Jim Baillie concluded that he could only tell the press that the report was 'somewhat academic, taking an ivory-tower approach to the problems,' but that the commission would nonetheless give the proposals the usual careful consideration.[51]

An investigation into Gordon Daly Grenadier, one of the few remaining members of the Broker Dealers Association still engaged in marketing penny mining stocks, revealed that a bunch of 'qualifiers' was as busy as ever telephoning at least seventy-five people a day seeking expressions of interest in new issues. About one-fifth of those called responded positively, but the cost of this promotional activity was so high that a company treasury would receive only 30 per cent of the sale price of the shares. When no significant discovery was made, the market for a stock would collapse, and the shares could often be bought back for much less than the original offering price. Gordon Daly Grenadier, for instance, had bought up the entire public issue of Pelican Mines and then resold the shares in the secondary market, with all the profits going to the broker-dealer, a technique known as 'lifting.' Failure to report these activities, of course, violated the disclosure requirements of the Securities Act.[52]

The OSC had not been aware of lifting until that time, but it immediately began an investigation. During the current year, when almost 9 million shares of junior mining stock had been offered in primary distribution, nearly 43 per cent of that had been resold in secondary markets. If only about a third of the funds raised ended up in a company treasury, then just 20 cents on the dollar would be available for exploration. Once again the commission began tinkering with its rules so that at least 30 per cent of the proceeds of sales by broker-dealers, not only of the underwritten stock but of secondary marketing by them as well, must now end up in the company treasury for use in actual exploration.[53]

The idea of a new stock exchange to handle junior mining issues refused to die. In the spring of 1979 Jim Baillie explained the risks involved to a group of cabinet ministers. The Windfall inquiry had revealed the size of the profits that insiders could make by the primary distribution of the shares of already-listed companies through the facilities of the Toronto Stock Exchange. As a result, the exchange and the OSC had imposed new rules, which had been in place long before the recent decline in amounts invested in junior mines. Should the proposals put forward by Natural Resource People Canada and others for an exchange devoted solely to trading in speculative resource stocks be accepted, the most likely result would be the recurrence of the kind of fly-by-night activity that had attracted so much criticism in the 1950s and 1960s.[54]

A few months later Baillie summed up his views on the regulation of markets for speculative mining shares, based upon fifteen years of experience and study in the field. George Jewett of the Ministry of Natural Resources had made the familiar complaint that over-strict rules were preventing money being raised from the public to fund mining exploration. Why was the 'unsophisticated speculator in the middle or low income brackets' no longer allowed to put money into penny mining stock promotions with the chance at a really big bonanza? After all, such people were no longer prevented from buying lottery tickets. Baillie's response was irate: all the studies showed that it was precisely this class of unsophisticated buyer that was targeted by the hard-selling broker-dealer, but this fact made it all the more important to protect such individuals. Lottery tickets cost little and people knew of the odds against winning money, while mining investments required enough to take them out of the 'pin money' class, and investors believed that there was a genuine chance any company might pan out.
    Jewett had asked why the OSC didn't require promoters to disclose their track records, since that alone was the best protection a share buyer could have; trying to protect the fool from his folly was otherwise largely futile. Angrily, Baillie pointed out that the OSC had been collecting more and more information about track records for over a decade, but unfortunately this data had proven 'largely meaningless.' 'What I resent is the implication that the Commission has overlooked this obvious disclosure technique in favour of a more aggressive regulatory posture.' Baillie took dead aim at the paradox lying at the heart of much of this rhetoric about reviving Ontario's depressed mining industry. While insisting that the greatest freedom to market speculative shares was essential, mining people were also demanding that the government do something to revive a flagging industry. Wrote Baillie, 'I have long felt that the decisive element needed to produce a change in success of Ontario's junior mining industry is another Kidd Creek or Texas Gulf discovery. Given this basis for optimism, the investment floodgates will open. Without it, they will not.'[55]

10

Foreign Ownership

By the late 1960s American brokers and investment bankers were eyeing Canada as a field for expansion. Many in the financial community were acutely nervous about the impact of competition from firms that were larger and better capitalized, and they looked to their regulators to protect them. These demands became part of a broader debate about the role of outsiders in the investment business. Should such people be permitted to invest in brokerage houses and investment dealers, or should they continue to depend upon internally generated funds and capital raised from senior management? Before long, the Ontario Securities Commission found itself faced with the need to develop policies regarding these issues.

I

Before 1960 the securities business in Canada had been a pretty cosy, close-knit place. Perched at the top of the hierarchy were the diversified investment dealers, led by three major underwriters that could trace their origins to the more distant past: A.E. Ames and Company (founded 1887), Dominion Securities (1901), and Wood Gundy (1905). The largest of these, Wood Gundy, acted as lead underwriter for many major government and corporate issues, while the other two divided up the management of most of the other important flotations. Outside this inner circle stood a cluster of other old-line houses: Royal Securities Corporation, McLeod Young Weir, Nesbitt Thomson, Harris and Partners, Greenshields, James Richardson and Sons, Burns Brothers and Denton, Midland Osler, and Pitfield Mackay Ross. As well as distributing securities to institutional and retail customers, they were the leading members of the stock exchanges in Toronto, Montreal, and Vancouver.

Whenever a corporation or a government sought to raise a substantial amount of new capital, a proposal would be requested from its customary adviser concerning the terms and conditions under which bonds and shares, common or preferred, might successfully be marketed. This lead underwriter would create an 'originating' or 'purchasing' group of major dealers who would agree as to the percentage of liability for the deal they would assume both jointly and severally. These firms might in turn take in other houses that would commit themselves to purchase a specified portion of the underwritten issue. Together all such parties were referred to as the 'banking' group or syndicate, with those added last being responsible only for their explicit commitments. The 'special bracket' firms (Ames, Dominion Securities, Wood Gundy) were almost always offered participation in the banking group for a major issue. The originating firm (or firms) would receive a higher 'step-up' commission, while the other special-racket houses usually got a more generous deal than most other members of the banking group.

The extent of the participation offered to a particular firm was very much a product of tradition and experience over decades. Less-favoured houses found themselves consigned to the 'selling' group, which received securities at a lower discount, or they might even have to go into the secondary market to purchase an issue if their own customers expressed interest in it. Members secured their places on the basis of the record of success in distributing previous offerings, combined with a judicious amount of mutual back-scratching, which together made it very difficult to alter one's rank in the pecking order except over a lengthy period of time. The capital that any firm commanded was not nearly as important as its connections, its expertise in certain industries or types of issues, and its ability to move securities off the shelf and into customer accounts when the time came. As investment dealer James Strathy put it, 'in Canada the "Establishment" is small, and everyone well known to each other.'[1]

Not that the this set-up was entirely written in stone. Some firms might find themselves losing ground, being offered a smaller share or a less desirable position, if they failed to take up a deal that was offered to them or were deemed to have done a poor job on a particular issue. The long-standing links between issuers and their underwriters were reasonably solid and jealously guarded, but relationships could change little by little as the personalities involved shifted over time. Still, young people coming up in the investment business quickly learned the ground rules and were assumed by their elders to value these historical connections too much to try to disrupt them. Most insiders shared Jim Strathy's view that this well-entrenched system was professional, expert, innovative, and (even) highly competitive.[2]

Critics saw a less rosy picture. J.H. Brown, the president of Gairdner and Company, complained privately that his firm had always felt strongly discriminated against, particularly by the banking syndicates that began to be formed in the 1930s to market bonds for the province of Ontario. The Ontario group had become a pace-setter, and deals for all other big issues had gradually come to be modelled upon it. In Brown's view, 'The managers of these syndicates are stronger than the masters they presume to serve. This is made possible and preserved by the fact that the same participants control the dominant syndicates.' For all the talk about expertise and professionalism, these factors were almost never put to the test since nobody could ascertain whether an outsider might have done a better job marketing a certain issue. '[H]ow can a dealer prove that his placing power is greater than others if he only has a nominal position with which to demonstrate[?]' Even on relatively tough sells, Brown claimed, Gairdner and Company had sometimes been compelled in recent years to go into the secondary market and make purchases in order to fill all its customer orders, which could be twice as large as the allotment it had received in a selling syndicate, so that it earned little or no profit on that issue. Unable to garner sufficient profits from the bread-and-butter business generated by the steadily growing financing requirements of corporations and governments, the up-and-coming houses could not realize enough, especially in difficult times, to create a large retail sales force and mount a challenge to the major firms. Brown insisted that the 'problems in the Canadian investment dealer industry stem from these antiquated historical syndication practices, which originated in the mid-thirties and ever since have operated to the disadvantage of those houses which were small or non-existent at that time.'[3]

Only on rare occasions did complaints about this system reach the public. In 1975 the federal government-controlled Canada Development Corporation proposed to make a sizeable issue of preferred shares to help finance its acquisition of businesses so as to ensure that they remained in Canadian hands. Some brokers disliked the deal in principle because of their hostility to a state enterprise going public, while others believed that CDC was not presenting its accounts properly. As a result of the controversy, the firm of Draper Dobie announced its withdrawal as a member of the banking group, which caused lead underwriter Wood Gundy to recast the terms of the CDC issue. The dividend on the preferred shares was raised from 7 to 8 per cent, and the stock was made retractable to enhance its marketability. But when Draper Dobie reapplied for a share of the syndication, it was told that it was no longer welcome to a piece of the estimated $5 million to be made by investment dealers, and instead it was offered a place only in the selling group of about one hundred firms handling odds and ends of the deal at a much reduced margin. When Daper Dobie complained publicly, Wood Gundy responded blandly that participation in the banking group had already been rearranged and nothing could be done. Most people in the industry, however, believed that Draper Dobie was being punished for its refusal to go along with the terms of the original deal and that it was not likely to crack the inner circle again. Protests about the high-handedness of the lead underwriter proved useless, however, since the rules in Canada, unlike those in the United States, did not even require that there be a meeting of the prospective members of the banking group where such issues might be aired.[4]

When an issue was not received with much enthusiasm, members of the syndicate might arrange to have it 'warehoused' in friendly hands so that the primary distribution could be declared complete, in hopes that the stock could be redistributed to a wider public at a better price some time in the future. When the Unity Bank of Canada sought to distribute 3 million shares at $9.25 in 1972, Gairdner and Company, the lead underwriter, was reported to have had to warehouse as many 500,000 of them when the stock slipped to around $8 in the aftermarket. An underwriter who was unable to sell or warehouse all of a firm commitment would have to 'ice' the unsold balance by putting it 'on the shelf' as part of inventory, with a view to placing it eventually.[5]

Critics of Canada's investment dealers pointed out that underwriters sometimes held back a portion of an offering that investors were eager to snap up. Particularly in buoyant times, stocks often shot to a large premium as soon as secondary trading began. For instance, in the bull market in late 1968 over half the new issues recorded quick gains of between 50 and 75 per cent over the issue price, and almost all the others rose handsomely in value. Since a typical offering was then between 150,000 and 250,000 shares of an established company, the small float helped to inflate prices artificially. Complaints were heard about preferential treatment being offered to key people who handled large institutional accounts or acted as legal advisers, as well as about the jiggering of allotments by underwriting syndicates to favour certain interests. In one or two cases there were charges that members of selling syndicates had simply parked their shares in house accounts for later resale when prices advanced. Unlike the National Association of Securities Dealers in the United States, the Investment Dealers Association had no rules banning 'free-riding or withholding' of new issues or their resale to other brokers above the issue price.[6]

Syndicate members argued that hot new issues always created problems for them. Their most closely guarded secrets were their allotment lists of preferred customers. A few dealers had rules that forbade withholding any part of an issue for the firm, its employees and partners, or any institutional customer, and they insisted that they preferred to see stock parked securely where it would not come back out. Notorious free riders could find themselves offered a crack only at the most unpromising deals, though aggressive investors might have accounts at several different brokers in hopes of getting a piece of every new offering. Small customers resented free riders since they were rarely offered the chance to buy the most desirable stocks at the issue price. Despite efforts to prevent the practice, however, up to half of every new issue was reportedly being resold within four days of issue, and some brokers were quite happy to see the free riders dumping their shares since this generated healthy commissions. The Ontario Securities Commission had rules intended to make it more difficult for underwriters to withhold stock by requiring them to declare as soon as a primary distribution was complete, but the critics complained that it was quite easy to conceal a block of shares that was being withheld if the underwriters desired.[7]

Brokers in Canada were determined to preserve the business of trading Canadian securities for themselves as far as possible. During the 1920s Laidlaw and Company had become the first foreign-controlled house to belong to the Toronto Stock Exchange. By 1952 there were eight foreign-controlled members, but when Bache and Company applied for a seat, it was approved on condition that there should never be more than eleven such members in all. In 1960 the governors of the Toronto and Montreal Stock Exchanges decided to refuse memberships to new American applicants.[8]

When Walter Gordon's 1963 federal budget proposed a takeover tax to discourage foreign investors from acquiring control of Canadian companies, brokers joined the rest of the financial community in attacking the idea. Three years later, however, the TSE board suggested the adoption of a rule formally requiring all of its members to be at least 55 per cent Canadian-controlled, with the exception of the nine American firms that already held seats. The New York Stock Exchange had a similar regulation, so that J.R. Timmins and Company, which had had a seat there since the 1920s, was its only Canadian-owned member. In 1967 the NYSE formally enquired whether the Montreal Stock Exchange would grant an American-based firm a seat if Canadians were permited to acquire memberships in New York. The MSE, however, replied that increasing competition for brokerage business in Canada meant that it could not agree, and the TSE's new president, J.R. Kimber, carried the same message to New York.[9]

The NYSE went ahead and altered its rules, but the Canadian exchanges continued to stand firm against admitting foreigners. The Vancouver Stock Exchange rejected two applications from American firms in the autumn of 1968, reportedly because the Toronto-based houses that held seats there swung all their weight against the requests. The TSE now insisted that any American firm seeking membership should sell a 55 per cent share to local interests.

The issue of foreign ownership was complicated by its connection to a larger debate about whether the investment business needed an infusion of capital, since some people were convinced that Canadian firms were underfunded for their volume of business. The rule of thumb was that an investment dealer required a capital base amounting to 10 per cent of adjusted liabilities, which in turn equalled 10 per cent of customers' debit balances. As the value and volume of deals rose, the strain would increase. Most firms still secured funds principally through loans and investments from partners, and Wood Gundy, the largest house in Canada, was believed to have no more than $8.5 million in capital. Yet many people were reluctant to see outsiders put money into the investment business. In particular, brokers remained strongly opposed to institutions such as mutual funds and insurance companies gaining control of exchange members or acquiring seats in order to capture commission income on their own trading. When Yorkshire Securities sought a TSE seat in 1966, it was rejected because of its close links to the financial conglomerate Power Corporation.[10]

The giant American brokerage firm Merrill Lynch felt particularly disadvantaged by the protectionist rules of the Canadian financial community. A predecessor of Merrill Lynch had acquired a TSE seat in 1925, and the house became a member of the Canadian Investment Dealers Association in 1952. Yet the firm complained that despite its capacity to distribute large blocks of shares to its retail customers and its access to plenty of resources to finance underwritings, 'Representatives of Merrill Lynch had in prior years been advised on a number of occasions, informally, that neither Merrill Lynch or any other American brokerage firm would be invited to participate generally in syndicate or banking groups in Canada.'[11]

By the late 1960s the Royal Securities Corporation found itself in need of an infusion of capital. Merrill Lynch seized the opportunity. In May 1969 came the announcement that it had acquired Royal Securities and applied to the Montreal and Toronto Stock Exchanges to take over the firm's memberships. Faced with a fait accompli, both exchanges approved the transfer of ownership. However, the major stock exchanges and the Investment Dealers Association soon announced a task force to inquire into the entire problem of the ownership and capitalization of the investment business, including foreign control. Chosen to head this committee was Trevor Moore, retired vice-president of Imperial Oil, who was joined by senior brokerage executives from across the country.[12] Until this report was received, it was agreed that none of the organizations would grant memberships to new foreign-controlled applicants.[13]

This investigation, of course, coincided with a number of other inquiries into the issue of foreign ownership in the Canadian economy, such as the federal task force on the control of Canadian industry headed by Melville Watkins and Joel Bell's report for the federal department of Consumer and Corporate Affairs. All of these studies reflected growing public concern about foreign direct investment, particularly amongst Liberals loyal to Walter Gordon and members of the New Democratic Party.[14]

The Moore committee's report, delivered in May 1970,[15] began by describing the current state of the industry. As well as being stock brokers, many firms also acted as merchant bankers, underwriters, money-market dealers, and investment advisers, though in recent times over 60 per cent of their gross revenues had come from brokerage commissions. Altogether the IDA and the three exchanges counted 182 members, many of them belonging to more than one of the organizations. Of these, fifteen houses were foreign-controlled. The committee's request for financial data produced responses from 114 Canadian and 11 American-controlled firms. These returns showed that the former had total capital of $183 million, used to finance underwritings, bond and money-market operations, margin trading, and accounts receivable, as well as their own-account dealings, which absorbed about one-quarter of the funds. The typical firm was a relatively small partnership or private company, of whom 79 were capitalized at less than $1 million, and 21 at between $1 and $3 million. Just 14 had capitalizations higher than $3 million, accounting for 56 per cent of the grand total, while the small and medium-sized houses each represented 22 per cent, with gross earnings in roughly the same proportions.[16]

These lightly capitalized undertakings depended for funds principally upon their retained earnings, supplemented by loans and investments from partners and employees, who typically held shares covered by buy-sell agreements at book value or some multiple thereof.[17] To date, such sources of capital had proven adequate, but concern was expressed about the longer term, which might dictate resort to outside investors. The problem was that the requirements imposed by governments and self-regulatory organizations seemed to make it inadvisable for any sizeable interest in a firm to be acquired by outsiders, for fear that they might demand special treatment or create conflicts of interest. One possible solution was to permit firms to sell their own shares to the public, something that the NYSE's Donaldson, Lufkin and Jenrette had recently announced an intention of doing. The Moore committee, however, strongly opposed this idea, arguing that outside control might reduce competition between firms or create brokers captive of other interests such as mutual funds or insurers. Underwriters and distributors of securities could also find themselves in conflicts of interest if compelled to worry about fluctuations in their own share prices.[18]

How could firms in the securities industry obtain more capital if going public was ruled out? The Moore report suggested that outside parties approved by the regulators might be permitted to acquire an interest up to 40 per cent, but that no one person should hold more than 10 per cent of the voting stock, and the insiders should have three-quarters of the board seats to ensure control. And what of foreigners seeking to enter the business? The report pointed out that other countries considered the securities business a key sector and refused to allow any outsiders in. The Royal Commission on Banking and Finance had recognized the special importance of the financial sector, and amendments to the Bank Act in 1967 had made it impossible for non-Canadians to take over a chartered bank. The majority of the committee was quite firm that new foreign entrants should be blocked by denying them membership in the self-regulatory organizations such as the exchanges and the IDA. Only Moore and one other committee member were ready to permit foreigners to buy even a 10 per cent interest in a Canadian firm, while the rest of the members wanted a total ban.[19] To throw open the doors might lead to a wave of American takeovers as domestic firms seized the opportunity to sell at a premium, leaving companies and governments at the mercy of outsiders and subject to the extraterritorial application of U.S. law. The Moore report concluded, however, that foreign firms already on the scene should not be penalized unless control switched from one party in the United States to another. Should an American broker with a Canadian subsidiary go public, however, its membership in all self-regulatory organizations ought to be withdrawn so that domestic firms would not face competition from deep-pocketed outsiders.[20]

Even the *Financial Post* complained that the Moore report seemed extremely cautious and conservative, quoting one source who dismissed its recommendations as 'very unimaginative.' How could the committee conclude that current sources of capital for brokers were adequate, while at the same time admitting that many firms had faced considerable financial pressures during the bull markets of 1968–9? Nothing was said about the desire of many firms to take liability positions using their own capital, which might require substantial additional funds. Refusing to endorse any further foreign investment in the Canadian securities business on the grounds that this might impair the efforts of governments to borrow seemed too protectionist and head-in-the-sand.[21]

While the Moore committee was at work, a sharp decline in trading volume on the stock exchanges in 1969–70 left many brokerages struggling to break even. At the peak in 1968 TSE members had been doing 14,000–16,000 trades daily, but now business had fallen back to about 6,000. Small and medium houses that depended on retail business had been hardest hit, and as a result, talk of mergers between brokerages filled the air.[22] Representatives of the IDA and the stock exchanges agreed to extend the freeze on considering foreign-controlled applicants for membership to permit them to draw up recommendations to provincial regulators for permanent rules.[23]

Early in 1971 Merrill Lynch announced its intention to go public by selling about 4 million shares, equal to one-eight of its total capitalization. This infusion might permit the firm's Canadian subsidiary to seize business from financially weaker domestic rivals, although the head of Merrill's local office tried to defuse this objection by promising that the amount of capital in use in Canada would be frozen at least until the moratorium ended. Another New York house, F.I. DuPont, Glore, Forgan, revealed that it too was seriously considering acquiring a Canadian subsidiary.[24]

In June 1971 a Joint Industry Committee of the IDA and the three exchanges finally agreed on how to regulate the ownership of investment firms.[25] Canada must 'have a viable national securities industry amenable to the needs of its community.' Limitations on foreign participation in this 'key sector' were entirely justified. Outsiders to the industry should therefore be limited to a 25 per cent share in any house, with any single interest restricted to 10 per cent (the 25–10 rule). The JIC agreed that dealers with foreign parents should not be permanently grandfathered, as the Moore committee had recommended, but compelled to reduce the amount of foreign capital employed in their businesses over the next fifteen years. The current capitalization of foreign-controlled securities firms would be frozen, and contributions from their parents limited in future to 1 per cent of net earnings annually, so that their rate of growth did not outpace their Canadian rivals. Increasing domestic capitalization at an average of 5 per cent annually would mean that all the foreign firms would comply with the requirement to be 75 per cent Canadian-owned by 1986.

The JIC pointed out that these proposals should also settle the question of whether or not securities dealers would be permitted to become public corporations. Public financing was not appropriate in Canada, and if the investment business required additional capital, it could be raised by permitting non-industry investors to acquire up to 40 per cent of the capital in any firm, provided that they held no more than 25 per cent of the voting stock. In that way Canadian dealers would not be left competing against powerful American operators, while at the same time the amount of capital available to the securities industry could be greatly increased.

At this point the government of Ontario suddenly seized the initiative. Financial and Commercial Affairs Minister Arthur Wishart pointed out that Merrill Lynch had a capital base of $360 million, dwarfing the largest Canadian investment dealer, Wood Gundy, which could then mobilize a mere $14 million. Merrill was moving ahead with its plans to go public, and its long-range aims were crystal clear: the firm would strenuously oppose any effort to prevent it going public, restrict the growth of its assets, or end its control of Royal Securities. If something was not done speedily, Merrill might persuade Washington to enter the fray on its behalf. On 13 July 1971 Premier William Davis announced to the legislature that henceforth all investment houses would have to conform to the 25–10 rule. Merrill Lynch and the other U.S.-controlled firms operating in Ontario would be grandfathered to continue operating for the moment; only if there was a change in ownership would the foreign interest have to be reduced to 25 per cent.[26] Prior to the imposition of permanent rules by the government, the Ontario Securities Commission was ordered to undertake a study of the entire issue of ownership and control in the securities business.[27]

II

Directed by OSC vice-chair Harry Bray, with chair E.A. Royce and commissioner James Strathy as the other members, the task force quickly discovered that more information was required about the cost structure of the securities industry, the amount of capital employed in various activities, and the rates of return received. The Moore committee had collected lots of data, but its queries had been vague, calling for a mixture of fact with opinion in the answers, and some key issues had not even been addressed. The problem was that most dealers could not estimate what percentage of their capital was distributed amongst the different functions such as brokerage, underwriting, and money-market operations 'because the cost accounting methods are too poor in most firms.' The sums required for a particular activity such as liability trading might vary dramatically from day to day. Some firms that had enjoyed rapid growth in recent years had been screaming about a lack of capital, yet the need for long-term investment must be carefully distinguished from cash-flow requirements. A questionnaire was quickly dispatched to all members of the industry.[28]

The Toronto Stock Exchange replied with a lengthy and elaborate brief.[29] Not surprisingly, the exchange came down firmly against any increase in foreign competition. On the question of securities houses seeking outside investment, it argued that there seemed to be no shortage of capital since the value of trading on the exchange had doubled between 1966 and 1969 without creating serious problems. Moreover,

TSE members were now permitted to have $1 worth of subordinated loans from outside the industry for every $3 worth of equity capital, so that altogether the capital employed could be increased enough to meet anticipated future requirements. Nor should going public be permitted, because it might only create conflicts of interest between investment dealers and their underwriting clients.The Ontario section of the Investment Dealers Association expressed similar views.[30]

American-controlled firms such as Laidlaw and Company and Dean Witter strongly opposed ownership restrictions as little more than a cover for a self-interested desire to give the Canadian securities industry protection without regard for investors.[31] The heaviest fire came from Merrill Lynch. Foreign participation in the industry would create more competition and ensure greater efficiency. Not only that but Merrill noted ominously that American regulatory agencies might react adversely to the retroactive and discriminatory requirements upon parent companies ordered to roll back investments in their Canadian subsidiaries.[32]

The OSC Ownership Study Committee also held four days of public hearings in November 1971; it then retired to deliberate. Its members approached the issues from differing perspectives. Coming as he did from the investment dealer Dominion Securities, Jim Strathy was inclined to stand pat; he contended that investment dealers in Canada did their job well and probably should be left alone.[33] The chair of the commission, E.A. Royce, argued that the provincial government's decision to impose a 25–10 rule on new entrants should be made permanent. But that still left thirty-eight firms operating in Ontario grandfathered so long as their ownership did not change. Should there be a roll-back to make all of them comply? If nothing was done, a giant like Merrill Lynch might come to dominate before long, but the IDA proposals to freeze capitalization and require a steady Canadianization might be too self-interested and protectionist. On the matter of going public, too, Royce thought that there could be no objection in principle since the Moore committee itself had recommended allowing outsiders to invest in securities dealers. The OSC would continue vetting and approving the backers of investment dealers to make sure that no 'repugnant' individuals manoeuvred themselves into a controlling position.[34]

Harry Bray, chair of the ownership study, believed that the status quo was not satisfactory. All the talk about the dangers of letting American 'giants' into Canada might be mere scaremongering. 'The disturbing spectre raised through the Moore and Joint Industry reports is ... whether the findings ... were in reality protectionist rather than taking an objective view of the needs of the Canadian capital market.' Bray also wanted the 25–10 rule retained, but he thought that complaints from Merrill Lynch and others that it was practically impossible to crack the inner circle of Canadian underwriters should be carefully considered. How could one criticize American firms for not doing enough to raise capital for business in Canada when they were not given any opportunity to show what they might do?[35]

The report of the ownership committee,[36] delivered in April 1972, began by repeating the assertion that the securities industry was a key sector: 'It is important that the investment community be responsible and responsive to the particular needs of Canada. It is therefore essential that ownership remain substantially in the control of Canadian residents who are patently more responsive to these needs and aspirations.' Yet competition should be encouraged and efficiency rewarded. Was the industry equal to raising the large amounts of capital required for future growth? Firms felt mounting pressure to undertake costly commitments such as money-market dealings and liability trading in securities. With the exception of a few foreign-controlled firms, however, Canada's investment dealers were organized as proprietorships, partnerships, or private companies whose capital was supplied by staff members, so high dividends were needed to allow junior employees to pay off the heavy debts incurred to purchase their shares. The conclusion was unmistakable: additional sources of capital were urgently required.

Responses to the OSC's questionnaire had revealed deep divisions on how to procure these funds. Seventy-seven respondents wanted to continue the ban on going public, while forty-four were opposed. Among investment dealers the split was much narrower, forty to twenty-nine, with the latter group including the five largest firms, who were most conscious of undercapitalization. If other jurisdictions were to permit securities dealers to go public, how could Ontario hold out? The committee recommended that outsiders be permitted to invest in brokerage firms.

Finally, there was the sticky question of how to deal with the existing foreign-controlled firms. There were thirty-eight grandfathered companies, and they should be allowed to continue operating unless their ownership changed hands. Rather than rolling back foreign investment, a capital base would be established for each dealer as of 1971, and such firms would be permitted to expand this base no more rapidly than the current rate of increase in capital of Canada's thirteen leading investment dealers unless the new money was raised domestically. Early in 1973 the Ontario government announced that it would accept the recommendations of the OSC study, including the 25–10 rule.[37]

Yet regulators in other provinces did not acknowledge the need for such strict controls over the ownership of investment houses. In particular, a study commissioned by the government of Quebec recommended in mid-1972 that outsiders be permitted to acquire up to 49 per cent of the shares in an investment firm, provided that no more than 10 per cent was held by a single interest and 25 per cent of the voting shares were controlled by Quebec residents. If adopted, such changes might shake the dominance of Toronto-based firms over the securities business, particularly if some European houses could be induced to enter the province along with American ones.[38]

Within the industry, however, the desire for even greater protection against foreign competitors remained strong. In July 1973 the Investment Dealers Association and the stock exchanges released a brief calling for the securities industry to become 'substantially Canadian' in order to respond to national priorities. The brokers complained about unregistered American firms selling Canadian securities to local buyers, rather than confining themselves to marketing American issues to exempt purchasers such as pension and mutual funds, insurers, and trust and loan companies. The investment dealers even suggested that underwriters for companies and governments in Ontario should be required to register there, whether or not the securities in question were being offered for sale within the province.[39]

The OSC's Harry Bray warned that acceding to demands for even tighter restrictions on foreigners would be foolish: 'This is certainly not an area where one would consider unilateral amendments to the legislation, the result of which would be to move all of the institutional trading desks to Montreal.' As it was, exempt purchasers often traded securities, even Canadian ones, outside the country when prices were better. The demand to channel all local underwritings through firms registered in Ontario was certain to be controversial. The OSC ownership study had made 'no comment or recommendation which would in any way restrict an Ontario issuer from seeking financing in a foreign jurisdiction.' Strong protests could be expected from domestic issuers, including the provincial government, about any attempt to control who should float their securities issues abroad. Bray concluded, 'These proposals appear to be designed as a kind of protectionism under the guise of bringing under regulation areas of activity in which no need for regulation has been demonstrated.' Another commission member, G.R. Guillet, agreed that these suggestions seemed 'unnecessarily restrictive' and only likely to attract retaliation by the Americans if the OSC went along with them.[40]

At a meeting in September 1973 officials from the IDA and the TSE again tried to persuade the OSC that it ought to register any foreign firm which tried to market non-Canadian securities to exempt purchasers or even handle an underwriting in Ontario to be distributed abroad. The exchange president, Jack Kimber, argued that any action concerning a deal in securities which occurred in Ontario was sufficient to establish the province's jurisdiction. Thus if a local securities issuer agreed upon an underwriting with a firm in Boston, or a mutual fund in Toronto telephoned New York to order shares purchased, a transaction had occurred in the province, which could bring the house involved under the OSC's licensing control. The commissioners were highly sceptical: did the brokers really believe that American firms would be willing to obtain an OSC licence? The industry representatives blustered: it wouldn't really cost the foreigners anything simply to register, and institutional investors should actually welcome rules that forced all dealers to set up branches in Canada since doing so would strengthen links to them. As neither of these groups was represented at the meeting, there was nobody to point out the implausibility of such claims.[41]

Meanwhile, the Ontario government was working to turn the recommendations of the OSC ownership study into law. When the final snags had been worked out, a new regulation was promulgated under the Securities Act in February 1974 by which the 25–10 rule on the ownership of securities firms operating in Ontario was made permanent.[42] The new regulation was quickly put to the test when the grandfathered firm of DuPont, Glore, Forgan announced that it wanted to sell off its Canadian operations to Paine, Webber. Both the Montreal and the Toronto Stock Exchanges opposed granting permission for the transfer, and the OSC ordered a hearing. Paine, Webber was a major U.S. securities firm with plans to expand its operations, and the commission found that the DuPont firm provided no services to Canadians that were unique. The ruling observed that nothing stood in the way of a sale of the major part of the equity in the branch operation so that it would comply with the 25–10 rule. The application for a transfer of ownership was flatly rejected, and the company decided to close up its Canadian business altogether as a result.[43]

In the autumn of 1976 Baker Weeks and Company was acquired by Reynolds Securities, and Baker Weeks of Canada applied to the commission to continue operating under the protection of the grandfather clause. In this case the OSC concluded that the transfer would not be contrary to the public interest, citing evidence that Reynolds could provide important services to investors by allowing them access to markets in other countries. The commission's decision noted that the ceiling on the amount of capital supplied by the parent to its Canadian subsidiary seemed sufficient protection against unfair competition with domestic brokerage firms. Yet when Reynolds approached the Toronto Stock Exchange (which had taken no part in the commission hearings) to request the transfer of the seat owned by Baker Weeks since 1956, the exchange staff recommended rejection. Reynolds was a large public company, significantly different from Baker Weeks, and the change of ownership might have serious consequences. Noting that they considered foreign ownership 'a topic of very great importance,' the exchange governors decided that they should adhere to the recommendations of the Moore report, to which the TSE had been committed since 1970. A material change in ownership of a grandfathered firm would terminate its exemption, and since Reynolds did not comply with the 25–10 rule, it should not control a seat.[44]

Baker Weeks immediately appealed to the OSC for an order to compel the exchange to grant its request for a seat. Since any lengthy delay could seriously harm the firm's ability to do business, the commission heard the appeal immediately and within a few weeks delivered a stinging rebuke to the TSE. After reviewing the history of the debate over foreign ownership of brokerage firms in the past few years, the OSC took issue with the claim that the exchange had adopted the principles of the Moore report in 1970 and adhered to them ever since. In fact, the TSE board had never formally endorsed the Moore recommendations. Moreover, both Merrill Lynch and Bache and Company had gone public in the United States, but in neither case had its Canadian subsidiary been deprived of its exchange seat. Laidlaw and Company had also changed parents but retained its membership.

The TSE had the right to question the owners of firms seeking membership to determine their fitness, but the OSC pointed out that nothing indicated that Reynolds would not pass such a test with flying colours. Even if the exchange had once been a self-regulating monopoly with the right to refuse membership to foreign-controlled firms, that authority had ended in 1971 when the government of Ontario first imposed the 25–10 rule. The OSC was particularly scathing about the argument that if the exchange's board had made a mistake, the matter should be referred back to the entire membership for a secret ballot. The commission decision clearly implied that it believed the TSE's foot-dragging was aimed at hurting Baker Weeks, which had already lost seven employees as a result of the uncertainty about its future. To force it to wait for a ballot and likely another unfavourable decision would only compound the damage, so the OSC ordered the exchange to grant the seat transfer.[45]

Within less than a year, however, the new Reynolds Securities Canada created more controversy when its U.S. parent merged with Dean Witter. The OSC held hearings at which both the TSE and the Investment Dealers Association weighed in heavily against approval of the merger. Focusing upon the argument that the firm could offer local investors access to foreign markets, the exchange pointed out that at least ten Canadian firms already had offices in Tokyo or London. This time the OSC allowed itself to be convinced that Dean Witter Reynolds had no unique services to offer which would justify the foreign-controlled firm from having continued registration, and the OSC refused a licence.[46]

In 1978 the drive for protection against competition from outsiders came to focus upon American firms that offered services without registering in the province. Local people referred to them as 'suitcase brokers,' harking back to the American salesmen who had moved north during the 1930s under pressure from the newly created SEC and set up shop in hotel rooms to sell shares by telephone. In fact, the firms complained of included some of the most prestigious names in the financial world, such as Morgan Stanley and Goldman Sachs. Since the 25–10 rule forbade those foreign-controlled brokers who were not grandfathered under the 1971 rules from applying for registration in Ontario, there were complaints that they enjoyed a competitive advantage in doing business by ignoring local regulation altogether. A strong lobby led the government to order the OSC to hold hearings on whether the interlopers ought to be permitted to continue to sell Canadian issues listed abroad in Ontario or to arrange the private placement of securities with institutional buyers.[47]

A call for submissions produced about twenty responses. The TSE and the IDA stuck to their long-standing position that all foreign-controlled firms wishing to operate a general business in Canada must comply with the 25–10 rule, but they accepted that new entrants who sought only to sell foreign issues to Canadian institutions and to distribute Canadian stocks abroad might be granted a limited registration which would forbid them from dealing with the general public. The OSC issued its own position paper, pointing out that Ontario was the only Canadian province that had so far adopted restrictions upon foreign-controlled securities dealers, even those grandfathered having been limited to a growth in the rate of capital assets equal to the average rate of expansion in the industry. Four unnamed firms had recently indicated a desire to start operations in Ontario, and the OSC proposed that limited registration be offered to them which would restrict them to dealing in foreign securities. Those dealers who had no desire to have offices in Ontario should at least be required to make an irrevocable commitment to accept legal service in the province in the event of disputes.[48]

At an OSC hearing in held October, 1978 representatives from the IDA and the Canadian stock exchanges repeated their calls for tighter restrictions upon foreign operators. The president of the TSE pointed out that in future both European and Japanese firms might try to push their way into Canada. Half of all trading in interlisted issues was already being done in the United States, so that the future of the local exchanges was at increasing risk. The IDA insisted that Canadian capital markets were more efficient than American ones, and that the need for new investment was being more than adequately met at present. By contrast, the U.S. Securities Industries Association put the case for speedy internationalization, demanding that American brokers be permitted to underwrite and distribute domestic issues to Canadians while also handling interlisted issues, which were predominantly traded abroad exempt from OSC rules.[49]

Reviewing the submissions, James Baillie, who had recently become chair of the OSC, expressed disappointment at the protectionist attitude displayed by the Canadian securities industry. The OSC's position paper had proposed that new foreign-controlled firms might be admitted to do certain types of business in Canada, as a quid pro quo for requiring the registration of suitcase brokers if they wanted to establish offices in Ontario and enter the retail business. Baillie pointed out that the response had been an attack on the 'quid,' while the 'quo' was simply ignored; the local industry simply viewed the situation 'as an opportunity to increase the level of protection available to it against competition from non-residents.' Why should the OSC impose rules to shelter domestic brokers when there was no evidence that such rules were required either to protect investors or to preserve Canadian control of capital markets?[50]

Consensus on how to ensure that Ontario investors would be adequately protected against the operations of foreign-based investment firms proved elusive. In the summer of 1979 the OSC sent out draft regulations to the TSE and the IDA. After several months of deliberations the securities industry produced strong criticisms of the plan to register new outsiders even to undertake certain specialized functions such as the marketing of foreign securities in Ontario. The response of the brokers was that this would be like permitting 'limited pregnancy,' and that such entrants would eventually take over entire sectors of the business. Clearly, the securities industry was bent upon sticking to the highly protectionist strategy of the past decade, despite the plain warning from the OSC that it could not ignore the increasing internationalization of the financial sector and the need for a full review of the situation within the next few years.[51]

11

Mergers

Corporate mergers created a whole new set of regulatory problems for the Ontario Securities Commission during the1970s. Though the Securities Act of 1966 required much greater disclosure concerning the internal affairs of companies, questions still arose about how the interests of investors, particularly small shareholders, might be protected in the event of a takeover. Should everyone be paid the same price for his or her stock, or could the owners of control blocks receive a premium from an acquirer? In the early 1970s pressure arose for another major overhaul of securities legislation, but eventually the drive stalled because of disagreements over such issues. The OSC often found itself powerless to control the merger-makers, but it was not until 1978 that a revised act was finally passed to deal with these problems.

I

In the United States there were 250 corporate acquisitions during 1967, followed by 390 the next year. Buoyant economic growth produced generous cash flows which assisted the financing of acquisitions, while institutional investors accumulated sizeable pools of loanable funds for these purposes. Such takeovers often raised corporate earnings sharply, so that further mergers occurred in hopes of emulating these early successes. By the end of the decade a number of conglomerates such as Seaway-Multi Corporation, Dylex Diversified, and Neonex International had been created in Canada, grouping together sizeable numbers of companies, often in quite unrelated fields, which were supposed to benefit from managerial expertise and greater efficiency to outperform their independent competitors.[1]

For instance, in January 1969 Seaway-Multi, which originally operated hotels, sought control of Levy Industries, a steel fabricating
firm, $25 million being raised through a private placement of 1 million
Seaway-Multi shares with a group of exempt purchasers. Such buyers,
institutional investors like mutual funds, trust companies, pension
managers and insurers, were permitted to acquire blocks of securities
worth at least $97,000 without the seller making the kind of disclosure
by prospectus that would be required to market stock to the public.
Aggressive operators like Norton Cooper of Seaway-Multi were naturally attracted to such deals because they did not entail the expense
and delay of a standard flotation. However, OSC director Harry Bray
became concerned that this privilege might be abused, particularly if
the securities were resold to the public within a short period of time. In
the United States, where 'go-go' funds that quickly turned over their
portfolios in search of the maximum rate of return were proliferating,
the Securities and Exchange Commission compelled issuers to create
special 'letter' stock, which carried a written commitment not to redistribute for at least two years and sometimes longer. Bray began to wonder if similar time limits might have to be imposed on the resale of
private placement issues in Ontario.

Mergers created other regulatory problems. When a public company
acquired a private one (or another public company with fewer than fifteen shareholders) in exchange for shares of the purchaser, there was
also no requirement that a prospectus be issued. In the United States
the SEC demanded prospectus-like disclosure about takeovers, but in
Ontario a buyer could apply to the OSC for a ruling that the issue of
new stock did not constitute a primary distribution. If the sellers (however numerous) were deemed sufficiently sophisticated to retain lawyers and accountants to advise them on the negotiations, they were not
considered members of the public and an exemption on issuing a prospectus could be granted. Not only that but active acquirers frequently
returned with new applications for further purchases, leaving the regulators wondering whether the character of a conglomerate might not
have altered sufficiently that it should be required to issue a prospectus
or at least a takeover circular to inform its own shareholders.[2]

A study by OSC economist Dagmar Stafl of Neonex's 1969 bid for
Maple Leaf Milling pointed up some of the problems in assessing takeover bids. Since the most recent corporate information about either
company was its annual report for the year ending 31 December 1968,
almost twelve months prior to the bid, even the most knowledgeable

outside investor would have a hard time making an intelligent assessment of the offer. Neonex had filed some interim statements during the
year, but these did not reveal the assets acquired or the amounts paid
during a headlong rush of takeovers. What had been disclosed was in
keeping with current requirements, but Stafl noted that the passage
of time 'turns the annual report into a historical novel, and leaves
the investor completely in the dark as to the capitalization of the company and its balance sheet position.' Moreover, Neonex's method of
accounting for its acquisitions would make the picture available to any
outsider 'very hazy.'[3]

Bray thought that other 'startling developments' might also necessi-
tate changes to the Securities Act. For instance, cash takover bids did
not require the buyers to reveal their identity. Though the Kimber committee had endorsed anonymity in 1965, the recent wave of takeovers
had shown this to be a mistake since 'the name of the offeror becomes
increasingly important in a consideration of whether the offeror is in
earnest, or whether its real purpose is to achieve a short-swing market
play or de facto manipulation.' Was the buyer able to raise the required
funds for the acquisition, and could it effectively manage the merged
company that would result? Minority shareholders in the acquirer
might find their equity diluted by the issuing of a large amount of
additional stock for a purchase, yet a control group was under no obligation to disclose this situation to anyone.

Insiders or major shareholders on both sides of a deal often seemed
to be the principal beneficiaries. Buyers could make private agreements with individual shareholders without offering the same terms to
everyone, so that takeovers were often locked up by paying a 'control
premium' to a small group alone. Not only that but these privileged
groups got a chance to dispose of their entire holdings, while others
who tendered shares might not have them taken up. Bray recognized
that requiring much more disclosure and the production of elaborate
takeover circulars was bound to be attacked by impatient entrepreneurs. Yet in both the United States and Canada 'there is much concern
amongst regulators as well as the industry about the mushrooming
conglomerates, and the unrealistic (in many people's view) prices at
which these stocks are trading.'[4]

Henry Langford, the chair of the OSC, shared these concerns. In the
spring of 1969 he created a task force headed by Bray, together with
commissioners John Willis and D.S. Beatty, to look into the situation.
At the outset this Merger Study Committee decided not to concern

itself with the wider economic and social impact of the concentration of corporate ownership in Canada and abroad. No attempt would be made to define 'good' and 'bad' mergers and conglomerates or to recommend giving regulators the power to intervene and prevent them as a blue-sky law might have done. Instead, the study would focus upon the extent of disclosure that ought to be required though registration, circulars, and prospectuses. That meant defining a number of key terms and concepts. What was the definition of a 'takeover bid'? What constituted 'control' of a public company? Should the owners of control blocks of shares be entitled to receive a premium price, and what protections were required by minority shareholders? A request for comments was sent out to a number of well-known conglomerates and financial advisers; later on over four hundred letters went to lawyers and accountants, and briefs were solicited from fifty organizations such as the stock exchanges, the Canadian Bar Association, and the Investment Dealers Associations.[5]

While waiting for responses, the committee staff busied itself studying the American scene as described in the Securities and Exchange Commission's recent study of disclosure to investors.[6] The 1934 Securities Exchange Act required persons who acquired more than 10 per cent of a company's shares to notify the issuer, the exchanges, and the SEC of their identity. During a visit to Washington Harry Bray was briefed on the elaborate system by which all 'reporting companies' that had at least five hundred shareholders and over $1 million in assets were required to file annual reports, semi-annual reports, and timely disclosure reports within ten days from the start of the month following a material change. Confined essentially to companies with shares listed on the stock exchanges, these rules left it to those bodies to order trading halts when disclosure seemed to be required.[7]

By the autumn of 1969 submissions were beginning to flow in to the OSC study group. James Kay of Dylex Diversified[8] supplied the most elaborate rationale for mergers, arguing that the continued growth of acquisition-minded companies was highly desirable. Why place any obstacles in the way of these deals? Much of his argument was pitched on a nationalistic basis, including the claim that mergers were safeguarding Canadian firms from foreign control. Rather than stifling competition, consolidations increased corporate stability, as Dylex was developing talented managers and preventing any 'brain drain' to the United States. James Pattison of Neonex International also argued for the maintenance of the existing rules. He raised funds using private placements with exempt purchasers and urged that no additional restrictions be imposed upon them. Parties ready to make cash take-over offers should be entitled to keep their identities secret. William I. Turner, the president of Power Corporation, a more traditional holding company, contended that there was nothing wrong with paying a pre-mium price for a block of shares carrying control. He regarded control as an asset of the owners of the shares rather than of the corporation because controlling shareholders could find themselves with obliga-tions not demanded of others, such as the need to pledge other per-sonal holdings from time to time. Thus the members of a control group might deserve a premium price in a takeover.[9]

The study committee was also particularly interested in hearing from stock exchange members about how requirements to disclose a proposed takeover would affect the price of publicly traded shares. At what stage should an announcement be mandatory, and would it be necessary to suspend trading on the exchange in order to disseminate the news? What would happen if an acquirer undertook a concerted campaign to secure a controlling interest in the stock of a target through buying on the exchange? When would that information need to be disclosed to protect the rights of potential sellers?[10]

The Toronto Stock Exchange supplied a formal brief in November 1969, pointing out that near the end of 1968 the exchange and the OSC had already worked out a new set of rules requiring timely disclosure of material changes in corporate affairs which might be expected to affect share prices significantly. Beyond that, however, market forces should be interfered with only when necessary to prevent abuses that might undermine investor confidence. For instance, paying a premium for a control block might actually be to the benefit of the other share-holders in inflating the price of all the stock. The brief strongly defended the practice of financing takeovers by private placements, pointing out that listed companies had raised over $140 million in this way during the past fourteen months, and that there seemed to be no need to require the exempt purchasers who took these securities to hold them for any minimum period. The exchange did admit that it might be necessary to stiffen the rules governing insider trading in the shares of companies involved in mergers or takeovers. Otherwise, timely disclosure should solve most problems.[11]

The Investment Dealers Association, whose members were inti-mately involved in many deals as advisers to management and under-writers of new securities, formed a special committee to prepare a submission to the merger study. The wave of takeovers had arisen because conglomerates could install more efficient and economical management, diversify the sources of their corporate earnings, and raise their share prices. The IDA argued that the definition of a takeover should continue to be the acquisition of at least a 20 per cent interest, so that institutions could still take substantial equity positions in other companies without triggering other requirements. The investment dealers maintained that a cloak of secrecy should be permitted until a deal was finalized, but at that point full disclosure of the terms should be made to shareholders of the target company. When fewer than 100 per cent of the shares were being sought, the identity of the bidder ought to be revealed. The target board should then issue an information circular, even if no recommendation was made to other shareholders about acceptance of the offer. Premiums might be paid for control blocks since share prices usually rose, and other shareholders could then sell into that rising market or tender their stock to the bidder, even though all of them might not be taken up.[12]

The merger study also heard from a number of securities lawyers who revealed divided opinions. Partners James Tory and James Baillie raised questions about the assumptions the committee was making. Was it wise to depend so heavily upon the SEC's experience? The American federal legislation of the 1930s rested fundamentally upon the efficacy of disclosure, while Ontario law had always had a greater element of 'blueskying,' whereby regulators were allowed discretion to intervene for investor protection. Could the two approaches easily be combined? John Kirkpatrick of Montreal, however, complained because he thought that the OSC was moving steadily in the direction of 'some kind of blue sky authority,' which he totally rejected, preferring simply disclosure instead. '[N]o securities commission could afford to hire people capable of blueskying securities, even if such persons were available.'

Even about the value of prospectuses, the bread and butter of securities practice, there were conflicting views. Kirkpatrick said that they were of little use for disclosure since they appeared to be 'becoming more and more of a dodge, where the approach is to "put the language this way" so that it will be meaningless.' James Lewtas expressed similar cynicism about these documents, suggesting that they were 'largely therapeutic.' However, R.A. Davies, who had served on the Kimber committee, contended that in the hands of 'persons who count' – specialists – a prospectus was useful, even if it was not intended as reading for the general public. Tory and Baillie also thought that pro-spectuses had their value, but they observed that not even the brokers and the financial press were always well equipped to comprehend and distribute the information that they now received, a situation likely to get worse if more stringent disclosure requirements were to increase the flow.

Only on the question of how to separate the general public from those who needed much less formal protection was there a broader consensus amongst the lawyers. Tory and Baillie claimed that the $97,000 minimum on sales to sophisticated investors was 'both irrele-vant and arbitrary.' Why not develop a definition of such a buyer that bore no relation to the size of the purchase involved? Lewtas proposed dividing securities into 'market and non-market' and investors between the 'protected and the non-protected'; the latter would be per-mitted to buy any kind of security they wished without special disclo-sure by the issuer, while protected buyers of non-market securities ought to receive different treatment. Kirkpatrick, too, thought that any-one who wanted to declare him or herself sophisticated should be per-mitted to do so simply by filing a declaration with the OSC renouncing the right to receive the disclosure required under the Securities Act.[13]

As a busy bureaucrat, forced to spend most of his time on day-to-day administrative detail, Harry Bray observed that simply collecting these views had been valuable, since it was 'probably the first time I have been forced to sit down and examine in a practical way the underlying philosophy of our acts. There are so many things which like motherhood one assumes to be "good," which upon closer exami-nation appear to serve no useful purpose excepting to act as punish-ment for the entrepreneur. On the other hand, many of the policies and regulations are aimed at removing the incentive to manipulate while at the same time preserving a profit for the promoter.'[14] Perhaps, thought Bray, the OSC was taking a too 'timorous approach to truth and securi-ties.' Whom should a prospectus be aimed at? 'I suspect that many people rely on the fact that it is screened by the OSC, coupled with, perhaps, the face-page disclosure and the fact that the party offering the securities is registered and has some degree of expert knowledge. The burden, it seems to me, is on the dealers and salesmen more and more to review the material and to offer expert advice routinely.' They could pass on details to potential investors.[15]

The committee decided to have its research director, Peter Dey, draft an interim report in November 1969, to be distributed confidentially to securities regulators across Canada for comment without committing the OSC to any particular position. Dey's brief document argued that the problems created by mergers and takeovers could best be dealt with through a system of continous disclosure about corporate affairs based upon an initial filing with annual updates. A company issuing securities to the public for the first time would file a prospectus and thereafter be subject to continuous reporting requirements. Those already reporting would need only to file a simpler offering circular to raise additional funds. Because of concerns about the resale of securities privately placed, Dey suggested that the committee should consider imposing a fixed holding period of between six months and two years. If private placements were resold to the public, up-to-date information about the issuer would already be available to prospective buyers. The interim report noted that no final decision had yet been reached by the study group on whether cash bidders ought to be compelled to identify themselves or whether premium prices might be offered for control blocks. Bray requested comments on this document from other regulators across Canada and promised full consultation before any legislation was introduced.[16]

The final report of the merger study in the spring of 1970 adopted from the Americans the principle that there existed a general 'need to know' about corporate affairs on the part of shareholders and investors. Thus any issuer who sought to sell securities to the public should become a 'reporting company' by filing a 'cornerstone' prospectus, supplemented by regular quarterly statements. Whenever an acquisition was planned, there would have to be an 'offering circular' to keep the information 'evergreen.' As a result, investors would receive continuous disclosure about all material changes.[17]

Between 1967 and 1969, $500 million had been raised in Ontario by private placements of securities with the one hundred or so exempt purchasers to whom a prospectus need not be delivered. Of this sum $300 million had been raised in the past year alone, and much of this money had gone to finance acquisitions. The merger study pointed out, however, that many of these securities were ultimately being resold to the wider public. Rather than adopting the American system of distinguishing private placement shares as 'letter' stock, carrying an undertaking not to resell them for at least two years, the report recommended that only reporting companies should be allowed to make private placements, so that timely disclosure would automatically be required within ten days of such a sale. The owners of such shares would be permitted to redistribute them at any time since the public would have continuous disclosure about the affairs of the issuer in order to permit investors to value these securities.[18]

Control groups, or people in a position to buy or sell companies, were defined by the merger study as those with 20 per cent of the voting shares. Once a person acquired a 20 per cent interest, this fact must be announced within three days, along with notice whenever an additional 5 per cent of the shares was added. When an offer was made for a public company, a takeover circular must be issued to inform investors, but the board of the target company would not be required to pronounce publicly upon the acceptability of an offer. Otherwise the committee proposed the retention of the rules imposed in the 1966 Securities Act, setting out minimum periods during which offers must remain open to ensure equitable treatment for all shareholders. Cash bidders would still not be required to identify themselves provided that they sought 100 per cent of the shares. Despite much deliberation, there was no recommendation about whether or not a premium might be paid for a control block.[19]

At its June 1970 meeting the Canadian Securities Administrators proposed that the OSC should prepare a bill incorporating the principal recommendations of the merger study. This draft could then be circulated confidentially for comment. Over the next few months Harry Bray produced a document, which was sent out for discussion in the autumn.[20] By the end of the year responses had begun to be received. The following February the Ontario section of the Canadian Bar Association organized a symposium attended by sixty-six members of the securities bar to discuss the changes. Naturally, some of the lawyers complained about the costs of compliance for new or dormant companies, though, as Bray noted privately, it was often precisely these undertakings about which disclosure was lacking but most sorely needed. Other lawyers, however, supported even more stringent rules concerning takeovers to protect investors. Over all, reported Bray and the other OSC staff, there seemed to be a surprising willingness on the part of the securities bar to support the new system, which was also endorsed in principle by the Toronto Stock Exchange.[21]

The Canadian Securities Administrators reviewed the proposal in mid-1971, and after minor changes it was tabled in the Ontario legislature a year later with a request for comments from interested parties before the bill was proceeded with at the next session. If a consensus could be achieved, then all ten provinces could swiftly enact identical acts to create a uniform regime across the country.[22] By the end of 1972, however, this plan began to unravel, as doubts developed in the business community about the cost and complexity of compliance. Mutual-fund operator Warren Goldring (who had served on the Kimber committee) pointed out privately to Harry Bray that the rock-bottom price for a prospectus would be $20,000, plus at least $10,000 for each periodic revision. He calculated that of the 941 companies listed on the TSE, over 30 per cent failed to earn $100,000 per annum. Thus for 72 per cent of the listed mines, 49 per cent of the oils, and 14 per cent of the industrials the updates alone would be gobbling up more than 10 per cent of earnings. When people realized this burden, they would either revolt or try to sell out to larger, more profitable combinations, which would only reduce the liquidity of the market on the TSE.[23]

The new minister of consumer and commercial relations, John Clement, had already expressed reservations about the bill. OSC chair E.A. Royce realized that if Goldring's concerns reached the opposition parties in the legislature, they would create a huge outcry and the government would start to back away, making the commission's situation 'pretty well untenable.' Royce therefore accepted the minister's instructions to write to him and say that the OSC was starting to have second thoughts about the evergreen prospectus and intended to reconsider the idea. After the formal decision was taken by the commission to abandon the scheme, Clement would get the political credit for announcing the retreat.[24]

Regulators in the other provinces began to get cold feet too. One OSC staff member summed up the discussion at a meeting of the Canadian Securities Administrators in Toronto in May 1973 as follows: Quebec thought that the new requirements were too burdensome; Alberta, Manitoba, and Prince Edward Island felt that the cost of compliance outweighed the benefits; British Columbia had initially endorsed the new system but now thought that modifications to present legislation would be better; Saskatchewan was prepared to go along in the interest of uniformity but believed that there were better alternatives. The momentum behind the revision of securities legislation evaporated.[25]

II

By the mid-1970s a combination of slow growth and high inflation was driving down share prices below the break-up values for some companies. These declines only fuelled the appetite for mergers and takeovers. Ontario securities law provided that a bid for more than 20 per cent of the outstanding shares of a company must be announced by a public circular and left open for twenty-one days, during which time each shareholder had the right to tender stock but to withdraw in the event that a higher offer was received. Yet aggressive merger-makers chafed under such restrictions and began to seek ways of securing control of an unwilling target by means of a pre-emptive strike that left holdouts and rivals no defence.

Takeovers through purchases of shares on the stock exchange were not covered by these rules regarding offering circulars and time limits. When Acres Limited attempted to secure control of Great Lakes Power in 1972, the Toronto Stock Exchange imposed a fifteen-day trading halt on Great Lakes shares and the bid failed.[26] Afterwards the TSE board struck a committee to consider the problems created by people attempting to use 'the facilities of the exchange' in this way, but in 1974 Noranda Mines made the surprise announcement at 5 o'clock one evening that it had already acquired a 23 per cent interest in the Fraser Companies pulp and paper firm and intended to bid for an additional 28 per cent of the stock the following day. Between 10:00 and 10:30 a.m. on 9 April 1974 Noranda snapped up enough shares of the stock, which had been trading at $24.50 on the TSE, paying premiums of up to $4.25, and obtained firm control before either the exchange or the OSC could intervene. A subsequent analysis of insider trading reports filed with the commission showed that a large proportion of the stock that had changed hands had come from major shareholders of the Fraser Companies, who had been approached individually and had tendered their shares before many of the smaller investors had even heard of the bid, much less had time to respond to it.

Aggressive takeover artists clearly had the upper hand over securities regulators and stock exchange officials concerned about investor protection. In October 1974 a privately held company called Canadian Forest Products gave just twenty-four hours' notice of its intention to acquire a controlling interest in Cornat Industries. Its shareholders tendered 80 per cent of the stock, which was then taken up on a pro rata basis to give CFP a 50.12 per cent interest, though most Cornat shareholders lacked any knowledge about who controlled CFP. As a result, the three major stock exchanges in Canada decided that when there was a takeover bid for a listed company, trading should be suspended for at least three days to permit the dissemination of news to the investors concerned.[27]

In November Abitibi Pulp and Paper concluded that the cheapest way to add to its newsprint capacity was to take control of Price Brothers.[28] It therefore decided to make a bid for a 49 per cent interest in Price by offering $18 for stock then trading on the TSE at $13. Associated Newspapers in Britain held 17 per cent of Price's shares, while Domtar Limited had a 7 per cent interest; if these two companies could be induced to tender their stock, it would account for half what was required, and the rest would be secured on the Toronto and Montreal Stock Exchanges without the need to make a formal offer to all Price shareholders.

The key question was whether the exchanges and the OSC would go along. Robert Morgan of Wood Gundy (who was also the elected chair of the TSE board that year) was consulted but replied that he could not predict what the TSE's reaction to the plan would be. On 7 November Abitibi's lawyer, Jim Baillie of Tory, Tory, DesLauriers and Binnington, was despatched to lunch with exchange president Jack Kimber to try to discover his views without revealing the parties involved. When asked what he thought about buying stock through the exchange for a take-over, which might well provoke a counter-bid for the target's shares, 'Kimber winced and said: "Let's cross that bridge when we come to it."' Baillie advised Abitibi that the exchange did not rule out such a bid in principle, and the company decided to proceed. Company chairman Thomas Bell and Bob Morgan went to see Kimber and his officials on 11 November. Bell proposed an offer to be open only for two days, during which trading on the exchange in Price shares would be suspended, in hopes that the shareholders would be stampeded into accepting before any competing offer could be organized. As predicted, Kimber made no objection to the use of the exchange, saying only, 'I don't think we can justify [only] two days. A few weeks ago the three exchanges [in Toronto, Montreal, and Vancouver] agreed that any more takeover bids would be kept open for at least three business days.'[29]

Bell agreed that Abitibi's offer could be announced before the opening of the exchange on Thursday, 14 November, and would expire on the morning of Tuesday, 19 November, which would allow five days for the news to spread. Kimber was insistent, however, that the TSE would only go along if the OSC also gave its approval. How would the OSC's recently appointed chair, Arthur Pattillo, respond to such a proposal? Beforehand, Donald Bean of Wood Gundy recorded that 'our initial feeling is that there's a 50–50 chance the Securities Commission or the exchange would disallow it. It's a hard one to call. The commission didn't express very strong views about the exemption when Royce was chairman. There's a new chairman now and who knows what he thinks?' As it turned out, the offices of the OSC were closed for the Remembrance Day holiday on 11 November and Pattillo could not be reached at his home, but Abitibi did get in touch with Harry Bray. In journalist Philip Mathias's words, the vice-chair 'combined physical corpulence with a keen agile mind,' and after nearly a quarter-century at the OSC he was so well schooled in the intricacies of Securities Act administration that 'he'd virtually *become* the commission. Under an undistinguished previous chairman and in the midst of mediocre advisers, he had generally been the *tour de force* [*sic*].' When lawyer Jim Tory laid out the situation, Bray expressed no immediate objection, merely observing that a formal bid open for twenty-one days would be preferable for ordinary investors. 'But under the present law you have the right to go ahead. We won't stop you from doing this. We'll be a bystander, perhaps not an enthusiastic one, but we'll let you go.'[30]

The real problem was now financing the bid. On 6 November, when Abitibi approached the Royal Bank of Canada for a line of credit to pay for the shares tendered, its president replied that 'the Bank of Canada has recently given us instructions that because of the tight money supply in Canada, we should not be using it for frivolous purposes – and frivolous includes a takeover. You're not contributing anything.'[31] Eventually, however, the Royal concluded that the demand for loanable funds was low enough that it could grant Abitibi an $81 million line of credit if the company itself put up $14 million, which would more than cover the $86.9 million outlay for 4,380,000 Price shares at $18 each. The Royal granted the loan on 12 November. The next day the Tory law firm drafted a press release and showed it to TSE officials to ensure that it met the standards of disclosure required. Now all that remained was for the regular board meeting of Abitibi to give its formal approval to the offer in time to transmit it to the TSE and other stock exchanges before the opening for business on 14 November, so that trading in Price shares could be suspended for the next five days.

A regular meeting of Abitibi's directors began at 8:00 a.m. on Thursday, 14 November. Only one person, retired American general Lauris Norstad, questioned the ethics of a takeover raid using the stock market; he pointed out that this practice was not permitted in the United States or anywhere else that he knew of. A couple of directors responded that they saw nothing troubling in the proposal, and the rest remained silent. By 9:30 a.m. the board had given its approval, and the necessary documents were rushed to the TSE before its 10 o'clock opening so that trading in Price shares could be suspended. Meanwhile, Ross LeMesurier of Wood Gundy had been dispatched to England to brief Vere Harmsworth, the chief executive officer of Associated Newspapers, to seek to persuade him to tender his interest in Price. Hopes were high that Domtar would come along, too, since the $18 offer was the same figure at which the Price shares were carried on Domtar's books, meaning that they could be sold without a writedown. Domtar quickly announced that it would tender its stock, and on Monday, 18 November, Harmsworth agreed to sell his 1 million Price shares and take a seat on Abitibi's board; the deal was sealed with a handshake.

The management of Price was not so cooperative. By Friday news was circulating that the company's shareholders had been told that the book value of the stock was $19, plus 1974 earnings of $5 per share, so that it was worth at least $24. On Saturday Price's board met in Montreal and decided to wire all stockholders advising them not to accept the Abitibi offer. The bidder, meanwhile, did its best to get hold of the names of large Price shareholders so that they could be approached individually. Abitibi also took out newspaper advertisements explaining the deal and touting its merits.

Objections to the way the raid was being carried out came from a somewhat unexpected source. John P.S. Mackenzie, vice-president for investments at Canada Permanent Trust, had 157 clients with shares in Price, who together accounted for 2 per cent of its stock. He complained that contacting those for whom he lacked discretionary authority to deal with the shares was extremely difficult in such a short time. On Monday, 18 November, Mackenzie's assistant vice-president for portfolio management, Norman Halford, protested directly to the vice-president of the TSE, William Somerville, about the exchange's willingness to suspend trading for such a short period of time, but Somerville simply replied there could be 'no extension' of the deadline. Halford also complained to Harry Bray at the OSC, and that afternoon Mackenzie dispatched a stiff letter of protest to OSC chair Arthur Pattillo. Mackenzie insisted that the bid should remain open until 25 November, and he made the embarrassing charge that there was 'inadequate protection for the small investor in takeover bids of all kinds.'[32]

Stung by this criticism, Pattillo summoned Abitibi lawyer Jim Tory and TSE president Jack Kimber to an immediate meeting. Kimber pointed out that the exchanges had recently agreed to cease trading for three business days for such bids and they should stick to that rule. Pattillo, however, now threatened to issue a cease-trading order on Price stock for fifteen business days, which would have kept the bid open for twenty days in all. Tory agreed that Abitibi could accept a one-day extension, but that anything longer would require a board meeting whose outcome nobody could predict. Eventually Pattillo agreed to have the bid extended for just twenty-four hours.[33]

His counterpart, Robert Demers of the Quebec Securities Commission, thought that the OSC was being spooked. He placed the highest premium upon keeping markets liquid and thought that takeovers were beneficial since they improved managerial efficiency and usually increased share prices. Demers told Pattillo, 'If we react to Canada Permanent, the liquidity of the market will be reduced to its lowest common denominator.' But the OSC stuck to its guns, and the bid would remain open until the morning of Wednesday, 20 November.[34]

This apparently innocuous change had momentous consequences. As soon as Paul Desmarais of Power Corporation learned of the new deadline, he instructed William Turner, president of its subsidiary Consolidated Bathurst to make a counter-bid. Consolidated Bathurst offered $20 each for up to 4 million Price shares. Harmsworth announced that he was going back on his handshake deal with Abitibi and accepting a swap of Consolidated Bathurst's treasury shares for Associated Newspaper's interest in Price. On 21 November Abitibi announced that it was now ready to pay $25 each for 5 million Price shares, giving it a 51 per cent interest. Desmarais therefore decided to re-tender the 1 million Price shares obtained by Consolidated Bathurst from Associated Newspapers to Abitibi, making a nice profit of $10 million for one day's work. At the same time 95 per cent of Price's other happy shareholders were offering their stock to Abitibi at $25, an increase of over 100 per cent above the price just a week earlier.

The Abitibi-Price takeover left stock exchanges and securities regulators more concerned than ever about their inability to control such operations on the exchanges. The auction market had originally been seen simply as a means to allow an acquirer to secure a growing interest in another company over a considerable period of time. Some people argued that takeover bids should be permitted without any suspension of trading, since this actually benefited the target's minority shareholders because they were able to sell their holdings if they wished or to wait and see if a better offer came along. Others noted that if less than 100 per cent of the stock was being sought, those who wished to dispose of their entire holdings could do so, rather than be left with a tag end if a tender was only taken up pro rata. Critics of the takeover artists, however, complained that investors had too little time to learn the details of a bid, and that they never received the kind of detail that a circular must contain. Moreover, there was no chance for a seller to withdraw if a better offer came along.[35]

Because of its embarrassment over the Aibitibi-Price deal, the OSC began considering whether to impose new rules governing takeovers through the exchanges. Could the auction market be suspended only briefly when a bid was announced, then reopened once the news had been disseminated? How much information should bidders be required to provide, and should standards differ for well-known public companies like Abitibi versus little-known private firms like Canadian Forest Products? Should anonymous bids be allowed? How long did offers have to remain open? The stock exchanges, for their part, did not want to see such bids banned since they generated sizeable commissions for member brokers. Jack Kimber of the TSE argued that such a system was inexpensive, and that all shareholders were treated equally, provided that trading was halted.[36]

When representatives from the Toronto and Montreal exchanges began discussing possible new rules, however, they soon discovered that they and their respective regulatory bodies were in disagreement. Arthur Pattillo was under strong pressure from the Ontario government to impose fairly stringent standards, while Quebec took a much more laisser-faire view. The OSC eventually induced the Montrealers to agree that no more takeovers through the exchanges would be permitted until a common set of rules had been worked out.[37]

The growing sensitivity of public opinion about the economic and social implications of corporate takeovers became evident in the spring of 1975, when Paul Desmarais's Power Corporation attempted to acquire control of another conglomerate, Argus Corporation. The federal government responded by appointing a Royal Commission on Corporate Concentration. During the remainder of the year the OSC continued its consideration of new rules governing takeover bids through the TSE. Because it was primarily concerned with making sure that all investors were fully informed, the commission wanted offers to remain open for at least fourteen days. The exchange considered this an unduly long time to suspend trading; if the regulators hedged these deals around with too many restrictions, they would lose their appeal. The TSE also wanted to permit 'nibbling,' by which a buyer could accumulate an additional 5 per cent of the shares of any company during a thirty-day period until the total holding reached 10 per cent, which would require disclosure as an insider. In addition, the brokers thought that an unannounced bid for control should be possible if the purchaser paid a premium averaging not more than 5 per cent over the current market price, since stockholders would be under no pressure to make a quick decision about whether to sell or not.

Negotiations between the OSC and the exchange dragged on until December, when it was clear that an agreement was impossible. However, the Quebec Securities Commission agreed to approve the more relaxed rules proposed by the exchanges. Despite arguments that such deals helped to promote economic growth, the OSC refused to go along, claiming that the TSE plan gave the initial offerer too many advantages and would discourage counter-bids in the interests of shareholders. The commission threatened to ban all takeover bids through the Toronto exchange altogether. Though Jack Kimber pointed out that having looser regulations on other exchanges was only likely to shift business elsewhere, the OSC decided that it would not allow any more takeover bids through the TSE until stiffer rules had been settled on.[38]

An OSC committee consisting of Harry Bray, Stanley Beck, and David Johnston was appointed to try to reach some understanding with the exchange, but no agreement had been arrived at by the time another controversy arose in August 1976. Cornat Industries announced a bid to acquire a 50.5 per cent interest in Bralorne Resources. Because of the OSC's ban on using the TSE, the offer was made only through the Vancouver Stock Exchange. Bray's angry reaction was that this was a straight-out attempt to get around the Securities Act: 'the commission has said that this kind of offer would be considered by it as contrary to the public interest, in that there is no assurance that the shareholders of the target company would be adequately informed in sufficient time to enable them to make a reasoned decision as to whether or not they ought to tender their shares.' Cornat should not be allowed to challenge the authority of the OSC in this way, and Bray immediately canvassed the other members of the commission and obtained their consent to issue a stop-trading order on Bralorne. When D.A. Berlis, the chair of Bralorne's board, complained that he was only damaging the interests of the company's Ontario stockholders, Bray replied sharply that it was management's own fault for ignoring the 'substance' of the law in the province. Berlis insisted that no laws had been broken, and that he need hardly concern himself with one regulator's view of the substance of legislation. Jack Kimber added his voice, pointing out that 60 per cent of Bralorne shares were held outside Ontario, so that the deal could proceed regardless of what the OSC did, and reminding Bray that he had warned that this kind of thing was bound to happen if uniform rules were not in place all across the county. In the end the OSC had to back down and withdraw its order, since the deal was clearly going ahead anyway, but it continued to grumble about the TSE's refusal to agree to a proper set of rules.[39]

A few weeks later the OSC announced that it had finally approved a set of takeover rules proposed by the TSE, which were similar to those already in force in Montreal. The commission was compelled to admit that lack of uniformity across Canada had created problems; it was only consenting to provisional regulations to eliminate such confusion. Discussions about a final set of rules would have to resume. In the meantime, problems continued to occur with the new TSE by-laws, which required anyone who sought to increase a holding to more than 20 per cent of a company's stock to secure the permission of the exchange, even if the objective was simply to fight off a takeover. Loewen Ondaatje McCutcheon was called on the carpet by the OSC when it bought too many shares in Western Broadcasting for Frank Griffiths, who was worrried that the *Toronto Daily Star* was aiming to take over his company. How Griffiths could be planning a takeover bid by acquiring more than 20 per cent of the company that he already ran was not explained. The brokerage firm (which included TSE chair Fred McCutcheon) was forced to announce that it would give up the commission earned to charity in order to avoid punishment, yet it was still fined by the exchange for the rule violation. A few weeks later another brokerage firm was penalized when it failed to get approval for the acquisition of over 20 per cent of Na-Churs International as part of a takeover.[40]

At the end of 1976 the Toronto Stock Exchange finally passed a by-law setting forth new rules about takeovers similar to those in already force in Montreal and Vancouver. Shareholders who wised to increase their stake, seek control, or defend their interests against rivals were now permitted to buy up to 5 per cent of a company's stock on the exchange during any thirty-day period. If a bidder was seeking to make a takeover, there could be a request to suspend trading in the stock until 'takeup' day. Such people must state their intentions, disclose their financial standing, and reveal any inside information to the exchange. Another option was to offer to purchase a block of a given size after six business days, with the stock to continue trading until that moment.[41]

These rules seemed to settle most of the problems created by takeovers through the exchanges during the next eighteen months. On 10 June 1978, however, the recently created state oil company, Petro-Canada, made a cash bid of $45 for 80 per cent of Husky Oil's shares. Shunning this 'friendly' takeover, Husky promptly sought out an American firm, Occidental Petroleum, to act as a 'white knight' by offering $49. The auction heated up on 15 June when Petro-Canada raised its offer to $52 and Occidental to $54. Meanwhile, Alberta Gas Trunk Line, the provincial pipeline utility, revealed that it had now secured an 8 per cent interest in Husky through the open market and had ordered a buying blitz of Husky shares on the American Stock Exchange. In just two days, 26–7 June, AGTL secured another 27 per cent of Husky's stock, giving it a firm control position.

TSE president Pearce Bunting expressed outrage that a formal takeover bid had not been made through the exchange. AGTL president Robert Blair responded angrily that since a very large percentage of Husky shares were now held in the United States, there could be 'no embarrassment about our buying shares from US residents in whatever stock exchange was best suited for that purpose.' Anyone could have tendered Husky shares through an Amex member, and Blair remarked rudely that the only reason he could see for Toronto brokers to complain was that they had had lost out on the commissions, 'if that is an underlying point of interest to the Toronto Stock Exchange.'[42]

This 'street sweep' of Husky shares in New York led the OSC to announce an investigation into whether or not the rules regarding takeovers through the TSE needed to be imposed on all companies registered under the Securities Act, wherever they were listed. Blair of Alberta Gas Trunk Line was unrepentant: he insisted that when his buying started, 90 per cent of Husky shares had been owned in the United States, partly as a result of arbitrageurs who had bought up the stock in anticipation of profiting from the rising bids. The TSE had claimed that as much as 45 per cent of the stock was in Canadian hands, but it later conceded that this proportion might have fallen as low as 8 per cent. There was no evidence that a single minority shareholder of Husky had actually been hurt. AGTL should hardly be condemned for its actions when it had not broken any law.[43]

Though the OSC argued that this deal showed the need for more sweeping formal regulations, not many people agreed. The head of the British Columbia Securities Commission considered that the existing exchange rules, backed up by the regulators, were sufficient to protect the interests of minority shareholders. Federal officials complained that the OSC had developed a fetish about protecting 'small' investors, while it ignored the fact that many large institutions such as pension and mutual funds also acted on their behalf. Rules designed to ensure equitable treatment seemed primarily driven by a desire to channel takeover bids through the exchanges and capture commissions for their members. An even more serious question was whether the OSC even had the authority to try to control the dealings in shares that were listed on exchanges elsewhere, simply because the issuers also happened to be registered in Ontario. The chair of the Alberta Securities Commission politely pointed out that this effort to apply provincial laws extraterritorially seemed quite unlikely to be accepted by the courts as constitutional.[44]

The OSC responded defensively. Jim Baillie, one of the lawyers for Abitibi in the takeover of Price in 1974, had recently been appointed chair of the commission. When Robert Blair sharply criticized the OSC for trying to interfere in Alberta Gas Trunk Line's activities, Baillie admitted that what had been done was entirely legal, but he claimed that he had a responsibility to ensure that all investors were treated equally. He said that he was really just trying to encourage a debate on the conduct of takeovers in order to advise the Ontario government about whether new rules were needed. The commission soon issued a set of draft regulations which would have required anyone making a takeover bid anywhere for a company in which Ontario residents owned shares to comply with OSC rules. AGTL remained entirely unrepentant: 'We are proud that we were able to move quickly, in compliance with all applicable United States and Canadian laws, to repatriate Husky, and we remain astounded that the Commission is determined to see that "that never happens again."' At a meeting with Baillie in September 1978, Blair again pointed out that the OSC had no authority over transactions on stock exchanges located elsewhere. 'That the Ontario Securities Commission should at such a time purport to govern by its regulations, conduct not only outside Ontario but outside of Canada and to impose Ontario and Toronto Stock Exchange concepts of "morality" upon the established procedures of stock exchanges in other civilized jurisdictions, we find incomprehensible.' In the face of this trenchant critique the proposed new rules were dropped.[45]

Takeovers continued. In December 1978 the Hudson's Bay Company announced its intention to acquire control of the Simpson's department store chain. Simpson's response was a complex scheme to thwart the takeover by merging with Sears, Roebuck and Company, its American partner, and to distribute shares representing a 41 per cent interest in their joint venture, Simpson-Sears, as a dividend. The HBC therefore upped its offer to include the shares of Simpson-Sears as well as Simpson's, and the OSC imposed a cease-trading order on both stocks. A few days later the commission held an unprecedented joint hearing with its Quebec counterpart, and an agreement was reached by all parties to extend the takeover deadline by five more days. As a result, the OSC's Baillie announced that he did not intend to intervene, despite complaints about various rule violations, because none of these appeared to have been 'flagrant.'[46]

In the spring of 1979 a wrangle broke out over Brascan Limited, which had just received about $380 million for the sale of its Brazilian utility interests. Brascan's cash-rich treasury immediately attracted the attention of Edward and Peter Bronfman, who joined with Patino N.V. to form Edper Equities as a vehicle for a takeover bid. The chartered banks agreed to put up $210 million to buy preferred stock in Edper, the funds to be used to finance the acquisition of up to 45 per cent of Brascan's stock. When Edper privately revealed its plans to J.H. Moore, the chief executive of Brascan immediately persuaded his board to reject the offer and bid for control of Woolworth's, the American five-and-dime store chain, to fend off further advances. Edper decided to buy at least a 10 per cent interest in Brascan through the American Stock Exchange, where the company was not listed but merely 'admitted to unlisted trading privileges' under a long-standing exemption. Though Edper's initial order was for 1 million Brascan shares, fears that some other interest like rival might intervene led to the acquisition of 6.7 million shares over a two-day period. Edper eventually got more than half of Brascan's stock and secured complete control.[47]

Edper was not a listed company, so it did not fall under the TSE's rules, which now forbade using an exchange outside Ontario for a takeover that would not have been permitted at home. Nevertheless, the exchange argued that the Brascan deal had shown the need for more protection of shareholders to ensure that creeping takeovers did not occur through the gradual increase of an interest, and that shares would be taken up pro rata if more than the required amount was tendered. As a result, the Ontario government finally amended the regulations under the Securities Act after the Brascan coup to try once again to force Ontario-registered companies to use the TSE when making a takeover bid, despite well-founded doubts that these rules were really enforceable.[48]

III

Many of the problems in regulating mergers during the 1970s stemmed from the failure of the Ontario government to amend the Securities Act. After the draft legislation was withdrawn back in 1973, any sense of urgency about a new law largely evaporated. Timely disclosure of material changes in internal corporate affairs was required by the rules of the OSC and the TSE after 1968, and although this principle was not formally embedded in a statute, no serious problems seemed to arise on that score. Surrounding the issue of takeovers, however, there was a deep division of opinion certain to make new legislation politically controversial. Should the owners of a control block of shares in a company be permitted to sell for a premium price, or should takeover bidders be required to make the same offer to all the stockholders?

In the autumn of 1973 the Ontario legislature's Select Committee on Company Law delivered a long-awaited report on this subject.[49] The OSC's merger study had not recommended that a follow-up offer should be made to all other shareholders following the acquisition of a control block in a takeover, but now the commission staff argued that any bid should be open to everyone, the shares being taken up pro rata by the acquirer to the desired level. The Conservative majority on the committee opted for the status quo, contending that shareholders had the right to dispose of their property as they wished, and that changing the rules would discourage prospective buyers if they could not afford to take up all the stock of the target company. The Liberals and New Democrats disagreed, claiming that any control premium was an asset of the corporation which belonged to all the shareholders, and that an acquirer should be obliged to make a follow-up offer to everyone on the same terms within sixty days.

This division of opinion made it certain that any renewal of debate on a new Securities Act would see the opposition parties casting the government as the fat-cat friend of big business if it did not require such follow-up offers. Still, the OSC remained keen to see revised legislation in place. Harry Bray, along with commissioners Stanley Beck and David Johnston, worked to produce a draft bill, and in the summer of 1974 Consumer and Commercial Relations Minister John Clement tabled it, announcing that submissions from interested parties would be received before the legislature took up the matter in the autumn. No more was heard of the bill until it was reintroduced by a new minister one year later. But the government did nothing to push the legislation through, and the bill died when an election was called in September 1975. The result of the voting was a Conservative minority government outnumbered by the combined Liberal and New Democrat opposition, which helped to dampen any enthusiasm on the part of the cabinet for proceeding with the legislation.[50]

Not until the autumn of 1976 did another bill surface in the legislature, but it too was not proceeded with. Another provincial election in June 1977 again produced a minority government. That fall, however, Lawrence Grossman, who had taken over the portfolio of Consumer and Commercial Relations, finally announced that action would follow upon discussion of the details of the legislation with a new chair of the OSC, who would take office at the start of 1978.[51] Now chairing the commission was Jim Baillie, and his arrival seemed to supply the impetus for action. The government, said one OSC staff member, 'had been trying to get changes in the Securities Act for years and years ... When they really wanted them, they went out and got the best securities lawyer going, Jim Baillie. He came in and got things straightened up quickly.'[52]

The new bill, tabled in the spring of 1978, aimed to solve a number of thorny problems.[53] Under the current legislation an issuer was required to seek registration with the OSC and produce a prospectus when making a 'distribution to the public' of securities. Now a 'closed system' was to be created which required all 'reporting issuers' either to send out a prospectus or to procure an exemption. 'Private' or 'non-public' distributions (like the private placements used to finance many takeovers) could continue to be exempt from the prospectus requirement, provided that the number of buyers and sellers was tightly limited. Sales could still be made to 'sophisticated' purchasers or 'exempt' institutions, who were presumed to be in a position to acquire information for themselves.[54] An issue might be distributed without a prospectus if investors had no 'need to know' because they were already well informed about the issuer and the security, as in the case of a stock dividend paid to current shareholders. And securities could be sold in certain circumstances subject to 'hold' periods ranging from six to eighteen months, during which time it was assumed that investors could secure the necessary information to permit them to trade freely. Without one of these exemptions, however, any 'reporting issuer' who distributed securities or possessed a stock exchange listing was required to make continuing disclosure of material changes in corporate affairs, thus plugging up leaks from the closed part of the system.

The proposed legislation also dealt directly with takeover bids.[55] Acquisition of more than 20 per cent of the voting stock of a target company would still trigger a procedure requiring bids to be open for at least twenty-one days and offers to be delivered to all shareholders with addresses in Ontario. Anonymous bids would no longer be permitted. Those who tendered their shares during the first seven days that such an offer was open would have the right to withdraw if a rival bidder materialized later on. Should a bidder seek only a portion of the shares outstanding and receive tenders for more than that percentage, the tenders would be taken up pro rata so that no shareholders would be able to sell their entire holdings on a first-come, first-served basis, leaving others shut out entirely. Offers to purchase stock in a takeover through the facilities of the stock exchange would have to be approved by the OSC, which would have the authority to limit the size of the proposed premium over the current share price.

In an effort to settle the controversy over premium prices paid for shares held by small control groups, the new bill exempted private purchases from up to fifteen persons, provided that the premium over the current market price of the stock paid was no more than 15 per cent. Should a larger premium be offered, however, the OSC was given discretion to order a follow-up offer to other shareholders within six months and to fix the price to be paid for the shares. The Liberals in the Ontario legislature expressed general approval of the new proposals, but the New Democrats registered concern that the degree of discretion left to the OSC might subject it to efforts at capture by powerful interests in the financial community. The Toronto Stock Exchange, which had been struggling to come up with some means of securing control over takeover bids made through its facilities, expressed its support for the bill, though seven widely held public companies[56] prepared a brief arguing that the new rules were a serious infringement on the rights of the owners of control blocks to sell their shares at whatever price they wished.

Much of the debate in the legislature eventually focused upon what facts would have to be disclosed in a takeover battle. The OSC proposed to define a material fact as anything that might affect the market price of the securities involved. Both the Liberals and the New Democrats sought to broaden this definition to include any information that might affect the business or value of the corporation as a whole. Jim Baillie and the officials at the OSC argued that anything broader than their proposed 'market' test would make the new legislation unworkable, because it would require company officers to make judgments about the way in which markets might respond to events. After a long delay the legislative committee finally adopted the commission's point of view, and the new Securities Act was passed, sections of which began to be proclaimed into law on 15 September 1979.

Nevertheless, the issue of payment of premiums for control blocks in takeovers, which had done much to stall the passage of new legislation during the 1970s, continued to cause controversy. If the premium offered was more than 15 per cent over the current market price of the target company's stock, the bid was supposed to trigger a follow-up offer to all the other holders of that class of shares. Yet as one scholar has noted, 'the follow-up offer legislated by the 1978 act's takeover regime was the subject of continued resistance by corporate issuers and was abandoned as unworkable during the 1980s.'[57] Thus the attempt to create new rules governing the sale of control blocks proved little more successful than the previous regulations.

Mergers helped to spark the drive for a revised Securities Act in the late 1960s, but the first efforts in this direction foundered as a result of complaints about the cost and complexity of making continuous disclosure about internal corporate affairs. Meanwhile, takeover bidders short-circuited the previous requirements to give all shareholders of a target company the time and opportunity to tender their stock if they wished. Using the facilities of the stock exchange became a means for a pre-emptive strike to gain control, which made it much more difficult for a target to organize its defences. When the Securities Act was finally revised in 1978 to permit the OSC to require follow-up offers to all stockholders on the same terms offered to those possessing control blocks, the new provisions proved largely unworkable.

12

Competition

During the 1970s the Canadian financial community found itself under increasing pressure from competitive forces. As the rate of inflation rose, securities markets stagnated and brokerage profits declined. In an effort to deal with these problems, investment houses sought to improve their position by raising the uniform commission rates charged on stock trading. Yet these attempts encountered resistance. The movement for negotiated commission rates was gaining strength in the United States, and by trying to resist such changes, Canadian brokers risked seeing business shift away to American dealers and exchanges. The Ontario Securities Commission found itself pushed into the uncomfortable role of a rate-setting agency.

Like their counterparts in other countries, Canadian brokers had always been accustomed to charging their customers a fixed scale of commission on the share trades that they executed. By the time J.R. Kimber became president of the Toronto Stock Exchange in 1967, he found that inflationary pressures had created broad support for the first general revision of the rates in seven years. The exchange governors prepared a proposal designed to increase the gross revenues of members approximately 11 per cent by creating a smooth curve of charges which rose with the price of penny stocks, then descended again on issues priced above $8.[1] After discussions with the Montreal and Vancouver exchanges, the members of all three bodies readily agreed to the increases. Since the OSC had received expanded authority under the 1966 Securities Act to approve all TSE by-laws, it was now required to give its consent and did so without objection. As a result, the cost of trading a share worth $11 in Toronto (where the average trading price was $14) became 50 per cent higher than on the New York Stock Exchange, though shares worth less than $4 (of which the NYSE had almost none) still cost less to buy in Canada.[2]

Yet the brokers continued to find themselves under pressure to grant lower rates to mutual funds, insurance companies, and other big institutional investors that undertook large block trades. Exchange members, of course, preferred to have all trades carried out in the normal way because it increased the volume and liquidity of dealings as well as bringing in higher revenues. Yet brokers could not ignore the fact that in light trading large lots could seriously distort prices, so by the late 1950s the TSE permitted trades valued at over $25,000 to be handled off the floor at reduced commission rates; this minimum was increased to $50,000 in 1959 as big transactions became more common. Later on, the value of these 'special size' transactions which qualified for reduced commissions was raised to $100,000.[3]

When the TSE's new commissions were being considered in 1967, a committee was struck to consider lowering the rates on block trades. After discussions with the Montreal Stock Exchange, it was agreed that there should be a 30 per cent commission discount on all trades worth over $100,000. Introduced as a six-month experiment, the new rule was eventually made permanent.[4] The danger was that if such concessions were not made to institutional investors, they might shift their dealings away to a 'third market' (outside both the exchanges and over-the-counter dealings). Brokers were particularly keen to prevent mutual funds and insurance companies from acquiring control of exchange members through whom they could channel their business to capture commission revenues. The new rules did prove fairly successful in keeping block trading on the exchanges, yet there always seemed to be new challenges, the most serious of which came in 1969 from the Instinet computerized trading system in the United States. For a monthly fee, subscribers could post notices of stocks they were seeking and haggle over prices, while retaining the anonymity of the auction market. In 1970 the TSE board approved bigger commission discounts on large orders, 30 per cent on the first $250,000, 40 per cent on the next $750,000, and 50 per cent over $1 million.[5]

Before long, demands arose from the brokerage community for another across-the-board commission increase. In 1971 a TSE committee recommended that, rather than a percentage fee on the value of a trade, the number of shares involved should govern the rate for stocks worth under $10. Particularly controversial was the plan to reduce the special discounts offered to insiders, who were permitted to trade for one-fifth of the regular commission. Some exchange governors were vociferous in defence of the traditional 'dealer's turn,' claiming that paying commissions on their own trades merely involved taking money out of one pocket and putting it in another. Yet the refusal of the exchange to grant memberships to mutual funds or insurers made such arguments less convincing: 'The closed membership denies "negotiated commissions" for example to excluded classes of institutions, but it is now the privilege of many persons inside the membership.' In the end, the TSE board concluded that new rates would be more defensible if the privileges for partners and customers' men were eliminated. 'The only serious problem is obtaining the support of the membership.'[6]

The TSE governors formed a Strategy Committee to sell their proposals, but approval did not come easily. With a number of firms ceasing business,[7] brokers worried that raising commissions might only worsen matters. The Strategy Committee was asked to prepare a study showing the effects of the proposed changes on revenues during the last two months of 1971. The results suggested that among sixty-four firms studied, thirty-six would enjoy a rise of income, while for twenty-eight it would decline, but that overall revenues would fall 3.15 per cent. The key variable was the size of a typical transaction, since orders up to 1,100 shares (which produced 62 per cent of all commissions) would generate increased returns. Another factor was price: shares worth from ½ cent to $3 and over $30 would produce more revenue, those in between less. The new scheme would load the burden on penny stock buyers since shares at the $1–2 level would now return the largest commissions, rather than $17–18 stock as under the current schedule.[8]

Another study of the impact of the new rates divided seventy-three TSE members into five categories by type of business: (A) national multi-branch earners of diversified income; (B) institutionally oriented local firms; (C) multi-branch ones with large agency business in low-cost orders; (D) local houses with average to low-value trades; and (E) diversified local firms. The results showed the following impact on earnings: firms in group A: 6 down, 6 up; B: 13 down, 1 up; C: 0 down, 6 up; D: 5 down, 19 up; E: 5 down, 11 up; or 43 up and 30 down overall. Large retail traders in low-cost shares were the obvious beneficiaries, and the strongest opposition would come from group B firms serving institutions.[9]

Along with some dissidents in Toronto, many members of the Montreal and Vancouver exchanges were unenthusiastic about the proposal. Eventually a whole new plan was devised which tied commissions to the dollar value of each trade, the percentage tapering as the value rose to produce 5.24 per cent in additional revenue.[10] Most TSE members rejected the notion that a hefty rise in commissions might drive small traders away and seriously reduce liquidity. Others disagreed; one critic complained to the OSC that 'Canadian stock markets are over-burdened with too many brokers and others seeking to make their living ... Exchange members apparently plan to make no special effort to improve their services or the market generally, but rather plan to use the privilege of the regulated rate structure to insulate themselves from the real competitive world.' The new charges were 'excessive and outrageous,' 'a gross abuse of the privilege of regulation,' when the proper course was to tear down the barriers.[11]

Further wrangling between the three exchanges led to more negotiations, which finally produced a proposal in the spring of 1973, aimed at raising total revenues by 8 per cent. Since the Securities Act required the OSC to approve any changes in the TSE by-laws, the Torontonians asked the commission to pronounce on the plan before it went to a vote of exchange members.[12] For the first time hearings were ordered. President Jack Kimber presented the exchange's case. He argued that the anomalies in the current commission structure dated back to the merger of the TSE with the Standard Stock and Mining Exchange in 1934, when penny mining stocks had been charged lower rates than industrials in order to encourage speculative trading. Now the time had come to eliminate these discrepancies. At the same time he rejected the notion of making all commissions negotiable as of benefit only to large institutional investors.[13]

The OSC was by no means ready to rubber-stamp this proposal. Chair E.A. Royce noted that the TSE might be self-regulating, but that did not mean its desires automatically reflected the public interest. The proposed scale seemed designed to make concessions to institutional traders, even though 70 per cent of commission revenues came from individual investors. High rates on small orders would simply drive the little players into the arms of the mutual funds. Other businesses accepted that they earned less from certain types of orders, and brokers might have to live with losses on low-cost retail orders as the price of doing business in a field well insulated against competition. After all, observed Royce, 'This is a highly protected industry with no new foreign firms allowed under present policy.'[14]

For the first time the OSC staff prepared a briefing book containing thirteen briefs from the public and the industry, most of the latter hostile to the proposed changes.[15] Commission economist Dagmar Stafl raised a series of searching questions about the TSE proposal. Was a raise really needed? Wages and the cost of living might have gone up since 1967, but brokerage earnings had also risen handsomely because share-price rises had outpaced inflation. Why should it cost any more to execute a trade in a higher-priced stock than in a lower-priced one? Would the increases simply diminish trading volume by driving away small customers? There was no move towards a flat rate since new deviations were being introduced, and the sliding scale on transactions worth over $30,000 might not be enough to induce institutions to keep trading on the exchanges rather than resorting to the third market or a 'fourth market' where brokers, acting as principals, handled deals off the exchange.

Stanley Gorecki of the OSC's accounting staff pointed out that the fixed rate structure had simply evolved from the practices of the New York Stock Exchange, which had never been seriously questioned prior to the past decade or so. No effort had been made to propose a 'reasonable' rate of return for the securities industry as a whole or for its various components. Commissioner David Johnston argued that it was appropriate that a monopoly should have its rates regulated by government, but he also raised the more fundamental question of whether or not it would be more efficient to allow the market to set rates by permitting competition.[16]

The OSC held five days of hearings in May and June of 1973. Afterwards its decision noted, 'In Canada the securities industry enjoys some of the advantages of a combine since uniform commission rates are permitted across the country.' Yet 'The proposals ... are almost completely industry-oriented. Little effort was made to assess the impact of change on the investor, whether individual or institutional.' The demand for a continuation of fixed rates simply assumed that exchange members should possess a monopoly without supplying any arguments for its necessity, as could be made in the case of certain public utilities. With the inclusion of a $12 minimum charge on small orders, it was calculated that the industry proposal would mean an overall revenue increase of 8.85 per cent. The brokers had rejected a flat-rate system based on the value of trades because they claimed that it would be too disruptive for certain types of firms. Since 70 per cent of trades were small or medium-sized ones for individual investors, consideration must surely be given as to whether increased commissions might cause their withdrawal from the market, with serious consequences for the liquidity of trading on the exchanges. None of the evidence indicated that the proposed plan would provide better service for investors or that an increase as large as requested was necessary to the industry.[17]

Nevertheless, the OSC showed itself sympathetic to the brokers in many ways. The commission believed that it should not act as a rate-setting body, nor would it order a move to fully negotiated rates without some idea of the impact that that would have upon the structure of the industry. While rejecting an increase of the size demanded, the commission made it clear that a proposal like the one approved the previous December by the TSE, which would have raised rates by 5.24 per cent, would be acceptable. The OSC suggested that a fuller national study, based on accurate information about costs and profit levels, was required over the next couple of years to assess the impact of even more radical changes.[18]

Seizing the opportunity, the TSE staff got busy reworking its proposal and soon concluded that reducing the mandatory minimum charge and shifting the point at which the maximum percentage rate would apply should produce a revenue increase acceptable to the OSC. All three Canadian exchanges gave their support to this proposal, but at the same time inserted a catch: because of the delay in bringing the new rates into force, a temporary 5 per cent commission surcharge on all orders should be applied for a one-year period because of the number of firms that were presently losing money. The OSC agreed to the new schedule, with a $10 minimum charge and rates that rose as share prices increased to $14, then tapered downward again on orders worth between $60,000 and $500,000, leaving commissions on larger transactions to be negotiated. But it simply ignored the request for a surcharge. Despite some grumbling, members of each exchange gave their consent, and the new rates took effect at the end of November 1973.[19]

Even increased commissions failed to solve the financial problems being experienced by certain brokers. Among the ninety-one TSE members, sixty claimed to have lost a total of $17 million during the second quarter of 1974, while the rest earned a mere $1.5 million, an amount lower than the rate of inflation. The TSE therefore immediately renewed its request for a temporary surcharge, citing the difficulties created by slow trading and inflationary cost increases.[20] The OSC staff was not impressed. The commission had ordered the exchanges to get busy and collect more information so that they could propose a reason-able rate of return on capital invested in brokerages, but nothing had yet been done. Since there was no incentive for more efficient opera-tions, higher costs might reflect nothing more than the heavier interest charges required to finance inventories. Advised that the OSC was not prepared to consider any revision of the commission schedule, the TSE decided not to press for a hearing.[21]

How could the brokers persuade the commission to change its mind? Nine firms had withdrawn from the brokerage business during the past year, leaving the TSE membership at a twenty-five-year low. And there were plenty of other ominous portents: the New York Stock Exchange had finally been ordered by the SEC to bring in negotiated commissions for all trading on 1 May 1975, making a further shift of volume there likely. Meanwhile, Leonard Ellen had gained control of C.J. Hodgson Securities of Montreal at the same time as he controlled the institutional investors United Financial Management, though for the moment he insisted that his interest in United was purely an investment.[22]

In October 1974 the OSC was persuaded to hear an application from the TSE for an across-the-board surcharge to generate about 7 per cent more revenue for its members. At the in-camera hearings exchange representatives were insistent that even this increase would be far from sufficient to ensure that all firms would break even. Volume on the TSE was down 22 per cent between April and September, but revenues had fallen by a whopping 37 per cent. Capital employed in the brokerage industry had dropped from $209 million to $185 million, despite the injection of an additional $5.5 million in new investment. As a result, members had cut back staffing by about 11 per cent since March 1974, and over three hundred customers' men had disappeared since the start of the year. After hearing this tale of woe, the OSC concluded that small investors would be little harmed if it approved a flat 10 per cent surcharge on all orders worth over $5,000 from 1 January through 31 July 1975, which also meant that Canadian brokers would have three months to adjust after the NYSE switched entirely to negoti-ated rates.[23]

Arthur Pattillo, who had taken over as chair of the OSC in mid-1974, shocked the brokers by a speech in the spring of 1975, in which he argued that the Americans had rendered the end of fixed commissions in Canada inevitable unless brokers were prepared to see a substantial proportion of their business lost forever. One hundred and eighty-five issues listed in Toronto also traded on American exchanges, accounting for 25 per cent of volume and 43 per cent of the value of trading, and it seemed likely that much trading in them would shift to the United States. Yet TSE members were deeply divided: some preferred to cling to fixed rates and see what impact the changes in the United States had on the Canadian brokerage business. Their opponents, however, replied that this course of action would merely put off the day of reckoning for a few months while volume and liquidity ebbed away. After much dithering, the TSE governors finally voted five to one to endorse the principle of fixed commissions, while keeping a close eye on trading in interlisted stocks to see what was happened after the New York Stock Exchange went to negotiated rates on 1 May.[24]

Meanwhile, the TSE board began campaigning to have the surcharge extended beyond 1 July. The OSC did agree to extend the 10 per cent surcharge on orders over $5,000 until 30 November, but when the exchange submitted a request in the autumn to have this continued further, the OSC's patience was exhausted. The commission staff produced a dossier that strongly opposed the request, pointing out that only six firms relied exclusively upon brokerage commissions for revenue, and there was no evidence that continuing the surcharge would end the malaise from which the business was suffering. Arthur Pattillo therefore cancelled the premium as of 1 January 1976 and announced that the commission would begin full-scale hearings on the whole issue of charges at the end of May.[25]

A questionnaire sent to members by the TSE board indicated strong support for the continuation of fixed rates: two-thirds of all seat holders, doing half the business, strongly favoured this system, while another 12 per cent of seat holders, accounting for 20 per cent of trading, preferred it. Exchange staff set to work preparing an elaborate presentation for the OSC hearings, where public cross-examination of witnesses would occur for the first time.[26] The TSE brief contended that fully negotiated rates were not in the public interest, particularly for the small investor. While institutions might see their commissions cut by as much as 40 per cent, based upon American experience, trades involving two hundred shares or less would cost no less and probably more. The result would be fewer investors participating, creating less-efficient markets with wider price spreads between bids and asks as big traders took advantage of their greater access to flows of information for their own benefit.

The proponents of negotiated rates had their say too. As a large underwriter, Dominion Securities argued that greater efficiency would be achieved through the 'unbundling' of brokerage services which many customers did not require.[27] At the public hearings in July 1976, Edward O'Brien, president of the U.S. Securities Industry Association, endorsed negotiated rates, saying that total earnings in the U.S. brokerage business were down about 5 per cent, but most dealers had learned to live with the new regime, and a single boom year could change the picture entirely. After all, brokerage was a highly cyclical business tied to market volume, and sceptics might note that rationalization was already under way in Canada, with a fall in TSE membership of one-quarter since 1969. Irving Pollack of the SEC pointed out that, to date, institutions had been the principal beneficiaries of the new American rules, seeing their charges decline by about 30 per cent. Yet individual investors had seen commissions rise at less than the rate of inflation, while their business was now being eagerly courted, sometimes with the offer of unbundled services. After two weeks the hearings were the adjourned until October 1976.[28]

Following a final round of submissions, the six members of the OSC retired to consider their decision. Within a fortnight it was announced that fixed commissions would stay. Most members of the TSE were convinced that a move to negotiated rates would be harmful and would lead to amalgamations, which would reduce competition in the brokerage business. Chair Arthur Pattillo and commissioners R.M. Steiner and Robert Morgan were not persuaded that the change would benefit the small investor, while vice-chair Harry Bray concurred, though he proposed that negotiated rates be phased in over the next five years.

Most striking about this ruling was its defensive tone. The commissioners admitted that there were many good grounds for moving to negotiated rates, as American experience had shown. Some improbable claims were trotted out: brokers and exchanges actually did compete for control of people's funds against other kinds of institutions and securities. Yet, said the decision, 'After considering all of the facts relating to the competitive forces now in effect, and appreciating that hard evidence in support of either fixed or negotiated commissions is limited, the majority of us have concluded that it would not be in the public interest at this time to direct the immediate introduction of negotiated rates in whole or in part. We have concluded that the [Toronto Stock] Exchange and its members should be given a further opportunity to introduce a rate structure which would be perceived to be fair to the industry's clients, the general public and the commission.' Accordingly, the TSE was granted until 31 March 1977 to prepare a new proposal for further hearings, at which the OSC would consider whether or not the rates suggested seemed fair and reasonable or might permit some or all brokers to make undue profits. If the commission was not satisfied, it threatened to move to abolish fixed commissions.[29]

Still more notable was what followed: for the first time in its history the OSC *Bulletin* carried a lengthy minority dissent.[30] The two academic members of the panel, law professors Stanley Beck and David Johnston, took dead aim at both the evidence and the reasoning employed by the majority. In 1973 the TSE had been forced to admit that it was impossible to allocate members' costs among their different functions. When the exchange had asked for new rates to raise revenues nearly 9 per cent, the OSC had allowed it only 5.25 per cent on the grounds that firms doing primarily institutional trading would suffer serious problems. The next year the TSE had been granted a temporary 10 per cent surcharge on commissions, but the OSC had cancelled this a year later because it did not promote restructuring of the industry. Many firms had once again become profitable, thanks largely to new bond underwritings.

The dissenters noted that the TSE's case for uniform rates seemed to rest primarily on preserving the status quo, which at least supplied some stability and predictability at a time when pressures for change were strong. Claims had been made that competition would lead to predatory pricing, which might create an oligopoly that favoured institutions at the expense of individual investors, thus undercutting the liquidity of markets. And all of this at a time when investment houses supposedly needed to raise much new capital to meet future challenges. But how was the OSC supposed to judge the reasonableness of any proposed rate schedule, since what might seem fair at one point in the business cycle could look decidedly different at another? This problem was compounded by lags and leads in the markets and enterprises with very different arrays of profit centres. How could there even be a single rate of return on investment for firms that were 'in reality totally different businesses'?

Beck and Johnston noted that Irving Pollack of the SEC had highlighted the virtual impossibility of allocating costs to various revenue sources, when the same salesperson might conduct agency trading at one time and primary distribution of an issue being underwritten by the firm at another. Evidence of this difficulty was that brokerage houses going public in the United States had proven unable to meet the SEC's prospectus requirements on cost allocation, and the Canadian situation was no different. The TSE might insist that negotiated rates would lead to predatory pricing and destructive competition, ultimately creating the oligopoly power to push commissions higher, but economist Calvin Potter had contended, without refutation, that the securities business ill fit the theoretical conditions for predatory pricing, finding neither the capacity nor the incentive in the sector to engage in cut-throat competition. Yet brokers insisted that Canadians should continue to pay the world's highest trading commissions, rather than alter the rules and see as much as $18 million in savings reinvested to good effect, despite all the evidence that lack of price competition led to wastefulness and suppression of innovation.

The two professors also pointed out that none of the witnesses had suggested that the securities business in Canada was well suited for rate regulation: 'Indeed, it is doubtful if a witness with even a nodding acquaintance with the economics of rate regulation could be found to so testify.' Effective regulation of an industry required uniform accounting systems and accurate allocations of costs and capital employed, as well as the determination of rates of return on investment. 'No one of these things had been done by the industry itself.' Not only was there little evidence that the brokers intended to undertake them, but 'Most importantly, there is wide agreement that the necessary tasks are not possible of accomplishment given the nature of the industry.' All in all, the 'futility' of the OSC acting as a 'rate-approving' body was crystal clear when 'Such an industry is uniquely unsuited for rate regulation.' With a 'diversified industry serving an unstable market characterized by volatile demand,' the commission was going to find itself faced with incessant demands for readjustments, something now common even in the utilities business, where consumption was much more stable and predictable.

The practical problems of continued price-fixing were legion. Most people thought that the rates charged institutional traders were too high, but the OSC did not want rates that priced individual customers out of the market. How could both objectives be attained? Was it true that institutions would be content to see many brokers driven out of business in a Darwinian bloodbath? Most large money managers had cautiously refrained from plumping all out for negotiated rates. Already there were just four or five dominant firms in most financial-

service sectors such as banks, insurers, mutual funds, and trust companies, and they realized that it would be foolish to decimate the brokerage business and perhaps sacrifice sound research and advice. Fully
negotiable rates might actually reverse some of the slippage of business to American markets and strengthen Canadian brokers.

In an effort to guard against the inevitable counter-attacks upon
ivory-tower theorists, Beck and Johnston observed, 'Prudence and
common sense dictate that those who have no experience or background in the industry must listen to, and weigh very carefully, such
warnings.' Yet there seemed to be plenty of evidence on their side.
Withdrawals from the brokerage business might be healthy. Admittedly, negotiated rates had been introduced in the United States when
markets were buoyant, so that the impact of a downturn was difficult
to assess. For that reason Beck and Johnston wanted fixed commissions
phased out over the next two years, giving Canadian brokers time to
adapt. Change was both 'desirable and inevitable,' and since the OSC
majority had called for new proposals in five months' time, the industry had better begin preparing itself now.

Armed with the majority decision of the OSC, however, the stock
exchanges in Toronto, Montreal, and Vancouver created a joint committee near the end of 1976 charged with devising a new commission
schedule that could win approval. In order to meet the requirements
set forth by the regulators, a number of principles were to be followed.
First of all, there should be a single flat rate, so that trades would be
valued without reference to the cost of the shares involved, the intention being to show the OSC and the public undeniable fairness
towards all traders. Yet the rates were to sustain lively share markets in
Canada by encouraging greater volume, particularly from individual
investors, so that the brokerage industry would retain its vitality.
Before long, however, the notion of a single percentage rate had to be
abandoned, as many brokers insisted that while they could live with a
slight overall cut in revenues, their customers' men (now called registered representatives), whose numbers had already declined from
5,000 in 1973 to 4,300 at present, would face a sharp decrease in their
earnings from low-priced trades. The TSE board therefore instructed
its negotiators 'that rates on small orders should not be cut simply to
make the schedule more politically acceptable.' The committee recommended that trades in 100-share lots of stocks costing $5 or less would
pay an increased rate of 3 per cent, which would taper to 2 per cent on

shares valued up to $10 and to 1 per cent thereafter. In order to encourage more trading, customers would be offered a 'turnaround' rate when they reversed a trade within forty-five days, which could mean a cut of up to half the standard commission.[31]

Over all, brokerage revenues could be expected to fall 3.3 per cent. Small traders would pay more, but it was hoped that the cuts would be sufficient to keep Canadian exchanges roughly competitive with American ones and stem the steady drift of orders for interlisted shares out of the country. Such trades accounted for 37 per cent of the trading on the TSE, but since the United States had adopted fully negotiable rates, the number of orders from Canadian brokers for shares in New York had more than doubled, as discounts for large trades in highly liquid issues could reach as high as 80 per cent of the posted Toronto rate. Harry Bray thought that the willingness of TSE members to stomach an actual revenue cut was 'directly the result of the winds of competition which have become stronger since securities dealers in the United States went to fully competitive commission rates on May 1, 1975. The substantial profits of former years derived from brokerage commissions have long disappeared.'[32]

Hearings on the new plan opened before the OSC in June 1977. In order to meet the commission's demand for more data on the brokerage business, the TSE had prepared an elaborate 'Revenue and Market Analysis' together with a detailed study of thirteen of its members by accountants Clarkson, Gordon. This analysis indicated very marked fluctuations in income during 1976. The average trade now cost between $55 and $65 to process, and the new rates would generate about $60 in revenues, so that the most efficient firms would benefit without large trades cross-subsidizing small ones or vice versa.

The OSC staff challenged some of the figures submitted by the exchanges, arguing that the comparisons with New York Stock Exchange rates were not strictly accurate and insisting that the rate still remained excessive on shares priced between $5 and $30. Over all, however, the commissioners seemed satisfied that the proposal was a genuine attempt to meet the criteria set forth in the decision released the previous autumn. Since revenues were expected to fall overall by more than 3 per cent and sixty-four of the seventy-eight members of the TSE could expect to earn less from agency business, there was an impetus for brokers to compete with one another. Unless trading volume skyrocketed, no firms were likely to make unduly large profits.

The commission expressed some regret that the new schedule was not simply a flat percentage rate on the value of each trade, but it accepted that much trading in Toronto was in relatively low-value stocks which absorbed a high proportion of the fee, so that a single scale would have entailed considerable disruption in the industry. The proposed rates were roughly competitive with negotiated charges for low- and high-value shares in New York, though, as the OSC staff complained, somewhat inflated for mid-priced stocks. Still, the plan seemed fair in the main, as some price had to be paid to maintain a vigorous brokerage community in a period of depressed trading volume.[33]

Stanley Beck and David Johnston, who had dissented so forcefully from the approval given in principle to fixed commission rates a few months earlier, repeated their view that fully negotiated rates should be adopted. Both, however, agreed that if there was to be a fixed scale, this proposal was not contrary to the public interest. The new rates would come into force on 1 September 1977. The long-sought changes occurred at a time when the securities business was undergoing a number of other shifts. TSE president Jack Kimber had died suddenly the previous autumn during a trip overseas, and as of 1 July Pearce Bunting resigned from Alfred Bunting and Company and was named by the exchange board as Kimber's successor, the first full-time exchange president chosen from within the brokerage industry. Arthur Pattillo announced that he would retire as chair of the OSC on 15 October. Before the end of the year the TSE began the long-awaited experiment with its computer-assisted trading system (CATS), handling just five stocks for the time being. The aim was to free up much-needed space on the Toronto trading floor by eliminating three posts now devoted to stocks for use with new derivative securities such as options. Some people predicted that before long the old premises would be vacated entirely as traders dealt with one another solely through computer screens.

That prospect was only one aspect of a larger uncertainty about the future shape of the brokerage business. By the middle of 1979 profitability had improved, and some institutional houses that had been doing little more than breaking even a few years before were reporting returns on capital as high as 50 per cent. Still, the price of a seat on the TSE had fallen to a mere $21,000, a fraction of the $132,000 paid as recently as 1973, while in Montreal memberships were going for just $1,200. In the autumn the TSE responded to persistent sniping from its floor traders and returned some of the more active stocks that had been assigned to the CATS to the traditional trading floor, leaving only some lightly traded issues to be handled in this newfangled fashion.[34]

Granted the right to review all changes in the by-laws of the Toronto Stock Exchange in 1966, the OSC had found itself almost unwittingly drawn into new areas of regulation. The decisions of the commission taken during the 1970s in favour of the continuation of fixed commissions were conservative, aimed at preserving the financial community in Canada from the disruptive effects that had resulted from the shift to fully negotiated charges in the United States. In doing so, the OSC acceded to the demands of the financial community for continuing protection against competitive pressures, despite growing criticism.

Conclusion

'End near for penny-stock abuses,' blares the newspaper headline.[1] Not likely, the cynic replies. Crime does not cease simply because of the passage of new laws, and more than a couple of new rulings by the Ontario Securities Commission would be needed to stamp out operators using high-pressure methods to sell over-the-counter stocks at excessive markups. Securities regulators will continue to be required to protect investigators against fraud and deception for the foreseeable future.

When Ontario passed its new Securities Act in 1945, officials at the OSC believed that they now had the tools to clean up the business of marketing stocks. 'Full, true and plain disclosure' by prospectus would henceforth be demanded of anyone attempting to make a distribution of new securities to the public. Yet many Canadians, regulators included, were concerned that over-strict rules might kill off markets for speculative stocks. The myth-makers of Canadian mining cherished the notion that many great finds had been the work of visionary prospectors who had followed their dreams into the wilderness, and that if exploration was no longer to be financed by the sale of shares in speculative public companies, it would soon be monopolized by a few large mining corporations, deemed to be too unimaginative and conservative. Not only that but ordinary investors would be deprived of opportunities to buy penny stocks and to strike it rich when a major discovery was actually made. The regulators must not be too invasive: 'After the war there were several mining booms in Canada, and a lot of effort of the Canadian regulators, in particular the OSC, seemed to be to keep the lid on. There was a lot of talk about the north, the prospectors, gold, ... shibboleths.'[2]

As it turned out, such fears about regulators clamping down too hard proved greatly exaggerated. Shares of companies possessing little more than claims to some acres of moose pasture continued to be marketed aggressively during the next two decades. What, after all, did disclosure entail? As one OSC staff member observed, 'If a prospectus complied with the [Securities] Act, then it would go through even if you didn't believe a word of it.'[3] What such documents contained was firmly fixed by tradition, so that a prospectus need say nothing about matters such as competition or costs, much less about the size of the markup over their costs at which brokers and dealers were reselling such shares to the public. Even long-time OSC official Harry Bray later admitted that the 1945 legislation had been 'riddled' with exemptions and that the changes made over the succeeding fifteen years were no more than 'cosmetic.'[4]

Moreover, during the 1940s and 1950s the OSC often failed to step in, despite the fact that some registrants frequently violated the rules against high-pressure selling and marketed shares unregistered in the United States, to the annoyance of the American authorities. In theory, of course, discipline was supposed to be imposed by the self-regulatory bodies such as the Broker Dealers Association, but D.A. Oesterle has noted that such organizations exist in perpetual tension between the demands of their members and the interests of customers, so that the real purpose is often 'to *market* an image of honesty but to *operate* some accepted distance from the image for the benefit of their members.'[5] Other analysts have gone so far as to argue that the system was deliberately adopted in Ontario to create a relatively loose regulatory environment in which the financing of speculative mining ventures might proceed without much hindrance.[6]

Did this system, then, represent some kind of 'capture' of the regulators by the regulated? Was the OSC captured, or did it perhaps undergo the 'midlife crisis' posited for the Securities and Exchange Commission in the United States during the 1950s?[7] Arguments by analogy always have their appeal for historians, and anthropomorphic analogies can seem particularly persuasive. As well, one can certainly find suggestive comments, such as that by one-time Ontario securities commissioner John Willis, that 'regulatory tribunals usually come to understand the problems of their customers so well that they aren't hard enough on them. The longer I sat with the Commission, the more often did I have to be reminded by my colleagues that I must not make remarks like, "I don't see how we can expect a mining promoter to be really truthful about a bit of moose pasture he's trying to sell shares in."[8]

Yet closer analysis suggests a more nuanced conclusion.Throughout the period under study the relations between the regulators and those determined to push the rules to the limits were almost invariably adversarial. Broker-dealers, in particular, frequently complained that by clamping down upon them too tightly, the OSC ran the risk of making the distribution of junior mining stocks impossible. The commission did pursue those whom it adjudged guilty of serious fraud quite doggedly during the 1950s and the early 1960s. Yet both regulators and regulated existed in a kind of symbiotic relationship, so that O.E. Lennox, who chaired the OSC from 1948 through 1962, often said that the commission could not be expected to bring about changes in conduct single-handedly but must wait for the more reputable elements in the financial community to set higher standards which others could then be compelled to adhere to. Until the revelations about the Windfall scandal in 1964, the myths of Canadian mining were largely unchallenged. Thus regulation came to have a profoundly conservative function. Both regulators and registrants shared certain assumptions that too much interference in the marketplace was bound to have adverse consequences. If the marketing of speculative shares were stopped, then the development of the Canadian economy must suffer.

New problems emerged during the 1960s. Mergers too often seemed to benefit corporate insiders at the expense of small shareholders. Disclosure assumed new meanings when insider trading was prohibited by the Securities Act of 1966. Yet regulation still retained its conservative function: the financial community looked to the OSC for protection against competition from foreigners. At the same time the commission was persuaded to maintain the fixed commission scale on trades, which prevented brokers from engaging in price competition with one another.

Perhaps the most notable change in the realm of ideas was the growth of doubts about the virtues of self-regulation, upon which the OSC depended so heavily. William O. Douglas of the SEC had pointed out in the 1930s that regulators needed to have a 'shotgun in the closet,' well oiled and ready for use, if only to remind self-regulatory organizations of their responsibilities.[9] Having watched the Broker Dealers Association and the Toronto Stock Exchange pay scant attention to investor protection on occasion, the OSC gradually came to accept the accuracy of Douglas's dictum. In 1978 long-time commission staff member Harry Bray wrote, 'I accept the proposal without reservation that the recognized self-regulatory bodies should be given so much responsibility for regulation as is feasible, but retaining in the commission the ultimate responsibility for all registrants, and, in the public interest, the effectiveness of its supervision of the self-regulatory associations.' And on taking over as chair at the OSC in the same year, Jim Baillie concurred that 'to be credible and effective it is desirable that the self-regulatory organization be subject to supervision by an agency of government.'[10]

Ontario's new Securities Act of 1978 widened the requirements for disclosure. All distributors of securities (unless granted a narrow range of specific exemptions) must now file a prospectus with the OSC. This closed system was designed to ensure that these 'reporting issuers' would make continous disclosure to investors about all material changes in corporate affairs. Before long the commission also required 'universal registration' that removed the exemption from licensing requirements from virtually everyone considered to be a 'market intermediary' engaged in the business of trading securities, a system that would eventually be adopted with only minor variations in most other Canadian jurisdictions.[11]

The task of regulating the securities business after 1980 went on against a background of rapid and dramatic changes in the Canadian financial world. Enthusiasm for deregulation during the 1980s made it increasingly difficult to defend protectionist rules. One of the first casualties was fixed commissions for brokers. In 1982 the OSC decided to abandon the attempt to construct a 'fair' rate structure and leave the market to set fees, as the Americans had done seven years earlier.[12] Price competition in the brokerage business was ratcheted up another notch that same year when Gordon Capital brought the 'bought deal' to Canada, in which the underwriters purchased a new issue outright as principals and then undertook its distribution.[13]

Despite continuing concerns about a shortage of investment capital in the brokerage industry, the Toronto Stock Exchange still limited outside investors to 10 per cent of the voting shares in a member firm and required 40 per cent of the directors and partners of members to be active in the brokerage business. In 1982, however, the exchange's by-laws were altered to permit firms to go public (provided that they obeyed these ownership restrictions), and within two years four houses had made offerings of their own stock, raising $23 million. The OSC continued to require that no single shareholder control more than a 10 per cent interest, that 40 per cent of all directors be Canadians, and that all board members be approved by the commission and other self-regulatory organizations. Brokers were not permitted to diversify into the provision of other types of financial services.[14]

Still unsettled was the question of what to do about foreign investment in this sector. The takeover of Royal Securities by Merrill Lynch in 1969 had led the provincial government to limit outsiders to a one-quarter share in any securities firm, with no single interest having over 10 per cent (the 25–10 rule). Twenty-six foreign-controlled firms already operating were 'grandfathered,' eight of which belonged to either the stock exchange or the Investment Dealers Association, when the 25–10 rule 'effectively closed the door on any new non-resident entrants to the industry in Ontario.' Subject to restrictions on their rate of growth and the infusion of capital from their American parents, only three of the eight were still extant by 1985.[15]

The Canadian financial system had always rested upon 'four pillars': banks, insurers, trust companies, and securities dealers, each of which pursued its activities subject to different regulatory regimes.[16] The Securities Act itself contained no restrictions upon the ownership of registrants, but a study of diversification in 1982 led the OSC to recommend by a five-to-three margin that other types of financial institutions should still not be permitted to invest in dealers, the minority arguing that a 10 per cent interest could be allowed. In 1984 the provincial cabinet established a ministerial task force to consider whether or not the separation of the four pillars should be maintained, and within a couple of years the government announced that ownership of securities dealers would be opened up to domestic financial institutions in an unrestricted way on 30 June 1987.[17] That decision set off a stampede which saw each of the major banks acquire a brokerage subsidiary. Before long, Wood Gundy had been taken over by the Canadian Imperial Bank of Commerce, Dominion Securities by the Royal Bank, Nesbitt Burns by the Bank of Montreal, and McLeod Young Weir by the Bank of Nova Scotia, while the Toronto Dominion created its own discount brokerage operation from scratch. Within a decade there existed just a handful of independently owned brokerage and underwriting houses of any size. Throwing open the securities business to outsiders in 1987 also saw foreign-controlled investment dealers permitted to operate in Ontario without restrictions, though federal and provincial legislation still prohibited foreigners from controlling more than a one-quarter share of a Canadian financial institution.[18]

Investor protection remained important in view of the steady spread of share ownership in Canada during the 1990s, either directly or through mutual funds. A survey conducted by the Toronto Stock Exchange indicated that, while just 13 per cent of Canadian adults owned shares or mutual funds in 1983, that figure had risen to 23 per cent by 1989, 37 per cent by 1996, and 49 per cent by 2000. By the latter date about 43 per cent of Canadians had holdings in mutual funds, while 25 per cent also owned some stocks. Many of these holdings were comparatively modest, since 35 per cent of portfolios in the year 2000 were worth less than $25,000 and only 18 per cent were valued at over $100,000. Almost 30 per cent of investors reported that their household income was under $50,000 per year. Just over 40 per cent of investors used full-service brokerage houses also equipped to supply investment advice; more than 20 per cent now depended upon discount brokerages. And while the use of the Internet for stock trading was almost non-existent in 1996, 27 per cent of investors made use of this method in the 1999–2000 year, suggesting that an increasing number of them were managing their affairs directly.[19]

Even the myths of Canadian mining took on a new life during the 1990s with the huge nickel discovery at Voisey's Bay in Labrador and the even more improbable find of diamond deposits in the Northwest Territories. Once again life was breathed into the legend of the independent prospector pursuing his goal against all the odds. If investors could only get in on the ground floor, there were still fortunes to be made, it seemed, though such hopes were dented by the Bre-X scandal in 1997, when shares that had risen to 280 times their original cost collapsed amidst revelations about ore samples crudely salted with gold in faraway Indonesia.

Meanwhile, regulating securities markets has become even more challenging following the development of 'value-at-risk' models of portfolio management, which depend upon the pricing formulas developed by Fischer Black, Myron Scholes, and Robert Merton in the 1970s.[20] This theoretical breakthrough permitted the pricing of options, which in turn opened the way for the vast expansion of trading in financial derivatives in recent years. The complexities of 'hedges' and 'index funds' are such that compelling full disclosure about a mining claim or a takeover bid may seem almost simple by comparison, suggesting that there will be plenty for securities regulators to do for the foreseeable future.

Appendix:

Indexes of Common Stock Prices, 1940–1977

TABLE A.1 Index of common stock prices,
1940–56 (1935–9 = 100)

Year	Mines	Industrials, utilities, banks
1940	81.2	77.4
1941	72.4	67.5
1942	52.3	64.2
1943	70.1	83.5
1944	81.3	83.8
1945	95.2	99.6
1946	97.8	115.7
1947	86.7	106.0
1948	82.0	112.5
1949	87.4	109.4
1950	89.9	131.6
1951	99.2	168.3
1952	103.6	173.1
1953	92.1	160.3
1954	91.3	181.2
1955	116.9	232.7
1956	134.4	269.0

SOURCE: F.H. Leacy, ed., *Historical Statistics of Canada*, 2nd ed. (Ottawa, 1983), J490, J494

TABLE A.2 Indexes of common stock prices,
1956–77 (1975 = 1000)

Year	Mines	Oil and gas	TSE 300 composite
1956	829	586	568
1957	749	607	532
1958	616	499	495
1959	697	460	562
1960	684	342	514
1961	902	425	646
1962	824	423	625
1963	862	419	674
1964	1,076	493	797
1965	1,211	536	955
1966	1,233	571	835
1967	1,275	752	885
1968	1,286	905	931
1969	1,370	1,090	1,036
1970	1,280	857	911
1971	1,109	1,085	969
1972	1,088	1,267	1,136
1973	1,271	1,461	1,213
1974	1,070	1,069	1,018
1975	1,000	1,005	1,000
1976	1,191	1,069	1,039
1977	1,000	1,198	1,010

SOURCE: F.H. Leacy, ed., *Historical Statistics of Canada*, 2nd ed. (Ottawa, 1983), J481, J486, J489

Notes

Abbreviations

AG	Attorney General (including records)
BDA	Broker Dealers Association of Ontario
BM	Bray Material, Ontario Securities Commission Records, PAO
Canada, Justice Records, file A91-00058	Canada, Justice Department, Access to Information Act release (to author), file A91-00058
CBA	Canadian Bar Association
Corr.	Correspondence
DLR	*Dominion Law Reports*
DM	Deputy Minister
EA	Canada, External Affairs (now Foreign Affairs) Department (including records)
FP	*Financial Post* (Toronto)
IDA	Investment Dealers Association of Canada
MB	Minute Book
MSE	Montreal Stock Exchange
MUA	McGill University Archives
NAC	National Archives of Canada
NASD	National Association of Securities Dealers
NYSE	New York Stock Exchange
OLR	*Ontario Law Reports*
OSC	Ontario Securities Commission
OSCB	Ontario Securities Commission, *Bulletin*, 1949–
OSDA	Ontario Securities Dealers Association
PABC	Provincial Archives of British Columbia

PAM	Provincial Archives of Manitoba
PAO	Provincial Archives of Ontario
PDA	Prospectors and Developers Association
RR	OSC, Reviews of Registrations, 1946–8, 3 vols. (mimeos, University of Toronto Library)
SCR	*Supreme Court Reports*
SEC	Securities and Exchange Commission
Select Committee on Administration of Justice	Ontario, Legislative Assembly, Select Committee on Administration of Justice, 1951, Proceedings (typescript, PAO, RG 18)
SS	Secretary of State
TSE	Toronto Stock Exchange
USS	Under-Secretary of State
VSE	Vancouver Stock Exchange
U.S., SEC, FOIA #90-1128	United States, Securities and Exchange Commission, Freedom of Information Act release (to author), #90-1128
WSE	Winnipeg Stock Exchange

A Note on Sources

The single most important source for this study was the collection of records of the Ontario Securities Commission at the Archives of Ontario, in particular the files collected by long-time senior staff member H.S. Bray, described as the 'Bray Material.' In addition, the archives has the records of the office of the attorney general of Ontario, through whom the OSC reported to the legislature until 1967; these files contain much valuable material, especially for the earlier years discussed here. As well, the provincial archives holds the very extensive records generated by the royal commission inquiring into the promotion of Windfall Mines in 1964–5 (cited as RG 18, B-132, but now renumbered RG 18-149) and the transcript of the hearings of the committee of the Legislative Assembly that looked into share-selling practices in 1951. The library of the OSC has a small but useful collection of documents and publications dealing with the activities of the commission. At the National Archives of Canada are the records of the Department of External Affairs (now Foreign Affairs), which detail relations with the United States on the subject of the marketing of speculative Canadian stocks there and the efforts to revise the Extradition Treaty between the two countries as a means of regulating these operations.

Both the Montreal and Toronto Stock Exchanges have created important collections of records. The minute books of the MSE were seen at the exchange. While the TSE has donated many of its early records to the National Archives of

Canada, its minute books subsequent to 1968 were consulted at the exchange. The minute books of the Broker Dealers Association of Ontario are currently in my possession, but I intend to deposit them in the Archives of Ontario. The Securities and Exchange Commission in Washington and the Canadian Department of Justice released copies of certain records to me under freedom-of-information legislation. Finally, the *Financial Post* newspaper provided highly valuable stories on many different aspects of the business world.

Introduction

1 Joel Seligman, *The Transformation of Wall Street: A History of the Securities and Exchange Commission and Modern Corporate Finance*, rev. ed. (Boston, 1995), 622

2 The literature on the United States is particularly extensive; for Canada see Christopher Armstrong and H.V. Nelles, *Monopoly's Moment: The Organization and Regulation of Canadian Utilities, 1830–1930* (Philadelphia, 1986).

3 See Mary G. Condon, *Making Disclosure: Ideas and Interests in Ontario Securities Regulation* (Toronto, 1998), chapter 1, 'Frameworks for Regulation: An Interpretive Approach.'

4 Because of her concentration upon formal documents and decisions, Condon sometimes neglects the interplay of interests. For example, in discussing the failure to revise the Ontario Securities Act during the 1970s, she notes only, 'The viscissitudes of the proposed legislation become somewhat harder to trace as final enactment in 1978 is approached ... Securities legislation was not apparently considered a priority for the Ontario government during this period' (*Making Disclosure*, 206–7). This comment neglects the fact that the ruling Conservatives were reduced to a minority in the legislature in 1975 and remained in power with support from opposition Liberals and New Democrats, some of whom opposed certain provisions in the proposed law. See chapter 11 below.

5 F.H. Leacy, ed., *Historical Statistics of Canada*, 2nd ed. (Ottawa, 1983), F13

6 The mining stock index had, however, surpassed its pre-crash values, thanks principally to a boom in gold stocks during the late 1930s.

7 The term 'over the counter' derived from the transfer of share certificates through the offices of brokers; lacking exchange quotations, such brokers served customers by telephoning one another to ascertain current prices for stocks in which they wished to deal.

8 See Christopher Armstrong, *Blue Skies and Boiler Rooms: Buying and Selling Securities in Canada, 1870–1940* (Toronto, 1997) chapter 4.

9 Ibid., chapter 11

10 Seligman, *Transformation of Wall Street*, chapters 1–3

11 The OSC could close the TSE altogether, but doing so would have thrown the financial world into chaos.
12 Seligman, *Transformation of Wall Street*, chapter 11, 265, 273, 349–50
13 The New York Curb Exchange had operated outdoors until the end of the First World War, with no effective listing requirements; even after it moved inside and was renamed the Amex in 1953, its listing requirements remained very relaxed. See Robert Sobel, *The Curbstone Brokers: The Origins of the American Stock Exchange* (New York, 1970).
14 Seligman, *Transformation of Wall Street*, 288–9
15 Ibid., 299. The full title was *Report of the Special Study of Securities Markets of the Securities and Exchange Commission*, submitted to the House of Representatives Commerce Committee (House Doc. no. 95, 88th Congress, 1st Sess., 1963).
16 Seligman, *Transformation of Wall Street*, 327–35. The NYSE successfully resisted this effort to abolish floor trading.
17 Ontario, *Report of the Royal Commission to Investigate Trading in the Shares of Windfall Oils and Mines Limited* (n.p., September 1965), 101
18 See Kennth G. Patrick, *Perpetual Jeopardy: The Texas Gulf Sulphur Affair, a Chronicle of Achievement and Misadventure* (Toronto, 1972)
19 John Brooks, *The Go-Go Years* (New York, 1973)
20 See note 4 above.
21 Seligman, *Transformation of Wall Street*, 167
22 Quoted ibid., 382
23 Michael Bliss, 'Another Anti-Trust Tradition: Canadian Combines Policy, 1889–1910,' in Glenn Porter and Robert D. Cuff, eds., *Enterprise and National Development: Essays in Canadian Business and Economic History* (Toronto, 1973), 39–50
24 Seligman, *Transformation of Wall Street*, 373
25 Ibid., 349
26 Ibid., 350
27 See Joel Seligman, *The SEC and the Future of Finance* (New York, 1985), 197; chapter 7, 'The Corporate Disclosure Debate,' 195–274, summarizes the literature.
28 Seligman, *Transformation of Wall Street*, 185–7
29 Ibid., 439–40
30 Ibid., 490

Chapter 1: 'The Canadian Problem'

1 Liz Lundell, *The Estates of Old Toronto* (Toronto, 1997), 166–7

2 Memorandum by Chalmers, 'Re: H.R. Bain and Company,' 4 April 1940, and section of MS autobiography by Chalmers entitled 'Post-Lude to the Mining Scandals,' (quoted), both lent to the author by John T. Saywell
3 NAC, TSE, MB, 1, 6, 9, 13, 20, 22, 27 February, 19 March, 23 April (quoted)1940
4 OSC, RR, vol. 1, Re H.R. Bain and Co., 27 January 1946
5 FP, 18 May, 8 June, 20 July, 17 August 1940
6 FP, 30 November 1940; U.S., SEC, FOIA # 90-1128, SEC Assistant General Counsel Robert E. Kline to R.B. Whitehead, 4 November 1940
7 PAO, AG, 4-02, file 35.1, Memorandum from R.B. Whitehead to AG Leslie Blackwell, 3 September 1943
8 Ibid., file 12.8, text of speech by Conant to Legislative Assembly, 7 April 1941
9 FP, 16, 23, 30 March 1940
10 Chalmers MS autobiography, 4–6 (quoted), and memorandum by Chalmers, 'Re: Security Frauds Legislation,' 4 April 1940, lent to the author by John T. Saywell
11 FP, 13, 20 April 1940
12 FP, 30 November, 14 December 1940
13 The old agreement did cover the offence of 'obtaining by false pretences,' but the American courts defined this so narrowly as to make convictions difficult to obtain. The United States had signed a new Extradition Treaty with Britain in 1931, and discussions with Canada commenced the following year. A draft treaty was prepared in 1933, but the talks stalled and no agreement was reached.
14 U.S., SEC, FOIA #90-1128, Frank to Hull, 30 January 1941. The need for treaty changes increased in February 1940 because the Alberta Supreme Court refused an application to extradite Edward P. Lamar on charges of fraudulently selling securities by mail on the grounds that mail fraud was not an offence specified by the treaty. See In re Lamar (1940), 2 Western Weekly Reports, 471–7.
15 Canada, Justice Records, file A91-00058, Treaty Series, 1942, no. 10, 'Treaty for the Extradition of Criminals concluded between Canada and the United States of America at Washington, April 29, 1942'
16 NAC, EA, vol. 2690, file 12216-6-40, part 1, Pierpont Moffatt to Mackenzie King, 14 July 1941; J.E. Read to O.D. Skelton, 29 April 1942; Read to DM of Justice, 30 June 1942
17 NAC, TSE, MB, 23, 30 June 1942; Canada, Justice Records, file A91-00058, Slaght to Justice Minister Louis St. Laurent, 26 June 1942
18 NAC, EA, vol. 3329, file 12216-6-40, part 2, A.N. Wolverton (VSE) to

Mackenzie King, 14 October 1942; T.A. Richardson and H.M. Chisholm (TSE) to King and Louis St Laurent, 15 October 1942; Brief from Montreal SE/Curb, 19 October 1942; H.E. Cochrane (IDA) to King and St Laurent, 14 November 1942; MSE, Governors' MB, 21 October 1943; NAC, TSE, MB, 22 September, 20 October 1943

19 Canada, Justice Records, file A91-00058, C.R. Magone to M.F. Gallagher, 4 September, 18 November (quoted) 1942; Conant to St Laurent, 18 November 1942

20 Ibid., St Laurent to M.F. Gallagher, 30 October 1942

21 *FP*, 16, 30 January 1943; *Globe and Mail* (Toronto), 15 January 1943; Canada, Justice Records, file A91-00058, OSDA Submission to King and St Laurent, 7 January 1943; Crerar to St Laurent, 16 January 1943; NAC, EA, vol. 3329, file 12216-6-40, part 2, G.A. MacMillan (PDA) to King, 16 January 1943; Norman Vincent to King, 18 January 1943

22 Canada, Justice Records, file A91-00058, TSE president T.A. Richardson to St Laurent, 19 January 1943; H.G. Kimber to St Laurent, 28 January 1943; Richardson to Finance Minister J.L. Ilsley, 29 January 1943; NAC, TSE, MB, 9 February 1943

23 NAC, EA, vol. 3329, file 12216-6-40, part 2, Memorandum from N.A. Robertson to J.E. Read, 20 January 1943; Canada, House of Commons, *Debates*, 29 January 1943, 8

24 Drew Pearson was technically incorrect since Canada refused to participate in Lend-Lease formally, though American defence purchases in Canada were certainly vitally important; Callahan had to be told that since the briefs had been submitted to the prime minister, they could not simply be forwarded, but a summary would be prepared. See NAC, EA, vol. 3329, file 12216-6-40, part 2, L.B. Pearson to N.A. Robertson, 22 January 1943.

25 U.S., SEC, FOIA #90-1128, Robertson to J.T. Callahan, 8 February 1943, Confidential; NAC, EA, vol. 3329, file 12216-6-40, part 2, J.E. Read to M.F. Gallagher, 3 March 1943

26 NAC, TSE, MB, 6, 20 April 1943

27 NAC, EA, vol. 3329, file 12216-6-40, Memorandum from R. Gordon Robertson re Statement concerning the Canada–United States Extradition Treaty, 6 February 1943; Norman Robertson to Mackenzie King, 16 February 1943 (both quoted)

28 Ibid., part 2, Memorandum from A.D.P. Heeney to Norman Robertson, 6 May 1943; J.C. McRuer, CBA, to St Laurent, 14 May 1943; Memorandum from R.G. Robertson re representations before a cabinet committee by organizations opposed to certain existing terms of the Extradition Treaty, 24 May 1943; NAC, TSE, MB, 11, 19 May 1943

29 NAC, EA, vol. 3329, file 12216-6-40, part 2, Memorandum from Robertson to J.E. Read, 8 June 1943; PABC, AG Corr., GR 1723, reel B7487, file S-338-3, Memorandum from DeBeck to AG, 9 June 1943; Canada, Justice Records, file A91-00058, Eric Cross to Louis St Laurent, 28 June 1943

30 PABC, AG Corr., GR 1723, reel B7487, file S-338-3, Memorandum from DeBeck to AG, 16 June 1943

31 U.S., SEC, FOIA # 90-1128, Memorandum re conference between J.E. Read, legal adviser, External Affairs; R. Forsyth, Justice; M.H. Wershof, Canadian Legation, Washington; Green Hackworth, legal adviser, State; and E.H. Cashion and James W. Deer, SEC, 9 June 1943, re Proposed Treaty of Extradition with Canada

32 NAC, EA, vol. 3329, file 12216-6-40, part 2, Minute sheet from Washington legation, 11 June 1943

33 Ibid. Memorandum from Read to W.C. Clark, 1 July 1943

34 Ibid., part 3, Clark to Norman Robertson, 9 November 1943

35 Ibid., Memorandum from R.G. Robertson to Norman Robertson, 29 January; Memorandum from Read to DM of Justice, 8 March 1944

36 FP, 27 November 1943; 15 January 1944; PAO, AG, 4-02, file 35.2, Memorandum from E.H. Clark to AG Leslie Blackwell, 23 February 1945, shows the following sums ordered repaid to the public: 1936, $5,077.07; 1937, $14,073.94; 1938, $36,376.86; 1939, $21,194.36; 1940, $39,491.65; 1941, $23,924.49; 1942, $29,787.29; 1943, $35,020.19; 1944, $19,378.64; total, $205,945.85.

37 PAO, AG, 4-02, 35.2, Grant to Blackwell, 12 January 1944 (quoted); FP, 8 January 1944

38 FP, 1 January 1944

39 PABC, AG Corr., GR 1723, reel B7487, file S-338-3, Memorandum from DeBeck, 4 August 1944

40 See Christopher Armstrong, Blue Skies and Boiler Rooms: Buying and Selling Securities in Canada, 1870–1940 (Toronto, 1997), chapter 8

41 Report of the Royal Ontario Mining Commission, 1944 (Toronto, 1944). The commissioners appointed 27 October 1943, in addition to Urquhart and Jowsey, included Kenneth C. Gray (Kirkland Lake), J. Roy Gordon (Copper Cliff), Homer W. Sutcliffe (New Liskeard), H. Chipman McCloskey (Toronto), Charles G. Williams (Toronto), and Henry Jessup (North Bay), with Douglas A. Mutch as secretary; other areas to be examined were the promotion of exploration, taxation, and employment.

42 PAO, AG, 4-02, file 35.2, J.A. Kingsmill to Blackwell, 12 January 1944, enclosing memorandum submitted by the Central District of the IDA, 12 January 1944; FP, 29 January 1944

43 FP, 29 January 1944

44 PAO, AG, 4-02, file 35.2, Grant to Blackwell, 12 January 1944
45 PAO, RG 8, series 1-7-B-2, unpublished Sessional Paper no. 47, 1944, Preliminary report of Royal Ontario Mining Commission, 18 March 1944; see also *FP*, 25 March, 1 April 1944
46 PAO, AG, 4-02, file 35.2, Submission by Gordon Jones for a group of mining lawyers, TSE members, unlisted dealers, and OSDA following meeting on 25 March 1944, 29 March 1944
47 *FP*, 1, 8, 22 (quoted) April 1944; PABC, AG Corr., GR 1723, reel B7487, file S-338-3, Memorandum from DeBeck, 4 August 1944
48 *Report of the Royal Ontario Mining Commission, 1944*
49 *FP*, 13 May, 10 June 1944
50 *FP*, 4, 11 March, 22 April, 20 May 1944
51 This appeal body, composed of a master of the Ontario Supreme Court, the judge of the Mining Court, and the deputy minister of mines, had been created in 1941.
52 *FP*, 20 May, 1 July 1944
53 *FP*, 15 July 1944
54 PAO, AG, 4-02, file 35.2, Blackwell to British Columbia AG R.L. Maitland, 31 October 1944; Blackwell to Joseph Sedgwick, 29 December 1944; 'A Summary of Misrepresentations of Fact Made to the Public by the *Financial Post* relating to the Securities Commission and the Government' by Acting Commissioner [Leslie Blackwell], ' n.d. [January 1945]
55 *FP*, 30 December 1944; 6 January 1945
56 PAO, AG, 4-02, file 35.2, 'A Summary of Misrepresentations of Fact ...'
57 PAO, AG, 4-02, file 35.2, R.L. Healy to Drew, 23 December 1944; Blackwell to Healy, 3 January 1945
58 NAC, TSE, MB, 7 November 1944, 16 January 1945. Though Blackwell was credited as the 'principal architect' of the bill, it was Roy Whitehead and lawyer Eric Silk who burnt the 'midnight oil' preparing the draft; see PAO, AG, 4-02, file 35.4, Memoranda from C.P. McTague to Blackwell, 17, 22 December 1947.
59 PAO, AG, 4-02, file 35.2, British Columbia AG R.L. Maitland to Blackwell, 20 September 1944; Blackwell to Maitland, 3, 31 October; 15 December 1944; file 36.1, Blackwell to Quebec premier Maurice Duplessis, 6 January 1945
60 Ibid., W.P.J. O'Meara to Blackwell, 1 November 1944; PABC, AG Corr., GR 1723, reel B7487, file S-338-3, Memorandum from E.K. DeBeck, 15 February 1945. O'Meara claimed that it was his department's 'firm belief that our role ought not to go beyond that of facilitating the meeting from time to time of provincial officials and that there is no need of any federal security frauds prevention law.'

61 Manitoba's public utilities commissioner (who also regulated securities) fell ill and was not able to attend, while Nova Scotia's AG expressed the view that these matters could be handled just as well by correspondence; see PAO, AG, 4-02, file 36.1, Nova Scotia AG J.H. MacQuarrie to Blackwell, 23 January 1945; Blackwell to Manitoba AG James McLenaghen, 19 February 1945.

62 Shares in primary distribution were those sold to the public from the company treasury or resold as part of a block which could be used to control the affairs of the company.

63 Canada, Justice Records, file A91-00058, Memorandum from Robert Forsyth to DM, 20 September 1945; PAO, AG, 4-02, file 36.1, Memorandum from E.H. Silk to Blackwell, 24 November 1944

64 FP, 13 January, 10 February, 3 March (quoted) 1945; PABC, AG Corr, GR 1723, reel B7487, file S-338-3, Memoranda from DeBeck, 19 January, 15 February 1945

65 Ontario, Legislative Assembly, Debates (mimeograph, hereafter Ontario, Debates), 26 February 1945, 298–301

66 Ibid., 5 March 1945, 693–5

67 Ibid., 5 March 1945, 703–4; see also TSE, Historical files, S-6, 'Stock promotions,' Toronto Better Business Bureau, Financial Bulletin, April 1945; FP, 17 March 1945.

68 Ontario, Debates, 5 March 1945, 834–48, 850–8, 866–8 (834, 848, 854 quoted)

69 PAO, AG, 4-02, file 36.1, T.M. Mungovan to Blackwell, 5 March 1945; Blackburn to Blackwell, 6 March 1945; Viola MacMillan, PDA, to Blackwell, 19 March 1945; FP, 17, 24 March 1945. In the Globe and Mail, 7 March 1945, Wellington Jeffers and Sidney Norman attacked the ban on telephone selling.

70 Ontario, Debates, 16 March 1945, 1551–67, 1572–1603 (1584 quoted); Ontario, Statutes, 1945, c. 22. After a meeting of members, Arthur Trebilock of the TSE staff appeared before the committee, but the exchange generally supported the bill; see NAC, TSE, MB, 13 March 1945.

71 FP, 30 June 1945

72 FP, 23 December 1944

73 TSE, Historical files, S-6, 'Stock promotion,' Bulletin of the Pennsylvania Securities Commission, 1 April 1945 (quoted). Copies of Callahan's letters, dated 20 November 1944 through 29 October 1945 and sent to AG Leslie Blackwell, may be found in PAO, AG, 4-02, file 36.2; some people received several such letters.

74 PAO, AG, 4-02, file 36.2, Redmond and Co. to Blackwell, 9 April 1945; McLean and Co. to Callahan, 14 May 1945; Eugene Stevens to Callahan, 10 May 1945

75 When his Conservative political master, R.L. Maitland, complained that
    such comments would make it hard for him to get along with the Drew
    government, DeBeck was unrepentant; he reiterated all of his complaints
    that Blackwell had promised full consultation before the new Securities Act
    was drafted but had refused to make changes at the Toronto conference in
    January, despite unanimous objections from the other provinces. If any-
    thing, said DeBeck, Drew owed Maitland an apology for his 'arrogant' han-
    dling of the issue. See PABC, AG Corr., GR 1723, reel B7487, file S-338-3,
    DeBeck to Maitland, 1 August 1945, addressed to 'Dear Pat.'
76 See *Toronto Daily Star*, 13, 14, 15, 16, 18 June 1945; *Globe and Mail*, 20 June
    1945; *FP*, 23 June 1945 (quoted).
77 New York *Times*, 16, 18 May 1945
78 On the life and times of the fictional J. Rufus Wallingford, see Armstrong,
    Blue Skies and Boiler Rooms, chapter 4.
79 PAO, AG, 4-02, file 36.2, R.F. Parkinson, *Ottawa Journal*, to Leslie Blackwell,
    15 June 1945, attaching a copy of the flyer and asking advice on reproduc-
    ing it
80 Ibid., Michigan securities commissioner Howard M. Warner to Blackwell,
    18 June 1945; Blackwell to Warner, 9, 20 (quoted) July 1945; Pennsylvania
    Securities Commission secretary I.G. Myers to Blackwell, 25 June 1945;
    Blackwell to Myers, 28 June 1945; Memorandum from E.H. Clark to Black-
    well, 25 June 1945. Warner claimed that failure to register was a felony
    under Michigan law whether or not fraud was involved, while Myers
    pointed out that cease-and-desist orders required proof of violation of the
    Pennsylvania criminal code, both of which ought to be grounds for suspen-
    sion or cancellation of registration in Ontario; see ibid., Warner to Black-
    well, 9 July 1945; Myers to Blackwell, 11 July 1945.
81 Ibid., Memorandum from C.P. Hope to Blackwell, 23 June 1945
82 Ibid., Blackwell to R.F. Parkinson, 23 June 1945
83 Ibid., Memorandum from Blackwell to C.R. Magone, 29 June 1945. Michi-
    gan officials denied being part of any organized campaign for the treaty,
    but Blackwell refused to be convinced; see ibid., Howard M. Warner to
    Blackwell, 9 July 1945; Blackwell to Warner, 20 July 1945.
84 NAC, EA, vol. 3329, file 12216-6-40, part 3, M.M. Mahoney to Norman Rob-
    ertson, 21, 27 June 1945
85 Canada, Justice Records, file A91-00058, Memorandum from R. Forsyth to
    F.P. Varcoe, 11 June 1945; Varcoe to USS for EA, 13 June 1945; Memorandum
    from Varcoe, 3 August 1945 (quoted); Memorandum from R. Forsyth to DM
    of Justice, 26 November 1945
86 NAC, EA, vol. 3329, file 12216-6-40, part 3, Memorandum by J.E. Read re

Extradition Treaty between Canada and the United States, 16 August 1945

87 Ibid., PDA president Viola MacMillan to Mackenzie King and Louis St Laurent, 31 October 1945; VSE president K.L. Patten to King and St Laurent, 21 November 1945; ibid., Acc. 86-7/159, file 12216-6-40, part 4, Brief from TSE to House of Commons on Extradition Treaty, 1 November 1945; NAC, TSE, MB, 10, 15, 16 October 1945; PABC, AG Corr., GR 1723, file B7487, file S-338-3, Memorandum from E.K. DeBeck to AG, 12 December 1945

88 Canada, House of Commons, Standing Committee on External Affairs and National Defence, *Minutes of Proceedings and Evidence*, no. 5, 22 November 1945, testimony of Read, 77–94; Canada, Justice Records, file A91-00058, Memorandum from R. Forsyth to DM of Justice, 26 November 1945 (quoted)

89 Canada, House of Commons, Standing Committee on External Affairs and National Defence, *Minutes of Proceedings and Evidence*, no. 5, 22 November 1945, testimony of Slaght, 95–104 (quoted, 95); ibid., no. 6, 23 November 1945, testimony of Sedgwick, 129–49 (quoted, 145)

90 Ibid., no. 6, 23 November 1945, testimony of Salter, 151–8 (quoted, 155)

91 The allegation that the SEC maintained an agent in Toronto drew a refutation from External Affairs, which argued that although SEC staff visited Toronto from time to time with the OSC's consent, the Americans had no permanent representative; see NAC, EA, vol. 3329, file 12216-6-40, part 3, John Read to A. Plouffe, 27 November 1945.

92 Canada, House of Commons, Standing Committee on External Affairs and National Defence, *Minutes of Proceedings and Evidence*, no. 7, 26 November 1945, testimony of Norman, 186–93 (quoted, 187, 190)

93 U.S., SEC, FOIA #90-1128, Callahan to SEC General Counsel E.H. Cashion, 7 December 1945; Canada, House of Commons, Standing Committee on External Affairs, *Minutes of Proceedings and Evidence*, no. 9, *Third and Final Report*, 11 December 1945; Canada, House of Commons, *Debates*, 17 December 1945, 3711–2; NAC, EA, vol. 3329, file 12216-6-40, part 3, extract of letter from Adamson to Pearson, n.d. [February 1946]; R.M. Macdonell to Canadian ambassador, Washington, 18 March 1946

94 Gordon Carroll, 'Canada's New Gold Boom, ' *Saturday Evening Post*, 19 January 1946. Carroll had visited Yellowknife to see the Giant gold mine, which he admitted was a valuable find, but he was highly critical of securities regulation in Canada.

Chapter 2: Self-Regulation

1 *FP*, 27 October 1945

2 PAO, Select Committee on Administration of Justice, testimony of McTague, 24 August 1951, 2669–70 (quoted); *FP*, 24 November 1945
3 Rickaby was the deputy minister of mines; he had sat on the OSC's Board of Review since its creation in 1941 and was well versed in mining matters. Lennox, a master of the Supreme Court of Ontario, had experience in the field of securities law, having handled the long-running bankruptcy proceedings against I.W.C. Solloway of the Solloway, Mills brokerage firm during the 1930s.
4 *FP*, 6 April 1946; NAC, TSE, MB, 1, 21 March 1946; OSC, RR, vol. 1, Re H.R. Bain and Co., 26 March 1946
5 PAO, AG, 4-02, 35.4, Roberts to Blackwell, 28 June 1946; Blackwell to Roberts, 2 July 1946
6 Ibid., Harold J. Awde to Blackwell, 31 May 1946 and reply (quoted)
7 OSC, RR, vol. 1, Re Ivan Israel, 11 January 1946; *FP*, 9 March, 11 May 1946
8 *FP*, 18 May 1946
9 *FP*, 18 May 1946. Gamble asked for a new hearing and submitted additional evidence about his earlier problems which the OSC did not find entirely convincing, but because of a reasonable record in mining promotion the two Gambles and their firm were given the benefit of the doubt and relicensed; see *FP*, 24 August 1946.
10 *FP*, 8 June 1946; 'Re the Securities Act and Morton, ' *OLR*, 1946, 492–7
11 OSC, RR, vol. 1, Re Davison and Co., 29 January 1946
12 *FP*, 13, 20 April 1946
13 OSC, RR, vol. 1, Re Jack Rosen, 11 January 1946
14 Ibid., Re J.W. Armstrong, 4 February 1946
15 Ibid., Re H.R. Bain and Co., 27 January 1946; *FP*, 23 November 1946
16 *FP*, 23 November 1946. O.E. Lennox voted against this decision by McTague and Rickaby.
17 *FP*, 18 May, 15 June 1946; see PAO, AG, 4-02, file 35.4, which contains letters to Blackwell from Wheeling, West Virginia, the District of Columbia, Arcadia, Louisiana, and Washington Springs, South Dakota, and to McTague from Alhambra, California, dated May–June, 1946.
18 OSC, RRBS, vol. 2, Re A.E. DePalma, 13 May 1947
19 Ibid., vol. 3, Re Robert Mitchell and Co., 13 January 1948
20 *FP*, 17 May 1947
21 'Re the Securities Act and Gardiner et al.,' *OLR*, 1948, 71–80
22 *FP*, 6, 13 April 1946; Ontario, *Statutes*, 1946, c. 86. On McTague's views, see PAO, Select Committee on Administration of Justice, testimony of McTague, 24 August 1951, 2918.

23 *FP*, 16 March, 29 June (quoted) 1946
24 *FP*, 5 October 1946
25 PAO, Select Committee on Administration of Justice, testimony of McTague, 27 August 1951, 2998–3002
26 O.E. Lennox, 'The Operation of the Ontario Securities Commission,' *OSCB*, January 1949
27 PAO, Select Committee on Administration of Justice, testimony of McTague, 24 August 1951, 2915–21
28 NAC, TSE, MB, 9 May, 25 June 1946; *FP*, 29 June 1946
29 PAO, AG, 4-02, file 68.4, McTague to AG Leslie Blackwell, 13 May 1948; Blackwell to McTague, 25 May 1948
30 NAC, TSE, MB, 29 October, 5, 13, 26 November 1946
31 *FP*, 11 January 1947. Besides Tom the committee consisted of TSE manager A.J. Trebilcock, the OSC's William Wismer, and securities lawyer W.R. Salter, along with J.H. Batten, Louis Cadesky, D.E. Cushing, Gordon Jones, R.S. Lampard, William Lawson, E. McDonnell, Brian Newkirk, Irving Picard, and Arthur White; see NAC, TSE, MB, 7 January, 25 February, 5 March 1947.
32 PAO, Select Committee on Administration of Justice, testimony of Wismer, 29 August 1951, 3430–1; NAC, TSE, MB, 26 March, 9 September 1947; see also *FP*, 7, 28 June, 1 November 1947; Ontario, *Statutes*, 1947, c. 8 (Broker Dealers Association), c. 98 (Securities Act)
33 BDA, MB, 25 February 1948. The other members of the board were Louis Cadesky, Sidney Davidge (representing salespeople), Harry W. Knight, R.S. Lampard, Irving Picard, E.H. Pooler, J.M. Rogers, and Cecil Tom (vice-chair), who had not yet even received copies of the orders-in-council formally appointing them. The BDA minute books covering the entire history of the organization until 1985 are currently in the author's possession and will eventually be deposited in the PAO.
34 BDA, MB, 3, 10, 24 March, 2, 3 April 1948
35 Brokers based in the largest cities, Ottawa, Toronto, Hamilton, London, and Windsor, paid an annual fee of $150, those in cities with a population over 25, 000 paid $75, and the rest paid $25; associates (salesmen) paid fees of $10 and were required to post a bond of $1, 000. Companies wishing to market their own securities to the public directly could also register with the OSC for a fee of $150; see BDA, MB, 10, 24 March 1948.
36 Ibid., 5, 21, 28 April, 5, 19 May, 9 June, 18 August 1948
37 Ibid., 2, 9 June, 14 July 1948
38 Ibid., 9, 16, 28 June, 7, 14 July 1948; *FP*, 11 December 1948; PAO, Select Committee on Administration of Justice, testimony of William Wismer,

28 August 1951, 3151. The board also agreed to allow members to be represented by counsel when appearing before it since the TSE's Managing Committee did so, even though the NYSE did not. The BDA refused to release its bulletins recording disciplinary actions to the press and soon ceased to record the amount of fines levied; see BDA, MB, 15 December 1948.

39 BDA, MB, 5, 19, 27 May, 16, 21, 28 June, 4, 18 August 1948
40 Ibid., 28 April, 5 May, 27 May, 16 June 1948
41 PAO, AG, 4-02, file 68.4, McTague to AG Leslie Blackwell, 13 May 1948; Blackwell to McTague, 25 May 1948; OSC, vol. 3, 11 March 1948. FP, 3 July 1948. A.S. Marriott became vice-chair.
42 PAO, Select Committee on Administration of Justice, testimony of Lennox, 24 July 1951, 1936; 25 July 1951, 1977 (both quoted); BDA, MB, 8, 22 September 1948
43 BDA, MB, 22, 29 September, 29 December 1948; OSCB, February 1949, 'Re L.V. Trottier and Co.'
44 PAO, Select Committee on Administration of Justice, testimony of Lennox, 24 July 1951, 1936; 25 July 1951, 1977, 2013–4; BDA, MB, 8, 22 September, 13 October, 3 November, 1 December 1948
45 OSCB, March 1949, 'The Operation of the Ontario Securities Commission'
46 OSCB, April 1949, 'Securities Legislation'
47 OSCB, February, March 1949, 'Operation of the OSC'; April 1949, 'Securities Legislation'
48 OSCB, March 1949, 'Operations of the OSC'
49 BDA, MB, 10 March 1948
50 OSC, RR, vol. 3, Re Canadian Securities and Re G.H. Cockburn and Co., 1 March 1948
51 BDA, MB, 22 September 1948; PAO, Select Committee on Administration of Justice, 27 July 1951, testimony of Lennox, 2049
52 BDA, MB, 7 July, 6, 27 October, 29 December 1948. Two governors voted against any discussion of the issue at the annual meeting but were defeated six to two.
53 PAO, Select Committee on Administration of Justice, testimony of Lennox, 22 August 1951, 2742–8. Interestingly, the BDA MB contains no reference to this 'armistice.'
54 BDA, MB, 10, 16 February 1949; PAO, Select Committee on Administration of Justice, testimony of Lennox, 25 July 1951, 2059–60 (quoted)
55 FP, 23 July, 3, 24 September 1949
56 BDA, MB, 24 August, 21, 29 September 1949

57 Ibid., 4 April, 11 May 1949; PAO, Select Committee on Administration of Justice, testimony of William Wismer, 29 August 1951, 3314–5

58 PAO, Select Committee on Administration of Justice, testimony of Wismer, 29 August 1951, 3314–5, 3335–4; testimony of Lennox, 27 July 1951, 2297–9 (quoted), 2303

59 BDA, MB, 10 March, 5 May (quoted) 1948; PAO, Select Committee on Administration of Justice, testimony of William Wismer, 28 August 1951, 3168–9, 3195–6, 3200–2

60 BDA, MB, 4 April 1949; PAO, Select Committee on Administration of Justice, testimony of William Wismer, 28 August 1951, 3200–3; testimony of O.E. Lennox, 25 July 1951, 2024, 2031–3 (quoted)

61 *OSCB*, February 1950, 'Re Junior Golds Securities Corp.'

62 BDA, MB, 4, 6, 13 February, 6, 10 March 1950

63 *OSCB*, April 1950, 'Re Junior Golds Securities Corp.'; PAO, Select Committee on Administration of Justice, testimony of Lennox, 25 July 1951, 2011–2 (quoted); 23 August 1951 2801–4

64 PAO, Select Committee on Administration of Justice, testimony of Lennox, 25 July 1951, 1977, 2068; 22 August 1951, 2650 (all quoted)

65 BDA, MB, 24 August, 2 November, 5 December 1949, 11, 25 January, 13 February 1950

66 PAO, Select Committee on Administration of Justice, testimony of Lennox, 25 July 1951, 2064; 22 August 1951, 2743

67 Ibid., testimony of Lennox, 25 July 1951, 2068 (quoted); BDA, MB, 2, 23 November (quoted), 5 December 1949, 11 January 1950; *FP*, 21 January 1950

68 NAC, TSE, MB, 13 December 1949

69 PAO, Select Committee on Administration of Justice, testimony of Lennox, 25 July 1951, 2063–4; testimony of William Wismer, 29 August 1951, 3374; BDA, MB, 4 January 1950

70 BDA, MB, 11 January 1950. Lampard was a partner in a TSE member firm, even though he sat on the BDA board as a representative of a non-member firm. Picard's firm had recently joined the TSE, but he had remained a BDA member.

71 BDA, MB, 25 January 1950

72 Pooler, Lampard, and Picard had not stood for re-election; Louis Cadesky and William Seaford were defeated. James A. Lumsden, Albert A. Perrin, and Clifford D. Wilson joined Allen C. McLean and Arthur White as the brokers' representatives, while Jerome Henley was the lone salesman.

73 BDA, MB, 11 January, 6 March 1950. Speaking for the departing board members, Picard observed that a firm foundation on which to build had

been laid but that 'great courage would be required, especially to prevent government bureaucracy from ruining the securities business.'

74 PAO, Select Committee on Administration of Justice, testimony of Lennox, 25 July 1951, 2068

75 BDA, *Self-Government in the Securities Industry: A Survey of the Broker-Dealers Association of Ontario, Its Functions, Responsibilities and Achievements* (n.p., 1 March 1950)

76 O.E. Lennox, *Securities Legislation and Administration* (n.p., n.d. [1950])

Chapter 3: Moose Pastures

1 See Fred Bodsworth, 'How the Stock Crooks Operate, ' *Maclean's*, 15 June 1951.

2 U.S., SEC, *17th Annual Report* (1951), 159

3 NAC, EA, vol. 3322, file 10895–40, part 1, W.D. Matthews to USS for EA, 11 July 1949; Wrong to A.D.P. Heeney, 18 October 1949, Confidential

4 PAO, AG, 4-02, Memorandum from Lennox to file, 1 September 1949; Memorandum from Lennox to Col. E.J. Young, 19 December 1949 (quoted)

5 *Globe and Mail* (Toronto), 5 October 1949, contains a list of the names of thirteen Toronto promoters and eleven brokers and the stocks covered by banning orders issued by U.S. postmaster general Jesse Donaldson.

6 Canada, House of Commons, *Debates*, 29 March 1950, 1350–1; 18 April 1950, 1638–9

7 BDA, MB, 6, 22, 29 March, 5, 12 April, 7 (quoted), 14, 21, 27 June 1950; see also Canada, House of Commons, *Debates*, 9 May, 27 June 1950, 2347–9, 4207–8.

8 PAO, Select Committee on Administration of Justice, testimony of Lennox, 22 August 1951, 2708–24

9 Ibid., testimony of Wismer, 29 August 1951, 3352–3

10 NAC, EA, vol. 3322, file 10895-40, part 1, USS for EA to Washington embassy, 16 October 1950, Confidential; Washington embassy to USS for EA, 26 October, 9 November 1950, Confidential, the last enclosing U.S., SEC, 'Deficiencies in Extradition Arrangements between Canada and the United States for Securities Frauds,' 1950, Confidential

11 Canada, Justice Records, file A91-00058, Memorandum from H.C. K[eenleyside] to Robert Forsyth, 13 June 1946; Memorandum from Forsyth to DM of Justice, 25 January 1947; NAC, EA, Acc. 86–7/159, box 62, file 12216-6-40, part 4, Memorandum from K.J. Burbridge to USS for EA, 10 September 1949; Memorandum from Burbridge to F.B. Roger, 26 September 1950

12 NAC, EA, Acc. 86–7/159, box 62, file 12216-6-40, part 4, Memorandum

from F.B. Roger to K.J. Burbridge, 29 September 1950, Secret (quoted); vol. 3322, file 10895-40, part 1, Memorandum from D.F. Kennedy to Burbridge, 28 November 1950; Acc. 84–5/150, box 185, file 10895-40, part 2, Memorandum from Burbridge re Securities Frauds Offences, 29 December 1950
13 PAO, Select Committee on Administration of Justice, testimony of Lennox, 25 July 1951, 2111–2; 22 August 1951, 2743–4; BDA, MB, 29 November, 13 December 1950; NAC, EA, Acc. 86–7/159, box 62, file 12216-6-40, part 4, W.D. Matthews to USS for EA, 4 January 1951; Acc. 84–5/150, box 185, file 10895-40, part 2, Washington embassy to SS for EA, 7 February 1951
14 *OSCB*, February 1951; BDA, MB, 3 January, 7, 14 February 1951
15 *OSCB*, April 1951. Glass's registration was cancelled.
16 *FP*, 19 May 1951
17 BDA, MB, 2, 9 May 1951
18 Ibid., 2 May 1951
19 Ibid., 4, 18, 25 April 1951
20 PAO, Select Committee on Administration of Justice, testimony of Lennox, 25 July 1951, 2068–9; BDA, MB, 24 January 1951; NAC, TSE, MB, 16 January, 20 February 1951; Corr. 1949–59, file 343.23, Beverly Matthews to A.J. Trebilcock, 14 February 1951
21 NAC, EA, Acc. 85-5/150, box, 185, file 10895-40, part 2, Memorandum from Heeney, 22 February 1951; Memorandum from K.J. Burbridge to Heeney, 3 March 1951; Heeney to Washington embassy, 3 March 1951; Washington embassy to USS for EA, 10 March 1951
22 NAC, TSE, MB, 30 January, 6 , 20, 28 March 1951
23 The paper sent a reporter to Toronto, along with a representative of the St Louis Better Business Bureau, after the SEC supplied a list of actions by state and Ontario authorities between 1946 and 1949 and a copy of its 1950 annual report, where the problem was discussed. See U.S., SEC, FOIA #90-1128, Memorandum re conference between R.F. Milwee and J.L. Pritchett, manager of Fort Worth Better Business Bureau, 19 March 1951.
24 See TSE, Historical files, S-6, 'Stock promotion,' for a copy of the pamphlet, as well as a bulletin from the St Louis Better Business Bureau, 14 May 1951, applauding the newspaper's series.
25 Proofs of articles in St Louis *Star-Times*, 13–27 March 1951 (quoting Wismer), enclosed in NAC, EA, Acc. 84-5/150, box 185, file 10895-40, part 2, Washington embassy to USS EA, 13 March 1951; Wrong to Heeney, 16 March 1951; *FP*, 7 April 1951 (quoting Lennox)
26 NAC, EA, Acc. 84-5/150, box 185, file 10895-A-40, Jenner to Lester B. Pearson, 16 March 1951, enclosing transcripts of broadcasts on Buffalo's WBEN, 12–14 March 1951

27 BDA, MB, 18 April 1951
28 *FP*, 31 March 1951; U.S., SEC, FOIA #90-1128, Memorandum re Conference of E.T. McCormick, NY Curb Exchange; Edward Gray, executive vice-president of NYSE; W.H. Fulton, executive director of NASD; S. Rosenberry and G. Weiss, Bache and Co.; Wm O'Hara, Thompson and Mckinnon, W.E. Dugan; Laidlaw and Co. and Loss, Cohen; and O'Leary of SEC staff, 2, 18, 19, 22, 24, May [1951]; NAC, EA, Acc. 84-5/150, box 185, file 10895-40, part 2, SS for EA to Washington embassy, 16 March 1951; Heeney to DM of Justice W.R. Jackett, 20 March 1951
29 Canada, Justice Records, file A91-00058, draft letter from DM of Justice F.P. Varcoe to EA's J.P. Erichsen-Brown, 21 March 1951
30 NAC, EA, Acc. 86-7/159, box 9, file 1415-40, part 2, Memorandum from Erichsen-Brown re 'Relations with the United States, Sale of Securities "Across the Border" (by telephone, telegraph and mail),' 30 March 1951, Restricted
31 NAC, EA, Acc. 86-7/159, box 162, file 12216-6-40, part 4, Memorandum from Pearson to cabinet, 20 March 1951, Confidential; Acc. 84-5/150, box 185, file 10895-40, part 2, Note for Heads of Divisions Meeting, 23 April 1951; NAC, TSE, Corr. 1949–59, file 339.1, Wismer to A.L.A. Richardson, 30 March 1951
32 *FP*, 5 May 1951; NAC, EA, Acc. 84-5/150, box 185, file 10895-40, part 2, Minutes of Informal Discussion between Canadian and Ontario Officials, 1 May 1951, 11 a.m.
33 NAC, EA, Acc. 84-5/150, box 185, file 10895-40, part 2, Minutes of an Informal Meeting of Officials of the United States, Canadian and Ontario Governments, 1 May 1951, 2 p.m.; Continuation of meeting, 2 May 1951, 10 a.m.; Continuation of meeting, 2.30 p.m.; ibid., part 3, Memorandum from E.R. to L.B. Pearson, [5] May 1952. The Americans warned, however, that short-form registration might run into congressional opposition on the grounds that there would soon be pressure to extend it to South American nations; see Canada, Justice Records, file A91-00058, Memorandum from minister to cabinet, 5 June 1951, Confidential.
34 Canada, Justice Records, file A91-00058, Memorandum from minister to cabinet, 5 June 1951, Confidential; Notes for use of minister in parliamentary debate on Criminal Code amendments re Extradition Treaty, 6 June 1951; NAC, EA, Acc. 86-7/159, box 62, file 12216-6-40, part 4, Memorandum for Mr Garson, 8 August 1951
35 Ontario, Legislative Assembly, *Debates*, 21 March 1951, A-2-A-4, B-2. The other members were Conservatives A.W. Downer, C.E. Janes, and O.F. Villeneuve, CCFer W.J. Grummett, and Liberal W.L. Houck.

36 PAO, Select Committee on Administration of Justice, testimony of Lennox, 24 July 1951, 1925 (quoted), 1935–49 (1935 quoted); 26 July 1951, 2202–4, 2253–4 (quoted); 21 August 1951, 2520; 27 July 1951, 2347 (quoted); 23 August 1951, 2805–7

37 Ibid., testimony of Lennox, 25 July 1951, 1977 (quoted), 2053 (quoted), 2060–8 (2068 quoted)

38 Ibid., testimony of Lennox, 27 July 1951 2297–307, 2420 (quoted 2304, 2420); ibid., Exhibit no. 126 for the affadavit

39 Ibid., testimony of Lennox, 22 August 1951, 2685–8, 2738

40 Ibid., testimony of Lennox, 25 July 1951, 2105, 2118, 2144, 2152 (latter two quoted); 26 July 1951, 2215–16

41 Ibid., testimony of Lennox, 26 July 1951, 2143 (quoted), 2162–7, 2189–90

42 Ibid., testimony of Lennox, 25 July 1951, 2128–30 (quoted); 26 July 1951, 2274–6; 27 July 1951, 2154–60; 21 August 1951, 2517 (quoted)

43 Ibid., testimony of McTague, 24 August 1951, 2914–23, 2993–4; 27 August 1951, 2998–3002 (quoted), 3066–8

44 BDA, MB, 4 April 1949

45 PAO, Select Committee on Administration of Justice, testimony of McTague, 27 August 1951, 3047–51, 3054–5, 3072 (each quoted)

46 Ibid., testimony of McTague, 28 August 1951, 3085–96

47 Ibid., testimony of McTague, 24 August 1951, 2925–7 (quoted), 2931, 2941–2; 28 August 1951, 3097–8, 3103

48 Ibid., testimony of Wismer, 28 August 1951, 3151–2; 29 August 1951, 3236–7, 3263–8

49 Ibid., testimony of Wismer, 28 August 1951, 3154–5, 3172–5; 29 August 1951, 3357–8

50 Ibid., Exhibit no. 127, McEntire to Porter, 17 August 1951

51 Ibid., testimony of Lennox, 21 August 1951, 2440, 2458–66

52 Ibid., testimony of Lennox, 21 August 1951, 2544–8 (quoted); 22 August 1951, 2731–2

53 Ibid., testimony of Lennox, 24 August 1951, 2984–5; 27 August 1951, 3072 (both quoted)

54 Ibid., testimony of Wismer, 30 August 1951, 3472–6

55 Ibid., testimony of Cadesky, 3 October 1951, 3785–3895 (3856, 3895 quoted)

56 PAO, Select Committee on Administration of Justice, testimony of Lennox, 4 October 1951, 3903–29; ibid., box 1, W.M. Vickers to Alex C. Lewis, 28 November 1951

57 *FP*, 22 September 1951

58 Canada, Justice Records, file A91-00058, Memoranda from DM of Justice

368 Notes to pages 99–103

F.P. Varcoe to Stuart Garson, 3 April (quoted), 7 April 1952; Varcoe to Deputy AGs, 12 September 1951 (quoted); Varcoe to USS for EA, 18 October 1951; O.M.M. Kay to Varcoe, 22 October 1951
59 Ibid., D'Arcy M. Doherty, TSE, to Garson, 11 September 1951; W.J. Borrie, IDA, to Garson, 13 September 1951; Varcoe to Hayden, 14 September 1951, Confidential (quoted); NAC, TSE, Corr. 1949–59, file 348.10, Slaght to F.J. Crawford, 2 August 1951; MB, 11, 18 September 1951
60 NAC, TSE, Corr. 1949–59, file 343.23, Beverly Matthews to A.J. Trebilcock, 24 September 1951; file 350.8, Trebilcock to V.A. Simons, 28 September 1951; MB, 2 October 1951, confirming a decision at an informal board meeting on 26 September; MSE, MB, 2 October 1951
61 BDA, MB, 10, 17 October 1951
62 NAC, EA, Acc. 86-7/159, box 162, file 12216-6-40, part 4, copy of order-in-council, PC 5736, 25 October 1951; Canada, Justice Records, file A91-00058, Memorandum from A.D.P. Heeney for Prime Minister's press conference, October 1951
63 U.S., SEC, FOIA, # 90-1128, Anthon Lund to R.R. Taylor, 30 January 1952
64 Canada, Justice Records, file A91-00058, Memorandum from Garson to · Varcoe, 8 March 1952; Memorandum from D.G. Blair to Garson, 19 April 1952; NAC, EA, Acc. 84-5/150, box 185, file 10894-40, part 3, Washington embassy to SS for EA, 25 April 1952; Memorandum from E.R. to L.B. Pearson, [5] May 1952
65 Canada, House of Commons, Standing Committee on External Affairs, *Proceedings and Evidence*, no. 10, 13 May 1952, 267–86 and appendix B for the letters of endorsement; ibid., *Fourth Report*, 14 May 1952
66 Canada, Justice Records, file A91-00058, Memorandum from Varcoe, 27 May 1952
67 NAC, EA, Acc. 84-5/150, box 185, file 10894-40, part 3, Washington embassy to SS for EA, 23 May 1952; SS for EA to embassy, 26 May 1952 (quoted); Memorandum from F.J.Burbridge to press officer, 27 May 1952; Burbridge to Varcoe, 29 May 1952 (quoted)
68 Ibid., SS for EA to Washington embassy, 24 June 1952; Canada, Justice Records, file A91-00058, copy of Privy Council minute 3500, 8 July 1952; *OSCB*, June 1952, note on inside cover (quoted); *FP*, 19 July 1952
69 *OSCB*, April 1952
70 BDA, MB, 12 March, 4 June 1952; NAC, EA, Acc. 84-5/150, box 185, file 10894-40, part 3, McTague to Pearson, 3 July 1952; SS for EA to Washington embassy, 9 July 1952; Washington embassy to SS for EA, 14 July 1952
71 NAC, EA, Acc. 84-5/150, box 185, file 10894-40, part 3, Erichsen-Brown to

Douglas Lepan, 21 July 1952, Personal; Washington embassy to SS for EA, 29 July 1952

72 Ibid., Memorandum from A.J. Pick to Legal Division, 22 July 1952; Memorandum from K.J. Burbridge to Reid, 1 August 1952 (quoted); Reid to McTague 5 August 1952; BDA, MB, 13 August 1952

73 BDA, MB, 25 September 1952, appendix A; *FP*, 6 September, 18 October 1952

74 NAC, TSE, Corr. 1949–59, file 347.23, 'Suggestions of BDA re Proposed Exemption for Canadian Offerings, ' 23 September 1952; BDA, MB, 10, 17, 29 December 1952; 4 March 1953; NAC, EA, Acc. 84-5/150, box 185, file 10894-40, part 3, McTague to Garson, 2 March 1953 (quoted)

75 NAC, EA, Acc. 84-5/150, box 185, file 10894-40, part 4, Washington embassy to SS for EA, 11 April 1953; Canada, Justice Records, file A91-00058, copy of SEC release 3467, 6 March 1953

76 BDA, MB, 8 October 1952, 11, 18 February, 11 March 1953

77 Ibid., 18, 25 March 1953; NAC, TSE, Corr. 1949–59, Lennox to W.L. Somerville, 27 March 1953, enclosing BDA circular to members, 26 March 1953, Confidential; *OSCB*, June 1953

78 BDA, MB, 6 May 1953, containing Garson to McTague, 23 April 1953

79 Ibid., containing McTague to Garson, 29 April 1953; NAC, EA, Acc 84-5/150, box 185, file 10895-40, part 4, Garson to McTague, 6 May 1953.

80 *FP*, 30 January 1954; BDA, MB, 2 February 1954. Commissioner Paul R. Rowan wanted the deadline postponed to October 1955, but Ralph Demmler persuaded his colleagues to accept the earlier date.

81 Canada's GNP grew from $24.6 billion in 1952 to $25.8 in 1953 but only reached $25.9 in 1954; see F.H. Leacy, ed., *Historical Statistics of Canada*, 2nd ed. (Ottawa, 1983), F1-13. See also BDA, MB, 13 April, 4 May, 17 November 1954; *FP*, 10, 17 (quoted) July 1954.

82 O.E. Lennox, 'Statement of Policy,' 16 November 1954, in *OSCB*, November 1954

83 Ibid.

84 NAC, EA, Acc. 84-5/215, vol. 41, file 12216-Z-1-40, USS for EA to DM of Justice, 4 October 1954; Montreal *Gazette*, 17, 26 November 1954; *FP*, 25 December 1954

85 *USA v. Link and Green* (1955), 3 *DLR*, 386. Both men were promptly arrested and charged with violating Canadian law.

86 NAC, EA, Acc. 84-5/215, vol. 41, file 12216-Z-1-40, Memorandum from F.M. Kirk re Extradition Proceedings re Link and Green, 5 January 1955, Confidential; Memorandum from H.C. Kingstone re the Extradition Convention with the United States, 23 October 1957, Confidential, annex A; *USA v. Link and Green* (1955), *SCR*, 183; *FP*, 12 March 1955; NAC, EA,

Acc. 84-5/150, box 185, file 10895-40, part 4, Washington embassy to SS for EA, 13 May 1955 (quoted)

87 NAC, EA, Acc. 86-7/160, box 174, file 12216-6-40, part 5, Wiley to A.D.P. Heeney, 16 April 1955; M.H. Wershof to DM of Justice, 6 May 1955, Confidential; R.A. Farquharson, Washington, to Archibald Day, 6 May 1955 (quoted)

88 Canada, Justice Records, file A91-00058, Memorandum from D.H. Christie to A.J. MacLeod, 5 May 1955. One problem in discussing the situation with Wiley was that any correspondence was certain to be published and had therefore to be fairly innocuous to avoid creating 'undue alarm' in the Canadian financial community; see ibid., Memorandum from MacLeod to DM of Justice F.P. Varcoe, 9 May 1955.

89 NAC, EA, Acc. 86-7/160, box 174, file 12216-6-40, part 5, Washington embassy to SS for EA, 18 June 1955, and to USS for EA, 30 June 1955; Canada, Justice Records, file A91-00058, Memorandum from A.J. MacLeod to Justice Minister Stuart Garson, 25 June 1955

90 NAC, EA, Acc. 86-7/160, box 174, file 12216-6-40, part 5, Heeney to SS for EA, 18 July 1955; Washington embassy to USS for EA, 22 July 1955; Memorandum from R.M.M. to Minister [Pearson], 10 August 1955, Confidential; Memorandum from E.A. Ritchie to M.H. Wershof, 29 August 1955, Confidential, enclosing SEC statement

91 PAO, AG, 4-02, file 76.13, Memorandum from Lennox to AG Kelso Roberts, 31 October 1955, enclosing OSC press release, 16 November 1955; William H. Timbers and Irving M. Pollack, 'Extradition from Canada to the United States for Securities Fraud: Frustration of the National Policy of Both Countries,' *Fordham Law Review* 24 (Autumn, 1955): 301–25

92 NAC, EA, Acc. 86-7/414, box 158, file 12216-6-40, part 6, A.D.P. Heeney to L.B. Pearson, 18 November 1955, Personal and Confidential, enclosing memorandum by Heeney on Security Frauds: Extradition: Link and Green Case, 8 November 1955, Confidential; Memorandum re Canada-U.S. Extradition Treaty: Reference to Supreme Court, 23 December 1955, Confidential; Heeney to Garson, 31 January 1956, Personal and Confidential; Heeney to Pearson, 7 February 1956, Personal and Confidential (quoted); Heeney to Garson, 15 June 1956, Personal and Confidential; Memorandum from H.C. Kingstone re the Extradition Convention with the United States, 23 October 1957, Confidential

93 Also convicted and fined $2, 000 plus two months in jail was former BDA member George F. Caldough, who had once sought to employ Link in his Malvern Trading Corporation in Toronto before moving his boiler-room operations to Montreal; see BDA, MB, 24 April 1956.

94 NAC, EA, Acc. 86-7/414, box 158, file 12216-4-40, part 6, Heeney to Stuart Garson, 2, August 1956, Personal and Confidential; Memorandum from M.H. Wershof to acting USS for EA, 4 September 1956, Confidential (quoted); Memorandum from J.S. Nutt to USS for EA, 12 October 1956, Confidential; Memorandum from Wershof to Jules Leger, 14 November 1956

Chapter 4: Regulating the Stock Exchange

1 NAC, TSE, MB, 25 June 1946
2 See Christopher Armstrong, *Blue Skies and Boiler Rooms: Buying and Selling Securities in Canada, 1870–1940* (Toronto, 1997), 224–6
3 Long-time TSE official A.J. Trebilcock explained that North American exchanges had originally followed the European practice of describing only government bonds and a few other gilt-edged issues as 'listed,' other shares only being 'admitted to trading.' Over time, however, any issue recommended by two members was accepted for listing, with price and trading volume recorded in the exchange's daily summary; other stocks could still be traded on the 'unlisted' or 'curb' sections of the exchange. The TSE Curb survived the merger in 1934, but no new issues were added, so that the original 196 stocks on the Curb had fallen to 58 by 1957; see *FP*, 14 September 1957.
4 TSE, Historical files, A-1, 'TSE-SSME Amalgamation,' in 'History of the Development of Listing Standards on the TSE,' n.d. [1964]
5 NAC, TSE, MB, 17, 20 May, 4, 26, 27 June 1946
6 OSC, RR, vol. 1, Report by T.P. O'Connor and J.H. Collins re Beaulieu Yellowknife Gold Mines, October 1946; *FP*, 2, 9, 23 November, 21 December 1946, 8 February 1947
7 In June 1947 lawyer J.J. Robinette did report that an investigation into the affairs of Harold A. Prescott and Company had revealed that it was paying out a large share of its profits to two outsiders, for whom it might have been a front, and it was ordered to cease these affiliations or face expulsion from the exchange; see NAC, TSE, MB, 26 June 1947.
8 NAC, TSE, MB, 19, 26 November, 3 December 1946, 14 January, 11 February 1947; MUA, MSE, MSE-TSE Meetings, MB, 14 March 1947, recording A.J. Trebilcock's report on the matter to a meeting between the exchanges. The TSE auditor's investigation uncovered only a single instance of a transaction that might have been intentionally aimed at affecting the market price of the shares; it was then referred to the OSC for study.
9 NAC, TSE, MB, 22, 23 September 1947

10 OSC, RR, vol. 3, Report of OSC senior solicitor T.P. O'Connor, auditor J.H. Collins, and auditor L.E. Wetmore, 15 April 1948; Re Eldona Gold Mines, 20 April 1948; NAC, EA, Acc. 84-5/215, vol. 41, file 12216-Z-1-40, director, Criminal Law Section, Department of Justice to USS for EA, 3 August 1955
11 NAC, TSE, 21, 29 October 1947, 27 April, 4, 11 May 1948
12 *FP*, 15 November 1947
13 NAC, TSE, MB, 29 October 1947; 22 June 1948; *FP*, 15 November 1947 (quoted)
14 NAC, TSE, MB, 8 May 1952; *FP*, 26 April, 2 August 1952
15 NAC, TSE, MB, 30 September 1952; ibid., Corr. 1949–59, file 348.10, Trebilcock to M.M. Schwebel, 10 December 1952 (quoted); file 347.23, Trebilcock to Milton Kroll, 15 December 1952; file 343.16, Trebilcock to Dr George Light, 8 January 1953
16 *FP*, 22 November 1952
17 NAC, TSE, Corr. 1949–59, file 336.7, A.J. Trebilcock to R.W. Scrimgeour, 14 February 1952; file 336.8, W.M. Ketchen to Calgary Stock Exchange, 16 February 1953; file 339.20, Ketchen to Dattels and Co., 20 October 1954; file 343.25, W.L. Somerville to McCarthy and McCarthy, 30 May 1955; *FP*, 26 April 1952. The maximum markup was 20 per cent on shares between 51 cents and $1.00, 18 per cent from $1.01 to $2.00, 15 per cent from $2.01 to $5.00, and 10 per cent above $5.00.
18 *FP*, 15 May 1954
19 Details of the Pontiac case may be found in *OSCB*, May 1955 and PAO, AG, 4-02, file 141.5, 'Final Report on Pontiac Petroleums–Frank Kaftel Investigation and Rittenhouse and Co.' by W.W. Cameron, 3 May 1955
20 When Kaftel tried to get a TSE listing for an oil promotion in 1952, a private note from a TSE insider to its manager, Arthur Trebilcock, observed' 'Dear A., The action is a corker, for [the] reason that F[rank] K[aftel] has never been allowed to operate on an Ontario basis from the west, and it [the listing request] discounts a lot of hard work'; see NAC, TSE, Corr. 1949–59, file 348.10, Stewart Smith to Trebilcock, 5 May 1952 (attached note quoted).
21 NAC, TSE, Corr. 1949–59, file 341.14, 'Special investigation of trading in Pontiac Petroleums Limited' by exchange auditor Holland Pettit, 15 August 1955, ibid., MB, 30 August, 27 September, 4 October 1955
22 NAC, TSE, MB, 22, 23, 24, 26, 29 August 1955; BDA, MB, 25, 29 August 1955; *FP*, 3 September 1955
23 NAC, TSE, 20 September 1955, 7 February 1956; *FP*, 3 September, 8 October 1955
24 *FP*, 22 September 1956; NAC, TSE, Delisting files, file 81.5, Lawson to

Trebilock, 12 July 1956; Memorandum from OSC counsel W.W. Cameron to file, 16 October 1956

25 NAC, TSE, Delisting files, 81.5, Memorandum from William Wismer to W.L. Somerville, 10 September 1956; Final Report on Morrison Brass investigation from W.W. Cameron to O.E. Lennox, 7 January 1957

26 *Torny Financial Corporation Ltd. v. Marcus et al.*, 4 *DLR* (1951), 762

27 PAO, AG, 4-02, file 122.13, Memorandum from Assistant Deputy AG Silk to AG Kelso Roberts, 27 February 1958

28 *OSCB*, April 1956, 'Important Notice'

29 NAC, TSE, Delisting files, file 81.5, Memorandum from Lennox to AG Kelso Roberts, 22 October 1956

30 NAC, TSE, Corr. 1949–59, file 346.5, Lennox to A.J. Trebilock, 25 October 1956; ibid., MB, 30 October, 20, 27 November, 4 December 1956; BDA, MB, 8 November 1956. The TSE MB for 20 November reports that seven lawyers who were consulted all opposed the plan.

31 NAC, TSE, Corr. 1949–59, file 346.6, Lennox to W.L. Somerville, 20 May 1958; Somerville to Lennox, 26 May 1958

32 NAC, TSE, MB, 23 October, 12 November 1956; ibid., Corr. 1949–59, file 338.23, A.J. Trebilcock to William J. Cook, 13 May 1957

33 NAC, TSE, Delisting files, file 135. 2, 'Findings and Opinion of SEC re Great Sweet Grass Oils and Kroy Oils,' 8 April 1957; ibid., MB, 30 April , 7 May 1957; 'Beware Those Phony Stock Salesmen, ' *Saturday Evening Post*, 22 June 1957

34 *FP*, 27 February 1965; NAC, TSE, MB, 11 January, 20 February 1962; PAO, AG, 4-02, file 248.8, Memorandum from H.S. Bray to AG Frederick Cass, 24 January 1964

35 NAC, TSE, MB, 22 May 1957

36 *FP*, 10 August, 23 November 1957; NAC, TSE, MB, 17, 20, 24 September, 1, 22 October, 13, 14 November 1957

37 The TSE eventually changed its rules so that any member of the Listing Committee whose firm had a direct or indirect interest in shares of an applicant company must declare this, and unless the interest was only small, retire from the committee's deliberations, though he might be interviewed by the committee regarding the application; see NAC, TSE, MB, 26 April 1960.

38 *FP*, 23, 30 November 1957; *Northern Miner*, 19 December 1957

39 *FP*, 11 January 1958. The phrase quoted is from the OSC's Harry Bray; see PAO, OSC, BM, box 47, file 975, Memorandum from Bray to D.N. Omand, 24 January 1967.

40 NAC, TSE, MB, 7 January 1958; *FP*, 11 January 1958. In 1960 the TSE added entering into any management contract as one of the material changes that

must be reported; see NAC, TSE, MB, 1 November 1960. The TSE did not, however, publish a list of non-exempt companies for the information of investors.

41 PAO, AG, 4-02, file 141.5, Memorandum from Lennox to AG Kelso Roberts, 17 March 1959
42 NAC, TSE, MB, 23 May, 5 June 1956; FP, 26 May 1956. Trebilock had joined the Standard Stock and Mining Exchange as legal counsel in 1927 and come over to the TSE in the merger of 1934.
43 NAC, TSE, MB, 23 September 1958
44 PAO, OSC, BM, box 47, file 975, Memorandum from Harry Bray to D.N. Omand, 24 January 1967 (quoted); NAC, TSE, MB, 20 April , 29 November 1960
45 NAC, TSE, MB, 30 May 1961
46 Ibid., 26 September, 17, 31 October 1961
47 FP, 4, 11, 18 March 1961; NAC, TSE, MB, 16 February, 2, 7, 14 March 1961; PAO, AG, 4-02, file 168.1, Memorandum from Roberts, 6 March 1961, Confidential; Memorandum from A. K. R[oberts], 11 March 1961
48 Ontario, Legislative Assembly, *Debates*, 28 March 1961, 2674–82, contains a speech by Donald MacDonald of the CCF alleging anti-Semitism.
49 FP, 8, 29 April, 13 May 1961, 16 May 1964, 25 September 1965; *Toronto Daily Star*, 14 May 1963; NAC, TSE, MB, 4, 11, 25 April, 9 May 1961; *Posluns v. Toronto Stock Exchange and Gardiner* (1964), 2 OLR 547; (1966), OLR 285
50 FP, 4 March 1961
51 FP, 11, 18 February, 17 June 1961; NAC, TSE, MB, 24 May 1961
52 NAC, TSE, MB, 1 August, 3 October 1961, FP, 12 August 1961, 11 August 1962
53 PAO, OSC, BM, box 47, file 975, Memorandum from Bray to D.N. Omand, 24 January 1967

Chapter 5: Fighting Fraud

1 BDA, MB, 28 February 1956. The policeman became involved innocently enough, because Wacker secured his confidence through an expression of interest in a Boys' Club he ran, then used the man's name as the supposed vendor of a property acquired by Triton.
2 BDA, MB, 28 February, 13 (quoted), 27 March, 8 May 1956; PAO, AG, 4-02, file 92.4, Memorandum from Lennox to AG Kelso Roberts, 24 July 1956 (quoted)
3 *OSCB*, May 1962; PAO, OSC, BM, box 32, file 664, Memorandum from H.S.Bray to J.R. Kimber and J.F McFarland, 21 December 1962 (quoted)

4 PAO, AG, 4-02, file 105.7, In re Securities Act and Joseph S. Wacker, 14 March 1957; Memorandum from Lennox to AG Kelso Roberts, 11 March 1957 (quoted)
5 BDA, MB, 4, 17 September 1957
6 Ibid., 1 October 1957
7 *Toronto Daily Star*, 9 March 1958; PAO, AG, 4-02, file 122.13, Memorandum from Lennox to AG Kelso Roberts, 29 July 1958
8 *Toronto Daily Star*, 14 May 1959; PAO, AG, 4-02, file 144.2, 'In re Securities Act and Lyle Francis Smith,' decision by Hughes, J. in Supreme Court of Ontario, 21 January 1959; Memorandum from H.S. Bray to O.E. Lennox, 22 January 1959; Lennox to AG Kelso Roberts, 27 January 1959; Memorandum from Common to Roberts, 4 February 1959; file 105.7, Memorandum from Lennox to Roberts, 22 March 1957; file 122.14, Memorandum from Lennox to Roberts, 29 July 1958; *Smith v. R.* (1961), *SCR*, 25 *DLR*, 2d, 225.
9 *OSCB*, May 1962; PAO, AG, 4-02, file 122.13, Memorandum from Lennox to AG Kelso Roberts, 31 December 1958
10 *OSCB*, May 1962; PAO, AG, 4-02, file 141.5, Memorandum from Lennox to Roberts, 26 June 1959; Roberts to Lennox, 2 July 1959; Memorandum from H.S. Bray to Lennox, 28 October 1959. On the 1951 decision on *Torny Financial Corp. v. Marcus* upholding section 23, see chapter 4 above.
11 *OSCB*, May 1962; PAO, AG, 4-02, file 141.5, Memorandum from Bray to Lennox, 28 October 1959; Memorandum from Lennox to Roberts, 28 October 1959 (quoted)
12 PAO, OSC, BM, box 1, file 10, H.S. Bray to W.C. Bowman, 8 March 1963
13 W.W. Cameron, 'Securities Legislation, Administration and Marketing in the Province of Ontario,' *OSCB*, September 1954; Harry Bray, 'Ontario's Proposed Securities Act: An Overview, Its Purposes and Policy Premises,' *OSCB*, August 1975, 235–70
14 PAO, AG, 4-02, file 68.5, Memorandum from Lennox to E.J. Young, executive assistant to Premier Leslie Frost, 27 April 1951
15 PAO, Select Committee on Administration of Justice, testimony of Lennox, 21 August 1951, 2532–5
16 PAO, AG, 4-02, file 68.5, Memorandum from Lennox to AG Dana Porter, 19 September 1951; Proposed Agenda for Conference of Securities Officials, Toronto, 28 November 1951; Further Items Suggested for Conference of Provincial Securities Officials, 28–30 November 1951
17 All the provinces except Newfoundland and Prince Edward Island were represented, along with officials from the SEC; delegations from the Investment Dealers Association, the Toronto Stock Exchange, and the Broker Dealers Association were invited to join the second day of meetings.

18 PAO, AG, 4-02, file 68.6, 'Proceedings of Conference of Provincial Securities Commissioners under the auspices of the Ontario Securities Commission held in the Parliament Buildings, Toronto, Ontario, November 28th, 1951 et seq.' (typescript, 406 pp.)

19 Ibid., Memorandum from Lennox to Porter, 8 January 1952

20 'Verner,' as told to Earl Beattie, *Saturday Evening Post*, 12 January 1952

21 PAO, AG, 4-02, file 68.5, Memorandum from Lennox to Frost, 14 January 1952

22 Ibid., Memorandum, n.d. [February 1952], probably by Lennox

23 Porter might have been less sanguine if he had known that Robertson, the financial editor of the *Toronto Telegram*, had been placed on a salary of $2, 000 per annum to advise the BDA on public relations less than a year earlier and had sat in on at least one board meeting in a 'listening capacity'; see BDA, MB, 4 April 1951.

24 Ontario, Legislative Assembly, *Debates*, 29 February 1952, vol. 8, A-5–B-6

25 The identical words appear in PAO, AG, 4-02, file 68.5, Memorandum re 'Solicitations in the United States by Mail and Telephone,' unsigned, n.d.; see above note 2.

26 Ontario, Legislative Assembly, *Debates*, 28 February, vol. 7, B-6–B-14 (B-6-7 quoted); 29 February 1951, vol. 8, D-8–D-9

27 A few days after the article appeared, BDA governor Jerome Henley went to the offices of Cardigan Securities and confronted Stafford E. Harriman, claiming that he was Marcus Verner. In profane language Henley threatened to have Harriman's registration taken away, promising, 'I'll see you never work on the street again.' Harriman, who had ten years' experience as a salesmen, complained about this treatment to the BDA board. Following a lengthy discussion (with Henley present throughout), executive secretary William Wismer was directed to write to Harriman and advise him that his registration was not in jeopardy. Nevertheless, Henley refused to let the matter drop, and he made two further efforts to persuade the other governors to have the BDA investigate Harriman's role, or at least to have him and another salesman, Bruce McDonald, hauled before the board for a grilling. Wary of the repercussions if such an inquisition were to become public knowledge, the other governors refused to accede to Henley's demands. See BDA, MB, 23 January (quoted), 20 February, 5 March 1952.

28 Ontario, Legislative Assembly, *Debates*, 29 February 1952, vol. 8, C-8–D-6 (Salsberg); D-11–D-13, 26 March 1952, vol. 25, G-12–G-13; Ontario, *Statutes*, 1952, c. 96

29 PAO, AG, 4-02, file 68.5, Memorandum from Roland O. Daly to Porter, 5 March 1952

30 BDA, MB, 28 February 1952; PAO, AG, 40-02, file 68.5, Memoranda from Lennox to Porter, 7 March, 17 May 1952
31 *FP*, 15 December 1956, reporting the American decision to permit disclosure of reserves and production figures from 30 June 1955 onward
32 *Revised Statutes of Ontario*, 1950, c. 351, s. 52
33 BDA, MB, 2 February, 30 March 1954
34 Ibid., 2, 23 July, 12 November 1957; PAO, AG, 4-02, file 120.10, Petition from BDA to Roberts, n.d. [November 1957]. At the least the BDA suggested testing the constitutionality of the law by a reference to the courts.
35 PAO, AG, 4-02, file 120.10, Memoranda from Lennox to Roberts, 2 December 1957, 2 January 1958 (quoted)
36 *OSCB*, September 1957; PAO, AG, 4-02, file 105.7, Memorandum from Lennox to Roberts, 20 November 1957. Gregory then shifted his operations to New Brunswick, where he used Canam Investments to sell $4 million worth of shares in St Stephen Nickel Mines; see New Brunswick, *Report of the Acting Administrator under the Security Frauds Prevention Act upon Investigation in Canam Investments, St. Stephen Nickel Mines, etc.* (n.p., 30 November 1960).
37 *OSCB*, December 1958; PAO, AG, 4-02, file 122.13, Memorandum from Lennox to Roberts, 9 September 1958; Memorandum from A.W. Nicol to Roberts, 9 September 1958; Memorandum from H.S. Bray to Roberts, 17 October, 10 December 1958
38 *FP*, 15 March 1958; PAO, AG, 4-02, file 105.7, Memorandum from Lennox to Roberts, 24 January, 15 August 1957; file 122.13, Memorandum from Lennox to Roberts, 29 July 1958; PAO, OSC, BM, box 1, file 10, H.S. Bray to W.B. Common, 2 December 1960
39 BDA, MB, 21 August, 4, 20 (quoted) September 1956
40 Ibid., 24 April 1957; U.S., SEC, FOIA #90-1128, Gemmell to Philip Loomis, 24 May 1957 (both quoted)
41 BDA, MB, 16 October 1957
42 PAO, AG, 4-02, file 122.13, Memorandum from Lennox to Roberts, 5 August 1958
43 *Globe and Mail* (Toronto), 17 March 1959; *Toronto Telegram*, 19 March 1959; *FP*, 21 March 1959; PAO, AG, 4-02, file 141.5, Memorandum from Lennox to AG Kelso Roberts, 17 March 1959 (quoted)
44 BDA, MB, 13 March, 21 April 1959; *OSCB*, September 1959, February 1960
45 BDA, MB, 6 October, 3 November 1959, 12 January, 10 August, 13 September 1960
46 Ibid., 29 September (quoted), 25 October, 8, 22, 29 November 1960, 7 March 1961

378 Notes to pages 150–6

47 NAC, TSE, MB, 24, 28 March 1961
48 *FP,* 1 April 1961; NAC, TSE, MB, 11 April 1961. The immediate response from Washington was favourable: the chair of the SEC wrote the TSE to welcome this initiative.
49 BDA, MB, 28 March 1961
50 Ibid., 11 April 1961; *OSCB,* October 1961 (quoted)
51 *FP,* 22 April 1961; BDA, MB, 25 April 1961
52 BDA, MB, 25 April, 9 May, 27 June, 18 July 1961; PAO, AG, 4-02, file 167.12, James P. Manley, T.P. O'Connor, W.C. Campbell, and B.N. Apple to AG Kelso Roberts, 22 June 1961; *FP,* 22 July 1961
53 *FP,* 7 April 1962
54 *FP,* 13 January 1962; BDA, MB, 13, 27 March 1962
55 BDA, MB, 12 April, 8 May 1962; *OSCB,* May 1962
56 BDA, MB, 13 March, 12 April 1962
57 Ibid., 23 May, 5 June (quoted), 20 July 1962; PAO, AG, 4-02, file 218.5, Jones to George Wardrope, 24 December 1962
58 BDA, MB, 19 June, 4, 20 July, 8, 21 August, 11 September 1962: NAC, TSE, MB, 24 July, 28 August, 5 September 1962
59 PAO, OSC, BM, box 28, file 556, Bray to J.H. Campbell, 15 June 1964
60 PAO, AG, 4-02, file 168.1, Memorandum from Lennox to AG Kelso Roberts, 18 May 1961; ibid., OSC, BM, box 47, file 957, Memorandum from Bray to D.N. Omand, 24 January 1967 (both quoted)

Chapter 6: Windfall

1 PAO, RG 18, B-132 (now renumbered RG 18-149), Records of the Royal Commission to Investigate Trading in the Shares of Windfall Oils and Mines Limited (hereafter PAO, Windfall Commission), General Files, box 11, William Dennis to Mr Justice Arthur Kelly, 9 June 1965. This record group also contains the records of a parallel inquiry into Windfall by the OSC (hereafter cited as PAO, Windfall Commission, OSC Inquiry). Testimony was taken from the many of the same people by both inquiries, the commission testimony being cited here by volume number, the OSC transcripts (which are arranged alphabetically) by box number.
2 E.K. Cork, *Finance in the Mining Industry: A Staff Study for the Royal Commission on Banking and Finance* (n.p., n.d.), 37
3 Ontario, *Report of the Royal Commission to Investigate Trading in the Shares of Windfall Oils and Mines Limited* (n.p., September, 1965; hereafter *Windfall Report*), appendix A, Harold O. Siegel, 'The Role of the Geologist and Geophysicist in Mineral Exploration'

4 Ibid., Hugh D. Carlson, 'Brief History of Mineral Exploration and Development in the Porcupine Area, Ontario'

5 Anyone holding a mining licence could stake up to ninety claims per year on open lands, eighteen in any one of the province's fourteen mining divisions; each mining claim was a square of forty acres extending from its northeast corner, the boundaries being marked by blazing trees and clearing underbrush or by erecting pickets or cairns. Claims had to be filed within thirty-one days of staking with the division's mining recorder, and at least twenty days work had to be performed during the first year to avoid forfeiture. See *Windfall Report*, appendix A, J.F. McFarland, 'Staking Requirements under the Mining Act, ' 134–5.

6 Kenneth G. Patrick, *Perpetual Jeopardy: The Texas Gulf Sulphur Affair, a Chronicle of Achievement and Misadventure* (New York, 1972), 33–43; PAO, Windfall Commission, OSC Inquiry, box 40, testimony of Darke, 24 September 1964, 94–5; box 41, testimony of Walter Holyk, 22 February 1965, 12 (quoted)

7 Graham Ackerly of the *Northern Miner* was given an exclusive story on the discovery for the issue to appear on April 16.

8 See text of Sinclair's broadcast on CFRB, 26 February 1963; and 'In Memoriam,' *Canadian Magazine*, April 1963, in PAO, OSC, BM, box 11, file 198.

9 PAO, AG, 4-02, file 218.5, William Price to Cass, 7 January 1963, Personal, enclosing BDA memorandum; file 209.2, Price to Cass, 29 January 1963, Personal, enclosing memorandum from Price to Cass, 22 January 1963, Personal; Memorandum from the Board of Governors of BDA re Problems faced by Broker-Dealers in raising speculative mining capital ..., n.d. [spring 1963]; A.B. Whitelaw to Cass, 8 March 1963; Price had been attorney general in the early 1930s when the OSC was created and now acted for many mining promoters.

10 *FP*, 13 August 1938

11 PAO, Windfall Commission, vol. 38, testimony of Viola MacMillan, 13 May 1965, 4570–6; vol. 11, testimony of George MacMillan, 17 March 1965, 1352

12 *Windfall Report*, appendix A, J.F. McFarland, 'Staking Requirements under the Mining Act'; PAO, Windfall Commission, vol. 11, testimony of George MacMillan, 10 March 1965, 1363–4; ibid., OSC Inquiry, box 43, testimony of Viola MacMillan, 21 August 1964, 422–6

13 *Windfall Report*, 13–4, 21–2; PAO, Windfall Commission, vol. 38, testimony of Viola MacMillan, 13 May 1965, 4577, 4589

14 *Windfall Report*, 22; PAO, Windfall Commission, vol. 25, testimony of Donald Lawson, 22 April 1965, 2967; vol. 38, testimony of Viola MacMillan, 13 May 1965, 4591–4. Viola MacMillan testified that Lawson had suggested that she take an additional $100,000 from the company in salary over a

five-year period, but as an indication of her determination to make a mine, 'I wouldn't hear of it.'

15 PAO, Windfall Commission, vol. 9, testimony of Fenton Scott, 11 March 1965, 1163–4; ibid., OSC Inquiry, box 45, testimony of Stanley Tallon, 10 December 1964, 3–5; box 43, testimony of MacMillan, 13 August 1964, 145–7, 175

16 Ibid., box 42, testimony of Larche, 15 September 1964, 33–4; box 40, testimony of Darke, 24 September 1964, 89–90; box 44, testimony of Schlitt, 14 January 1965, 22–7

17 *Windfall Report*, Chronology

18 PAO, Windfall Commission, OSC Inquiry, box 43, testimony of McKinnon, 15 September 1964, 13–5

19 Viola MacMillan later denied this incident, but others present definitely recollected it; see PAO, Windfall Commission, vol. 11, testimony of MacMillan, 17 March 1965, 1388.

20 *Windfall Report*, Chronology; PAO, Windfall Commission, vol. 38, testimony of Viola MacMillan, 17 March 1965, 4610–1 (quoted); ibid., OSC Inquiry, box 43, testimony of Viola MacMillan, 20 August 1964, 463, 474 (both quoted); box 39, testimony of Bradley, 11 December 1964, 26

21 PAO, Windfall Commission, OSC Inquiry, box 41, testimony of Jones, 23 November 1964, 20–8; box 39, testimony of Bradley, 9 December 1964, 23, 27

22 Ibid., box 41, testimony of Jones, 23 November 1964, 30–40

23 *Windfall Report*, Chronology, 72; PAO, Windfall Commission, OSC Inquiry, box 43, testimony of McKinnon, 15 September 1964, 30; box 40, testimony of Dennis, 24 November 1964, 3, 10. Dennis sent out a wire to other Davidson and Company salesmen to this effect the following day.

24 PAO, Windfall Commission, OSC Inquiry, box 44, testimony of Schlitt, 14 January 1965, 16–7; testimony of Stollery, 9 December 1964, 6; box 43, testimony of McKinnon, 15 September 1964, 16

25 *Windfall Report*, Chronology, 19, 70–3; PAO, Windfall Commission, OSC Inquiry, box 41, testimony of G.A. Hunter, 18 February 1965, 5–6, 14, 22; box 42, testimony of Lawson, 5 October 1964, 25; PAO, Windfall Commission, vol. 42, summation of Joseph Sedgwick, 26 May 1965, 5103; vol. 38, testimony of Viola MacMillan, 13 May 1965, 4604–7 (quoted). P.S. Dodd said that 795, 000 of the shares taken down under options were immediately lodged by Viola MacMillan with the Bank of Nova Scotia for a loan of $247,000 (or 32 cents per share), to be repaid as they were sold to the public; see ibid., vol. 27, testimony of Dodd, 26 April 1965, 3321–5.

26 *Windfall Report*, Chronology; PAO, Windfall Commission, OSC Inquiry, box 44, testimony of Roberts, 17 September 1964, 6. Walwyn, Stodgell and Com-

pany reported that Windfall was claiming a find, while James Richardson and Sons said there were rumours of 175 feet of copper and zinc values in the core, though noting that doubts remained whether this was a commercially exploitable find.

27 *Windfall Report*, Chronology, 73; PAO, Windfall Commission, OSC Inquiry, box 43, testimony of George MacMillan, 13 August 1964, 195; box 42, testimony of Donald Lawson, 5 October 1964, 33–4; PAO, Windfall Commission, vol. 39, testimony of Viola MacMillan, 14 May 1965, 4857–8

28 *Windfall Report*, Chronology; PAO, Windfall Commission, vol. 28, testimony of Watson, 28 April 1965, 3365–71

29 *Windfall Report*, Chronology; PAO, Windfall Commission, OSC Inquiry, box 41, testimony of Graham, 14 September 1964, 29–30; PAO, Windfall Commission, vol. 17, testimony of Graham, 31 March 1965, 2069–70; vol. 21, testimony of Marshal Stearns, 12 April 1965, 2408–10

30 For instance, on Thursday both Walwyn, Stodgell and Moss, Lawson had wired their branches concerning the rumours; on Friday all J.H. Crang salesmen were told to recommend going long on the stock, which, though speculative, might involve a big find, and Moss, Lawson said the stock might go higher; see *Windfall Report*, Chronology.

31 *Windfall Report*, 112, notes that 34 per cent of the first 400,000 shares of Windfall traded on Monday, 6 July, were for brokers' own accounts. Albert Reid testified that as a floor trader for Waite, Reid and Company, he ran a house account in which he and the firm split the profits fifty-fifty, as well as a personal trading account on which he took the entire profit or loss and paid only 20 per cent of the regular commission rate. All floor traders could buy on their own account, provided that they did not disrupt business and upset the governor responsible for running that particular section of the floor. See PAO, Windfall Commission, OSC Inquiry, box 44, testimony of Reid, 4 March 1965, 6.

32 In May the exchange had passed a new rule that board or committee members who had a 'small' interest in a given security being discussed were required to disclose this interest and state that the 'amount will not influence my judgement'; see NAC, TSE, MB, 5 May 1964.

33 Windfall does not appear to have been discussed at the regular Thursday board meeting, which was devoted to the suspension of John Frame and Company for having been discovered to lack the required amount of free net capital; see NAC, TSE, 9, 10 July 1964.

34 *Windfall Report*, 61; PAO, Windfall Commission, vol. 17, testimony of Graham, 31 March 1965, 2071; vol. 21, testimony of Stearns, 12 April 1965, 2412

35 PAO, Windfall Commission, vol. 23, testimony of Campbell, 15 April 1965, 2729–30, 2742–3 (quoted)

36 Ibid., OSC Inquiry, box 39, testimony of Campbell, 9 September 1964, 238 (quoted); PAO, Windfall Commission, vol. 23, testimony of Campbell, 15 April 1965, 2744–9 (quoted)

37 Campbell did say that he had been so annoyed when the TSE stayed open for twenty-two minutes after the New York Stock Exchange had closed on the day of President John Kennedy's assasination the previous November, he had even suggested to J.R. Kimber that use of the 'bomb' should be threatened; see PAO, Windfall Commission, vol. 23, testimony of Campbell, 15 April 1965, 2732–3.

38 *Windfall Report*, Chronology, 52–3, 62, 66; PAO, Windfall Commission, OSC Inquiry, box 39, testimony of Campbell, 9 September 1964, 148; box 41, testimony of Graham, 14 September 1964, 24. Campbell himself seems to have given credence to the rumour of a bid by Texas Gulf when he mentioned to Graham on 12 July that a foreign takeover was a possibility, thus putting the idea of a bid by Texas Gulf in his mind; see ibid., 27.

39 *Windfall Report*, Chronology, 74–7

40 The underwriters, Moss, Lawson, were no longer required to maintain an orderly market.

41 NAC, TSE, MB, 14 July 1964, 12:30 p.m.; PAO, Windfall Commission, General Files, box 15, Memorandum by J.R. Kimber, 2 September 1964

42 *Windfall Report*, 82; PAO, Windfall Commission, vol. 14, testimony of Cole, 26 March 1965, 1730; vol. 25, testimony of Lawson, 22 April 1965, 3010; vol. 38, testimony of Viola MacMillan, 13 May 1965, 4630–1

43 PAO, Windfall Commission, OSC Inquiry, box 41, testimony of Graham, 14 September 1964; PAO, Windfall Commission, vol. 21, testimony of Stearns, 12 April 1965, 2425–9; vol. 21, testimony of Somerville, 12 April 1965, 2504–6; ibid., OSC Inquiry, box 43, testimony of Viola MacMillan, 21 August 1964, 587–9. Stearns recalled that the Windfall lawyer, Thomas Cole, did intervene in the talk about a takeover bid to point out that she couldn't possibly know the identity of the buyers of large blocks of its shares.

44 PAO, Windfall Commission, vol. 22, testimony of Kimber, 13 April 1965, 2586–7; ibid., OSC Inquiry, box 43, testimony of Viola MacMillan, 21 August 1964, 592

45 See PAO, Windfall Commission, OSC Inquiry, box 43, testimony of Viola MacMillan, 21 August 1964, 591, where she claimed that if she had made such a comment, she had not intended it to be taken as a confirmation of a discovery. A week earlier George MacMillan had flatly denied to OSC investigators that she had said either 'Everybody knows we have hit it;

Texas Gulf knows we have hit it' or 'We picked a very good name for the company, Windfall'; see ibid., testimony of George MacMillan, 14 August 1964, 330–1.

46 Suggestions were later made that the resident geologist in the Porcupine Mining District should simply have used his authority under the Mines Act to make a site inspection and demand to see the Windfall cores, but Hugh Carlson, the provincial geologist, said that it never occurred to him to order a visit without the company's permission, as he had instructions only to make such inspections on the minister's directions in extraordinary circumstances. See PAO, Windfall Commission, vol. 11, testimony of Carlson, 17 March 1965, 1407–8.

47 PAO, Windfall Commission, vol. 21, testimony of Frohberg, 12 April 1965, 2523; testimony of Somerville, 12 April 1965, 2503 (quoted); testimony of Stearns, 12 April 1965, 2429–31; vol. 22, testimony of Kimber, 12 April 1965, 2590; vol. 24, testimony of McFarland, 20 April 1965, 2893 (quoted)

48 Ibid., vol. 21, testimony of Marshal Stearns, 12 April 1965, 2435–9 (quoted); vol. 22, testimony of J.R. Kimber, 13 April 1965, 2590–2; ibid., OSC Inquiry, box 43, testimony of George MacMillan, 14 August 1964, 331 (quoted)

49 *Windfall Report*, Chronology, 82 ; PAO, Windfall Commission, OSC Inquiry, testimony of Larche, 15 September 1964, 44; PAO, Windfall Commission, vol. 15, testimony of Ackerly, 29 March 1965, 1935–8; *FP*, 18 July 1964

50 *Windfall Report*, 82; PAO, Windfall Commission, vol. 15, testimony of Ackerly, 29 March 1965, 1942–4; ibid., OSC Inquiry, box 39, testimony of Brown, 17 September 1964, 12–13; box 44, testimony of Gregory Reynolds, 13 October 1964, 50. Reynolds, a reporter for the *Timmins Daily Press*, recalled Bragagnolo's comment.

51 *Windfall Report*, Chronology; PAO, Windfall Commission, OSC Inquiry, box 41, testimony of Ezrin, 12 April 1965, 17; testimony of Fidler, 8 April 1965, 36

52 *Windfall Report*, Chronology, 82; PAO, Windfall Commission, vol. 11, testimony of MacMillan, 17 March 1965, 1369–70; vol. 17, testimony of Graham, 31 March 1965, 2111–2; vol. 16, testimony of Drewe, 30 March 1965, 2055

53 *Windfall Report*, Chronology; PAO, Windfall Commission, vol. 21, testimony of Stearns, 12 April 1965, 2441–2; vol. 22, testimony of Kimber, 13 April 1965, 2611–2; General Files, box 15, Memorandum by Kimber, 2 September 1964

54 PAO, Windfall Commission, OSC Inquiry, box 44, testimony of Scott, 16 Sepember 1964, 19–24; PAO, Windfall Commission, vol. 16, testimony of Scott, 30 March 1965, 1984 (both quoted)

55 *Windfall Report*, Chronology; PAO, Windfall Commission, OSC Inquiry, box, 39, testimony of Bragagnolo, 25 September 1964, 70

56 PAO, Windfall Commission, General Files, box 15, Memorandum by J.R. Kimber, 2 September 1964. The investigation also covered Bunker Hill Extension Mines and Glenn Uranium Mines, both of which had property in the Timmins area, because of the receipt of similar forged orders.

57 Ibid., OSC Inquiry, box 43, testimony of Viola MacMillan, 21 August 1964, 511. Bray was concerned about possible market manipulation or short sales.

58 PAO, AG, 4-02, file 218.5, Graham to AG Frederick Cass, 22 January 1963; Ian M. Rogers to Cass, 28 February 1963; *FP*, 28 July 1962

59 *R. v. Alberta SC, ex parte Albrecht* (1963), 36 *DLR*, 2nd, 199; PAO, OSC, BM, box 32, file 662, W.S. Irwin to H.S. Bray, 13 February 1963, enclosing memorandum, n.d.; file 209.2, Explanatory Notes to Securities Amendment Act, 1962–3, 10 April 1963; Ontario, *Statutes*, 1962–3, c. 131. The other important change was to permit the vice-chair to act in the absence of the chair, an omission that had created serious problems during O.E. Lennox's final illness.

60 Ontario, *Statutes*, 1962–3, c.131; *OSCB*, November 1963, 'Notice'; PAO, AG, 4-02, file 248.8, Cass to Campbell, 7 January 1964; Decision of Campbell in Re I. Richard Wookey and P.J. Anderson, 3 March 1964, with Common's minute

61 PAO, Windfall Commission, vol. 23, testimony of John Campbell, 15 April 1965, 2729–30; ibid., OSC Inquiry, box 39, testimony of Violet Campbell, 4 September 1964, 19–23, 44–54

62 PAO, Windfall Commission, OSC Inquiry, box 39, testimony of Violet Campbell, 4 September 1964, 60–73; testimony of John Campbell, 4 September 1964, 23, 199

63 PAO, Windfall Commission, vol. 23, testimony of Campbell, 15 April 1965, 2736–49; ibid., OSC Inquiry, box 39, testimony of Violet Campbell, 4 September 1964, 54; box 43, testimony of Viola MacMillan, 21 August 1964, 512–15

64 PAO, AG, 4-02, file 218.5, Memorandum from Kimber to Common, 14 June 1963; Memorandum from Common to Cass, 20 June 1963; Memorandum from Cass to Kimber, 7 November 1963, Personal and Confidential

65 PAO, Windfall Commission, OSC Inquiry, box 39, testimony of John Campbell, 9 September 1964, 1516, 35–6, 193. The final block of 3,000 shares was sold through an account in the name of a friend of Campbell's, Eleanor Berry.

66 Ibid., 195–6 (quoted), 202, 229; PAO, Windfall Commission, vol. 23, testimony of Campbell, 15 April 1965, 2802–3 (quoted), 2813

67 PAO, Windfall Commission, OSC Inquiry, box 39, testimony of John Campbell, 9 September 1964 (quoted); PAO, Windfall Commission, vol. 23, testimony of Campbell, 15 April 1965, 2821–5

68 PAO, Windfall Commission, OSC Inquiry, box 39, testimony of John Campbell, 9 September 1964, 142, 246

69 *Windfall Report*, 52–3. Campbell did not have a high opinion of many of his OSC colleagues: on 12 August, in a drunken moment, he had confided to an acquaintance that 'where he works he is surrounded by incompetent people, but he cannot fire them because of the Civil Servants Association'; see PAO, Windfall Commission, General Files, box 15, Memorandum from investigator W.K. Jewett to N.W.H. Cox, 8 September 1964.

70 Bray was apparently passed over when Campbell was chosen because both the attorney general and his deputy, Common, had doubts about his administrative abilities; see PAO, AG, 4-02, file 218.5, Memorandum from Common to Cass, 17 April 1963, Confidential.

71 *R. v. Campbell* (1967), 2 OLR 1; 2 *Criminal Reports New Series* 403

72 *Windfall Report*, 'Foreword,' xi; 'Chronology of Events,' xiii–xviii

73 PAO, Windfall Commission, vol. 2, testimony of Darke, 1 March 1965, 31; vol. 21, testimony of Frohberg, 12 April 1965, 2528, 2551; vol. 25, testimony of Buffam, 22 April 1965, 3046; vol. 9, testimony of Scott, 11 March 1965, 1159, 1164.

74 Ibid., OSC Inquiry, box 43, testimony of MacMillan, 13 August 1964, 188 (quoted); PAO, Windfall Commission, vol. 40, testimony of MacMillan, 18 May 1965, 4938–40, 4991; vol. 11, testimony of MacMillan, 17 March 1965, 1365–72, 1382 (both quoted)

75 *Windfall Report*, Chronology, 81; PAO, Windfall Commission, vol. 39, testimony of Viola MacMillan, 14 May 1965, 4810–1; vol. 10, 16 March 1965, testimony of Ambrose, 1308

76 *Windfall Report*, 28, 36, 63–5, 77

77 PAO, Windfall Commission, OSC Inquiry, box 43, testimony of George MacMillan, 13 August 1964, 200; PAO, Windfall Commission, vol. 39, testimony of Viola MacMillan, 14 May 1965, 4811–12

78 *Windfall Report*, 16–9, 81, 92

79 PAO, Windfall Commission, vol. 28, testimony of Watson, 27 April 1965, 3367; ibid., OSC Inquiry, box 41, testimony of G.A. Hunter, 18 February 1965, 5–6, 33; *Windfall Report*, 82–4

80 PAO, Windfall Commission, vol. 25, testimony of Lawson, 22 April 1965, 2977–9; *Windfall Report*, 85

81 *Windfall Report*, 84–5

82 PAO, Windfall Commission, OSC Inquiry, box 41, testimony of Humphrey,

23 September 1964, 34; PAO, Windfall Commission, General Files, box 11, transcript of staff conference, tape no. 4, 6 October 1964, 4; *Windfall Report*, 24–5

83 *Windfall Report*, 1–3, 66–7

84 Ibid., 13–6, 18–20; appendix B, 'Summary of Normal Procedures Followed by a Mining Company When Financing through Sale of Treasury Shares'

85 NAC, TSE, MB, 22 April 1964

86 Ibid., 25 February, 14 April 1964. Minimum listing requirements for oil companies were slightly higher since $200,000 in net working capital was required; see ibid., 28 April 1964.

87 *Windfall Report*, 88–93. Kelly paid particular attention to the effect of rumours, not only because of allegations that the MacMillans had deliberately propagated them but also because on 27 July fourteen telegrams with false signatures were sent from New York to George MacMillan, as well as to various journalists and brokers, in an attempt to affect markets; these wires mentioned not only Windfall but also Bunker Hill and Glenn Uranium. For this reason, among others, the two companies were included with Windfall in the OSC investigation order. Because the recipients were suspicious of these messages, whose source was never discovered, Kelly concluded that they had little effect upon share prices. See also PAO, Windfall Commission, vol. 22, testimony of J.R. Kimber, 13 April 1965, 2611–12.

88 *Windfall Report*, 63, 82, 101, 104–5, 111–14; PAO, Windfall Commission, General Files, box 11, transcript of staff conference, tape no. 1, 6 October 1964, 6

89 In January 1965 the PDA announced that Viola MacMillan would not stand for re-election, and the annual conference was cancelled to avoid criticism. In a letter withdrawing her name, she insisted that she would be vindicated. See *FP*, 16 January 1965.

90 PAO, Windfall Commission, vol. 25, testimony of Lawson, 22 April 1965, 2975; ibid., OSC Inquiry, box 38, testimony of Borthwick, 8 April 1965, 9

91 PAO, Windfall Commission, OSC Inquiry, box 38, testimony of Applegath, 30 November 1964, 42–3; PAO, Windfall Commission, vol. 16, testimony of Scott, 30 March 1965, 1989

92 PAO, Windfall Commission, General Files, box 15, Memorandum from investigator W.L. Jewett to N.W.H. Cox, 8 September 1964 [re interview with Mrs. Stephanie Gobel]; ibid., OSC Inquiry, box 42, testimony of Lawson, 5 October 1964, 16–17; vol. 25, testimony of Lawson, 22 April 1965, 2967 (both quoted)

93 PAO, OSC, BM, box 2, file 44, Memorandum [from Meinhardt] to Canadian Securities Administrators Mid-Year Meeting, 17 April 1964. Meinhardt continued, 'This raises a great problem since if this idea does not work out, the

responsibility will rest squarely on the shoulders of those administered [*sic*] with the securities legislation, unless the legislation be so changed that prospectors and Prospectors and Developers Association be taken completely out of our jurisdictions, which would, of course, create a great danger, in my respectful submission, to the public at large.'

94 On litigation concerning this issue that had arisen in a British Columbia case during the 1930s, see Christopher Armstrong, *Blue Skies and Boiler Rooms: Buying and Selling Securities in Canada, 1870–1940* (Toronto, 1997), chapter 12. In the case of *St. John v. Fraser* (1935) the Supreme Court ruled that witnesses in such investigations did not enjoy the protections of a court to know the precise allegations against them and to cross-examine witnesses.

95 PAO, Windfall Commission, OSC Inquiry, box 43, testimony of George MacMillan, 14 August 1964; testimony of Viola MacMillan, 21 August 1964, 591

96 PAO, Windfall Commission, vol. 11, testimony of MacMillans, 17 March 1965; ibid., General Files, box 13, Writ to Court of Appeal from Kelly, J., 2 April 1965; Decision of Court of Appeal, 6 April 1965

97 Ibid., vol. 39–40, testimony of George MacMillan, 14, 18 May 1965; Sedgwick's examination is found at 4875–908, with the 'joke' at 4897; and the discussion of house accounts at 4996–8; Hartt's cross-examination is at 4913–5002.

98 Ibid., vol. 38, testimony of Viola MacMillan, 13 May 1965; Sedgwick's examination is found at 4570–666; the quotations are from 4649 and 4658.

99 Ibid., vol. 39, testimony of Viola MacMillan, 13 May 1965, with Hartt's cross-examination at 4666–875; the quotations are from 4813, 1817, and 4825.

100 Ibid., vol. 42, summation by Sedgewick, 26 May 1965, 5098–133 (from which the quotation is taken)

101 PAO, OSC, BM, box 11, file 198, White to Campbell, 7 February 1964

102 PAO, Windfall Commission, vol. 14, testimony of Cole, 26 March 1965, 1727–8; vol. 25, testimony of Lawson, 22 April 1965, 3010

103 Ibid., vol. 21, testimony of W.L. Somerville, 12 April 1965, 2506; vol. 14, 26 March 1965, testimony of Cole, 1730

104 Ibid., vol. 16, testimony of Alexander Dow, 30 March 1965, 2033 (quoting Kimber); vol. 38, testimony of Viola MacMillan, 13 May 1965, 4587–8, 4658 (both quoted); ibid., OSC Inquiry, box 38, testimony of Ackerly, 10 September 1964, 24

105 PAO, Windfall Commission, vol. 38, testimony of Viola MacMillan, 13 May 1965, 4581

106 Ibid., OSC Inquiry, box 43, testimony of Viola MacMillan, 21 August 1964, 591
107 *R. v. MacMillan* (1968), 1 *OLR* 475, 66 *DLR*, 2nd (1968) 680
108 *FP,* 16 October 1965, 18 February 1967, 20 April 1968, 15 February 1969
109 *R. v. Breckenridge* (1969), *Oral Judgment,* no. 168
110 PAO, OSC, BM, box 35, file 707, Memorandum from Bray to Kimber, 18 October 1965

Chapter 7: Challenges

1 PAO, Ontario, Legislative Assembly, Unpublished Sessional Papers, 1968–9, no. 123, testimony of C.C. Carrothers to OSC, 18 August 1967, 23–4
2 Ibid., testimony of N.A. Rafuse to OSC, 23 August 1967, 30–2
3 Clarkson, Gordon and Company, 'Report on the Investigation into the Affairs of Prudential Finance Corporation and Allied Companies,' 8 March 1967, 2 vols. (typescript, University of Toronto Library; hereafter Clarkson, Gordon, Prudential Finance Report), vol. 1; Ontario Securities Commission, 'Prudential Finance Corporation Limited, Final Report (Pursuant to Section 21 (6) of the Securities Act, R.S.O. 1960, c. 363 amended),' by B.C. Howard, chief legal investigation officer, 12 October 1967, 2 vols. (mimeo, York University Library; hereafter OSC, Final Report on Prudential Finance), vol. 1, 12, 54–7, 79
4 PAO, AG, 4-02, file 209.2, AG Frederick Cass to J.R. Kimber, 28 December 1962; Memorandum from H.S. Bray to W.B. Common, 14 January 1962; Report of OSC solicitor C.J. Stiles, March 1963; Memorandum from Kimber to Cass, 8 March 1963
5 Ibid., Memorandum from Henry Langford to AG Frederick Cass, 11 January 1963; Memorandum from W.B. Common to Cass, 15 January 1963; Memorandum from J.R. Kimber to Cass, 31 January 1963 (quoted); Peter V.V. Betts to Cass, 12 February 1963
6 Ibid., Memorandum from Kimber to Cass, 31 January 1963; PAO, OSC, BM, box 32, file 662, Memorandum from Kimber to H.S. Bray, 1 February 1963; Memorandum from Bray to Canadian Securities Administrators, 21 February 1963 (quoted)
7 PAO, OSC, BM, box 32, file 662, R.A. Davies to W.B. Common, 21, 22 March 1963, with explanatory notes; Memorandum from Kimber to Bray, 21 March 1963; OSC, Corr., box 8, file 4, Kimber to H.L. Rowntree, 9 February 1967; PAO, AG, 4-02, file 209.2, Explanatory Brief for AG re drafts of the Deposits Regulation Act and an Act to Amend the Securities Act, 1 April 1963; Explanatory Notes to Securities Amendment Act, 1962–3, 10 April 1963; Ontario, *Statutes,* 1962–3, c. 131

8 PAO, AG, 4-02, file 209.2, Peter V.V. Betts to Cass, 12 February 1963; Cass to Betts, 15 February 1963; Memorandum to members of the Executive Committee re Bills 151, 152, 153, 28 May 1963 (quoted). Carrothers had acquired his interest in Prudential in 1936, and he remained on the board as corporate secretary even after Brien's takeover.

9 OSC, Final Report on Prudential Finance, vol. 1, appendix B, 'The Ontario Securities Commission and the Prudential Finance Prospectus of June 14th, 1963'

10 Clarkson, Gordon, Prudential Finance Report, vol. 1

11 PAO, OSC, BM, box 4, file 74, Kimber to Wishart, 25 August 1966

12 'In the matter of the Securities Act and ... Prudential Finance Corporation Limited ...,' Interim Report by B.C. Howard to J.R. Kimber, 13 March 1967 (typescript, University of Toronto Library; hereafter OSC, Interim Report on Prudential Finance)

13 Statements by Wishart on 2 and 21 December 1966 are quoted in A.K. McDougall, *John P. Robarts: His Life and Government* (Toronto, 1986), 158–9.

14 PAO, OSC, BM, box 47, file 975, Press release by Rowntree, 12 January 1967; Press release by Trotter, 12 January 1967; Press release by MacDonald, 12 January 1967; Kimber to Rowntree, 9 February 1967

15 McDougall, *John P. Robarts*, 159–60

16 PAO, Ontario, Legislative Assembly, Unpublished Sessional Papers, 1968–9, no. 123, testimony of Carrothers to OSC, 18 August 1967, 48–59

17 The account of the affairs of Prudential Finance in this and the following paragraphs is drawn from Clarkson, Gordon, Prudential Finance Report; OSC, Interim Report on Prudential Finance; and OSC, Final Report on Prudential Finance; only the sources of the quotations are cited specifically. The quotation above is from OSC, Final Report on Prudential Finance, vol. 1, 109.

18 Clarkson, Gordon, Prudential Finance Report, vol. 1

19 PAO, Ontario, Legislative Assembly, Unpublished Sessional Papers, 1968–9, no. 123, testimony of DesLauriers to OSC, 1 September 1967, 67

20 PAO, OSC, BM, box 4, file 68, Kimber to Wishart, 7 January 1966

21 PAO, Ontario, Legislative Assembly, Unpublished Sessional Papers, 1968–9, no. 123, testimony of Jonak to OSC, 1 September 1967, 18, 59

22 Clarkson, Gordon, Prudential Finance Report, vol. 1

23 Ibid.

24 OSC, Final Report on Prudential Finance, vol. 1, 108

25 PAO, OSC, BM, box 47, file 975, Kimber to H.L. Rowntree, 24 January, 9 February 1967 (both quoted); the first quotation, from the February letter, was actually taken from the 1949 Cohen report in Britain.

26 According to PAO, OSC, BM, box 47, file 977, Langford to Rowntree, 20
April 1967, Confidential, the breakdown for all the creditors was as follows:

Number of creditors	Amount owing ($)	Losses ($)
3,884	1– 5,000	11,652,000
899	5,000–10,000	6,742,000
343	10,000–20,000	5,145,000

For Ontario residents only:

2,365	1– 5,000	7,095,000
518	5,000–10,000	3,885,000
224	10,000–20,000	3,360,000
?	20,000–25,000	410,000

27 Ibid., file 978, clipping from *Globe and Mail* (Toronto), 25 September 1967;
Rowntree to association president Harold Westlake, 25 September 1967;
Westlake to Langford, 5 October 1967; Langford to Westlake, 12 October
1967. This pressure probably explains the very defensive tone of appendix
B of volume 1 of the OSC's Final Report on Prudential Finance, quoted
above; see note 13 above.
28 PAO, OSC, BM, box 48, file 983, Press release by Rowntree, 12 January 1968;
Memorandum from Howard to Langford, 29 February 1968
29 Ibid., Memorandum from Langford to Rowntree, 10 July 1968
30 Statement by the Hon. H.L. Rowntree, QC, Minister of Financial and Commercial Affairs, regarding the Ontario Securities Commission's investigation into the affairs of the Prudential Finance Corporation Limited, n.d.
[September 1969] bound with OSC, Final Report into Prudential Finance
31 *Westlake at al. v. R.* (1971), 3 *OLR* 533
32 PAO, OSC, BM, box 26, file 516, Memorandum by Willis re 'Public Policy
and Canadian Securities Markets,' 22 January 1968
33 See Ontario, Royal Commission on Atlantic Acceptance, *Report* 4 vols. (n.p.,
12 September 1969; hereafter *Atlantic Acceptance Report*).
34 Ibid., 9–24, 1569–605; the quotations come from 1581, 1591–2, and 1605.
35 Ibid., 373–478; the quotations are from 373, 450, and 1597. See also NAC,
TSE, MB, 13 May, 18 June 1965, 26, 27 July, 17, 18 August 1966.
36 *OSCB*, March 1966
37 *Atlantic Acceptance Report*, 740–87; the quotation is from 744.
38 PAO, OSC, BM, box 8, file 4, Memoranda from Bray to Kimber, 20, 26 July
1965; box 4, file 71, Kimber to Samuel Hughes, 30 May 1966, Personal and

Confidential. In his letter to Hughes, Kimber criticized a study by John
Abel, commissioned by the royal commission, which argued that U.S. regulation was more stringent and might have prevented Atlantic's collapse.
39 Ibid., box 32, file 664, Memorandum from Kimber to AG Arthur Wishart,
   22 July 1965

Chapter 8: Disclosure

1 On the various meanings attributed to this term, see Mary G. Condon, *Making Disclosure: Ideas and Interests in Ontario Securities Regulation* (Toronto,
  1998), passim.
2 *FP*, 7 November, 12 December 1959
3 Falconbridge would take over all of Ventures assets (which also included
  interests in United Keno Hill, Giant Yellowknife, Kilembe Copper,
  Opemiska Copper, and other mines) in exchange for 600, 000 Falconbridge
  shares, to be added to the 2, 164, 753 Falconbridge that Ventures already
  owned; McIntyre would buy 280, 600 Falconbridge for about $60 and
  receive 728, 000 more Falconbridge in exchange for its 700, 000 Ventures
  shares in order to acquire direct control of Falconbridge rather than
  through Ventures; Ventures stockholders would receive 104 Falconbridge
  for each 100 shares held and Ventures would be wound up; see *FP*,
  5 August 1961.
4 NAC, TSE, MB, 1, 22 August 1961; *FP*, 5, 12 August, 9 December 1961
5 *FP*, 12 May 1962
6 PAO, AG, 4-02, file 220.1 Provincial Secretary John Yaremko to AG Frederick Cass, 13 February 1963; file 219.3, Memorandum from Kimber to Cass,
  5 September 1963
7 PAO, AG, 4-02, file 219.3, Memorandum from Lennox to Cass, 26 October
  1962; Report from OSC solicitor W.A. MacDonald re Shell Investments Ltd.,
  Canadian Oil Companies Ltd., etc., March 1963
8 PAO, AG, 4-02, file 291.1, Cass to Kimber, 2 January 1963; file 219.2, Memorandum from Kimber to Cass, 5 September 1963 (quoted)
9 *Toronto Daily Star*, 5 February 1963; NAC, TSE, MB, 23 October, 2 November
  1962
10 *Toronto Daily Star*, 20, 30 December 1963; PAO, AG, 4-02, file 219.3, Memoranda from Bray to Kimber, 23 August, 8 October 1963; Memoranda from
   Kimber to Cass, 29 August, 25 September, 9 October 1963; Memorandum
   from Kimber to Premier John Robarts, 18 December 1963; Press release
   from Cass, 20 December 1963; file 248.8, Decision of OSC director John
   Campbell in Re I. Richard Wookey and T.J. Anderson, 3 March 1964

11 PAO, AG, 4-02, file 219.3, Memoranda from Kimber to Cass, 5, 25 September, 18 December 1963; file 248.8, Decision of OSC director John Campbell in Re I. Richard Wookey and T.J. Anderson, 3 March 1964

12 NAC, TSE, MB, 11 December 1962, 15 January 1963; PAO, AG, 4-02, file 220.1, Provincial Secretary John Yaremko to Frederick Cass, 13 February 1963; Memorandum from Kimber to Cass, 19 February 1963; Memorandum from Common to file, n.d. [9 October 1963]; file 218.5, Memorandum from Deputy AG W.B. Common to Cass, 15 March 1963; Memorandum from Kimber to Cass, 15 May 1963; Memorandum from Cass to Common, 22 May 1963

13 PAO, AG, 4-02, file 218.5, Memorandum from Kimber to Cass, 10 October 1963

14 Ibid., file 220.1, Cass to Graham, 9 October 1963; Memorandum from Kimber to Cass, 18 October 1963; Cass to Mockridge, 18 October 1963; Mockridge to Cass, 23 October 1963; Press release by Cass, 29 October 1963; Graham to Cass, 29 November 1963; Cass to Graham, 10 December 1963; Ontario, *Report of the Attorney General's Committee on Securities Legislation in Ontario* (Toronto, 1965; hereafter *Kimber Report*), 6

15 The following paragraphs are drawn from Canada, Royal Commission on Banking and Finance, *Report*, chapter 17, 'The Stock Markets and Securities Legislation,' 334–54.

16 An earlier TSE study had fixed the level at 10–12 per cent.

17 The commission also recommended that company law be changed to require more disclosure of financial results, insider trading, proxies, and takeover bids.

18 The select committee was appointed on 8 May 1964 and reappointed on 22 June 1966; meetings were held during June and October–December 1964, January, June, August, and September 1965, and January 1966, and the report tabled in May 1966. Submissions and briefs, proceedings, files, and interim and final reports can be found in PAO, RG 18, D-I-69.

19 E.K. Cork, *Finance in the Mining Industry: A Staff Study for the Royal Commission on Banking and Finance* (n.p., n.d.)

20 PAO, Select Committee on Mining, 1966, Briefs, box 4, no. 14, United Steelworkers of America, 10 December 1964

21 The case is analysed at length in Kenneth G. Patrick, *Perpetual Jeopardy: The Texas Gulf Sulphur Affair, a Chronicle of Achievement and Misadventure* (New York, 1972)

22 'Brief to the Attorney General's Committee on Securities Legislation, Province of Ontario, submitted by the Toronto Stock Exchange, May 1964' (typescript, OSC Library; hereafter Kimber committee, TSE brief)

23 Ontario, Attorney General, Committee on Securities Legislation, Transcript of hearings, October 6–29, 1964, 6 vols. (typescript, York University Library; hereafter Kimber committee, Hearings), vol. 5, testimony of Grenier, 28 October 1964, 65; vol. 6, testimony of Sopha, 29 October 1964, 158
24 Ontario, Attorney General, Committee on Securities Legislation, Briefs (typescript, York University Library; hereafter Kimber committee, Briefs), Toronto Society of Financial Analysts, n.d. [1964]; Canadian Institute of Chartered Accountants, 12 February 1964; Kimber committee, TSE brief
25 *Kimber Report*, parts I, IV
26 Kimber committee, Briefs, CBA, part V; Kimber committee, TSE brief
27 *Kimber Report*, parts I (quoted), VI
28 Kimber committee, TSE brief
29 *FP*, 19 September 1964; Kimber committee, Briefs, CBA (quoted, 29); vol. 1, testimony of DesLauriers, 6 October 1964, 73
30 *Kimber Report*, part II. The committee rejected penalizing 'tippees' who profited from the use of such knowledge, as was alleged in the case of Texas Gulf Sulphur's discovery.
31 Kimber committee, Briefs, CBA, part VI; ibid., Hearings, vol. 1, testimony of R.J. Cudney and D.G.C. Menzel, 6 October 1964, 9–10, 97. The Canadian Institute of Chartered Accountants, however, favoured making the new code of ethics mandatory; see ibid., Briefs, CICA.
32 Kimber committee, Hearings, vol. 5, testimony of Grenier, 28 October 1964, 82; ibid., Briefs, CBA, part VI; Investment Dealers Association of Canada, 21 October 1964
33 Kimber committee, Briefs, CBA, part VI; IDA; ibid., Hearings, vol. 1, testimony of D.G.C. Menzel, 6 October 1964, 101–2. In its brief the CBA also made the convoluted argument that pro rata offers were too onerous for bidders since sophisticated investors would hold out until the last minute before tendering in hopes of an improved price.
34 *Kimber Report*, parts I, III
35 PAO, OSC, BM, box 32, file 664, Memorandum from Kimber to AG Arthur Wishart, 22 July 1965
36 Privately the OSC conceded this was true: an internal memorandum pointed out that there were 'unknown' policies, such as requiring issuers to submit a sales plan and forbidding underwriters to resell securities for more than 115 per cent of the price paid, though there was no statutory basis for these rules; see ibid., box 28, file 555, Memorandum from C.G. Ross to J.H. Campbell, 6 April 1964.
37 *Windfall Report*, 94–6
38 Ibid., 99–105

39 Ibid., 96–9
40 Ibid., 113, 118–21; PAO, Windfall Commission, General Files, box 11, transcript of staff conference, tape no. 1, 13 October 1964, 6–7 (quoted)
41 Kimber committee, Briefs, Pope and Company
42 Kimber committee, Briefs, Grenier; ibid., Hearings, vol. 5, testimony of Grenier, 28 October 1964, 58–62, 76–7 (quoted)
43 Kimber committee, Briefs, CBA, part I (quoted); ibid., Hearings, vol. 3, testimony of R.J. Cudney, 20 October 1964, 26–32
44 Kimber committee, TSE brief
45 Kimber committee, Hearings, vol. 6, testimony of Stearns et al., 29 October 1964, 83–94
46 Ibid., 6–10
47 *Kimber Report*, part VII
48 *Windfall Report*, 120–1
49 PAO, OSC, BM, box 47, file 975, Bray to D.N. Omand, 24 January 1967; box 4, file 68, Memorandum from Kimber to Wishart, 24 February 1966
50 Since Ontario had already established the McRuer commission to examine the procedures of all provincial administrative tribunals, Kimber claimed that it made little sense to alter other provisions of the Securities Act before that report was received; see PAO, OSC, BM, box 32, file 656, Kimber to AG Arthur Wishart, 4 February 1965; box 4, file 68, same to same, 24 February 1966.
51 Ibid., box 4, file 68, Memorandum from Kimber to Wishart, 24 February 1966
52 Ibid.
53 Ibid., file 74, Kimber to David Mishkin, 19 August 1966
54 Ibid., file 68, Kimber to Provincial Secretary John Yaremko, 25 February 1968
55 PAO, Windfall Commission, General Files, box 13, Memorandum from James Baillie to OSC director J.H. Campbell, 7 July 1964; NAC, TSE, MB, 26 October, 9, 16 November 1965
56 PAO, OSC, BM, box 4, file 73, Kimber to D.M. Peacock, 22 July 1966
57 Ontario, Legislative Assembly, *Debates*, 16 March 1966, 1578–9
58 *FP*, 26 March 1966; Ontario, Legislative Assembly, *Debates*, 29 March 1966, 2013–5, 2036
59 Ontario, Legislative Assembly, *Debates*, 29 March 1966, 2053–62
60 Ibid., 2043–53
61 Ibid., 2076–84
62 PAO, RG 49-193, Ontario, Legislative Assembly, Standing Committee on Legal Bills and Labour, Brief from Toronto Society of Financial Analysts to committee, 17 May 1966

63 Ibid., PAO, OSC, BM, box 4, file 72, Kimber to AG Arthur Wishart, 13 May 1966
64 PAO, RG 49–193, Ontario, Legislative Assembly, Standing Committee on Legal Bills and Labour, TSE vice-chair J.S. Deacon to committee, 11 May 1966
65 NAC, TSE, MB, 31 May 1966, containing Stearns to AG Arthur Wishart, 30 May 1966
66 PAO, RG 49-193, Ontario, Legislative Assembly, Standing Committee on Legal Bills and Labour, Brief from Shurtleff to committee, 2 May 1966
67 Ibid., Brief from Shurtleff enclosing Robinette to CMA Legislation Committee, 18 April 1966
68 In mid-1966 SEC chair Manuel Cohen announced that thirty-four Canadian companies had made voluntary filings in Washington, but that sixteen firms (BA Oil, Chemalloy Minerals, Cominco, Denison Mines, Dominion Bridge, Dominion Textiles, Hollinger Gold Mines, Imperial Tobacco, Jubilee Iron, Kirkland Minerals, Nickel Rim Mines, Power Corporation, Shell Canada, Stelco, Steep Rock Iron Mines, and Sherritt Gordon Mines) had so far declined to register; see FP, 20 August 1966.
69 PAO, OSC, BM, box 4, file 71, Kimber to Laskin, 24 May 1966, Personal; file 72, Kimber to A.R. Dick, 22 July 1966
70 PAO, RG 49-193, Ontario, Legislative Assembly, Standing Committee on Legal Bills and Labour, Fifth meeting, 3 May 1966; Sixth meeting, 10 May 1966; Eighth meeting, 17 May 1966; Tenth meeting, 24 May 1966; Twelfth meeting, 31 May1966; Fourteenth meeting, 7 June 1966; Fifteenth meeting, 9 June 1966; Sixteenth meeting, 14 June 1966; Seventeenth meeting, 19 June 1966, on which the following paragraph is based.
71 The BDA endorsed the CMFA position, having retained Patrick Hartt, who had served as counsel to the Windfall Commission, to put its case before the commitee; see BDA, MB, 26 April 1966.
72 PAO, OSC, BM, box 32, file 667, Memorandum from Kimber to H.E. Langford, 14 March 1967
73 Ontario, Legislative Assembly, Debates, 4 July 1966, 5542–60
74 PAO, RG 49-193, Ontario, Legislative Assembly, Standing Committee on Legal Bills and Labour, Seventeenth meeting, 16 June 1966; FP, 16 July 1966 (quoted)
75 PAO, OSC, BM, box 4, file 73, Memorandum from Kimber to Dick, 19 August 1966; file 76, Kimber to Cohen, 23 December 1966 (quoted)
76 Ibid., box 47, file 975, Memorandum from Bray to D.N. Omand, 24 January 1967
77 PAO, AG, 4-02, file 248.8, Press release from AG Arthur Wishart, 3 Decem-

ber 1964; OSC, BM, box 47, file 975, Memorandum from Bray to D.N. Omand, 24 January 1967. Bray was made acting director in September and confirmed in the post three months later.

78 PAO, OSC, Corr., box 7, file 9, Memorandum from Kimber to Wishart, 9 September 1965

79 PAO, OSC, BM, box 4, file 71, Proposed rules relating to the trading in securities by members of the Ontario Securities Commission and its staff, 2 June 1966; file 74, Kimber to Wishart, 6 September 1966; Memorandum from Kimber to H.S. Bray, 11 October 1966; Memorandum from Kimber to J. McFarland and J. Willis, 12 October 1966 (quoted); OSCB, October 1966, 'Rules Relating to the Trading in Securities by Members of the Ontario Securities Commission and Its Staff'

80 PAO, OSC, D.S. Beatty Committee Records, 1964–7, box 2, file 1, Memorandum from Bray to Kimber, 13 July 1965

81 PAO, OSC, BM, box 47, file 975, Memorandum from Bray to Omand, 24 January 1967

82 Price Waterhouse and Co., 'Ontario Securities Commission, Report on Organization, 7 January 1966,' 22 pp. plus appendices (typescript, York University Library), on which the following paragraphs are based.

83 PAO, AG, 4-02, file 248.8, Memorandum from E.K. Pukacz to Civil Service Commission chair D.J. Collins, 15 September, 19 October 1964. The commission granted Kimber the $1,500 raise recommended for chairing the committee but fixed the chair's maximum salary at only $18,000, while part-time commissioners were to have annual $6,000 retainers plus $50 per meeting attended.

84 PAO, OSC, BM, box 47, file 975, Memorandum from Bray to D.N. Omand, 24 January 1967

85 Ibid., box 4, file 68, Memorandum from Kimber to A.R. Dick, 15 February 1966

86 FP, 18 March 1967

87 PAO, OSC, BM, box 4, file 75, Kimber to Rowntree, 29 November 1966

88 Ibid., file 71, Kimber to Wishart, 27 April 1966, Personal and Confidential; file 75, same to same, 10 November 1966; FP, 16 July 1966

89 PAO, OSC, BM, box 4, file 75, Kimber to Wishart, 15 November 1966, Personal; NAC, TSE, MB, 26 January, 28 February 1967

Chapter 9: Decline of the Broker-Dealer

1 Canada, Royal Commission on Banking and Finance, Report, 346; BDA, MB, 26 February, 9 April, 28 May 1963

2 BDA, MB, 13 August, 10, 24 September, 8 October, 3 December 1963
3 *R. v. W. McKenzie Securities, West and Dubros,* 55 *Western Weekly Reports*
   (1966), 157–66
4 BDA, MB, 27 April, 8 June 1965
5 See note 3 above; the firm was actually acquitted because the statute provided only that 'no person' should trade without registration and did not
   refer to a company, but Philip West and the unnamed Dubros were found
   guilty.
6 *OSCB,* October 1965; BDA, MB, 24 August 1965
7 *OSCB,* November 1965. The BDA suspended Stewart's licence for sixty
   days; see MB, 19 October 1965.
8 PAO, OSC, BM, box 4, file 73, Kimber to AG Arthur Wishart, 29 September
   1966; *OSCB,* December 1965
9 *OSCB,* May 1966
10 BDA, MB, 30 March 1965
11 *OSCB,* November 1965
12 PAO, OSC, BM, box 4, file 68, Memorandum from Kimber to file, 1 March
   1966; Kimber to AG Arthur Wishart, 8 March 1966; Memorandum from
   Kimber to Bray, 10 March 1966; *OSCB,* June 1966
13 PAO, OSC, BM, box 11, file 213, Memorandum from Chief Legal Investigation Officer B.C. Howard to Director W.M. Duggan, 5 January 1970. On
   appeal, Rush's term was reduced to six years.
14 For an amusing account of a dishonest financier who allegedly turned the
   tables by swindling members of New York's Gambino crime family, see
   New York Times, 2 January 2000.
15 BDA, MB, 2, 15 November, 13 December 1966, 22 February, 7 March 1967
16 Ibid., 21 March, 11 April, 17 October, 5, 11, 19 December 1967; 9 January
   1968 (quoted); *OSCB,* 1968, 3, 'Statement of Commission Policy re Warnings
   in National Advertising'
17 PAO, OSC, BM, box 50, file 1033, Memorandum from H.S. Bray to H.E.
   Langford, 15 February 1968; Memorandum from E.C. Jaegerman, SEC chief
   investigative counsel, Division of Trading and Markets, to file, 10 March
   1968; Robert Assad, Quebec Dept. of Natural Resources, to J.C. Lyons,
   Quebec Securities Commission, 12 July 1968
18 Ibid., file 1028, Memorandum re interview with Dr Norman B. Rasky re
   Wee-Gee Uranium Mines, 11 March 1968; file 1033, Memorandum from
   Bray to Langford, 22 March 1968
19 Sales to 'a combination of persons or companies holding sufficient shares to
   materially affect the control of the company,' who in turn must disclose
   their activities by prospectus.

20 PAO, OSC, BM, box 50, file 1036, Memorandum from G.V. Bender to A.S. Wakim, 8 May 1968; Memorandum from S.S. Gorecki to W.M. Duggan, 13 August 1968; Memorandum from Wakim to B.C. Howard, 27 August 1968; file 1033, Memorandum from Bray to Langford, 20 August 1968; Ontario, *Statutes*, 1968–9, c. 116

21 PAO, OSC, box 50, file 1036, Memorandum from Langford to H.L. Rowntree, 20 March 1969 (quoted); Memorandum from Professor J. Willis re 'Personal Liability of Commissioners and/or Officials of the Commission for Acts Done by Them in Their Official Capacity: The Present Law and What Should Be Done,' 9 April 1970

22 Ibid., Burton Tait, McCarthy and McCarthy to OSC, 21 July 1971

23 *FP*, 26 May 1973; *OSCB*, 1975, 103–20

24 BDA, MB, 9 January 1973–15 December 1981, passim

25 OSC, *Report of Commissioner D.S. Beatty on Matters Relating to the Financing of Mining Companies and Development Companies* (Toronto: OSC, 23 September 1968; hereafter OSC, *Beatty Report*). The other members were Commissioners G.E. Grundy, D.F. McFarland, and John Willis.

26 PAO, OSC, BM, box 21, file 373, Memorandum from E.M. Browne to Beatty, 24 July 1967

27 PAO, OSC, Beatty Committee records, box 1, file 6, A.C. Mosher to Beatty, 28 November 1967; file 3, TSE to Beatty , n.d. [1968]; ibid., BM, box 21, file 373, Kimber to Beatty, 20 February 1968

28 OSC, *Beatty Report*

29 PAO, OSC, Corr., box 6, file 5, Memorandum from Bray to W.M. Duggan, 23 October 1969; file 9, Memorandum from Bray to Royce, 20 April 1970; ibid., BM, box 12, file 218, E.A. Royce to Lloyd Dolan, 4 June 1970

30 PAO, OSC, BM, box 36, file 734, Memorandum from John Kingsmill and Allan Leibel to S.E. Gorecki, 25 August 1970

31 PAO, OSC, BM, box 13, file 250, copy of the Prospectors and Developers Association, *P.D.A. Digest*, March 1972

32 PAO, OSC, BM, box 13, file 250, 'Background paper re financing junior mines' by Bray, 17 April 1972

33 Ibid., box 14, file 259, Watts to J.R. Rhodes, 4 August 1972; box 33, file 675, Memorandum from G.R. Guillet to Leo Bernier, 4 May, 1973; *OSCB*, 1973, Press release by Ontario Ministry of Natural Resources re OSC Policies on financing mining and oil exploration, 15 January 1973

34 PAO, OSC, BM, box 33, file 675, Memorandum from G.R. Guillet to Leo Bernier, 4 May 1973; *OSCB*, 1975, 35–40 (both quoted)

35 PAO, OSC, BM, box 14, file 258, Draft memorandum re OSC Policy 3-02,

Junior Mining and Exploration Companies, 14 March 1977, amended in
H.S. Bray's handwriting

36 See PAO, OSC, BM, box 13, file 253, Transcript of OSC Hearings re Junior
    Mining Companies, April–May 1975 by A.S. Pattillo, H.S. Bray, R.M.
    Steiner, and G.R. Guillet, assisted by C.R. Salter and Adelaide Lamey, coun-
    sel
37 Ibid., vol. 1, 22 April 1975, 2–4
38 Ibid., vol. 2, 23 April 1975, 266 (quoted), 286–8
39 Ibid., vol. 3, 24 April 1975, 421–4, 426–8, 437–50 (quoted); vol. 4, 29 April
    1975, 486–7 (quoted), 516-9 (quoted)
40 Ibid., vol. 2, 23 April 1975, 362–2 (quoted), 397–8
41 Ibid., vol. 6, 2 May 1975, 1090–4, 1127 (quoted), 1131 (quoted), 1148–52
    (quoted), 1158–60 (quoted)
42 *OSCB*, 1976, 82–92
43 PAO, OSC, BM, box 41, file 257, David D. Martin to Salter, 20 May 1975
44 *FP*, 15 December 1975; PAO, OSC, BM, box 14, file 257, Memorandum from
    T.O.P. Brown and Filing staff to C.R. Salter, 10 July 1975; file 27, box 529,
    Memorandum from Brown to Prospectus staff, 26 January 1976
45 PAO, OSC, BM, box 14, file 257, G.W. Thompson, executive director,
    Ontario Association of Professional Engineers, to A.S. Pattillo, 18 Septem-
    ber 1975; Donald McNeill, BDA executive secretary to G.H. Thornton,
    22 September 1975; *Globe and Mail* (Toronto), 6, 9 March 1976; *FP*, 13 March
    1976 (quoted)
46 *Toronto Daily Star*, 10 March 1976 (quoted); PAO, OSC, BM, box 14, file 258,
    Draft memorandum re OSC Policy 3–02, Junior Mining and Exploration
    Companies, 14 March 1977, amended in H.S. Bray's handwriting
47 PAO, OSC, BM, box 27, file 529, Reynolds to William Davis, 22 February
    1977; *OSCB*, 1977, 55–7
48 PAO, OSC, BM, box 27, file 531, Memorandum from Adelaide Lamey, n.d.
    [July 1977]
49 *OSCB*, 1977, 234–8, 'Explanatory Note re Amended OSC Policy 3-02, ' n.d.
    [September 1977]
50 PAO, OSC, BM, box 27, file 531, Memorandum from J.C. DaCosta to Baillie,
    27 January 1978
51 Ibid., box 14, file 258, Memorandum from Baillie to OSC members, 4 July
    1978
52 *OSCB*, 1978, 238–45
53 PAO, OSC, BM, box 14, file 259, draft letter from J.C. Baillie to Donald
    McNeill, BDA, 7 September; Memorandum from S.K, Dhawan, OSC inves-

tigation accountant, to H.W. Wilson, senior investigation accountant, 14 September 1978; Memorandum from Baillie to OSC, 5 October 1978
54 Ibid., file 260, Memorandum from Baillie to Larry Grossman, Frank Drea, Frank Miller, and D. (?) Crosbie, 23 March 1979
55 Ibid., Baillie to Jewett, 9 October, 13 November 1979 (both quoted)

Chapter 10: Foreign Ownership

1 This system, which was well understood by all insiders, was concisely described by Strathy of Dominion Securities when he had become a member of the OSC in 1971, in response to a request from H.S. Bray to compare the Canadian situtation to investment banking in the United States, where a similar hierarchy existed; see PAO, OSC, BM, box 12, file 231, Memorandum from Bray to Strathy, 30 November 1971, enclosing Samuel L. Hayes, 'Investment Banking: Power Structures in Flux, ' *Harvard Business Review,* March/April 1971; Strathy to Bray, 6 December 1971 (quoted).
2 See note 1.
3 PAO, OSC, BM, box 35, file 702, Brown to Bray, 16 September 1971, Private and Confidential (since Brown noted that disclosure of these views might prove detrimental to Gairdner and Company's continuing participation in the underwriting business)
4 *FP,* 6 September 1975. Some firms had also refused to participate in an underwriting for Texaco Canada in 1974 and were said to have been similarly disciplined.
5 PAO, OSC, BM, box 18, file 341, Memorandum from H.S. Bray to E.A. Royce, 17 November 1972; box 21, file 385, Bray to W.D. Kinsey, 26 February 1974 (quoted); *FP,* 18 November 1972
6 *FP,* 8 February 1969
7 Ibid.
8 NAC, TSE, MB, 14 June 1960
9 Ibid., 21 June 1966, 11 January, 2 February, 23 May, 6 September, 7 November 1967; MSE, MB, 18 October 1967; *FP,* 2 September 1967
10 *FP,* 11 June 1966; 19 October, 9 November 1968; 19 January, 29 March 1969; TSE, MB, 7 January 1969
11 PAO, OSC, BM, box 12, file 229, Submission by Merrill, Lynch, Pierce, Fenner and Smith, Inc., and Royal Securities Corporation Ltd. to the Ontario Securities Commission Industry Ownership Committee, September 1971
12 In addition to Moore, the members included Norman J. Alexander, managing partner of Richardson Securities; Gordon R.P. Bongard, executive vice-president of Bongard, Leslie and Company; W. Thomas Brown, president of

Odlum Brown and T.B. Read Limited; Peter Kilburn, vice-chair of Greenshields Incorporated; J. Ross LeMesurier, vice-president of Wood Gundy; Fred R. Whittall, president of C.H. Hodgson and Company; and as secretary, Roy W. Reid, economist, A.E. Ames and Company.

13 TSE, MB, 20, 27 May, 9, 17 June, 15 July 1969; MSE, MB, 20, 28 May, 11 June 1969

14 Canada, Privy Council Office, *Foreign Ownership and the Structure of Canadian Industry: Report of the Task Force on the Structure of Canadian Industry* (Ottawa, 1969); Canada, Consumer and Corporate Affairs, *Foreign Direct Investment in Canada* (Ottawa, 1977); Denis Smith, *Gentle Patriot: A Political Biography of Walter Gordon* (Edmonton, 1973), 346–52

15 Formally titled Investment Dealers Association of Canada, Canadian Stock Exchange, Montreal Stock Exchange, Toronto Stock Exchange, Vancouver Stock Exchange, *Report of the Committee to Study the Requirements and Sources of Capital and the Implications of Non-Resident Capital for the Canadian Securities Industry* (n.p., May 1970; hereafter *Moore Report*)

16 Ibid., 19–27, 43–7

17 Retirees were thus entitled to withdraw their capital if they wished.

18 *Moore Report*, 32, 59–69

19 Ibid., 139

20 Ibid., 124–46

21 *FP*, 20 June 1970

22 *FP*, 28 February 1970

23 TSE, MB, 18 August 1970; MSE, MB, 25 August 1970

24 TSE, MB, 2, 9, 23 March, 13, 27 April 1971; PAO, OSC, BM, box 45, file 940, Memorandum from E.A. Royce to file, 23 April 1971

25 TSE, MB, 11, 25 May 1971; Investment Dealers Association of Canada, Canadian Stock Exchange, Montreal Stock Exchange, Toronto Stock Exchange, Vancouver Stock Exchange, 'Report of the Joint Industry Committee on the Moore Report' (June, 1971; typescript, OSC Library)

26 PAO, OSC, BM, box 12, file 227, Memorandum from Wishart to Davis, 30 June 1971; *OSCB*, 1971, 83–4

27 *OSCB*, 1971, 95–100; *FP*, 24 July 1971; PAO, OSC, BM, box 12, file 227, Memorandum from Royce to F.J. Pillgrem, 20 July 1971; Memorandum from Bray to Barry Tocher, 21 July 1971; OSC press release, 29 July 1971

28 PAO, OSC, BM, box 12, file 227, Memorandum from David Johnston to Bray, 27 September 1971

29 Toronto Stock Exchange, 'Submission by the Toronto Stock Exchange to the Industry Study Committee of the Ontario Securities Commission' (October 1971; typescript, OSC Library)

30 Investment Dealers Association of Canada, Ontario District, 'Submission by the Ontario District of the Investment Dealers Association of Canada to Ontario Securities Commission Industry Ownership Study Committee,' October, 1971, (typescript, OSC Library)
31 PAO, OSC, BM, box 35, file 702, E.N. Jones to Bray, 15 September 1971; box 13, file 237, Bruce A. Gordon, vice-president, Dean Witter International, to Bray, 20 August 1971
32 Ibid., box 12, file 229, Submission by Merrill, Lynch, Pierce, Fenner and Smith, Inc., and Royal Securities Corporation Ltd. to the Ontario Securities Commission Industry Ownership Committee, September 1971
33 Ibid., file 231, Strathy to Bray, 30 November 1971
34 Ibid., file 227, Memorandum from Royce to Bray, 3 September 1971
35 Ibid., Memorandum from Bray to file, 17 September 1971
36 See OSC, *Report of the Securities Industry Ownership Committee of the Ontario Securities Commission* (Toronto: OSC, April 1972), on which the following paragraphs are based.
37 PAO, OSC, BM, box 31, file 637, Memorandum from E.A. Royce to file, 15 February 1973
38 Quebec, Ministère des institutions financières, compagnies et cooperatives, *Study on the Securities Industry in Quebec: Final Report* (21 June 1972)
39 PAO, OSC, BM, box 32, file 642, Brief of IDA and Canadian stock exchanges re participation of foreign-controlled firms in Canadian securities industry, 11 July 1973
40 Ibid., Memorandum from Bray to E.A. Royce, 24 August 1973; Memorandum from Guillet to Royce, 30 August 1973
41 Ibid., Memorandum from David Johnston to E.A. Royce, 14 September 1973; TSE, MB, 4, 18 September 1973
42 PAO, OSC, BM, box 32, file 642, Securities Act, 1970, Regulation 95/74, 13 February 1974
43 *FP*, 9 February, 18, 25 May, 27 July 1974; MSE, MB, 5 March, 23 April, 18 June 1974; TSE, MB, 30 April, 4 May 1974; *OSCB*, 1974, 133–8
44 *FP*, 25 September, 4 December 1976, 1 January 1977; *OSCB*, 1976, 284–8; TSE, MB, 19, 26 October 1976, 4 January 1977 (quoted). The MSE board voted by secret ballot nine to one to approve the transfer of the seat in Montreal; see MSE, MB, 14 December 1976.
45 TSE, MB, 18 January, 1 February 1977; *FP*, 5 February, 30 April 1977; *OSCB*, 1977, 32–52
46 *FP*, 11 February, 6 May 1978; MSE, MB, 14, 28 February, 4 April 1978; *OSCB*, 1978, 101–12

47 PAO, OSC, BM, box 35, file 728, Memorandum from H.S. Bray to R.J. Butler, 1 May 1978; *OSCB*, 1978, 17–20
48 *FP*, 24 June, 5 August 1978
49 *FP*, 14 October 1978
50 PAO, OSC, BM, box 35, file 727, Memorandum from Baillie to OSC, 10 January 1979
51 *FP*, 18 August, 22 December (quoted) 1979

Chapter 11: Mergers

1 PAO, OSC, BM, box 19, file 351, Draft report re 'Economic Background of Mergers and Acquisitions' by D.A. Stafl, 12 December 1969
2 Ibid., Corr., box 11, file 1, Memorandum from Bray to H.E. Langford, 13 February 1969
3 Ibid., BM, box 19, file 351, Memorandum from D.A. Stafl to Merger Study, 2 January 1970
4 Ibid., file 350, Memorandum from Bray to H.E. Langford, 5 March 1969
5 Ibid., box 20, file 362, Memorandum of minutes of Initial Study [*sic*] of Merger Study Committee, 25 April 1969; box 19, file 350, Minutes of 2nd meeting of Merger Study Committee, 1 May 1969; file 345, 'Ontario Securities Commission Merger Study,' 23 July 1969; file 342, 'OSC Merger Study Preliminary Position Paper,' 22 August 1969
6 SEC, *Disclosure to Investors: A Reappraisal of Administrative Policies under the 1933 and 1934 Acts* (Washington, 1969), otherwise known as the Wheat Report
7 PAO, OSC, BM, box 34, file 695, Memorandum from Bray and Peter Dey to file, 8 July 1969
8 Dylex then controlled twenty-one subsidiaries with 3, 000 employees in clothing, home furnishings, building products, and packaging.
9 PAO, OSC, BM, box 19, file 343, Kay to H.S. Bray, 29 August 1969; file 345, Memorandum of discussion over dinner with James Pattison, 29 September 1969; Memorandum of hearing for Power Corporation Ltd. – Montreal, 23 September 1969
10 Ibid., box 36, file 750, Peter Dey to David Johnston, 22 July 1969; Dey to Jack Lyndon, TSE, 23 September 1969
11 TSE, MB, 11 November 1969; PAO, OSC, BM, box 19, file 346, Toronto Stock Exchange, OSC Merger Study, Comments on Specific Topics Presented by the OSC, November 1969

12 PAO, OSC, BM, box 12, file 223, Investment Dealers Association of Canada, Brief to OSC re Mergers and Takeovers, October 1969
13 Ibid., box 19, file 345, Memorandum of hearing for J. Baillie and J. Tory of Tory, Tory, DesLauriers and Binnington, 10 September 1969; Memorandum of hearing for Mr John M. Godfrey and James L. Lewtas of Campbell, Godfrey & Lewtas, 26 September 1969; Memorandum of discussions with Messrs John G. Kirkpatrick and Pierre Legrand of Ogilvy, Cope, etc., 1 October 1969; Memorandum on hearing for R.A. Davies – Davies, Ward and Beck, 27 October 1969
14 Ibid., Corr., box 6, file 7, Bray to W.S. Irwin, 31 December 1969, Private and Confidential
15 Ibid., file 5, Memorandum from Bray to David Johnston, 17 October 1969
16 PAO, OSC, BM, box 19, file 352, Ontario Securities Commission, Merger Study, Interim Report by Peter Dey, 17 November 1969, Confidential; ibid., Corr., box 6, file 6, Bray to Marcel Lajeunesse (and other provincial regulators), 17 November 1969; file 7, Bray to W.S. Irwin, 31 December 1969, Private and Confidential
17 OSC, *Report of the Committee of the OSC on the Problems of Disclosure Raised for Investors by Business Combinations and Private Placements* (Toronto, 1970), 4–11, 19–20, 26–8, 87–9
18 Ibid., 59–73
19 Ibid., 51–7, 87–100
20 PAO, OSC, BM, box 3, file 49, Minutes of CSA meeting, 1–3 June 1970; box 5, file 78, Memorandum from Bray to E.A. Royce, 7 August 1970; box 33, file 675, B.C. Howard to T.C. Tapley, 5 October 1970
21 Ibid., box 33, file 673, CBA, Ontario Branch, 25 November 1970; box 5, file 81, Memorandum from Bray to file, 8 February, 1 March 1971; box 33, file 674, Memorandum from J.B. Johnston to Bray, 9 March 1971; box 33, file 673, Memorandum from TSE to OSC re cornerstone prospectus and offering circular, 26 April 1971
22 *OSCB*, 1972, 94–6, 'Statement to legislature by ... Eric Winkler,' 1 June 1972; 130–46, 'The Securities Act, 1972: Bill 154, Explanatory Notes'; PAO, OSC, BM, box 33, file 675, Memorandum from H.S.Bray to E.A. Royce, 22 November 1971
23 PAO, OSC, BM, box 33, file 676, Memorandum from Bray to file, 5 December 1972; file 678, Memorandum from John T. Clement to DM J.K. Young, 12 December 1972; Warren Goldring to Bray, 12 February 1973, Personal
24 PAO, OSC, Corr., box 2, file 1, Memorandum from Royce to file, 21 February 1973, Confidential

25 PAO, OSC, BM, box 33, file 677, Memorandum from W. Brian Trafford re Discussion of Bill 154 at CSA Conference, 2 May 1973

26 *FP,* 28 October 1972

27 *FP,* 28 December 1974; TSE, MB, 7 November 1972; PAO, OSC, BM, box 39, file 805, Memorandum from E.A. Royce, 9 April 1974; Memoranda from B.C. Howard, 1 August 1974, Confidential

28 The following paragraphs are derived from Philip Mathias, *Takeover: The 22 Days of Risk and Decision that Created the World's Largest Newsprint Empire* (Toronto, 1976), and *FP,* 23, 30 November, 28 December 1974.

29 Mathias, *Takeover,* 47, 65

30 Ibid., 28, 66–7

31 Ibid., 73

32 Mackenzie's letter is reproduced in Mathias, *Takeover,* at 260.

33 Some people noted the irony of Pattillo in the role of protector of minority shareholder rights, since as a practising lawyer in 1963 he had taken a case to the Supreme Court of Canada for Union Gas to wind up United Fuels over the protests of its minority shareholders.

34 Mathias, *Takeover,* 132

35 *FP,* 30 November 1974; PAO, OSC, BM, box 39, file 805, Philip Anisman to A.S. Pattillo, 11 December 1974

36 PAO, OSC, BM, box 39, file 805, Kimber to A.S. Pattillo, 30 November 1974; H.S. Bray to OSC, 4 December 1974

37 MSE, MB, 26 November, 3, 10, 17 December 1974; TSE, MB, 10 December 1974; PAO, OSC, BM, box 39, file 806, Excerpts from minutes of OSC, 5, 12 December 1974

38 PAO, OSC, BM, box 39, file 806, Excerpts from minutes of OSC, 9 July, 6, 13, 27 November, 4 December 1975; Position paper re stock exchange takeover bids by H.S. Bray, 15 November 1976; file 807, J.R.Kimber to A.S. Pattillo, 3, 23 December 1975; MSE, MB, 18 November 1975; TSE, MB, 2, 23 December 1975

39 PAO, OSC, BM, box 39, file 805, Memorandum from Stanley Beck to A.S. Pattillo, 7 September 1976; file 806, Memorandum from Bray to Pattillo, 27 August 1976; Bray to D.A. Berlis, 31 August 1976; Berlis to Bray, 31 August, 1 September 1976; Kimber to Bray, 2 September 1976; *OSCB,* 1976, 258–64; *FP,* 18 September, 2 October 1976

40 *OSCB,* 1976, 325; TSE, MB, 16, 30 November, 7, 16 December 1976; *FP,* 6, 27 November 1976

41 *FP,* 1 January 1977

42 PAO, OSC, BM, box 39, file 808, Blair to Bunting, 30 June 1978 (quoted); file

806, John L. Howard to J.C. Baillie, 12 July 1978, enclosing Draft paper re takeover bids, 12 July 1978, Confidential; *FP,* 1, 8 July 1978

43 Ibid., file 806, Blair to J.C. Baillie, 13 July 1978; file 808, Blair to the editor, *FP,* 19 July 1978; *FP,* 15, 22 July 1978

44 PAO, OSC, BM, box 39, file 806, Pearce Bunting to J.C. Baillie, 11 July 1978; W.S. Irwin to Baillie, 11 July 1978; Joanne B. Veit to Baillie, 12 July 1978; John L. Howard to Baillie, 12 July 1978, enclosing Draft paper re takeover bids, 12 July 1978, Confidential; Memorandum from D.W. Drinkwater to file, 13 July 1978

45 Ibid., Baillie to Blair, 14 July 1978; file 808, R.L. Pierce, Alberta Gas Trunk Line, to OSC secretary G.H. Thornton, 29 September 1978 (quoted); *FP,* 29 July 1978; *OSCB,* 1978, 173–4

46 *FP,* 23, 30 December 1978

47 *FP,* 14, 28 April, 5, 12, 19, 26 May, 2, 23 June 1979

48 PAO, OSC, BM, box 39, file 808, Memorandum from H[ugh] C[leland] re Stock Exchange Takeover Bids, 9 May 1979; OSC press release, 9 May 1979; Memorandum from J.C. Baillie to OSC, 14 May 1979

49 Ontario, Legislative Assembly, Select Committee on Company Law, *Report on Mergers, Amalgamations and Certain Related Matters* (n.p., 1973)

50 PAO, OSC, BM, box 33, file 680, Submission to the minister re Securities Act, 1974, n.d.; *OSCB,* 1974, 105–8; *FP,* 5 June 1975

51 *OSCB,* 1977, 270–2

52 Quoted in Mary G. Condon, 'Ideas and Regulatory Practice: The Ontario Securities Commission, 1945–78' (JSD thesis, University of Toronto, 1991), 481; she also quotes a former OSC chair as saying that 'Jim Baillie ... negotiated with Harry Bray at the Commission and was involved in all the changes.'

53 Mary G. Condon, *Making Disclosure: Ideas and Interests in Ontario Securities Regulation* (Toronto, 1998), 211–23, provides an extensive account, and the following paragraphs also draw upon David L. Johnston and Kathleen D. Rockwell, *Canadian Securities Regulation,* 2nd ed. (Toronto, 1998), chapter 8, 'Distribution Exemptions,' and Mark R. Gillen, *Securities Regulation in Canada* (Toronto, 1992), 178–91.

54 Readiness to purchase as a principal, securities worth more than $150, 000 (versus the previous minimum of $97, 000) was now deemed to be the mark of a sophisticated investor, while mutual funds, banks, and insurers were assumed to be able to acquire more disclosure than required by prospectus and were not permitted to resell to the public.

55 See Johnston and Rockwell, *Canadian Securities Regulation,* chapter 10, 'Takeover Bids.'

56 Algoma Steel, Inco, Macmillan Bloedel, Molson, Noranda, Stelco, and TransCanada Pipelines
57 Condon, *Making Disclosure*, 224

Chapter 12: Competition

1 The proposed rates were calculated as a percentage of the total value of a trade as follows: on shares worth less than 0.5 cents, 0.2 per cent; 5–10 cents, 0.35 per cent; 10–20 cents, 0.5 per cent; 20–30 cents, 0.65 per cent; 30–40 cents, 0.8 per cent, 40–50 cents, 0.9 per cent; 50–65 cents, 1.1 per cent; 65–75 cents, 1.4 per cent; 75–85 cents, 1.6 per cent; 85 cents – $1.00, 1.75 per cent; $1–8, 2.75 per cent minus 1 cent per share; $8–11, 2 per cent plus 5 cents per share; $11–15, 1 per cent plus 16 cents per share; $15–30, 0.5 per cent plus 23.5 cents per share; $30–65, 0.25 per cent plus 31 cents per share; above $65, 0.16 per cent plus 36.42 cents per share; see *FP*, 20 May 1967.
2 NAC, TSE, MB, 18 October 1966; 28 February, 25 April, 22 August 1967; MSE, MB, 9 May 1967; *FP*, 20 May, 3 June 1967, 14 September 1968
3 *FP*, 1 November 1958, 1 April 1961, 13 January 1962; NAC, TSE, MB, 14, 28 June 1960, 28 November 1961, 3 January 1962
4 NAC, TSE, MB, 11 July, 22 August, 5 December 1967; TSE, MB, 9 January, 2 February 1968; *FP*, 29 July 1967, 20 January 1968
5 TSE, MB, 12 March 1968, 4 February, 25 November, 23 December 1969, 3 February, 24 March, 30 June 1970; *FP*, 22 March 1969
6 TSE, MB, 6 April, 28 October, 2 November (quoted) 1971
7 In 1971 Mills, Spence merged with Burns, Fry, which also took over Playfair and Company; Barclay and Crawford was absorbed by Moss, Lawson; and Hevenor and Company and Jenkin Evans and Company closed up shop; while Malone Lynch went bankrupt; see *FP*, 11 December 1971.
8 TSE, MB, 21 December 1971, 22 February 1972
9 Ibid., 7 March, 11 April 1972
10 PAO, OSC, BM, box 36, file 760, 'A Proposal for a New National Commission Schedule' by MSE/CSE, TSE, and VSE, December 1972
11 Ibid., Brief to OSC from John S. Howard, 10 January 1973
12 *FP*, 3 February, 10 March, 28 April 1973; TSE, MB, 30 January, 13 March, 25 April 1973; MSE, MB, 3 May 1973
13 PAO, OSC, BM, box 36, file 761, Submission by TSE's J.R. Kimber re Proposed National Commission Rate Schedule, 22 May 1973; *FP*, 2 June 1973
14 PAO, OSC, BM, box 36, file 761, Memorandum from Royce re Review of Briefs on TSE hearings, 22 January 1973
15 Ibid., file 762, OSC briefing book, 22 May 1973

16 Ibid., file 761, Memorandum from D.A. Stafl re Proposal for A New National Commission Schedule, 23 January 1973; Memorandum Re Costs from Gorecki (?), n.d. [June, 1973]; Memorandum from Johnston to file, 8 June 1973

17 *OSCB*, 1973, 105–26

18 Ibid.

19 PAO, OSC, BM, box 36, file 760, Kimber to Royce, 26 September, 13 November 1973; Memorandum from S. Gorecki to Royce, 15 November 1973; *OSCB*, 1973, 148–9; MSE, MB, 18, 25 September, 12 October, 1973; TSE, MB, 20 November 1973

20 *FP*, 20, 27 July, 3 August, 12 October 1974; TSE, MB, 18, 25 June, 2, 9, 16 July 1974

21 PAO, OSC, BM, box 37, file 764, Submission by OSC staff re Proposal to Apply Commission Surcharge on Certain Orders, n.d. [July 1974]

22 *FP*, 12 October, 21 December 1974; TSE, MB, 1, 15, 18 October, 12 November, 3 December 1974

23 MSE, MB, 29 October 1974; *FP*, 10 November 1974; *OSCB*, 1974, 199–205

24 TSE, MB, 11, 14, 16, 22, 23 April 1975

25 Ibid., 27 May, 17 June, 8 July , 25 November 1975; *FP*, 31 May, 9 August, 29 November 1975; MSE, MB, 27 May, 25 November 1975; *OSCB*, 1975, 193, 278–82

26 TSE, MB, 3 February, 2 March, 16 March 1976; PAO, OSC, BM, box 37, file 770, Toronto Stock Exchange Documents Supplementing Brief to OSC on Commission Rates, 18 June 1976, Document no. 1, 'Evolution of the Canadian Securities Market with Particular Focus on the Equity Market,' by H.W.F. McKay, June 1976

27 PAO, OSC, BM, box 37, file 767, 'Submission of the Toronto Stock Exchange in the Matter of the Securities Act, R.S.O. 1970, c.426 ... and ... the TSE,' 18 June 1976; file 765, Submission from Dominion Securities–Harris and Partners, 18 June 1976;

28 *FP*, 31 July, 14 August 1976

29 *OSCB*, 1976, 289–303

30 Ibid., 303–24

31 TSE, MB, 30 November, 7 December 1976, 15 March (quoted), 4, 12 April 1977; *FP*, 16 April 1977

32 MSE, MB, 5 April 1977; *FP*, 16 April 1977; PAO, OSC, BM, box 37, file 774, OSC Staff Position Paper re Analysis of the New Rate Proposal for the TSE, by Calvin Potter, 7 June 1977; file 772, Bray to H. Skodny, 24 June 1977

33 *FP*, 18 June 1977; *OSCB*, 1977, 157–69. The precise scale approved was as follows: 3 per cent commission on 100 share lots valued at up to $500; 2 per

cent (plus 15 cents) on shares worth $5 to $15; 1 per cent (plus 35 cents) on shares worth over $15; 100 per cent on the first $500 in value; 90 per cent on the next $15,000; and 80 per cent on the next $20,000; rates on trades worth over $40,000 to be determined solely according to value and fully negotiable over $500,000.

34 *OSCB*, 1977, 157–69; TSE, MB 12 October 1976; 28 June, 2 August 1977; *FP*, 22 October 1976; 28 May, 3 December 1977, 17 March, 18 August, 27 October 1979

Conclusion

1 *Globe and Mail* (Toronto), 27 April 2000
2 OSC staff member quoted in 1987; from Mary G. Condon, *Making Disclosure: Ideas and Interests in Ontario Securities Regulation* (Toronto, 1998), 26
3 Quoted in Mary G. Condon, "Ideas and Regulatory Practice: The Ontario Securities Commisison, 1945–78' (JSD thesis, University of Toronto, 1991), 255
4 Bray, 'Ontario's Proposed Securities Act: An Overview, Its Purposes and Policy Premises,' *OSCB*, 1975, 235–70
5 D.A. Oesterle, 'Comments on the SEC's *Market 2000 Report*: On among Other Things, Deference to SROs, the Mirage of Price Improvement, the Arrogation of Property Rights in Order Flow and SEC Incrementalism,' *Journal of Corporation Law* 19 (1994): 491–3
6 Peter Dey and Stanley Makuch, 'Government Supervision of Self-Regulatory Organizations in the Canadian Securities Industry,' in Canada, Consumer and Corporate Affairs, *Proposals for a Securities Market Law for Canada*, vol. 3, *Background Papers* (Ottawa, 1979), 1420–3
7 See Joel Seligman, *The Transformation of Wall Street: A History of the Securities and Exchange Commission and Modern Corporate Finance*, rev. ed. (Boston, 1995), chapter 11
8 Quoted in Condon, 'Ideas and Regulatory Practice,' 270
9 See the introduction above.
10 PAO, OSC, BM, box 8, file 142, Memorandum from Bray to file, 15 February 1978; Baillie to Andrew Kniewasser, 10 April 1978
11 Such a system was recommended in OSC, *A Regulatory Framework for Entry into and Ownership of the Ontario Securities Industry* (Toronto, 1985; hereafter Dey Report); see also David L. Johnston and Kathleen D. Rockwell, *Canadian Securities Regulation*, 2nd ed. Toronto, 1998).
12 *OSCB*, 1982, no. 3, 136C

13 Gordon DuVal, 'The Bought Deal in Canada,' *Canadian Business Law Journal* 26 (1996): 358–90

14 Dey Report, 6–7; appendix 4 gives details of floations by Walwyn Stodgell and Midland Doherty (in 1983) and First Marathon and McNeil Mantha (in 1984) as the first publicly owned brokerage firms.

15 Dey Report, 3–5; appendix 1 shows that Bache and Company, Baker Weeks (having become Dean Witter Reynolds Canada), and Dominick Corporation belonged to the TSE or the IDA, and Drexel Firestone, DuPont Glore Forgan, Laidlaw and Company, Merrill Lynch, and J.R. Timmins and Company had surrendered registration, while Royal Securities had become Merrill Lynch Canada.

16 A brief account may be found in Mark R. Gillen, *Securities Regulation in Canada* (Toronto, 1992), 440

17 Dey Report, 9–21; OSC, *Annual Report, 1987*, 4

18 J.G. Mackintosh, 'The Role of Institutional and Retail Investors in Canadian Capital Markets,' *Osgoode Hall Law Review* 31 (1993): 419

19 *Globe and Mail*, 27 May 2000

20 For a brief popular account of the subject, see Peter L. Bernstein, *Against the Gods: The Remarkable Story of Risk* (New York, 1996).

Illustration Credits

City of Toronto Archives. Graydon Hall, SC 257, item 2379

Ontario Securities Commission. Charles P. McTague; J.R. Kimber; James Baillie

Toronto Stock Exchange. Exhibit Photos: Howard Graham telephones, box 99-008, file P-26

William Wismer. Broker Dealers Association of Ontario annual dinner, 1954; Toronto conference of securities regulators, 1951; touring the moose pastures; TSE governors in their boardroom, 1961

York University Archives. Toronto *Telegram* Collection: trading floor of the TSE, 1974-002, vol. 261; O.E. Lennox, 1974-002, vol. 382; Prospectors and Developers Association meeting, 1967, 1974-002, vol. 162; watching share prices, 1974-002, vol. 261; Windfall bubble bursts, 1974-002, vol. 261; MacMillans leave court, 1974-002, vol. 390; Prudential shareholders gather in a church, 1974-002, vol. 163; C. Powell Morgan, 1974-002, vol. 398; Harry Bray, 1974-002, vol. 142

.

Index

Royal Commission on Banking and Finance, 227–8, 288–9
Royal Commission on Corporate Concentration, 315
Royal Commission on Mining (Ontario, 1943–4), 36–9, 44, 45
Royal Commission on Windfall Mines, 177–98, 222, 233, 234–7, 244, 246, 254, 255, 256
Royal Securities Corporation, 15, 28, 287, 291, 344
Royce, E.A., 291, 292, 309, 328
Rush, David, 218
Rush, Myer (Michael), 218, 262, 263
Russell Steel, 223

St Laurent, Louis, 29–30, 31, 99
St Lawrence Cement, 223
St Louis Star-Times, 84, 90
Salsberg, Joseph, 143
Salter, Charles, 274
Salter, Ralph, 51, 65
Samuelson, Paul, 14
Santack Mines, 265
Saturday Evening Post, 52–3, 141, 142
Scarr, Charles, 121
Scarr, Tinkham and Company, 121
Schlitt, A.G., 162, 165
Scholes, Myron, 345
Scott, E.D., 130, 150, 151, 173
Scott, Fenton, 161, 183
Scott, James, 166, 176, 190, 192, 193
Scott, Chief Justice W.B., 107
Sears, Roebuck and Company, 320
Seaway-Multi Corporation, 300, 301
Securities Act (Ontario); 1937, 25, 90; 1945, 7–8, 41–6, 54, 56, 61, 63, 69, 90, 234–5, 340, 341; 1947, 65, 106, 117; 1951, 143; 1963, 178, 204, 215, 243; 1966, 11, 14, 222, 235–6, 242,

243–54, 256, 257, 308, 328, 342; 1969, 267; 1978, 13, 322–4, 343, 344
Securities Act (U.S., 1933), 7, 28, 42
Securities and Exchange Commission (U.S.), 7, 9, 10, 11, 12, 13, 14, 15, 16, 17, 18, 24, 27, 29, 32, 40, 42, 43, 48, 49, 52, 53, 71, 78–9, 80, 81, 84–5, 87, 89–90, 91, 93, 104–5, 109, 147, 148, 150, 152, 229, 303, 341; 'Canadian Restricted List,' 100, 150; *Special Study of Securities Markets* (1963), 10, 16
Securities Exchange Act (U.S., 1934), 7, 28, 42, 63
Securities Industry Association (U.S.), 333
securities regulators (Canada). *See* Canadian Securities Administrators
securities regulators (U.S.). *See* National Association of Securities Administrators
Security Frauds Prevention Acts, 6–7, 63, 68, 253
Sedgwick, Joseph, 51, 122, 123, 125, 136, 177, 191, 192, 193, 196
Select Committee on Company Law (Ontario), 321
Select Committee on Mining (Ontario), 228
Select Committee on the Administration of Justice (Ontario, 1951), 87–97
self-regulation, 8, 9, 54–77, 83, 88–9, 117, 228, 341, 342–3
Seligman, Joel, 4, 16, 17
shares: block trades, 13, 326; control blocks, 12; 'lifting,' 279; mail selling, 70–1, 79–82, 87, 88, 94, 96, 102, 149; options, 34–5, 39, 97, 107, 119,